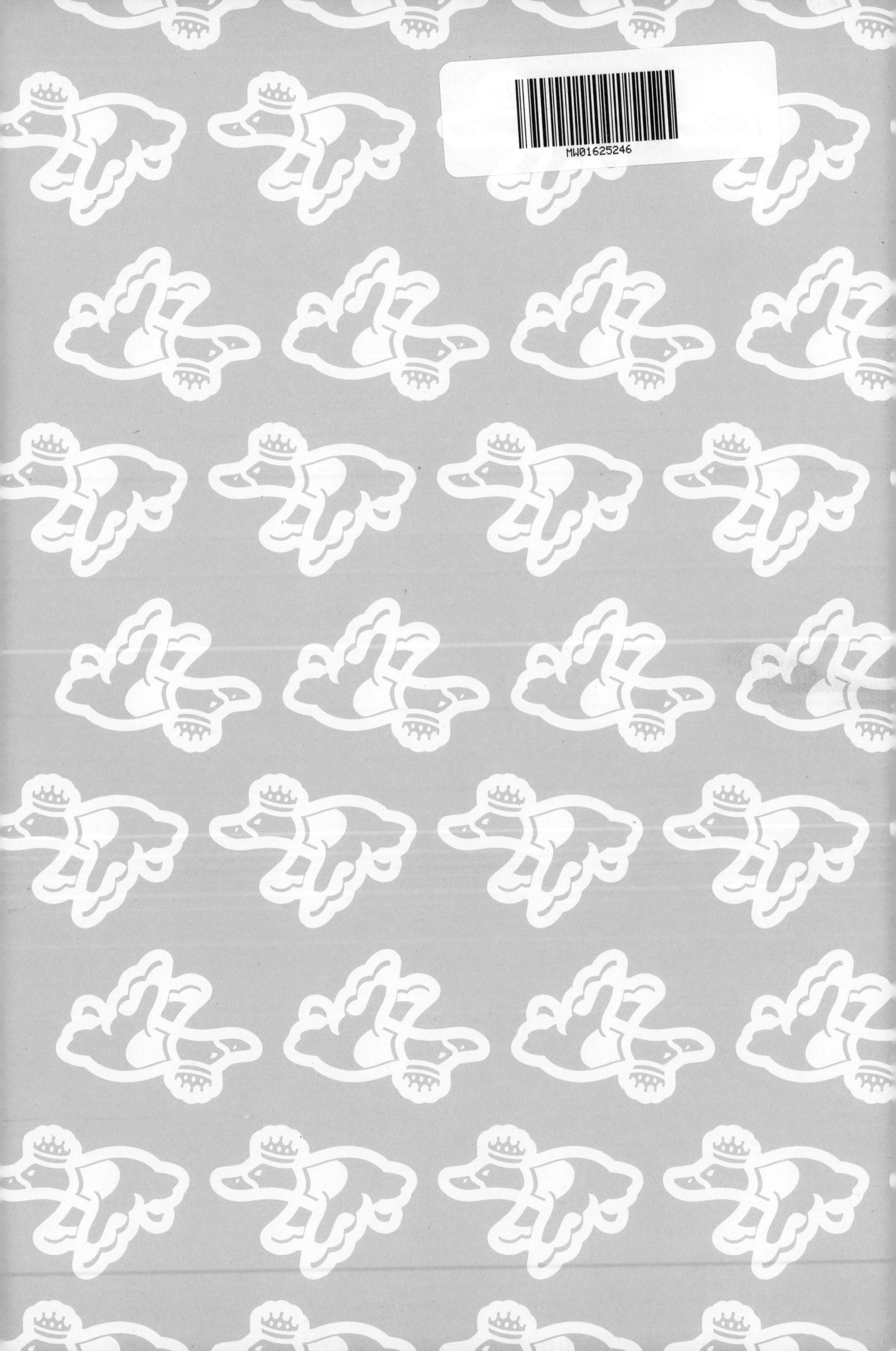
MW01625246

I know NIGO

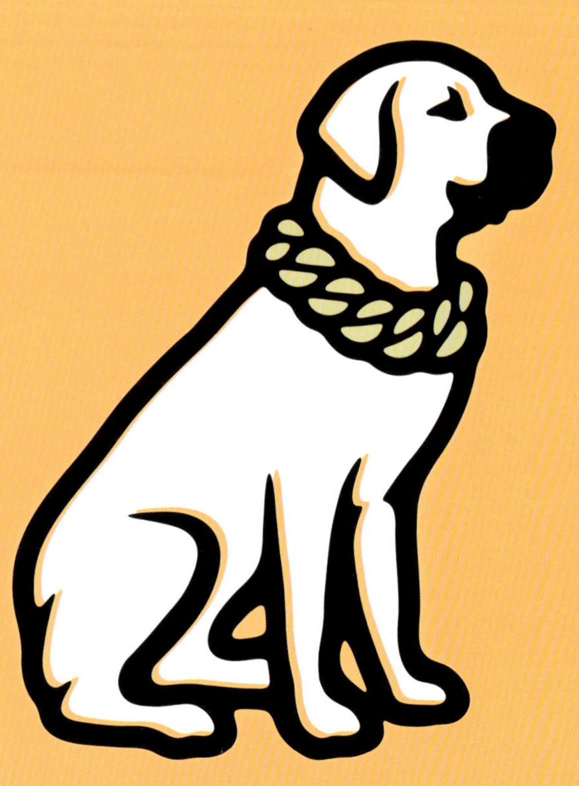

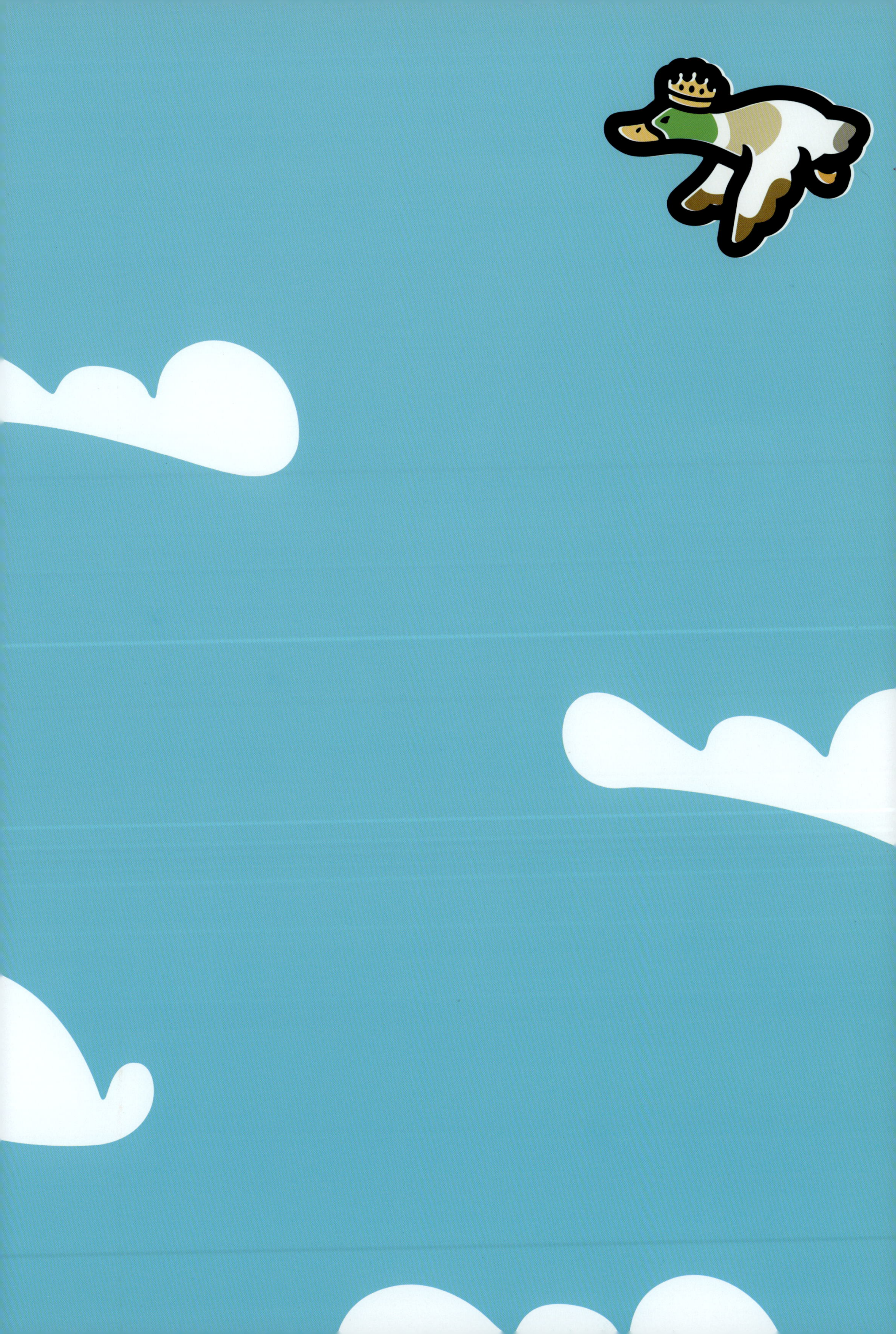

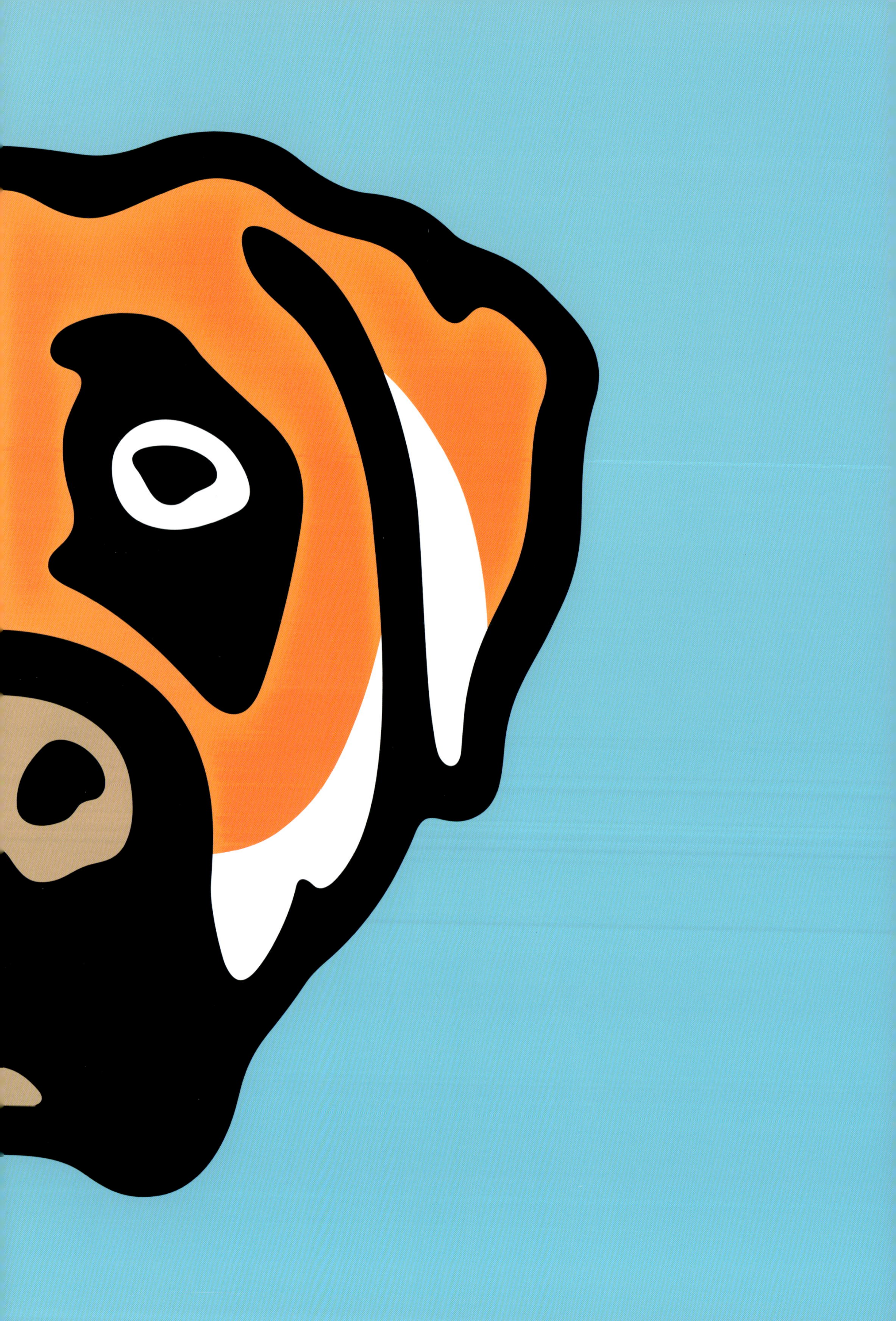

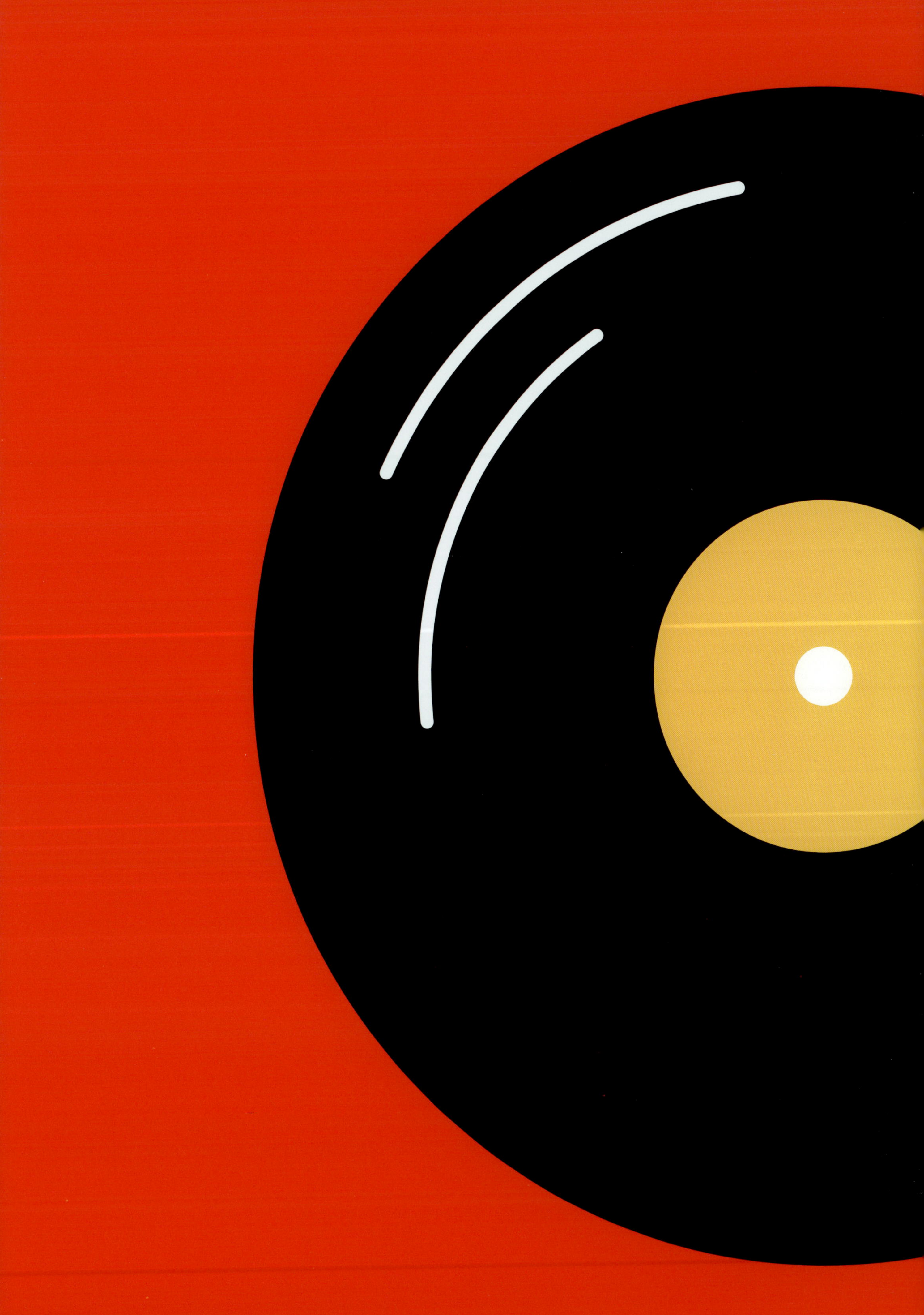

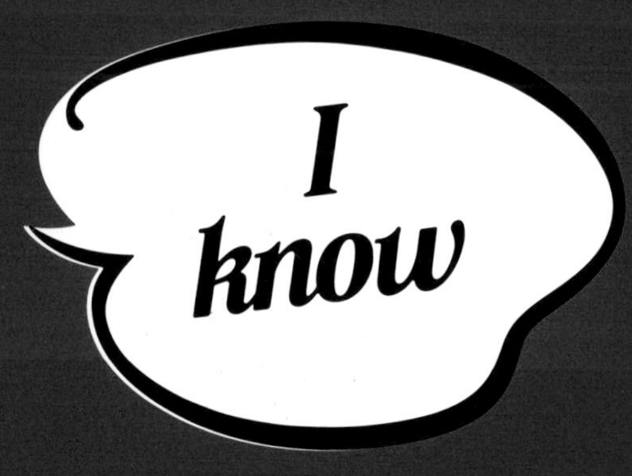
I know

NIGO

First published in the United States of America by
Rizzoli International Publications, Inc.

300 Park Avenue South, New York, NY 10010
www.rizzoliusa.com

I Know NIGO®

Rizzoli International Publications, Inc.:

Publisher: Charles Miers

Editor: Ian Luna

Project Editors: Joe Davidson and Meaghan McGovern

Production: Barbara Sadick & Eugene Lee

Design Coordination: Olivia Russin

Editorial Assistance: Lindsey Okubo

Transcription Services: Jane Dillingham

Proofreader: Mary Ellen Wilson

Publicist: Elizabeth Lagno

Book Design: Oliver Munday, with Paul Spella

Illustrations by NIGO® and Human Made

Additional illustrations by Oliver Munday
and Paul Spella

For NIGO® and Steven Victor:

Project Manager: Kevin McMullan

Project Coordination: Daniel Doyle and Toby Feltwell

The Editor would like to thank the following individuals for their assistance:
Kevin McMullan, Oliver Munday, Loïc Villepontoux, Hannah-joy Krishna, Daniel Doyle, Toby Feltwell, Mick Moreno and Mike Larson

Printed in Singapore

2024 2025 2026 2027 / 10 9 8 7 6 5 4 3 2 1

Library of Congress Control Number: 2023950607

ISBN: 978-0-8478-9918-0

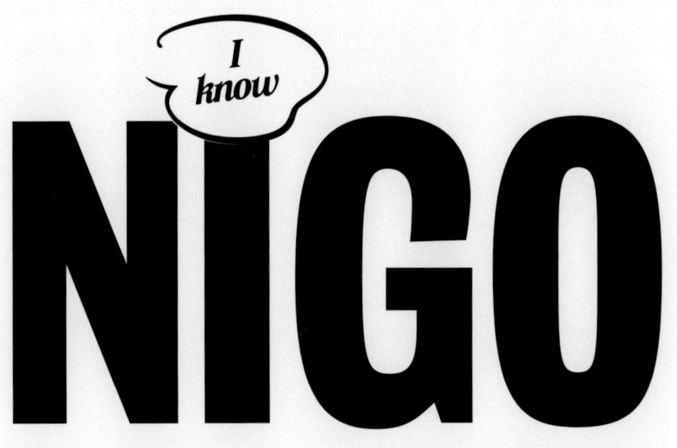

FOREWORD BY PHARRELL

NIGO®

WITH

STEVEN VICTOR
KAWS
VERBAL
SAMU TARO
KEVIN MCMULLAN

EDITED BY

IAN LUNA

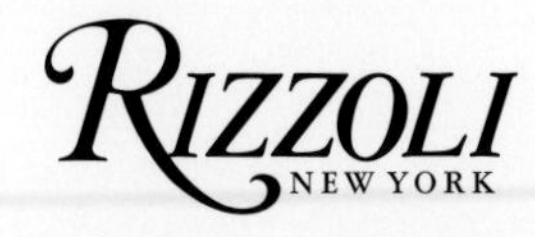

New York · Paris · London · Milan

FOREWORD BY PHARRELL

I'm terrible with times and dates, but I met NIGO® on a trip to Japan in 2002. We'd been looking for a studio to finish recording the *Clones* album project and he graciously lent us the one he had inside his Tokyo office at the time.

Since then, NIGO® has become my brother, collaborator and business partner. He is the general. He is an architect of dreams. He knows how to manifest those dreams and bring them to fruition. He has a very vivid perspective that I have been so lucky and privileged to be around. To be anywhere around him, to peer in, and to just learn.

He is my teacher.

He is definitely a Jedi, and I am a Jedi in intense study. I am a Jedi in training. My brother teaches me how to use the Force, and we will continue to cut through time and space. We will continue to find new ways to levitate, to elevate, and to share the journey with the rest of the spirits who really want to understand, to achieve enlightenment on the most luminous of levels.

My life has changed exponentially since I met him, and I never let a meeting of ours pass without me thanking him. I've been doing the same thing for over twenty years. I cannot begin to tell you the impact he's had on me, and you should really—politely—ask him.

Thanks, NIGO®-sama

—Paris, October 2023

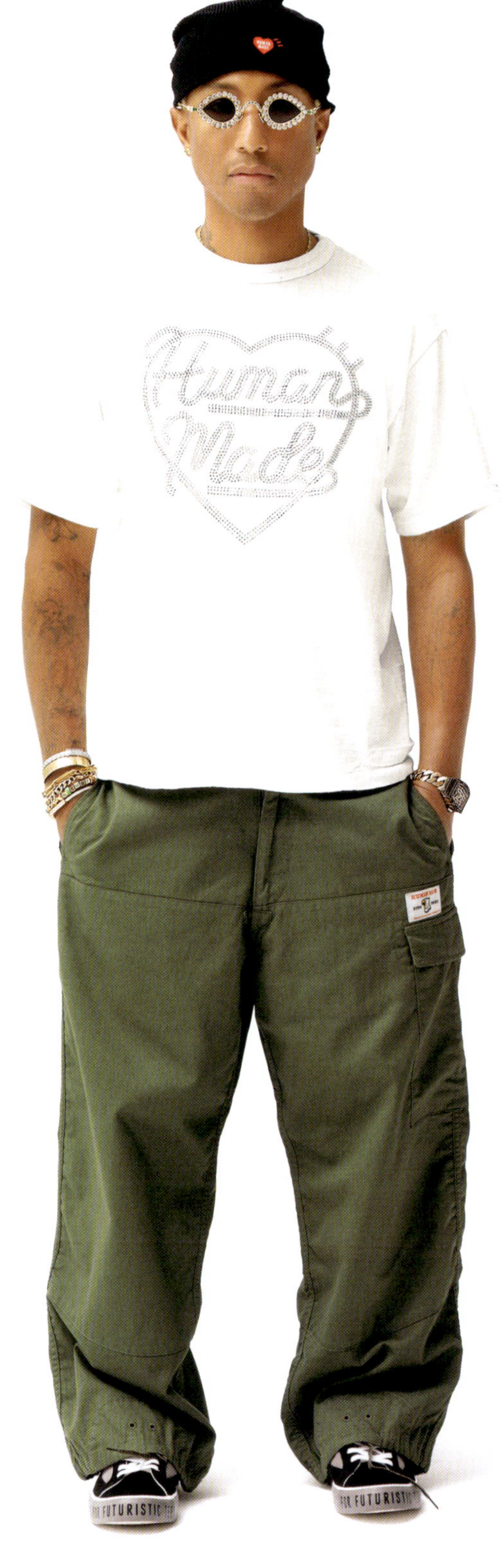

Pharrell and NIGO® wear Human Made, Spring-Summer 2023

TABLE OF CONTENTS

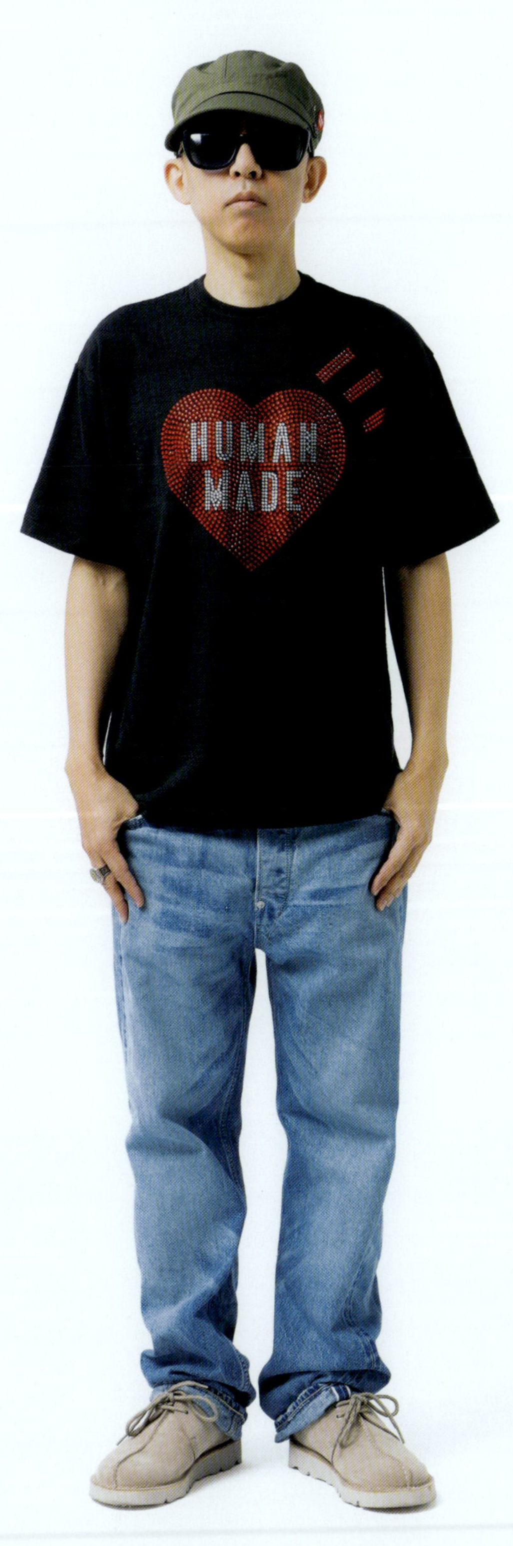

NIGO® IN CONVERSATION WITH STEVEN VICTOR

STEVEN VICTOR: Hi NIGO®

NIGO®: Hello Steven

SV: Thanks for taking the time! Firstly, what made you want to revisit music in 2021?

NIGO®: KENZO brought me back to fashion, and Steven brought me back to music. I'm very honored to continue to play a part in both worlds, as I think they go hand in hand. The fashion inspires the music, and vice-versa.

SV: What kind of music has influenced you the most in your life?

NIGO®: At first it was Buddy Holly and the Beatles. After that, I discovered hip-hop and my life really changed. I listen to all hip-hop—progressive to old school. Every era has always excited me.

SV: You are known to be a fan of The Beatles, but who is your favorite member? What is your favorite album?

NIGO®: I love the Beatles—all of them are my favorites; John, George, Paul, and Ringo. I like all of the albums. I started listening from the first album and listened to it over and over. I have listened to all in different periods and phases. *Let It Be* for a while, and then to *Please Please Me* again for a while. I've been listening to *Revolver* a lot lately—that's my latest phase.

SV: Do you pull influence from rock music?

NIGO®: I still listen to rock, but I am greatly influenced by hip-hop culture above all.

SV: If you had to name your biggest influence, one person in particular, who would it be?

NIGO®: Until I met my greatest ally, it has always been Karl Lagerfeld. But if I had to choose *one* person—it would be my ally, Pharrell Williams.

SV: That is why we had to have Pharrell involved in the album—it would have felt incomplete without him. I think you could say that *I Know NIGO®* was a dream project for me, that brings together all the artists that you have worked with and influenced you, and have also been influenced by you. Are there any other music projects or ideas that you are working on right now? Are there any current artists you would like to work on a project with?

NIGO®: Nothing in particular right now, because there is no project that can surpass this. If anything—it would have to be a sequel to *I Know NIGO®*. I like the idea of a sequel.

SV: I do too! *I Know NIGO®*, Two? In the context of music—what meaning did music have in your upbringing (especially from your childhood to your teens)? What music do you think was the most inspiring to you growing up?

NIGO®: Music always corresponded with fashion inspiration—it's something that makes life fun. It's still the same today for

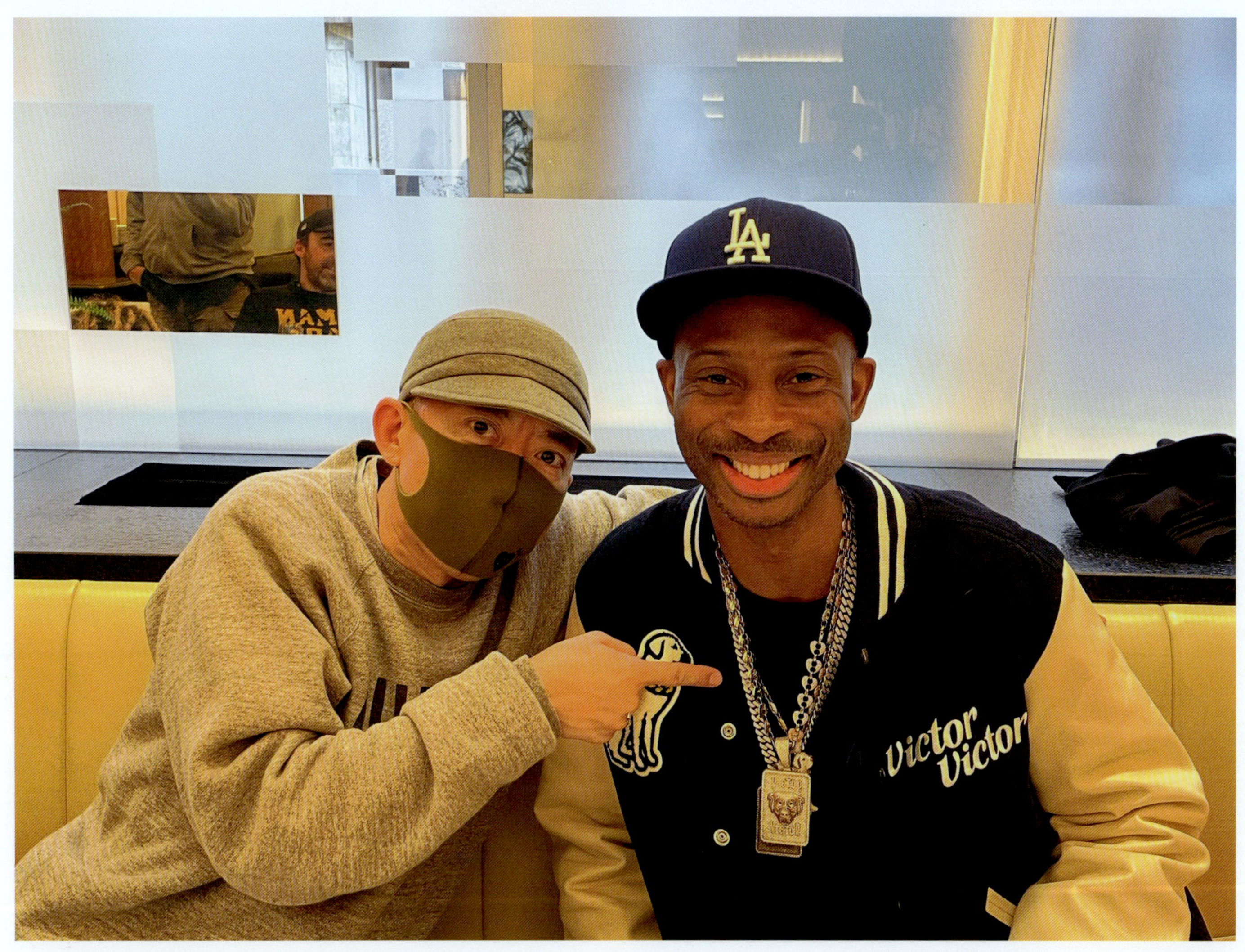

NIGO® and Steven Victor, 2021

me. My father was a police officer and played drums in a band. I always had a drum set at home. Before karaoke started up—I had a part-time job at a beer garden on the rooftop of a building where they played live music. My mother listened to hit Japanese pop songs on a vinyl record while preparing meals—and when the song ended, my role was to return the record needle to the beginning of the song.

SV: That's really interesting, with your dad being a musician and your mom being a fan of pop, it sounds like you grew up in a creative household. How do you perceive your own creativity, and how do you express it outwardly?

NIGO®: I think I'm most known for—outside of fashion and music—collecting. I am only interested in collecting things that I like or have a personal connection to. I like to collect things from different interests and find ways to store them for myself. I use my collections as a savings "bank" to draw from for each new project.

SV: So there is a ton of things on hand to always be inspired by!

NIGO®: Exactly. As I said earlier, I'm only interested in what I like. So I learn thoroughly about what I like and dig deeper and deeper.

SV: Was there ever a moment when you felt like your creativity was being suppressed?

NIGO®: When I was young, I had a lot of energy and did what I wanted, but now I'm fairly open creatively— I don't think I'm 100% right. I try my best to listen to what my team has to say, and if it's correct, I have to remember to suppress my own opinions.

SV: When you are feeling suppressed creatively—how do you deal with it? Any coping mechanisms?

NIGO®: Above all, I try to believe in what I have decided, and try it, even if I think it is different. If that doesn't work, there is a lesson to be learned. I believe that failure is not failure, but a lesson.

SV: Learning from your mistakes, it allows the creative process to be more informal. How does creativity for you strike? And what about your daily life? Do you have a pretty regimented schedule or is your life too hectic to keep a regimen?

NIGO®: I often spend time abroad or away from home, so even when I try to maintain a regular lifestyle, I can't quite do it. One thing I always do, no matter where I am is grind my favorite beans and brew my own coffee every morning. It's one of the routines I've been doing for twenty years.

SV: If you had to choose your favorite song from *I Know NIGO®*, which one would it be?

NIGO®: This is a great question. If there was a fire, and you could only escape with one item, which one would it be? I give up—There is no right answer. It is impossible to choose one song from the album. They are all my favorite songs!

SV: That's understandable, it is hard to choose one. It's like the album is your family. Do you think you could have pursued another career outside of fashion?

NIGO®: That's the only thing I am good at.

—Tokyo, November 2023

A$AP Rocky, Lil Uzi Vert, & NIGO® on set for the "HEAVY" music video, shot in December 2021, at Jacob & Co., New York City

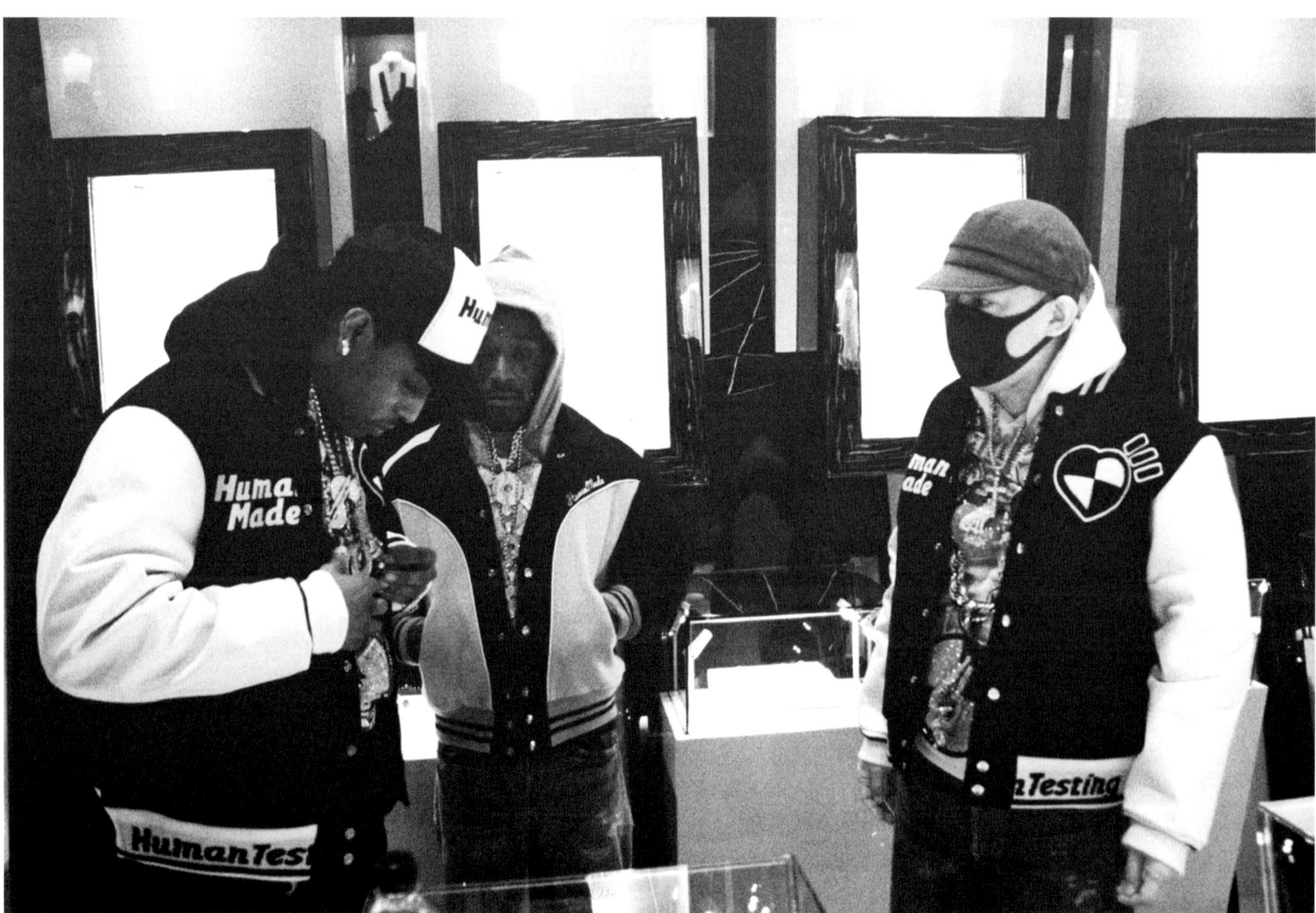

An Appreciation: by Samu Taro
The NIGO® Sound

In 2006, NIGO® appeared alongside Pharrell Williams on the red carpet at the 2006 MTV Video Music Awards in New York City. Dressed in a Bape tee, baggy IceCream jeans and a giant Jacob the Jeweler diamond pendant draped around his neck he looked just as much the part as the American rap icon and superstar producer he was standing next to. Though NIGO® wasn't yet a household name in the U.S., he would soon conquer the rap world and set a new trajectory in streetwear with his clothing line, *A Bathing Ape®.

Around this time, NIGO® was gearing up for the debut of TERIYAKI BOYZ®, the Japanese hip-hop supergroup he founded in Tokyo. Acting as the group's DJ and torchbearer, NIGO® had assembled four hip-hip artists from some of the biggest "J-Urban" groups around. Their Def Jam debut album, *Beef or Chicken*, pulled in producer credits from friends like Daft Punk, Ad-Rock, DJ Premier and of course the Neptunes. The album's initial lukewarm reception was soon forgotten when NIGO® called in a favor from Kanye West to jump on the remix of the single, "I Still Love H.E.R." in 2007.

It is NIGO®'s position as cultural ambassador in Japan that has enabled him to step into realms beyond fashion. Back in the 1990s, he played host to everyone from rappers like the Beastie Boys, to graffiti artists like Futura and Stash. But it was taste-making recording artists like James Lavelle, Cornelius and the Japanese singer CHERIE® who provided the necessary clout to connect Bape with the music industry. Lavelle, the legendary UK DJ, trip-hop pioneer and friend of NIGO® was instrumental in building hype around Bape during the brand's early years, particularly in Britain, where he was NIGO®'s go-to, alongside Stone Roses singer and solo artist Ian Brown.

As well as being one of the early influencers to endorse Bape overseas, Lavelle was also the first to debut NIGO®'s music. The duo quietly released *James* vs. NIGO®–*A Bathing Ape vs Mo'Wax* on the Mo'Wax imprint in 1997. The experimental record saw NIGO® attempt versions of the genres he liked: trip-hop, downtempo and drum and bass. Overseeing the song concepts, samples, and drum programming, NIGO® pulled together a constellation of producers and artists from Japan, America and the UK, including UNKLE, Scratch Perverts, DJ Shadow and Kan Takagi.

NIGO® would follow up with Mo'Wax in 2000 with *NIGO®—Ape Sounds*, a fascinating, experimental record that invited back collaborators from the first record along with other notable names like producer Cornelius. While it's easy to understand why the record didn't receive the level of international acclaim it deserved, what it did do was prove how NIGO® had always been ahead of the curve. In a *New Yorker* article from 2017, writer Matthew Trammell wrote: "What thrilled me was not just the confidence and ambition of the material—the punk rag-doll of 'Jet Set' or the Beatles wink of 'A Simple Song'—but how prescient NIGO®'s music sounded. His tracks 'Monster' and 'Freediving' nearly preempt N.E.R.D.'s coy pop-rock style, which would debut two years later, and the solar fuzz of 'Too Much' heralds the bright tones of Kid Cudi, a rapper who, years later, would get his start working at Bape's New York shop."

These early releases, along with *NIGO®: (B)ape Sounds* in 2004, demonstrate the limitlessness of NIGO®'s legacy. A master of taste and design, NIGO® has created an entire world and lifestyle off the back of his work in fashion, art, food and travel. His venture into music is just another string to his bow. Both *Ape Sounds* and *A Bathing Ape vs Mo'Wax* are now studied in detail. From the carefully curated list of musicians on the records to the cover art and packaging designed in collaboration with graffiti artist Futura, NIGO® showed how to turn a simple commodity like an album into a cultural artifact.

While these oddities are reserved for the most discerning fans, NIGO® has managed to amplify his visibility in the public eye through his relationship with Pharrell. Though they initially connected through a mutual love for jewelry, it was inside NIGO®'s recording studio at the former Nowhere offices in Tokyo where the two first met. Pharrell discovered NIGO® 's private museum, where he kept a slice of pop culture history, from original Beatles instruments, Andy Warhol art, vintage Jean Prouvé furniture, and the expansive Bape archive.

“I WOULDN’T BE WHO I AM TODAY IF I HADN’T MET [PHARRELL]. I DON’T THINK I COULD HAVE MADE IT OUT OF JAPAN: THAT WAS SOMETHING I WANTED TO ACHIEVE.”

From that moment on, the two friends became a creative powerhouse that impacted the history of streetwear and fashion worldwide. For the past twenty years, the dynamic duo have established themselves as a kind of Michael Jordan and Scottie Pippen of street culture, influencing not only one another’s creative output but also helping shape design, fashion and contemporary lifestyle in the process. In Pharrell’s first book with Rizzoli, *Pharrell: Places and Spaces I’ve Been*, NIGO® admitted “I wouldn’t be who I am today if I hadn’t met [Pharrell]. I don’t think I could have made it out of Japan: that was something I wanted to achieve.”

NIGO®’s appearances in Pharrell’s music videos like “Frontin’” as well as their frequent public appearances together throughout the early to mid-2000s helped propel NIGO®’s profile from a niche streetwear designer to a cultural phenomenon. NIGO®’s influence and presence in the music world have only grown stronger over the past two decades. Whether he’s outfitting big-name artists like Lil Uzi Vert in Human Made, having Tyler, the Creator and Ye sit front row at KENZO or continuing to make magic with Pharrell, NIGO® has created a multifaceted legacy, one rivaled by a very few. It’s easy to see why NIGO®’s peers, like A$AP Rocky describe him as being as important to hip-hop as Pharrell, Slick Rick or Kanye.

Given his status as a “god of culture,” in the Japanese press, it only makes sense that NIGO® drew on his cultural connections for the *I Know NIGO®* album. Released on Steven Victor’s Victor Victor imprint in 2022, the album marked NIGO®’s return to music after nearly two decades. This time around, he enlisted Pharrell to serve alongside him as co-executive producer, as well as a rotating cast of A-list rappers: Tyler, The Creator, A$AP Rocky, Kid Cudi, Pusha T, No Malice and Lil Uzi Vert were just a few names to grace the credits and receive the *I Know NIGO®* Human Made varsity jackets produced expressly for the album. More than anything, the project is a testament to NIGO®’s passion for all things hip-hop and his unique contribution to the culture.

—United Kingdom, October 2023

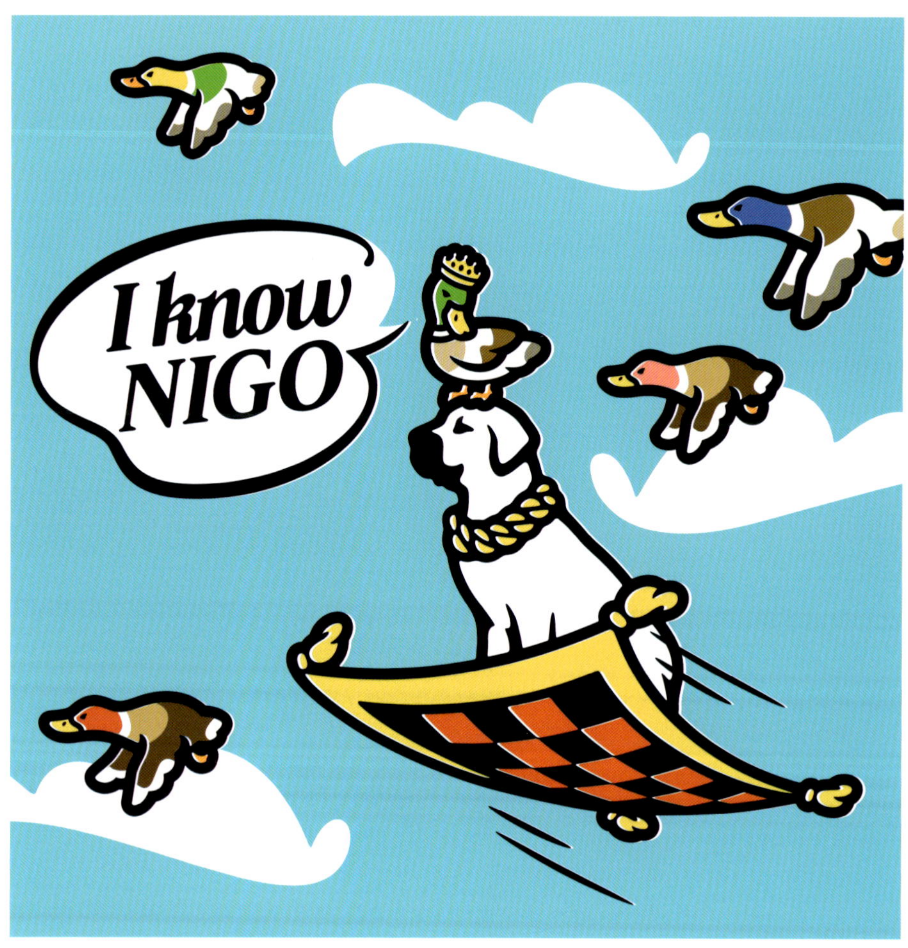

Cover art for the I Know NIGO® album. Designed by NIGO®, the iconography draws from Human Made, which uses mallard ducks extensively in its graphics, and references one of the most memorable advertising mascots of the 20th century, Nipper, the RCA Victor dog.

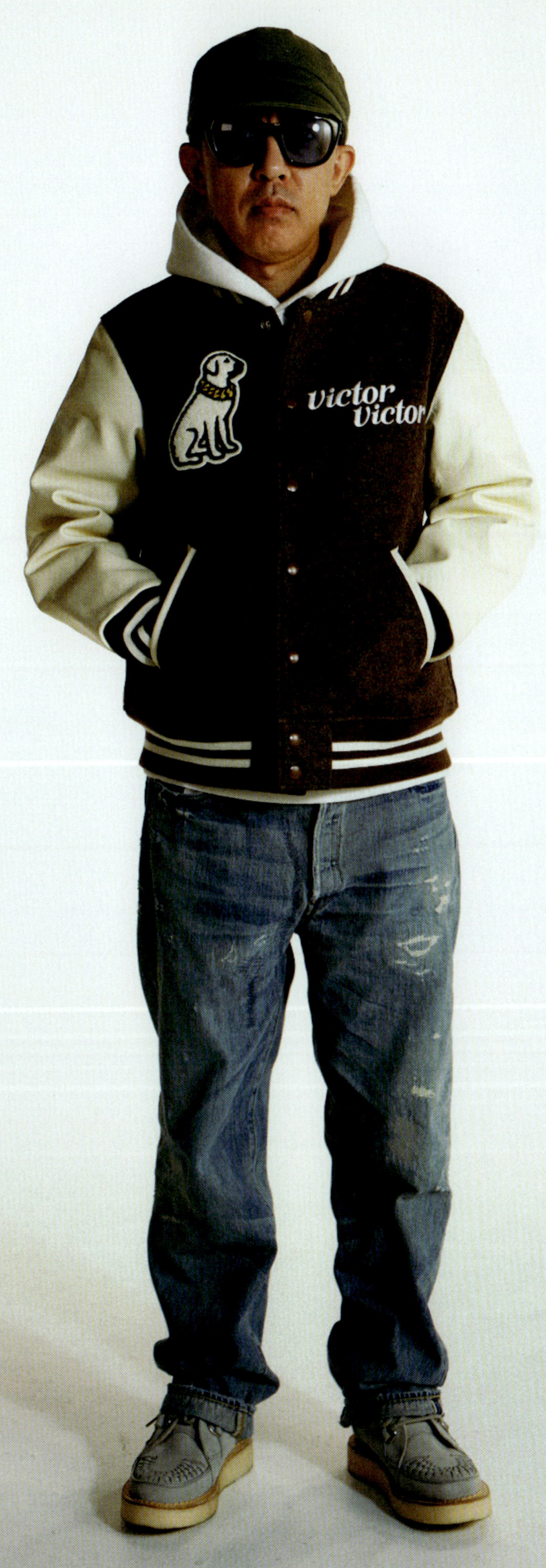
victor
victor

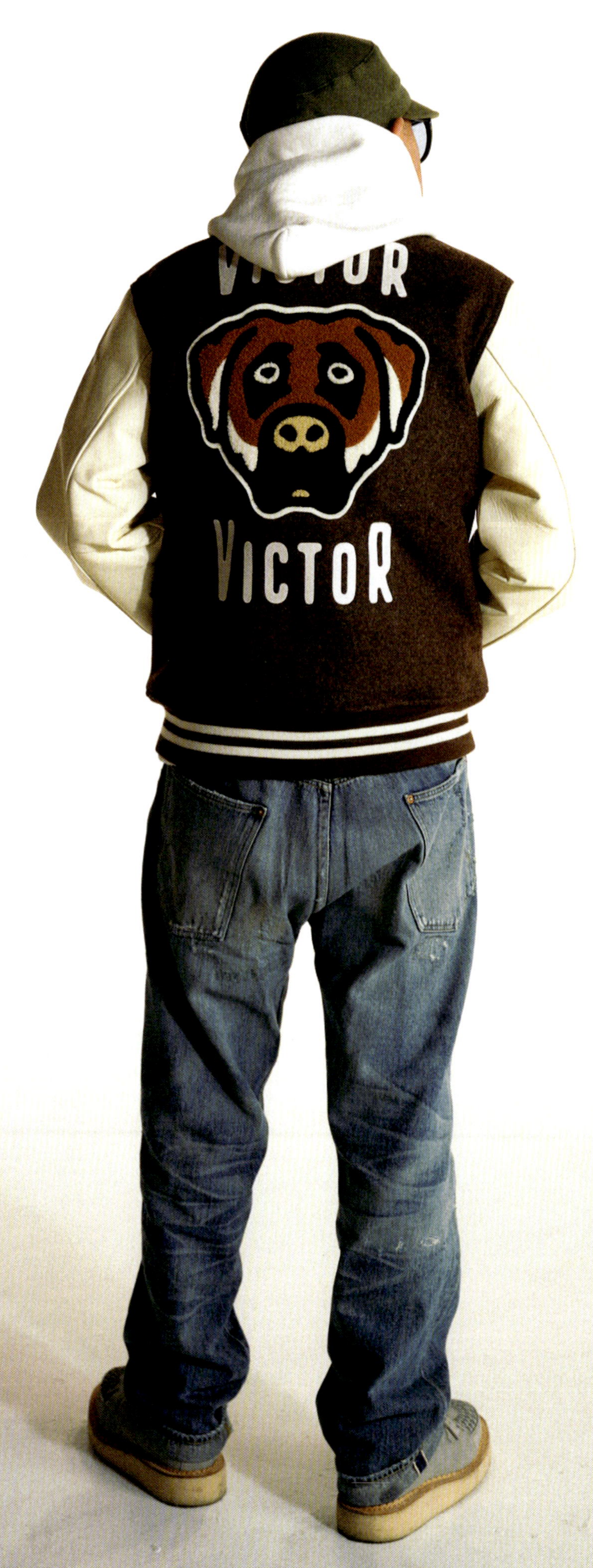
VICTOR

NIGO® wearing the VICTOR VICTOR varsity jacket produced by Human Made

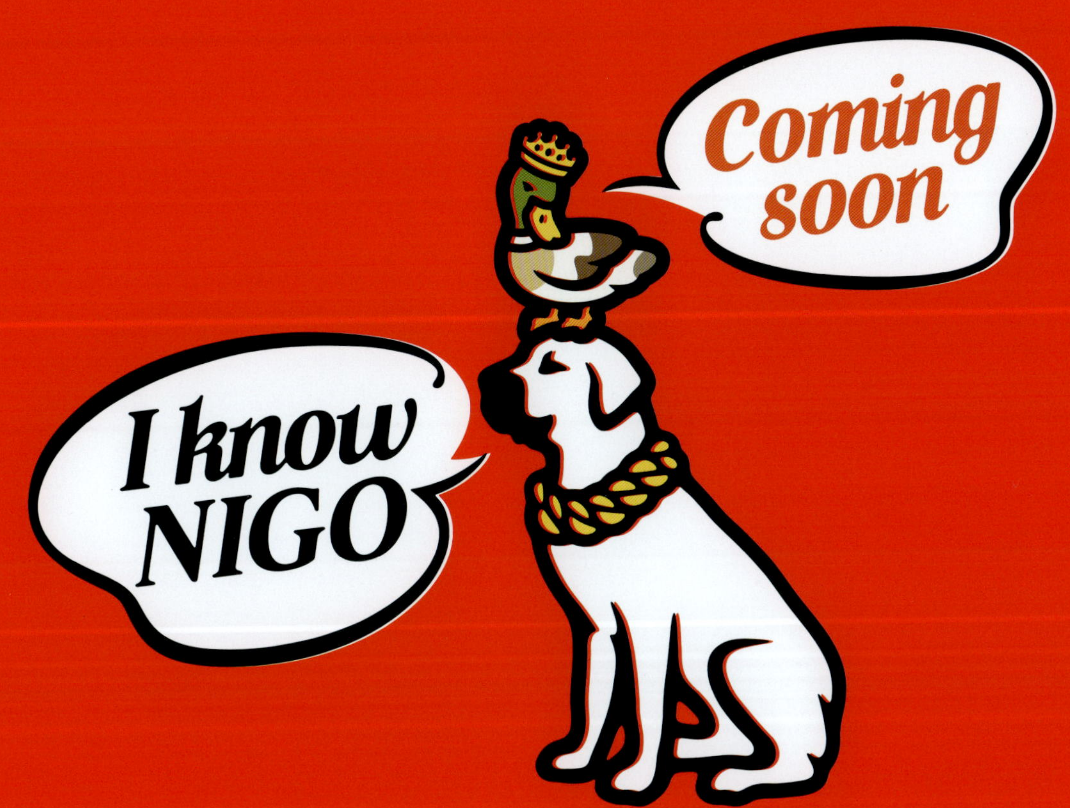

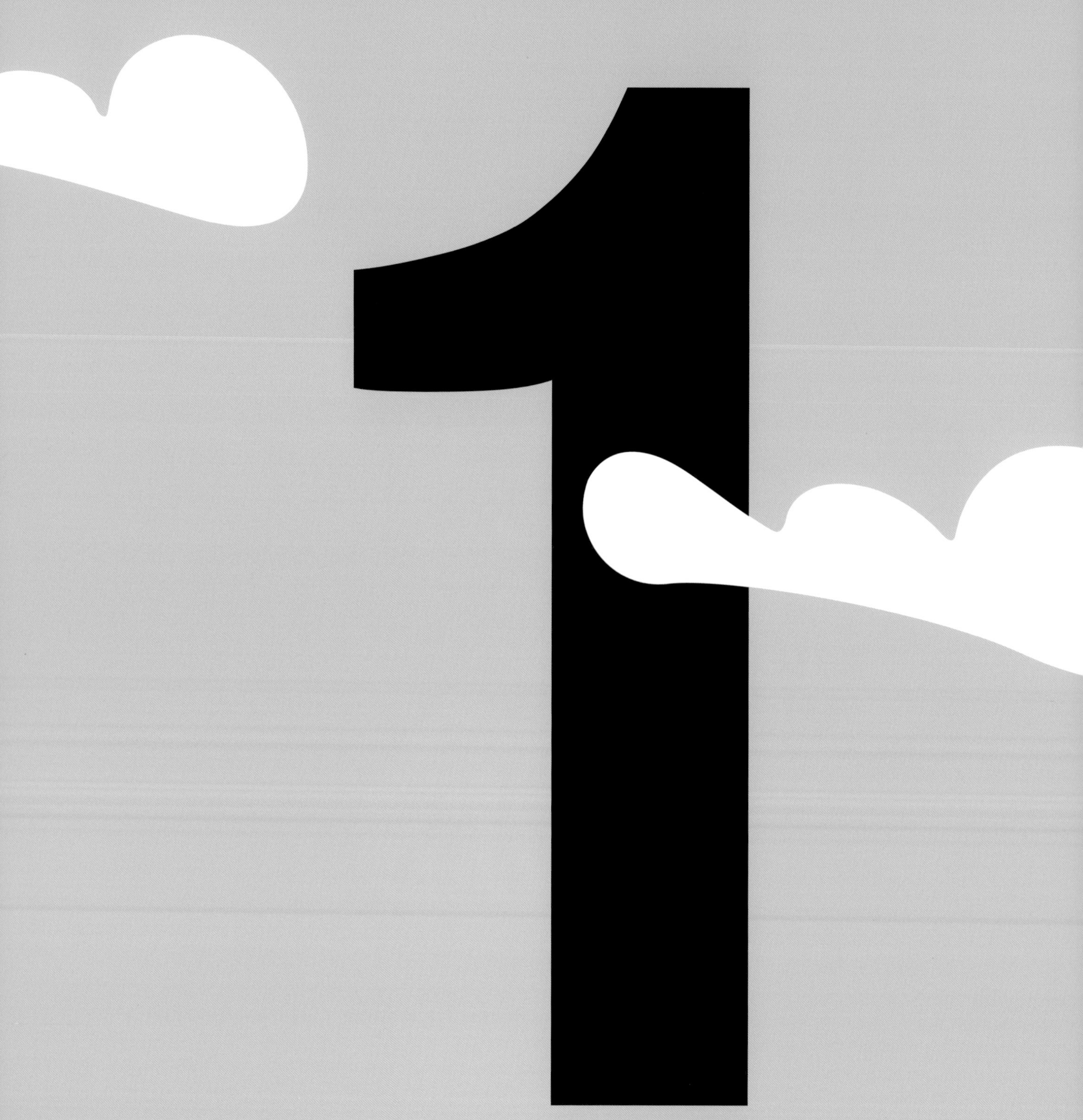

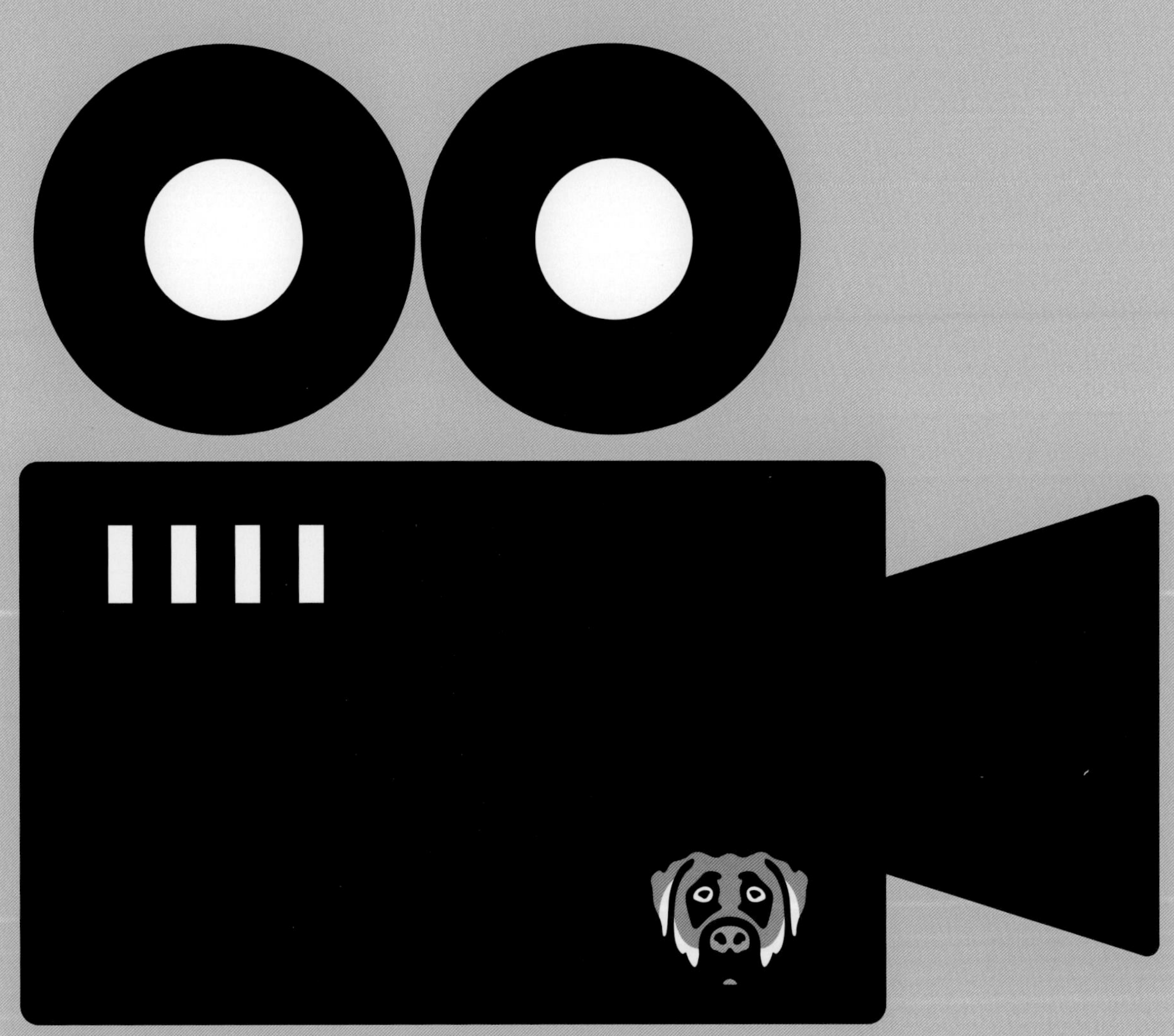

Album Track Listing

1. Lost and Found Freestyle 2019 (with A$AP Rocky & Tyler, The Creator)
(Rakim Mayers, Tyler Okonma, Willie James Clark, Bernard James Freeman, Clifford J. Harris, Clinton Darryl Mansell, Clarence Reid, Stayve Thomas, Leroy Williams, Sammie Norris, Donnell Prince, Micah Le Var Troy, Chad Hugo, Pharrell Williams) Sony/ATV Songs LLC / A$AP Rocky Publishing LLC (BMI)/a boy is a gun*, administered by Sony/ATV Ballad (BMI)/EMI Longitude Music (BMI)/Universal Music – Z Tunes LLC (ASCAP)/Pimp My Pen Int. c/o Universal Music Publishing Ltd. (PRS)/Domani And Ya Majesty's Music obo Sony/ATV Allegro (ASCAP)/Decca Music Group Ltd. c/o Universal Songs of PolyGram Int. (BMI)/EMI Longitude Music (BMI)/EMI Blackwood Music Inc. (BMI)/Slim Thug Publishing (BMI)/Noddfactor Publishing (BMI)/Reservoir 416 (BMI)/Donnell Prince Designee (ASCAP)/Pastor Troy Publishing (BMI)/Universal Music – Careers (BMI)/Slim Thug Publishing (BMI) c/o EMI Blackwood Music/Waters Of Nazareth Publishing (GMR) c/o Warner Chappell Music. Produced by Hector Delgado. Recorded by Hector Delgado at Westlake Recording Studios, Los Angeles, CA. Recorded by Vic Wainstein at COLDWATER STUDIOS, Los Angeles, CA; Westlake Recording Studios, Los Angeles, CA. Mixed by Hector Delgado at Clockwork Studios, Los Angeles, CA and assisted by Franky Kastle. Mastered by Tatsuya Sato at The Mastering Palace, New York, NY; Atmos mix by Fabian Marasciullo for That's A Dope Mix; A$AP Rocky appears courtesy of A$AP Worldwide/Polo Grounds Music/RCA Records; Tyler, The Creator appears courtesy of Columbia Records, a division of Sony Music Entertainment; Contains interpolation from "3 Kings" written by Willie James Clark, Bernard James Freeman, Clifford J. Harris, Clinton Darryl Mansell, Clarence Reid, Stayve Thomas, Leroy Williams, Sammie Norris, Donnell Prince, Micah Le Var Troy and published by EMI Longitude Music (BMI), Universal Music – Z Tunes LLC (ASCAP), Pimp My Pen Int. c/o Universal Music Publishing Ltd. (PRS), Domani And Ya Majesty's Music obo Sony/ATV Allegro (ASCAP), Decca Music Group Ltd. c/o Universal Songs of PolyGram Int. (BMI), EMI Longitude Music (BMI), EMI Blackwood Music Inc. (BMI), Slim Thug Publishing (BMI), Noddfactor Publishing (BMI), Reservoir 416 (BMI), Donnell Prince Designee (ASCAP), Pastor Troy Publishing (BMI) Used by permission. All rights reserved. Contains interpolation from "Like A Boss" written by Chad Hugo, Pharrell Williams, Stayve Thomas and published by Universal Music – Careers (BMI), Slim Thug Publishing (BMI) c/o EMI Blackwood Music, Waters Of Nazareth Publishing (GMR) c/o Warner Chappell Music. Used by permission. All rights reserved.

2. Arya (with A$AP Rocky)
(Rakim Mayers, Hector Delgado, Carter Lang, Westen Weiss) Sony/ATV Songs LLC / A$AP Rocky Publishing LLC (BMI)/Clockworklabs Music (BMI)/Carter Lang Publishing Designee, Warner Tamerlane Publishing Corp / Zuma Tuna LLC (BMI)/Universal Music Corp/ Electric Feel Music, LLC, Westen Weiss Productions, LLC (ASCAP); Produced by Lord Pretty Flacko Jodye, Hector Delgado, Carter Lang and Westen Weiss; Recorded by Hector Delgado at Westlake Recording Studios, Los Angeles, CA; Mixed by Hector Delgado at Clockwork Studios, Los Angeles, CA and assisted by Franky Kastle; Mastered by Tatsuya Sato at The Mastering Palace, New York, NY; Atmos mix by Fabian Marasciullo for That's A Dope Mix; A$AP Rocky appears courtesy of A$AP Worldwide/Polo Grounds Music/RCA Records.

3. Punch Bowl (with Clipse)
(Terrence Thornton, Gene Thornton, Pharrell) Sony/ATV Songs LLC/Neighborhood Pusha (BMI)/Gene Thornton Publishing Designee/EMI April Music, Inc. o/b/o itself and Even More Water From Nazareth (GMR); Produced by Pharrell; Additional Production by Chad Hugo; Additional Programming by Mike Larson for Hilldale Systems, LLC; Recorded by Mike Larson for Hilldale Systems, LLC at Criteria Recording Studios, Miami, FL, The Boathouse, Miami, FL, The Library Room, Miami, FL and assisted by Morgan David; Recorded by Robert Ulsh at Master Sound Studios, Virginia Beach, VA; Mixed by Manny Marroquin at Larrabee Studios, North Hollywood, CA and assisted by Zach Pereyra, Anthony Vilchis, and Trey Station; Mastered by Michelle Mancini for Demifugue Mastering at Larrabee Studios, North Hollywood, CA; Atmos mix by Fabian Marasciullo for That's A Dope Mix; Pusha T appears courtesy of Getting Out Our Dreams, Inc./Def Jam Recordings, a division of UMG Recordings Inc.

4. Functional Addict (with Pharrell & Gunna)
(Pharrell, Sergio Kitchens) EMI April Music, Inc. o/b/o itself and Even More Water From Nazareth (GMR)/Gunna Music / Administered by Songs of Kobalt Music Publishing (BMI); Produced by Pharrell; Recorded by Mike Larson for Hilldale Systems, LLC at The Library Room, Miami, FL; Recorded by Flo Ongonga at Home Studio; Mixed by Manny Marroquin at Larrabee Studios, North Hollywood, CA and assisted by Zach Pereyra, Anthony Vilchis and Trey Station; Mastered by Michelle Mancini for Demifugue Mastering at Larrabee Studios, North Hollywood, CA; Atmos mix by Fabian Marasciullo for That's A Dope Mix; Pharrell appears courtesy of i am OTHER/Columbia Records; Gunna appears courtesy of Young Stoner Life Records / 300 Entertainment.

5. Want It Bad (with Kid Cudi)
(Scott Mescudi, Pharrell) Universal Music Publishing Group (ASCAP)/EMI April Music, Inc. o/b/o itself and Even More Water From Nazareth (GMR); Produced by Pharrell; Recorded by William J. Sullivan and Andres Osorio at Moon Man's Landing, Los Angeles, CA; Recorded by Mike Larson for Hilldale Systems, LLC at The Library Room, Miami, FL; Mixed by Manny Marroquin at Larrabee Studios, North Hollywood, CA and assisted by Zach Pereyra, Anthony Vilchis, and Trey Station; Mastered by Michelle Mancini for Demifugue Mastering at Larrabee Studios, North Hollywood, CA; Atmos mix by Fabian Marasciullo for That's A Dope Mix; Kid Cudi appears courtesy of Republic Records, a division of UMG Recordings, Inc.

6. More Tonight (with Teriyaki Boyz)
(Verbal, Ilmari, Ryo-Z, Wise, Pharrell) Verbal Publishing Designee/Ilmari Publishing Designee/ Ryo-Z Publishing Designee/Wise Publishing Designee/ EMI April Music, Inc. o/b/o itself and Even More Water From Nazareth (GMR); Produced by Pharrell; Additional Vocals by Shurland Ayers; Recorded by Lucas Valentine at Ambush® Studio, Tokyo; Recorded by Mike Larson for Hilldale Systems, LLC at OTHER Island Studios, Miami Beach, FL; Mixed by Finis "KY" White at Club 25, Atlanta, GA; Mastered by Michelle Mancini for Demifugue Mastering at Larrabee Studios, North Hollywood, CA; Atmos mix by Fabian Marasciullo for That's A Dope Mix; Verbal appears courtesy of rhythm zone / AVEX ENTERTAINMENT INC.

7. Paper Plates (with Pharrell & Ferg)
(Pharrell, Darold Durard Brown Ferguson Jr.) EMI April Music, Inc. o/b/o itself and Even More Water From Nazareth; (GMR)/Fergenstein Music/Sony/ATV Songs LLC (BMI); Produced by Pharrell; Programming by Shelly Berg and OjiVolta; Additional programming by Mike Larson for Hilldale Systems, LLC; Orchestration by Shelly Berg and OjiVolta; Choir Vocal Production by Balint Sapszon; Choir Conductor: Marton Toth; Choir Vocals Recorded by Denes Redly; Recorded by Mike Larson for Hilldale Systems, LLC at Chalice Recording Studios, Hollywood, CA and assisted by Thomas Cullison; Mixed by Finis "KY" White at Club 25, Atlanta, GA; Mastered by Michelle Mancini for Demifugue Mastering at Larrabee Studios, North Hollywood, CA; Atmos mix by Fabian Marasciullo for That's A Dope Mix; Pharrell appears courtesy of i am OTHER/ Columbia Records; Ferg appears courtesy of A$AP Worldwide/Polo Grounds Music/RCA Records

8. Hear Me Clearly (with Pusha T)
(Terrence Thornton, Rennard East, Ye, Jahmal Gwin, Luca Starz, Lawrence Berment, Shawn Carter, William Roberts, Leigh Elliott, Johnny Mollings, Leonard Mollings, John Stephens) Neighborhood Pusha/Sony ATV (BMI)/Rennard East Publishing Designee/Please Gimme My Publishing, Inc./ EMI Blackwood Music, Inc. (BMI)/BoardMemberz Music LLC/Sony ATV (BMI)/Freibank (GEMA)/Mindkilla Music Productions (ASCAP)/Carter Boys Music (ASCAP) c/o Sony Music Publishing/4 Blunts Lit At Once (BMI) c/o Sony Music Publishing/Universal Tunes (SESAC) c/o Universal Music Publishing Group/First and Gold Publishing (BMI) administered by Songs of Kobalt Music Publishing (BMI)/Mollings Music (BMI) administered by Songs of Kobalt Music Publishing (BMI)/John Legend Publishing (BMI) c/o BMG Rights Management US LLC; Produced by Ye, BoogzDaBeast; Co-Produced by Luca Starz; Additional Production by ThaMyind; Recorded by Mike Larson for Hilldale Systems, LLC at Criteria Recording Studios, Miami, FL and assisted by Maximillian "Vandal" Deak, Morgan David and Nick Valentine; Mixed by Manny Marroquin at Larrabee Studios, North Hollywood, CA and assisted by Zach Pereyra, Anthony Vilchis, and Trey Station; Mastered by Michelle Mancini for Demifugue Mastering at Larrabee Studios, North Hollywood, CA; Atmos mix by Fabian Marasciullo for That's A Dope Mix; Pusha T appears courtesy of Getting Out Our Dreams, Inc./Def Jam Recordings, a division of UMG Recordings Inc.; Contains interpolation from "Free Mason" written by Shawn Carter, William Roberts, Leigh Elliott, Johnny Mollings, Leonard Mollings, John Stephens and published by Carter Boys Music (ASCAP) c/o Sony Music Publishing, 4 Blunts Lit At Once (BMI) c/o Sony Music Publishing, Universal Tunes (SESAC) c/o Universal Music Publishing Group, First and Gold Publishing (BMI) administered by Songs of Kobalt Music Publishing (BMI), Irocnasty Music (BMI) administered by Songs of Kobalt Music Publishing (BMI), Mollings Music (BMI) administered by Songs of Kobalt Music Publishing (BMI), John Legend Publishing (BMI) c/o BMG Rights Management US LLC Used by permission. All rights reserved.

9. Remember (with Pop Smoke)
(Bashar Jackson, Jose Luis Reynoso-Contreras, Angel Isaac Orozco, Samir Afuni, Kiesa Ellestad) Warner Chappell/Hozay Beats/Reddoe Beats LLC/Music Of Liberal Arts Publishing (BMI) and Afuni Music (BMI) c/o Songs Of Universal Inc. (BMI)/Stellar Songs LTD (BMI) and Elephant Eye Music (NS) c/o EMI Blackwood Music Inc (BMI); Produced by Hozay Beats and Reddoe Beats; Recorded by ZZ at Pass the Mic Sounds, New York, NY; Mixed by Jess Jackson at London Town Studios, Los Angeles, CA and assisted by David Bone; Mastered by Jess Jackson at London Town Studios, Los Angeles, CA; Atmos mix by Jess Jackson; Pop Smoke appears courtesy of Victor Victor Worldwide/Republic Records, a division of UMG Recordings, Inc.; Contains excerpts from "Sounds of a Woman" written by Samir Afuni, Kiesa Ellestad and published by Music Of Liberal Arts Publishing (BMI) and Afuni Music (BMI) c/o Songs Of Universal Inc. (BMI), Stellar Songs LTD (BMI) and Elephant Eye Music (NS) c/o EMI Blackwood Music Inc (BMI) Used by permission. All rights reserved. "Remember" contains excerpts from "Sound of a Woman" performed by Kiesza courtesy of UMG used by permission.

10. Heavy (with Lil Uzi Vert)
(Symere Bysil Woods, Manalla Yusuf Abdul-Aziz, Brandon Veal, Kevin Gomringer, Tim Gomringer) ASCAPUZI/WB Music Corp (ASCAP)/Sony ATV/Sony Music Publishing (BMI)/ UMPG; Produced by AxL, Brandon Finessin and CuBeatz; Recorded by Benjamin Thomas at Jungle City, NY; Mixed by Don Cannon at Generation Now and assisted by Benjamin Thomas; Mastered by Colin Leonard at SING Mastering, Atlanta, GA using SING Technology® (Patented); Atmos mix by Fabian Marasciullo for That's A Dope Mix; Lil Uzi Vert appears courtesy of Generation Now/Atlantic Recording Corporation

11. Come On, Let's Go (with Tyler, The Creator)
(Tyler Okonma, Pharrell) a boy is a gun*, administered by Sony/ATV Ballad (BMI)/EMI April Music, Inc. o/b/o itself and Even More Water From Nazareth (GMR); Produced by Pharrell; Arranged by Tyler Okonma; Additional Vocals by Reign Judge; Recorded by Tyler Okonma and Vic Wainstein at COLDWATER STUDIOS, Los Angeles, CA; Recorded by Mike Larson for Hilldale Systems, LLC at The Library Room, Miami, FL; Mixed by NealHPogue for 411 E 9th Ave at HotPurplePettingZoo, Los Angeles, CA; Mastered by Michelle Mancini for Demifugue Mastering at Larrabee Studios, North Hollywood, CA; Atmos mix by Fabian Marasciullo for That's A Dope Mix; Tyler, The Creator appears courtesy of Columbia Records, a division of Sony Music Entertainment

Each featured artist on the album was given a custom designed duck to represent their contribution to the collaborative project.

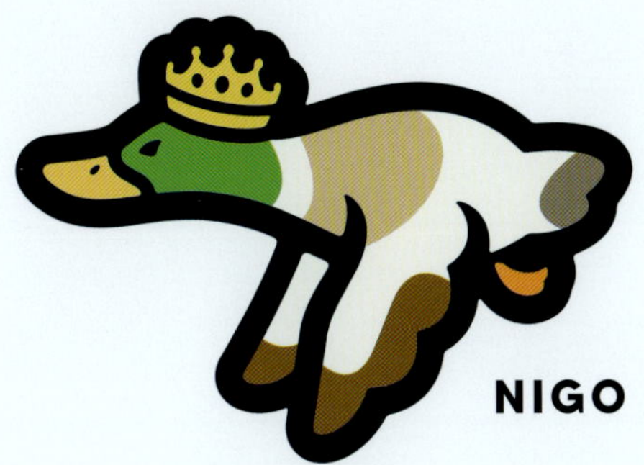

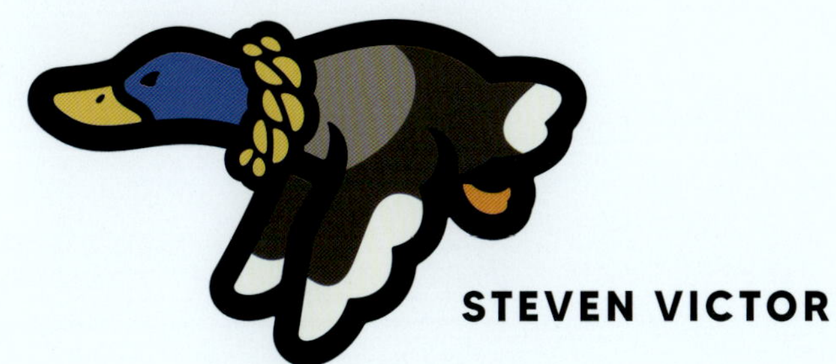

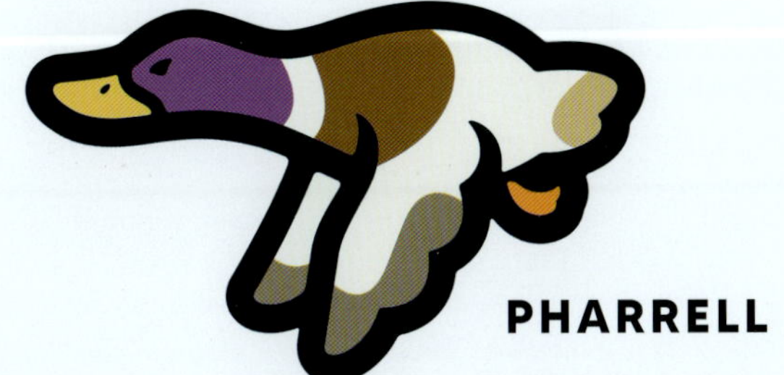

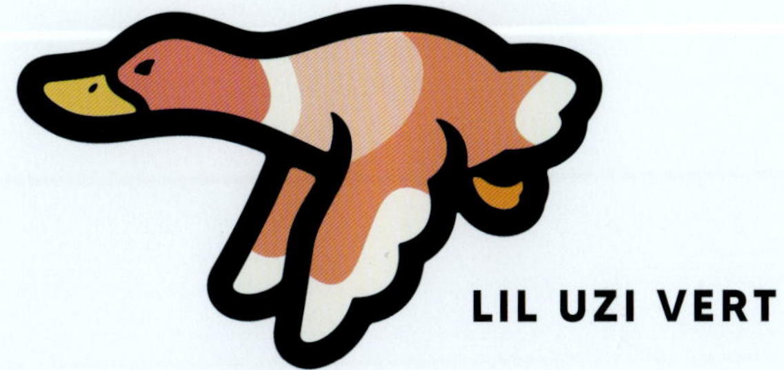

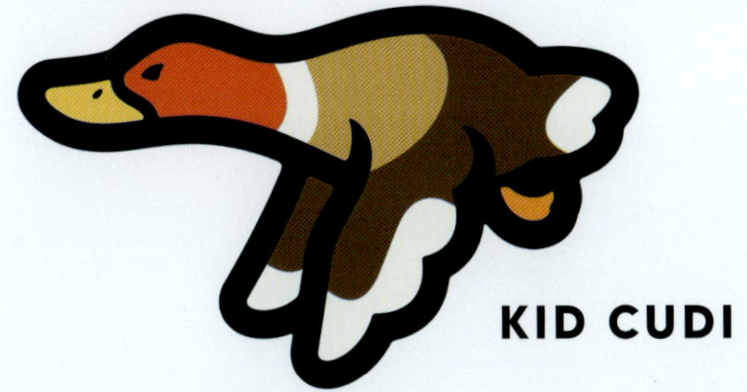

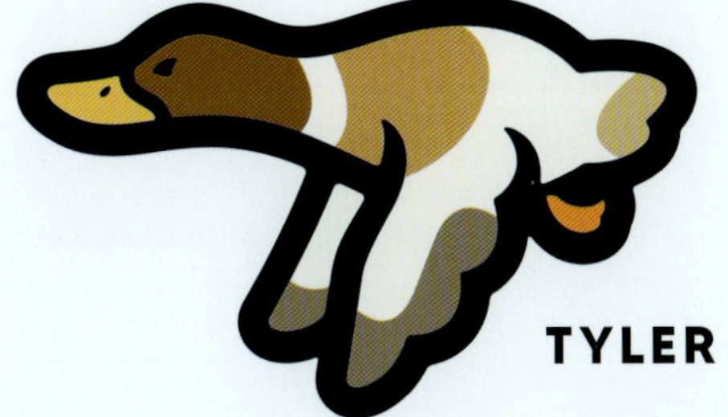

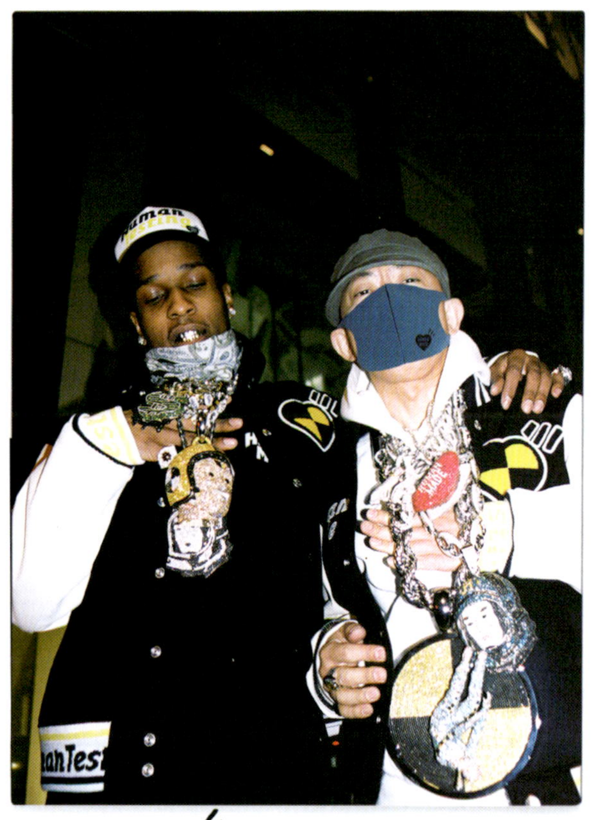

NIGO

A$AP ARYA

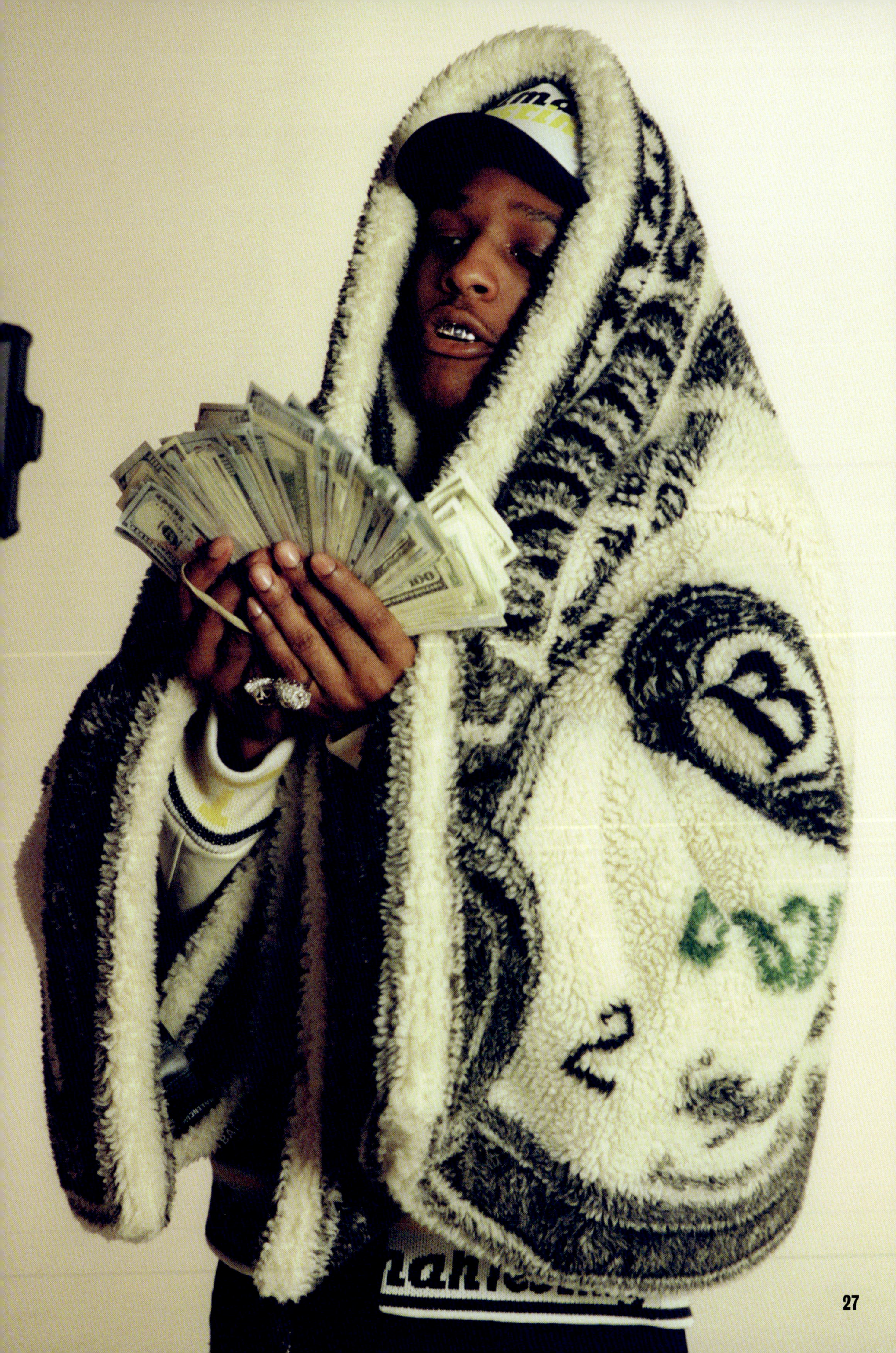

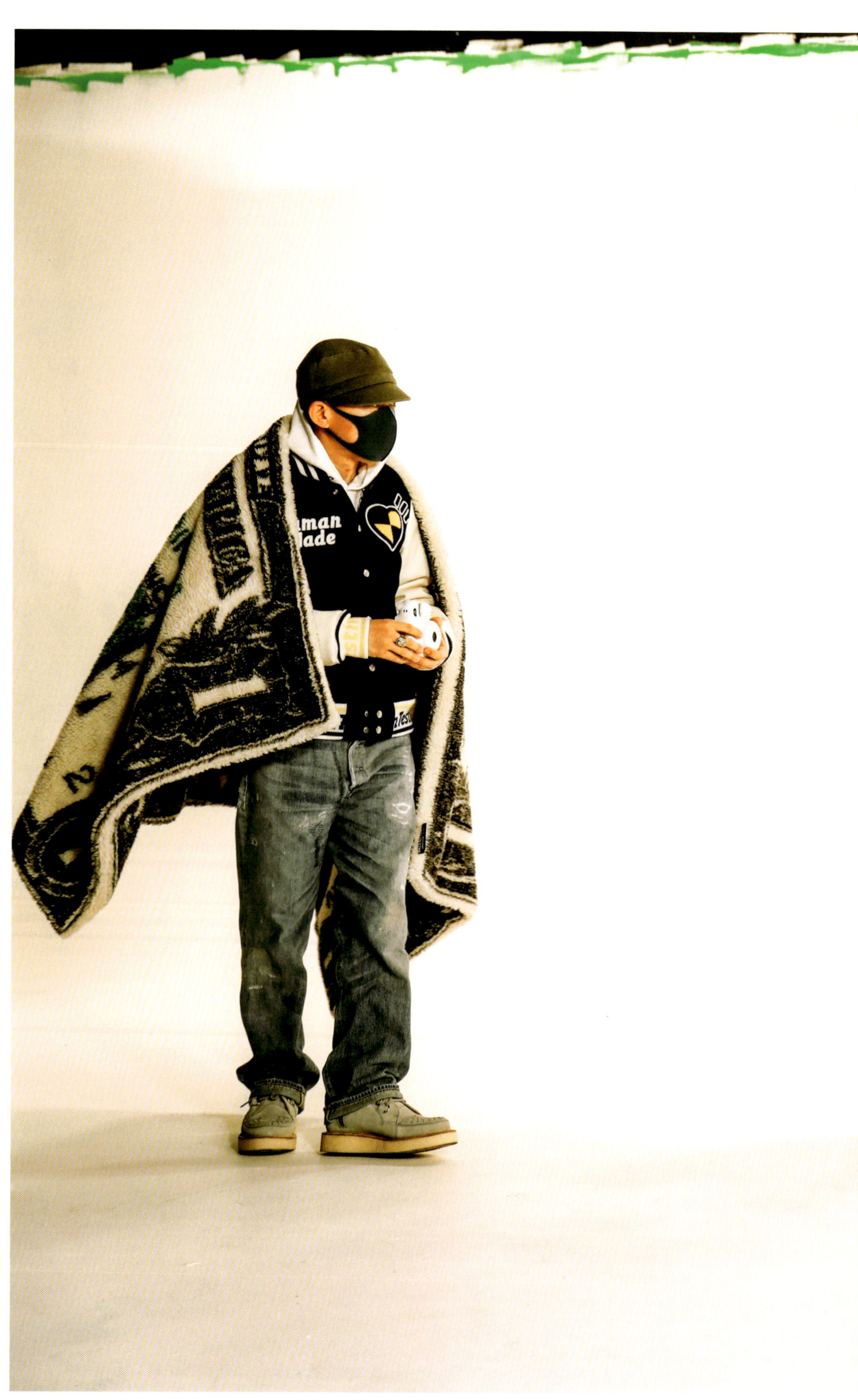

An impromptu appearance by Kid Cudi on the set of "ARYA"

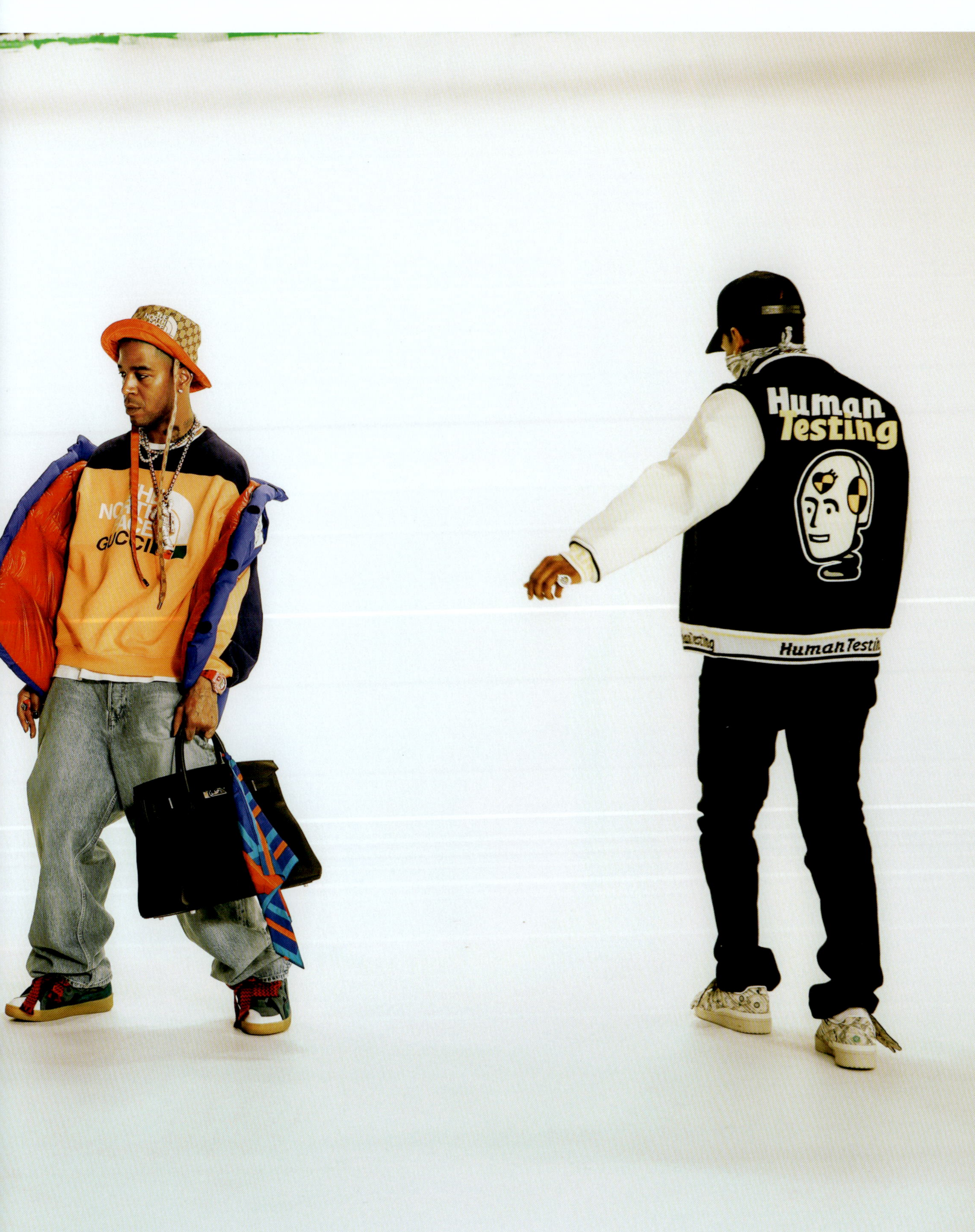
Human
Testing
HumanTesting
GUCCI

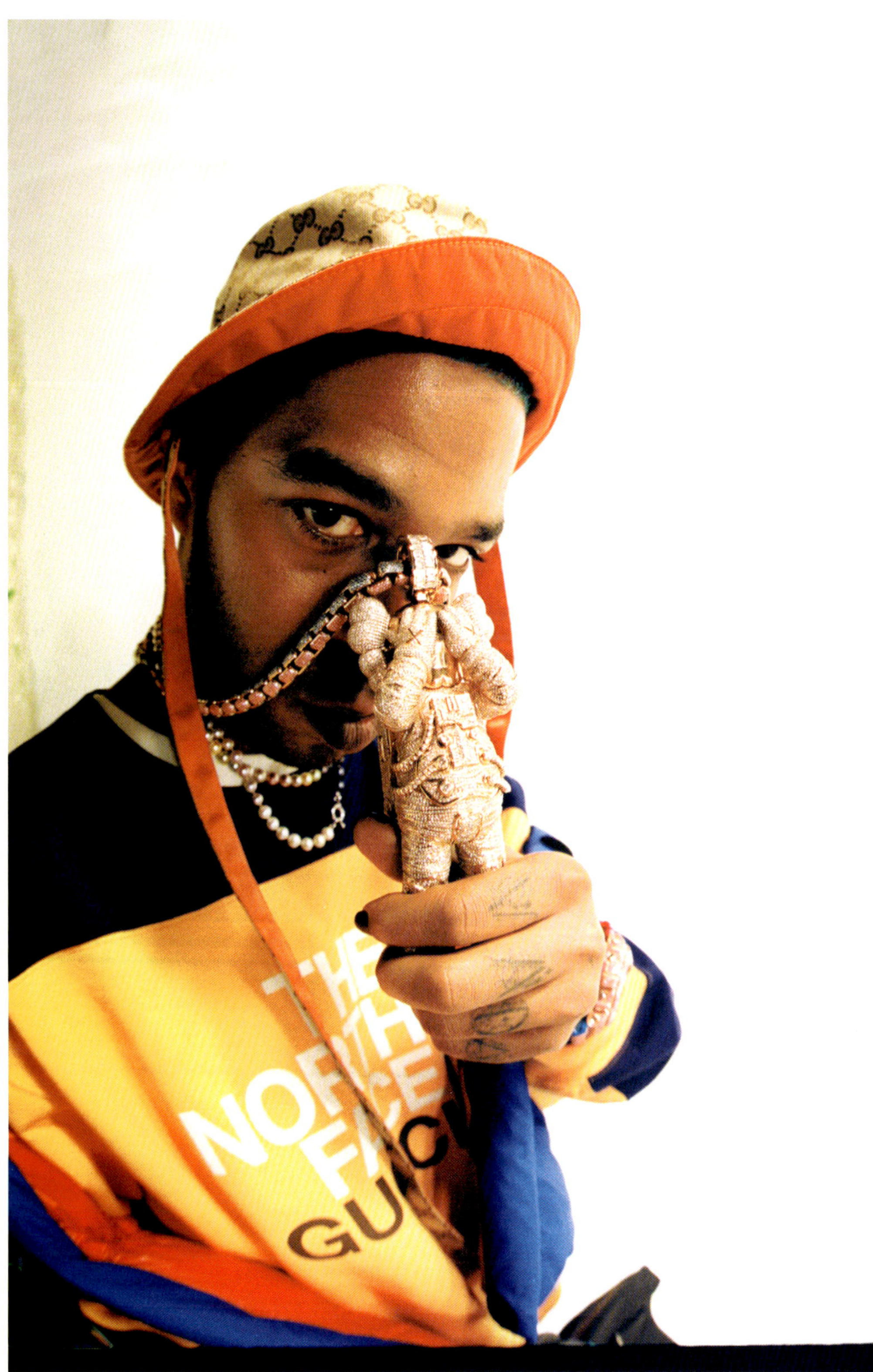

Kid Cudi x Ben Baller x KAWS Custom Pendant

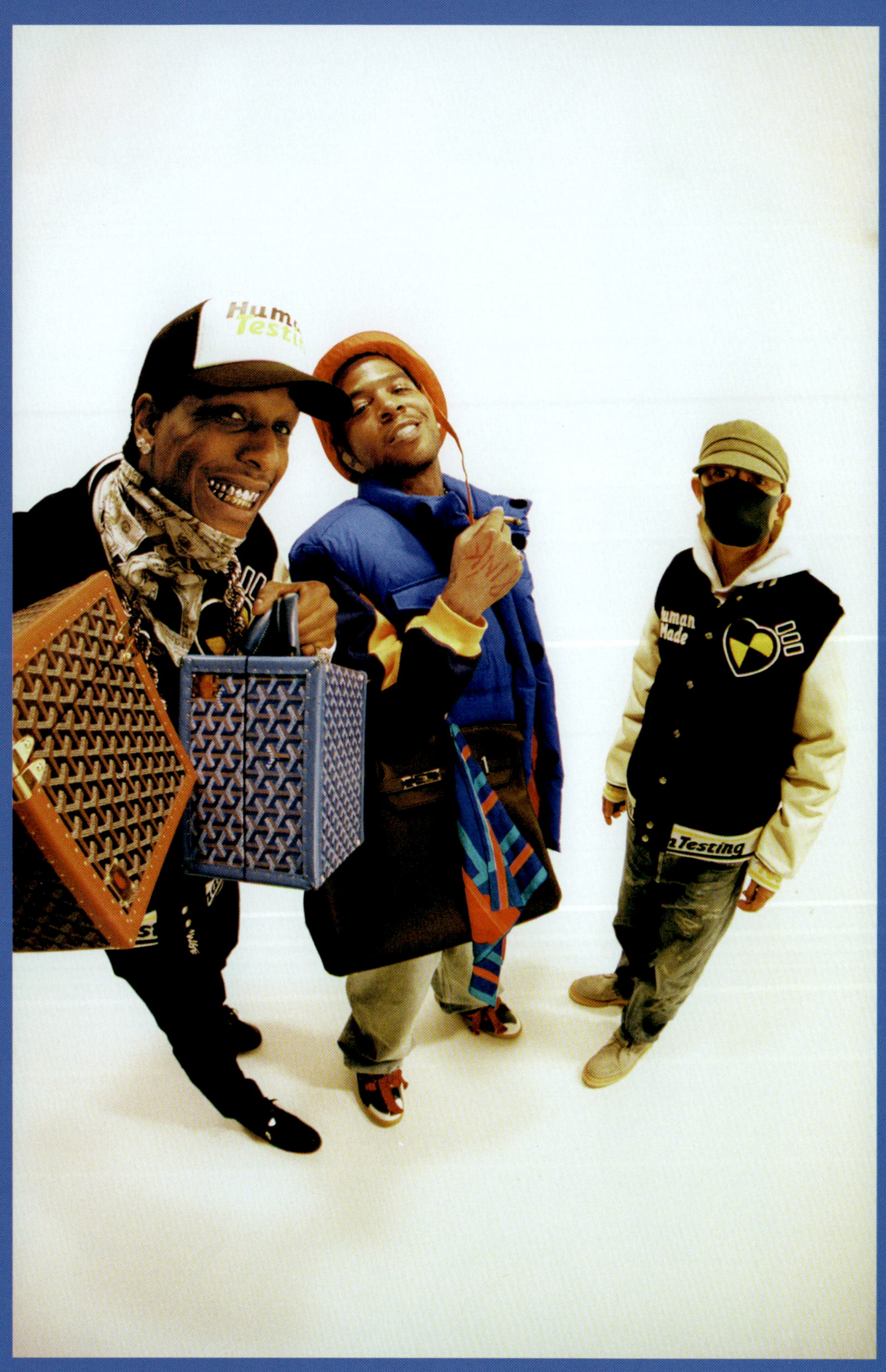

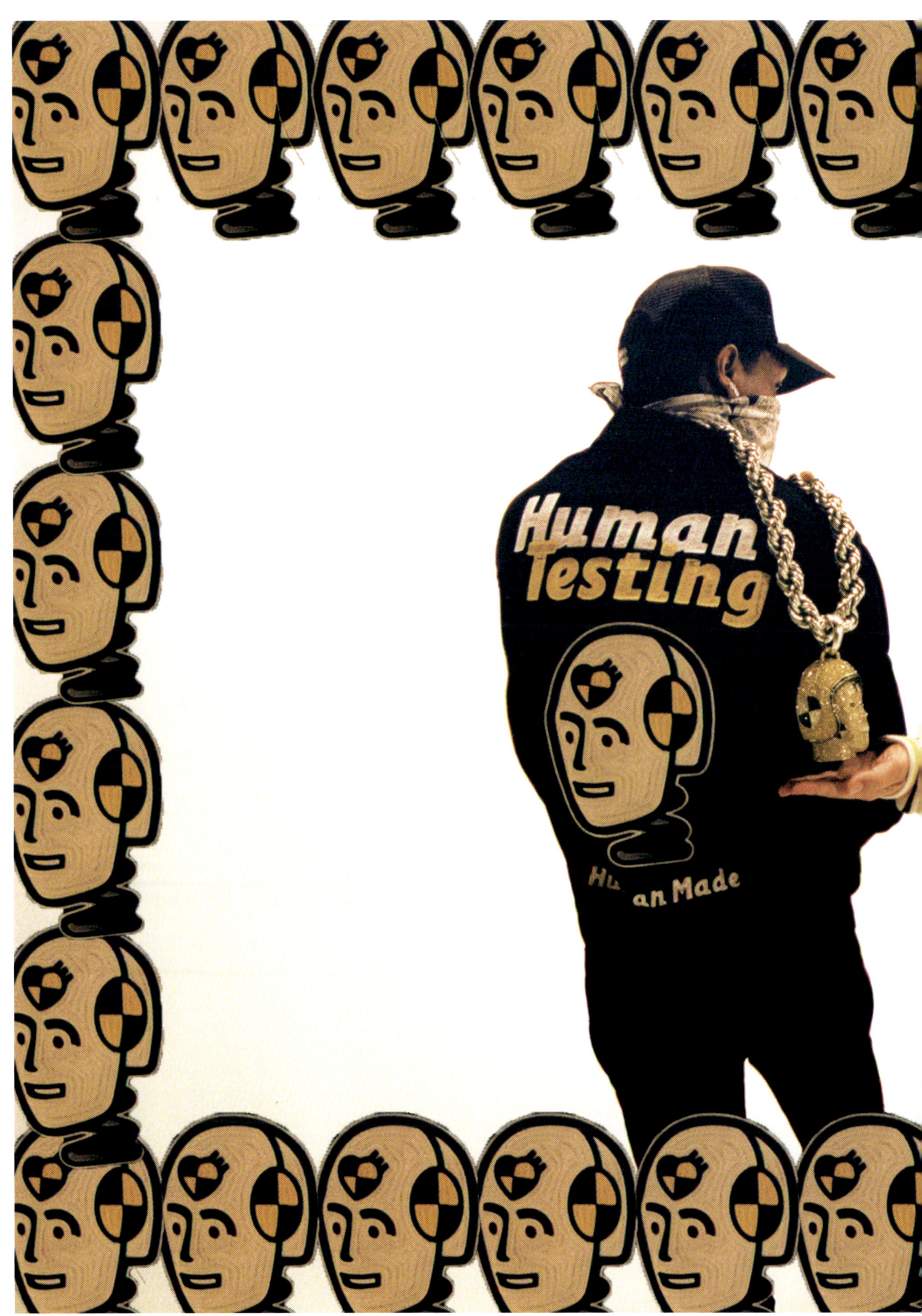
Human
Testing
Hu an Made

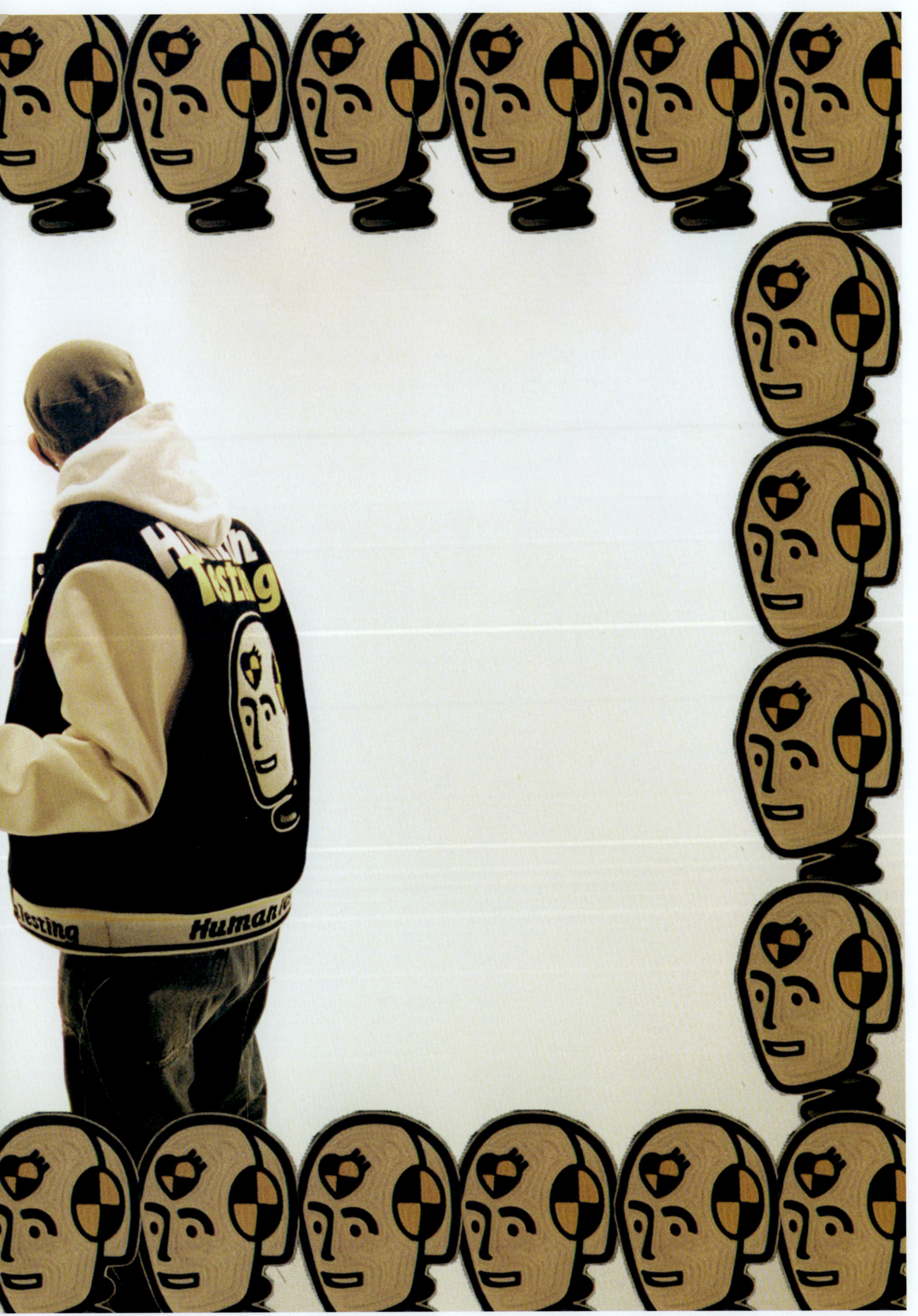
Testing

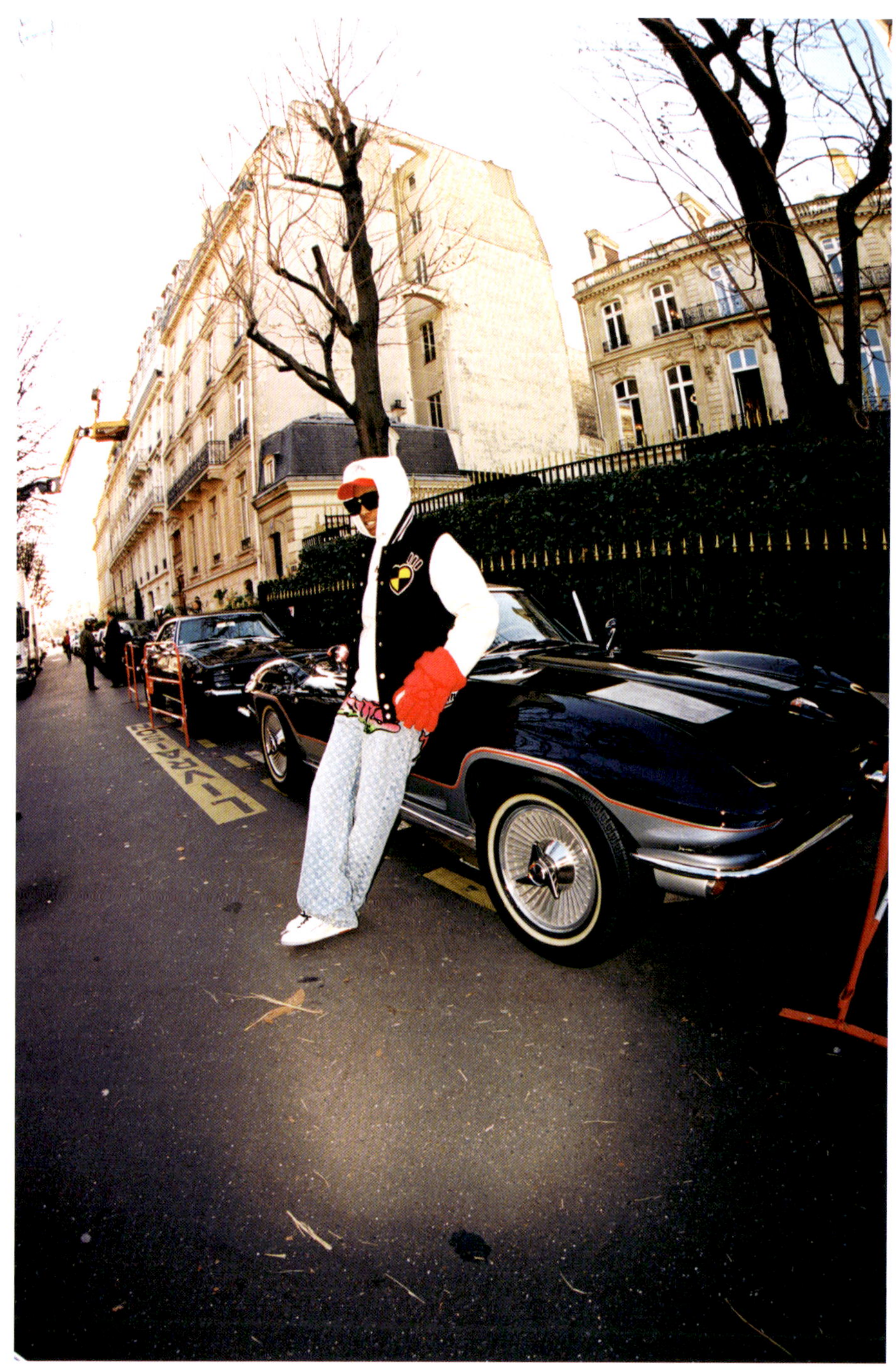

Pages 34-45: A$AP Rocky, Pharrell, Kevin McMullan and Steven Victor on the Paris set of the "ARYA" video shoot, December 2021

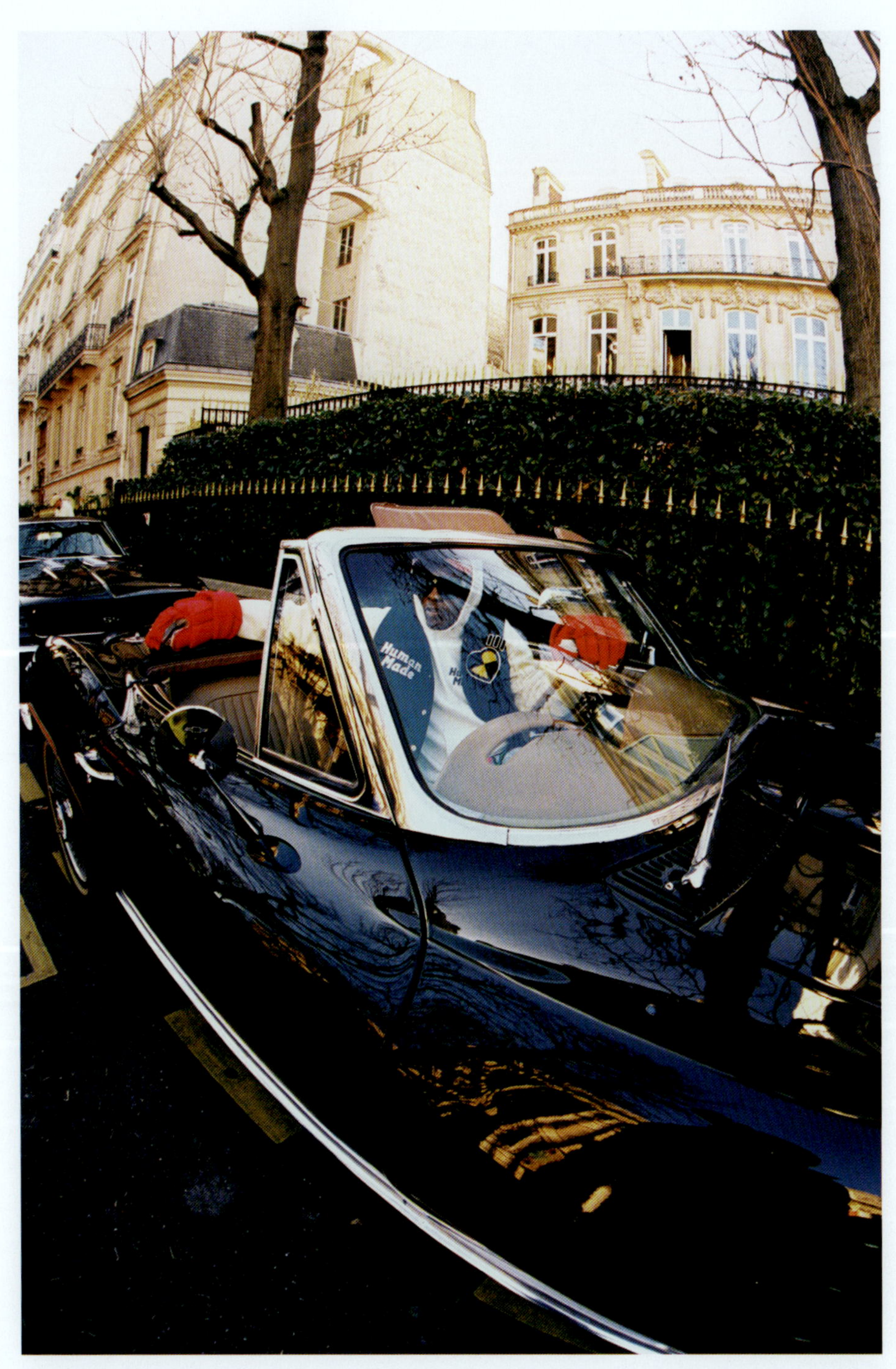
Human Made

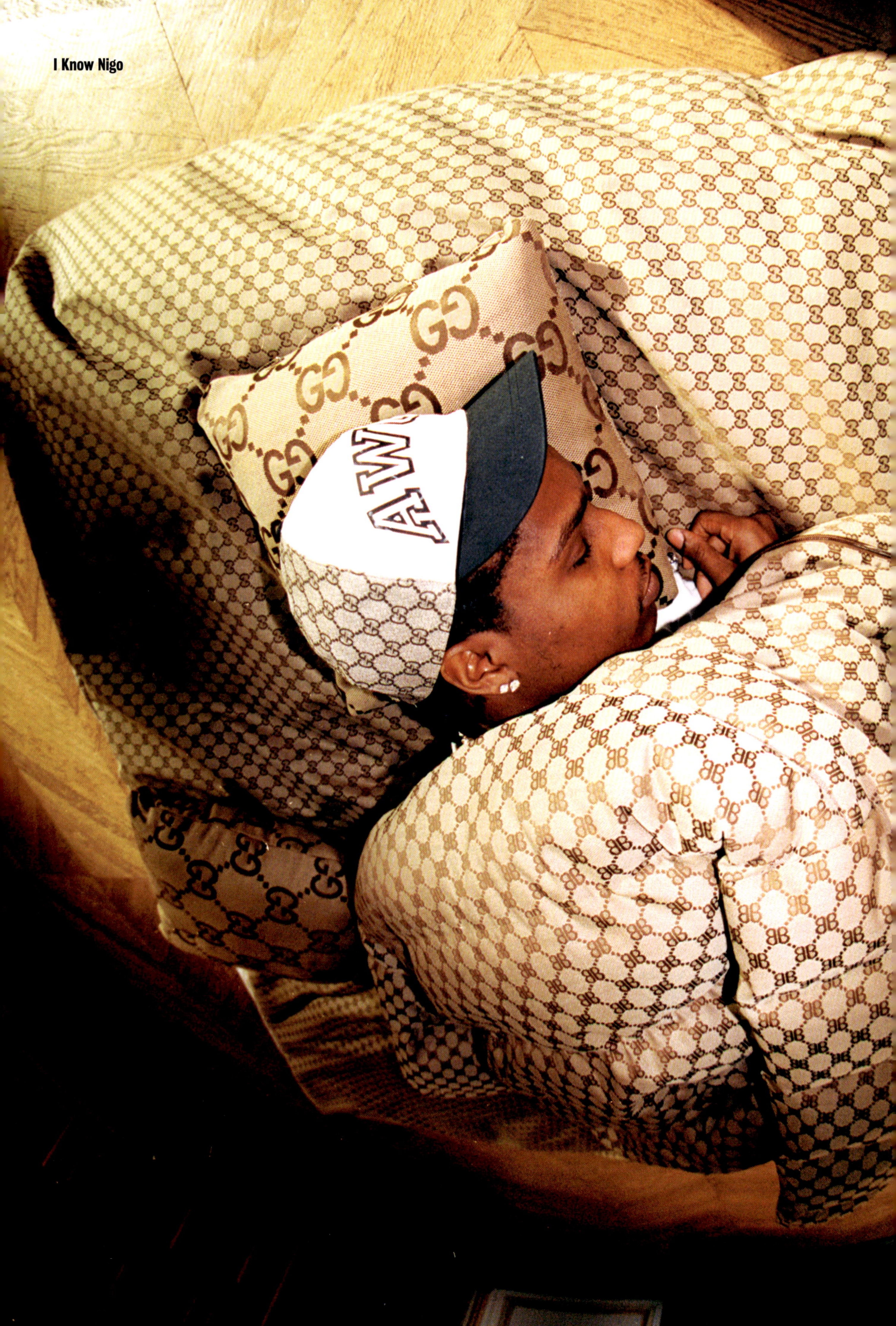
AW

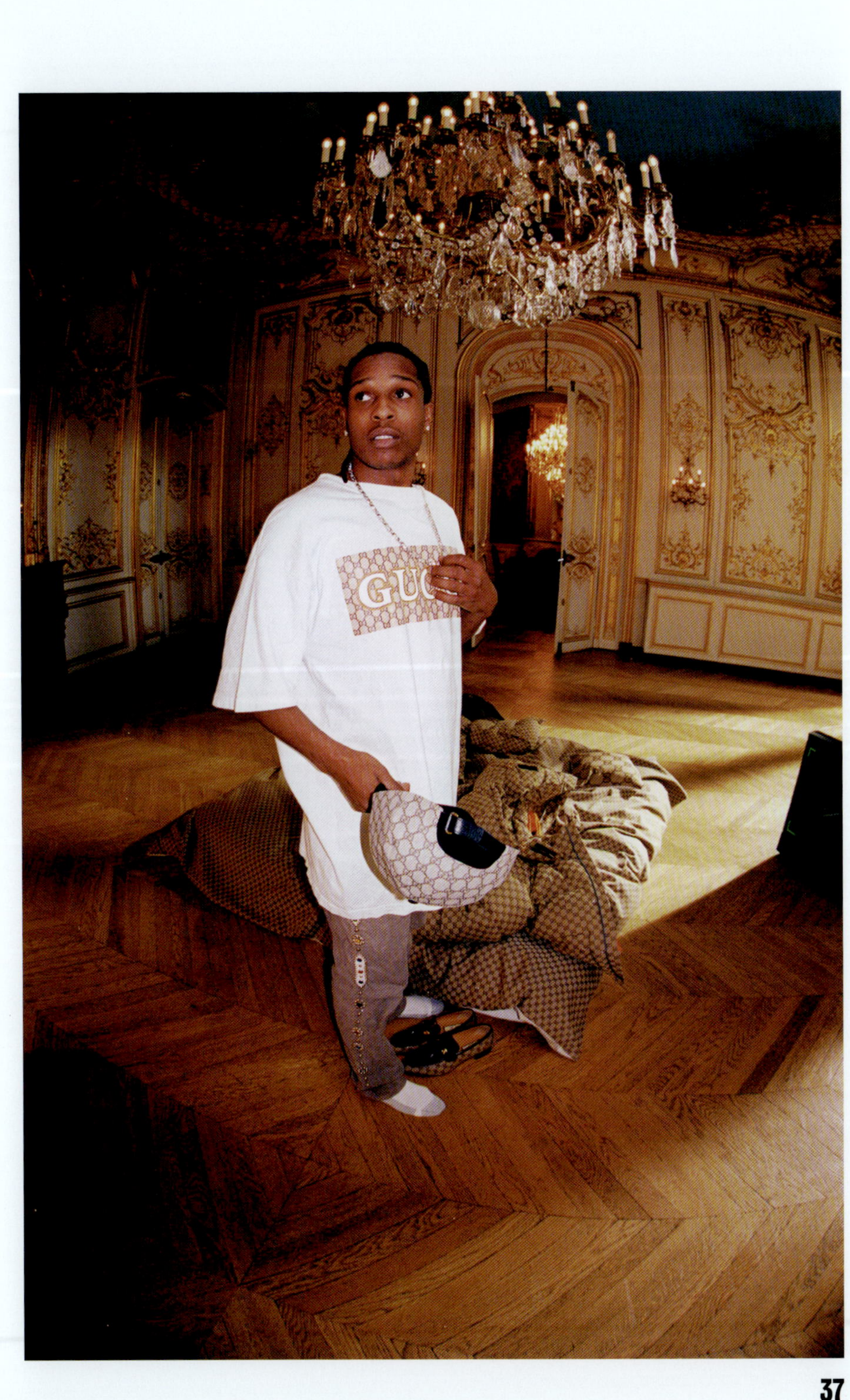

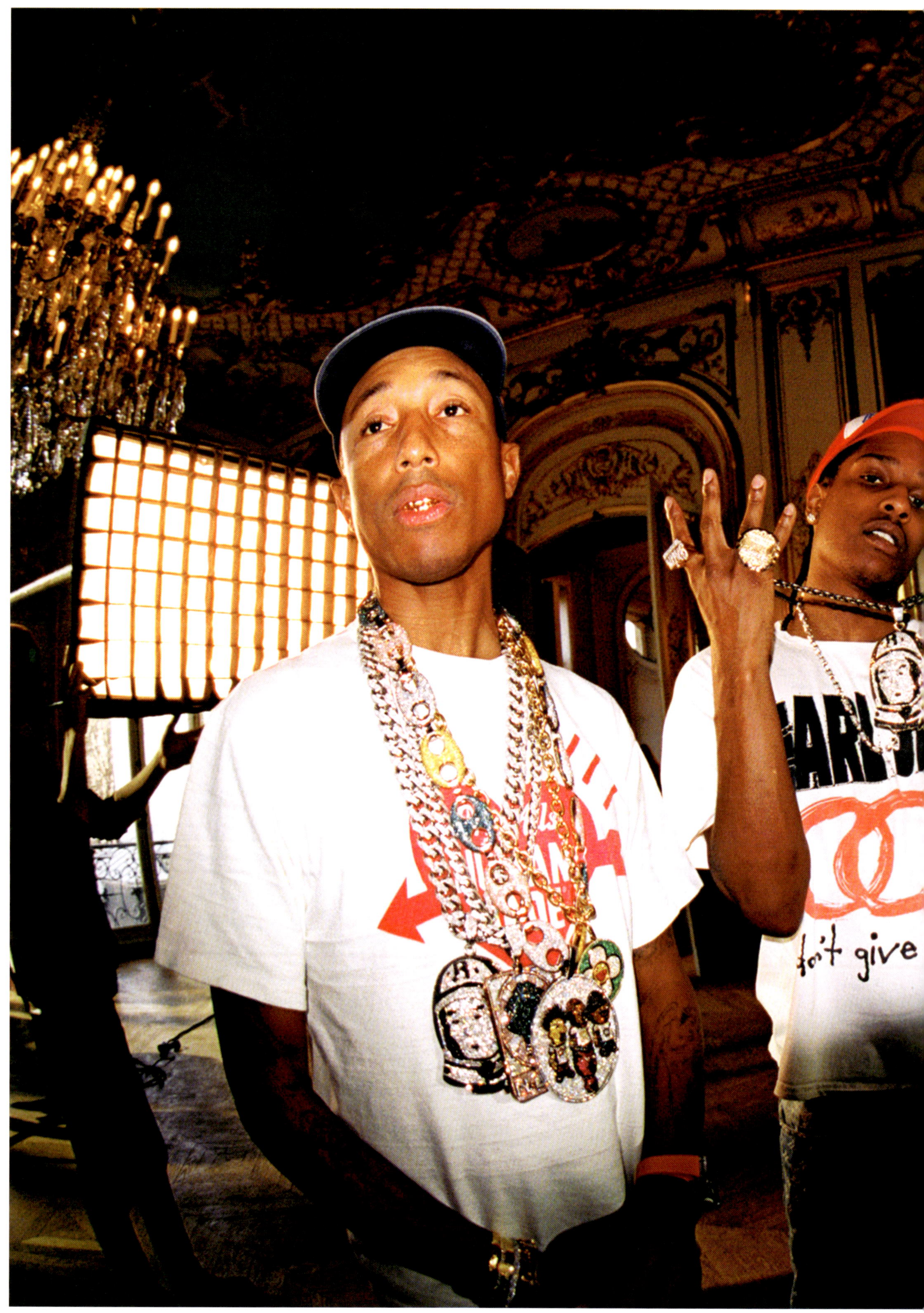

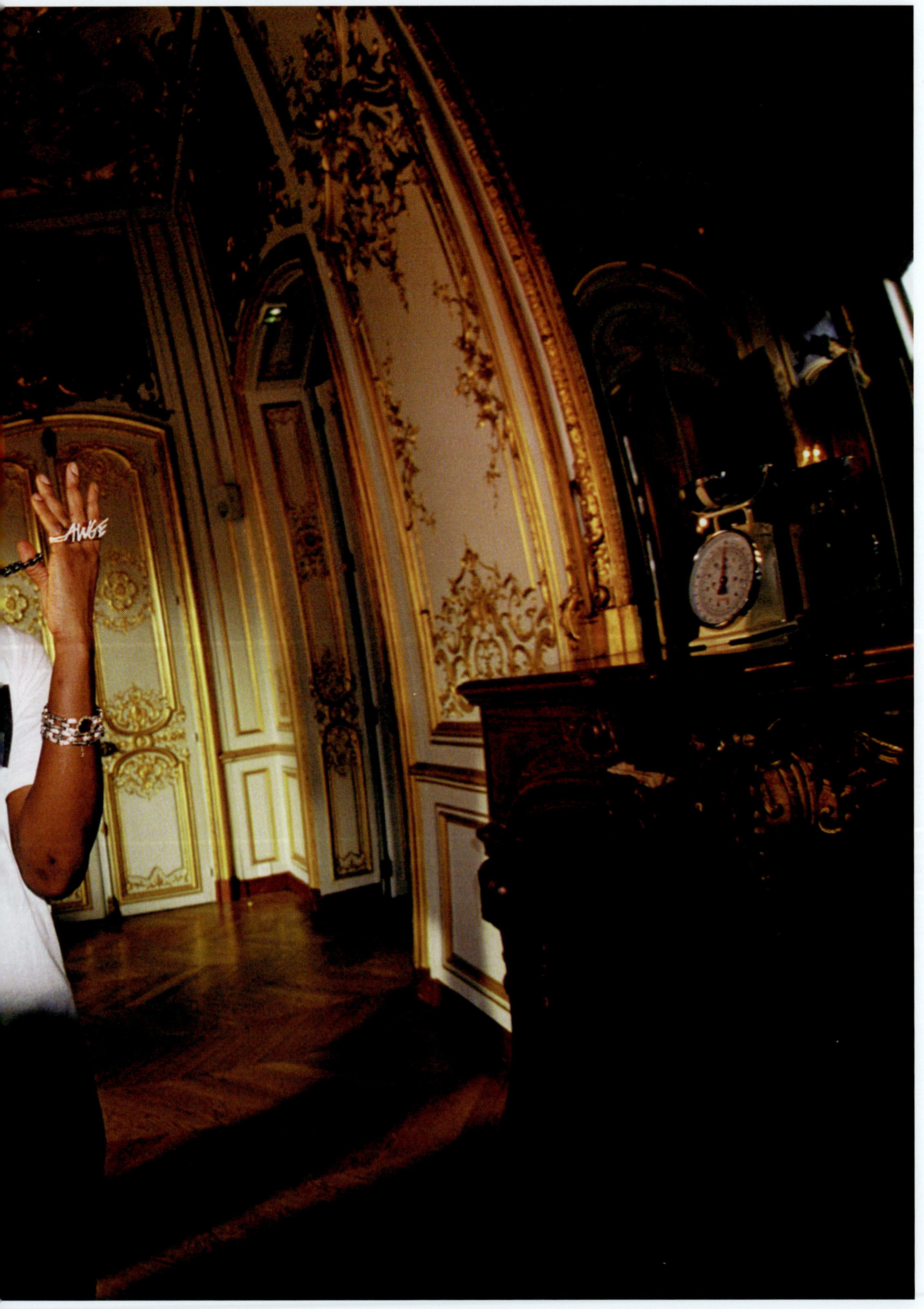
AWGE

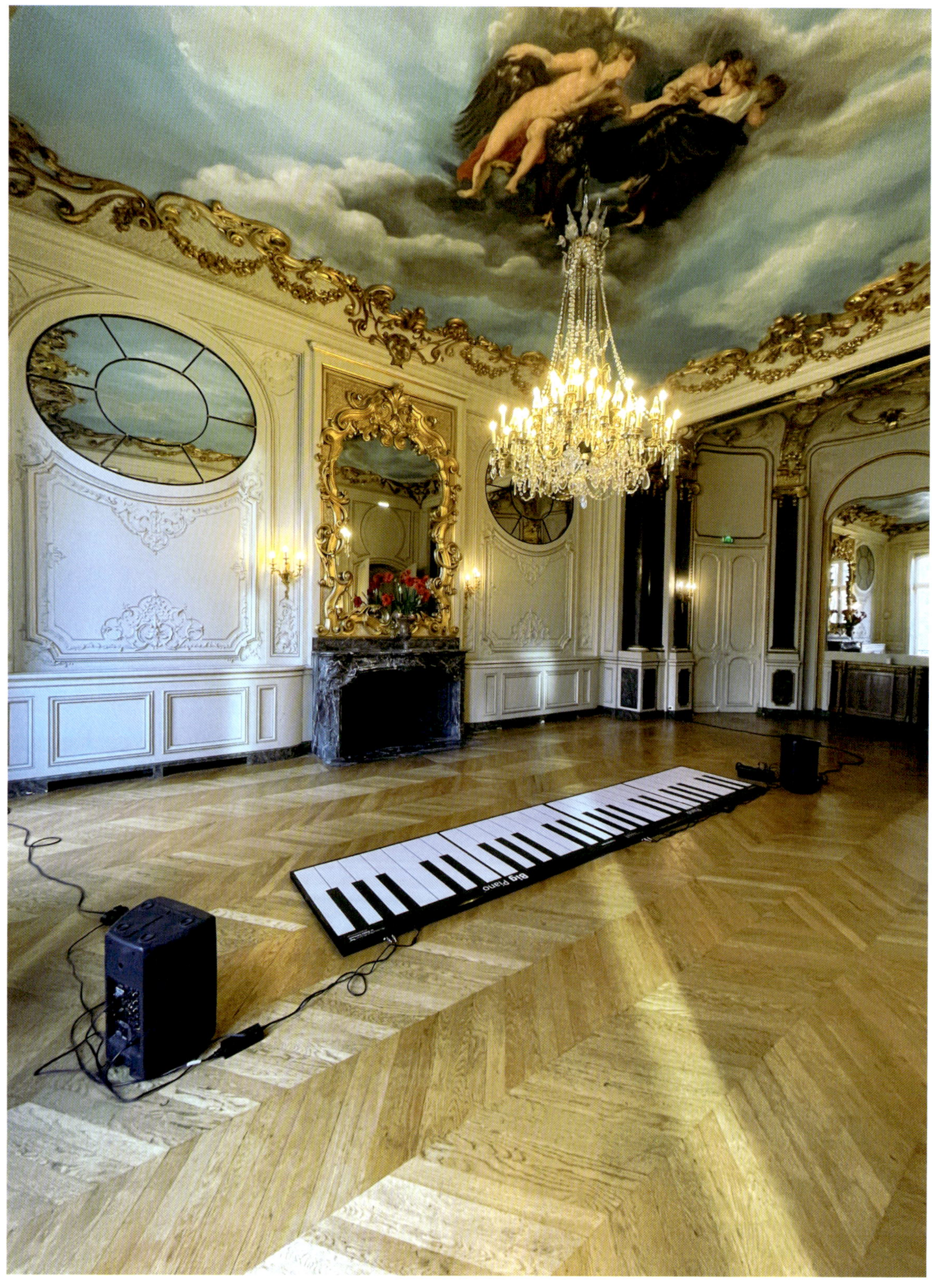
Big Piano

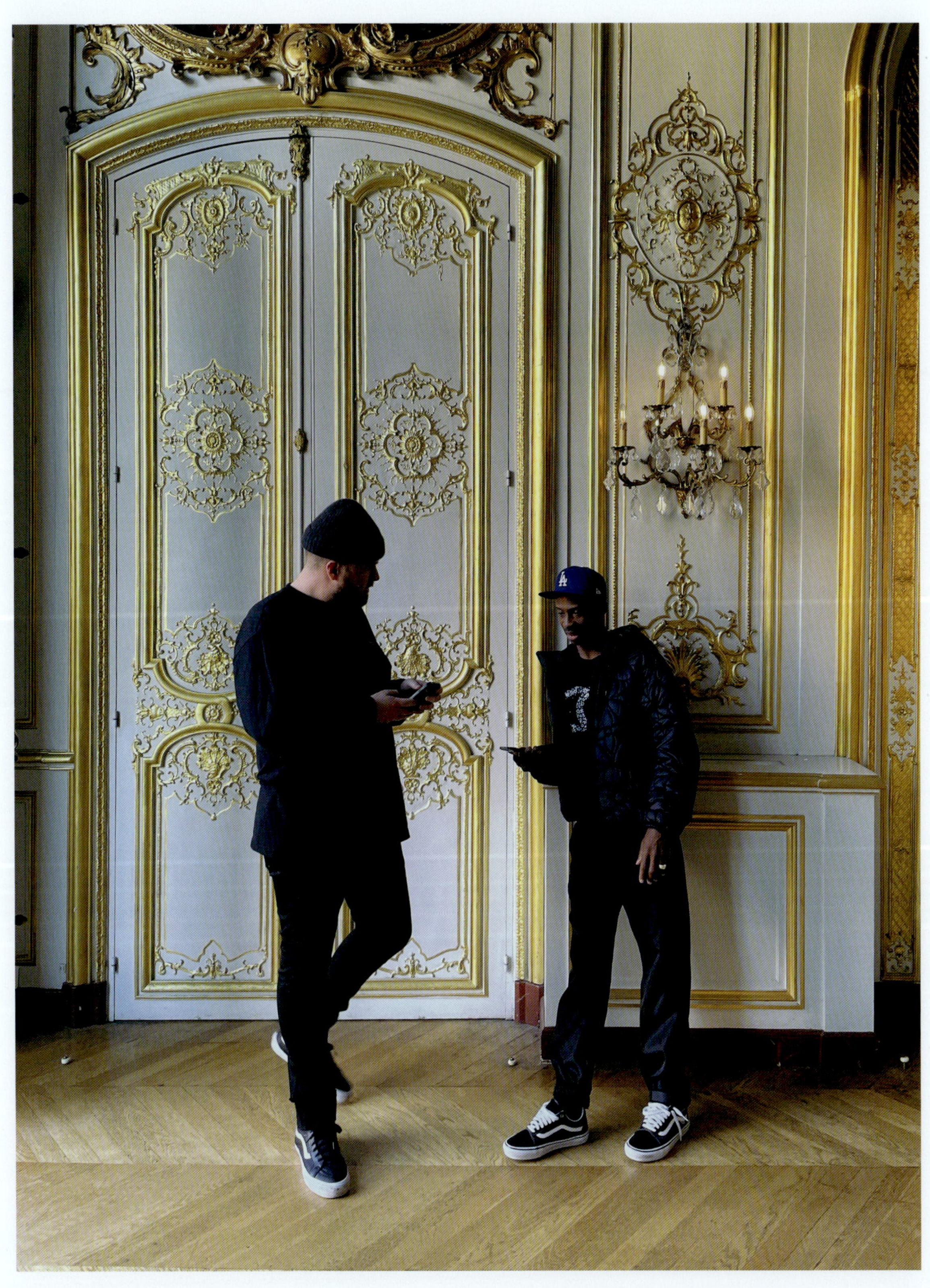

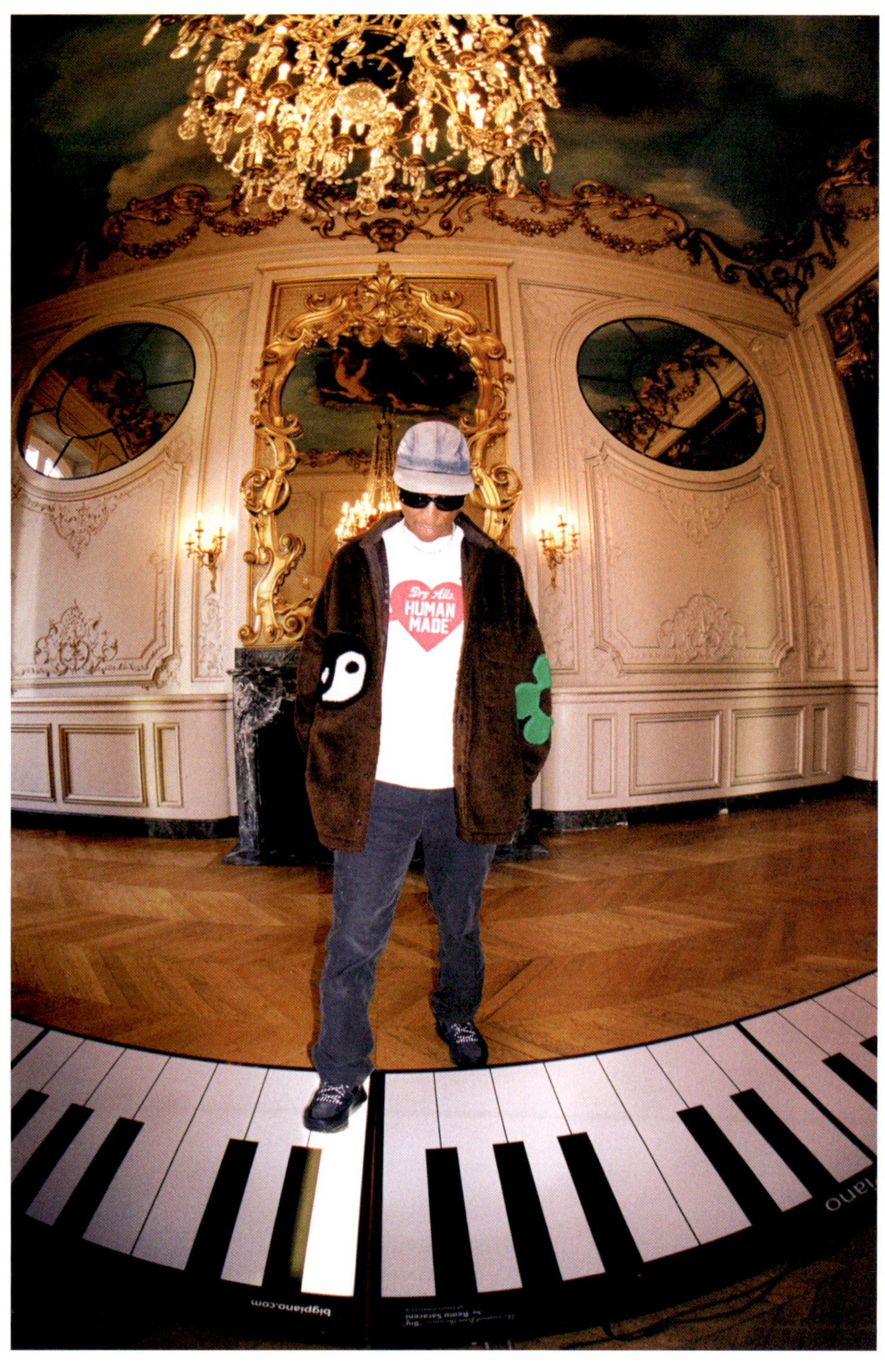
Dry Alls.
HUMAN MADE
bigpiano.com

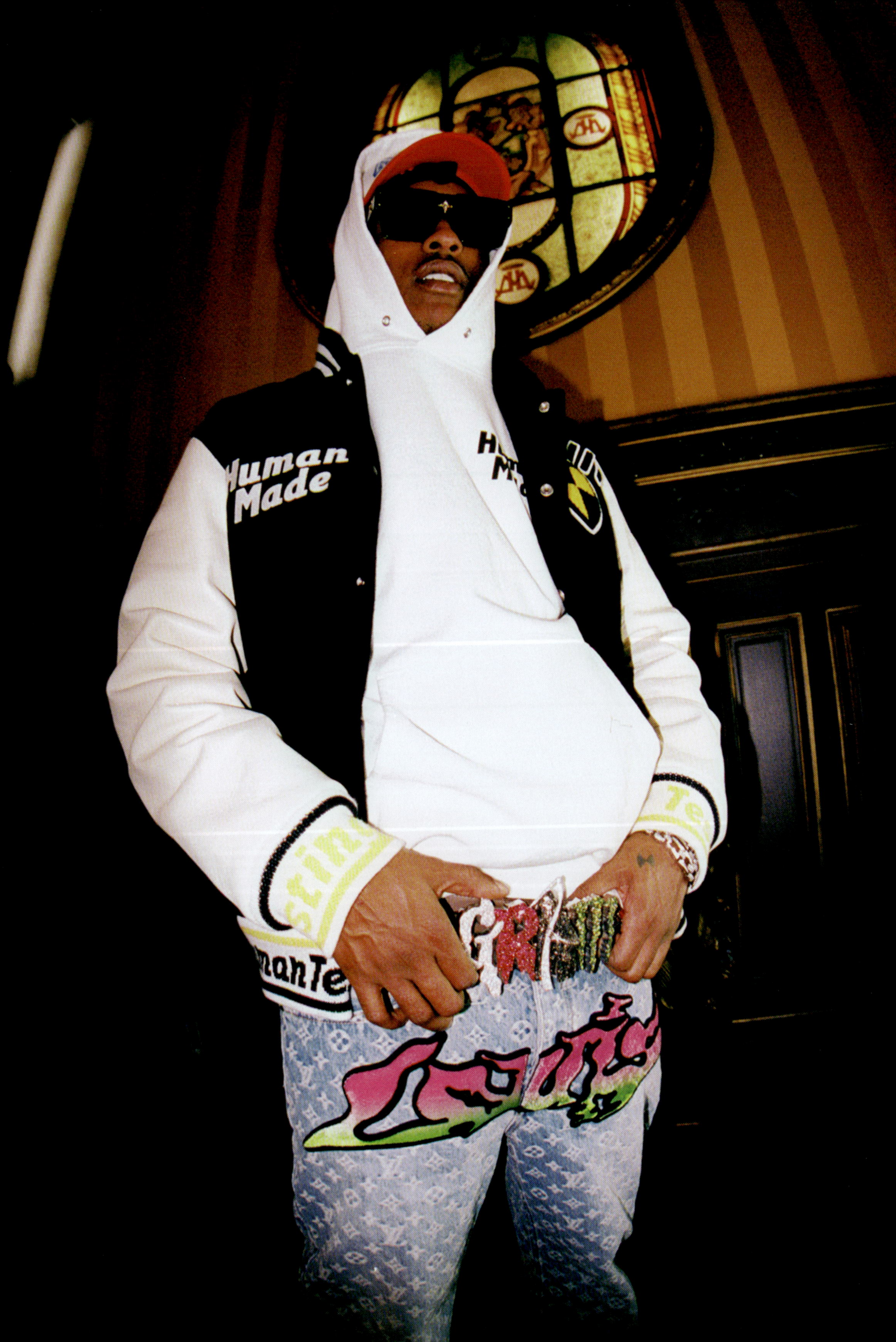
Human
Made

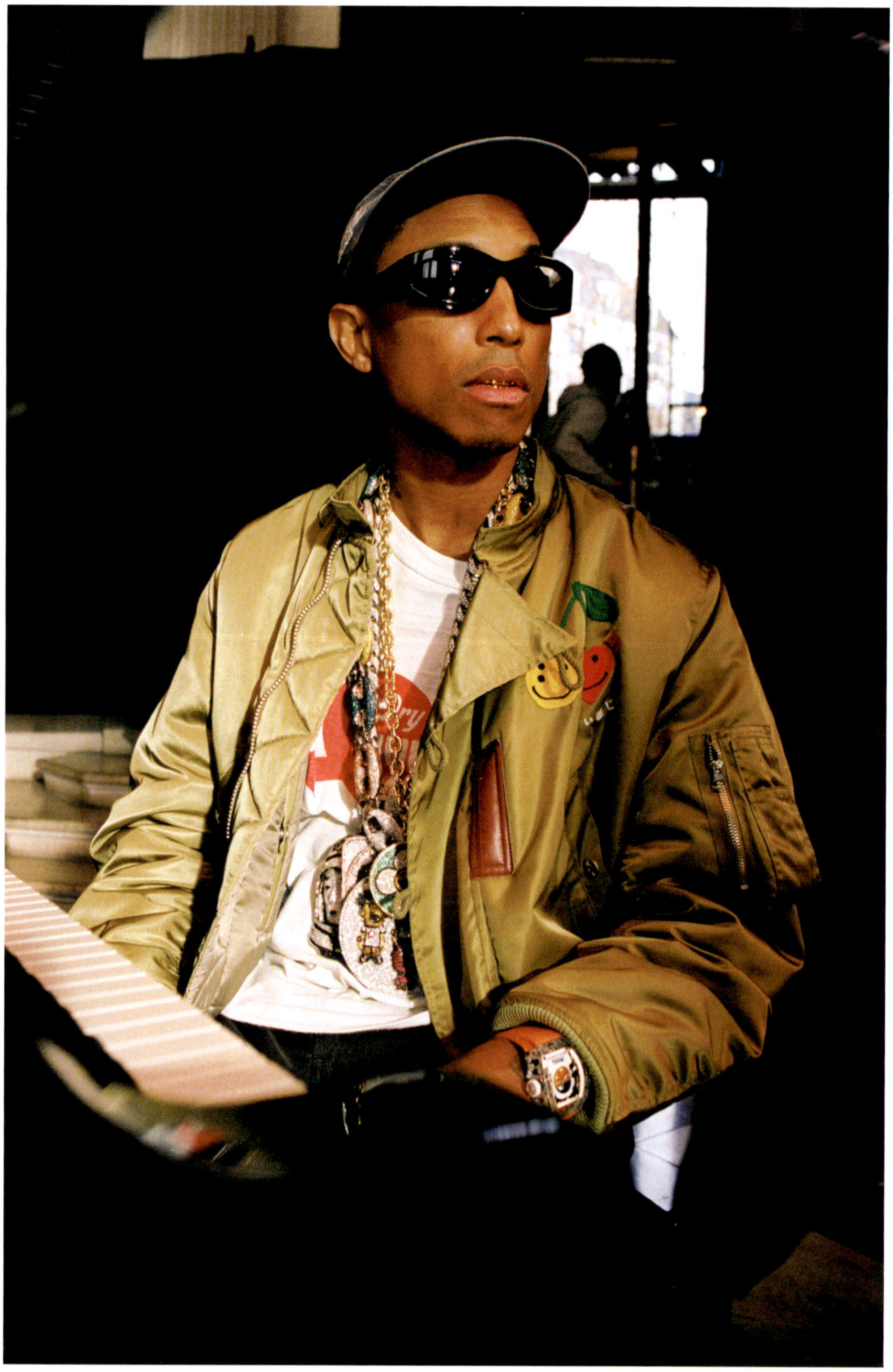

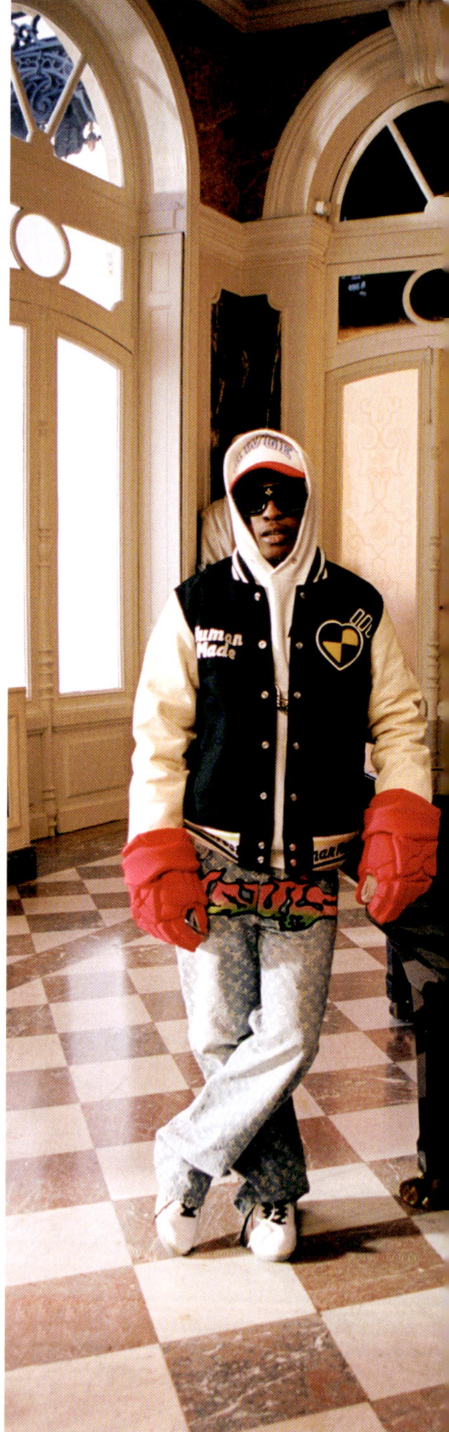
Human
Made

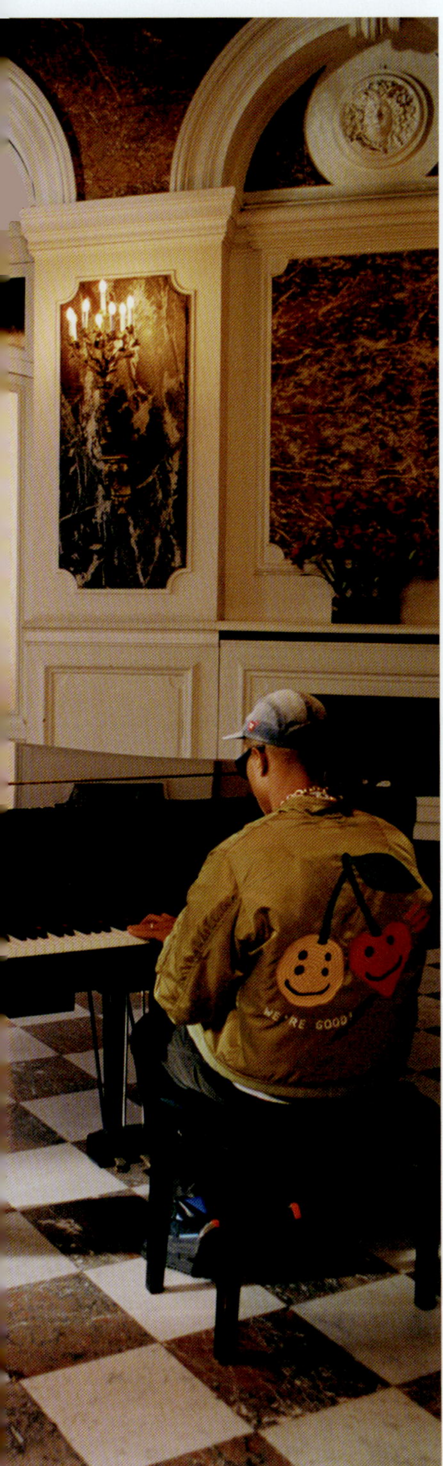

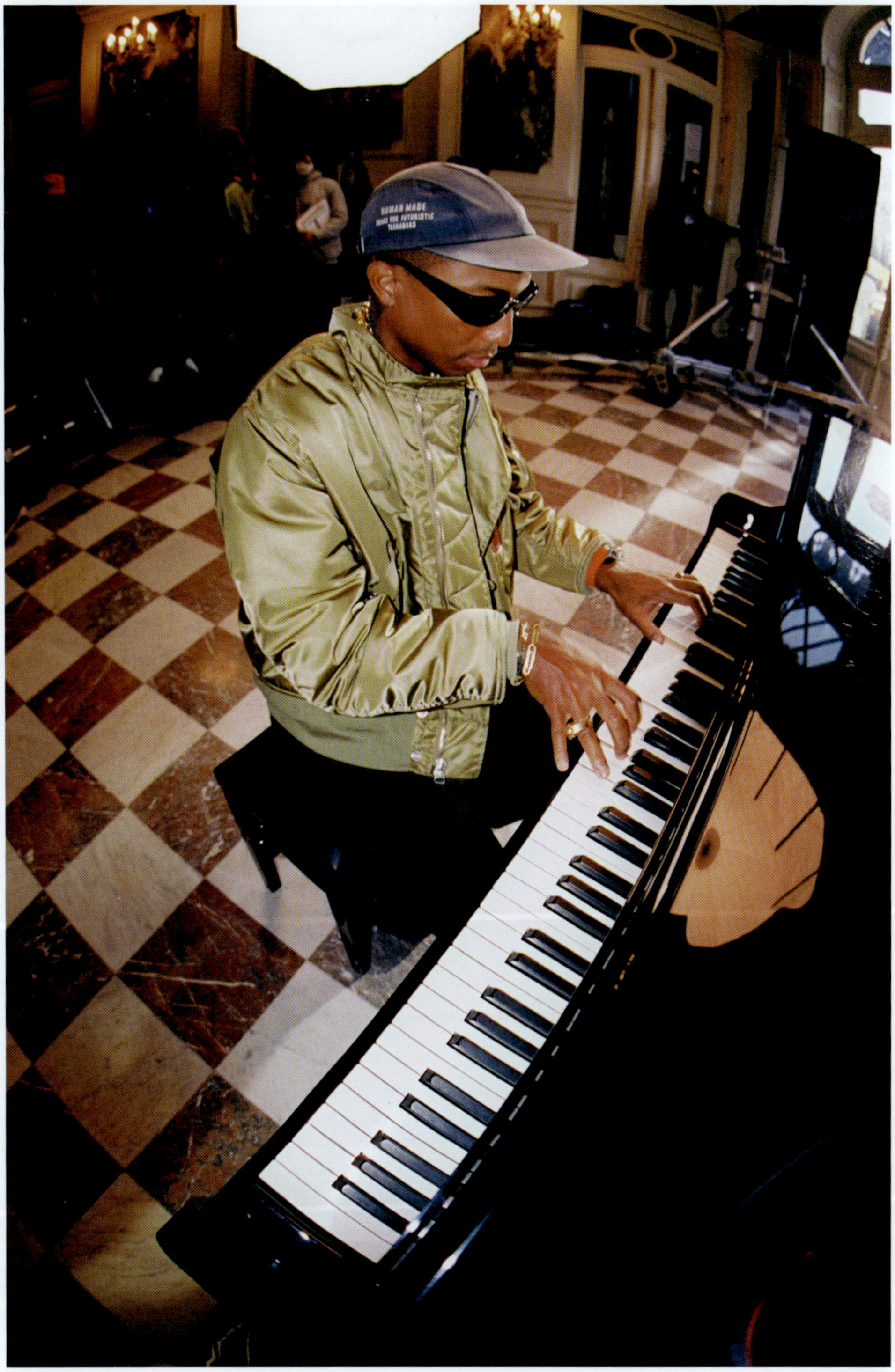

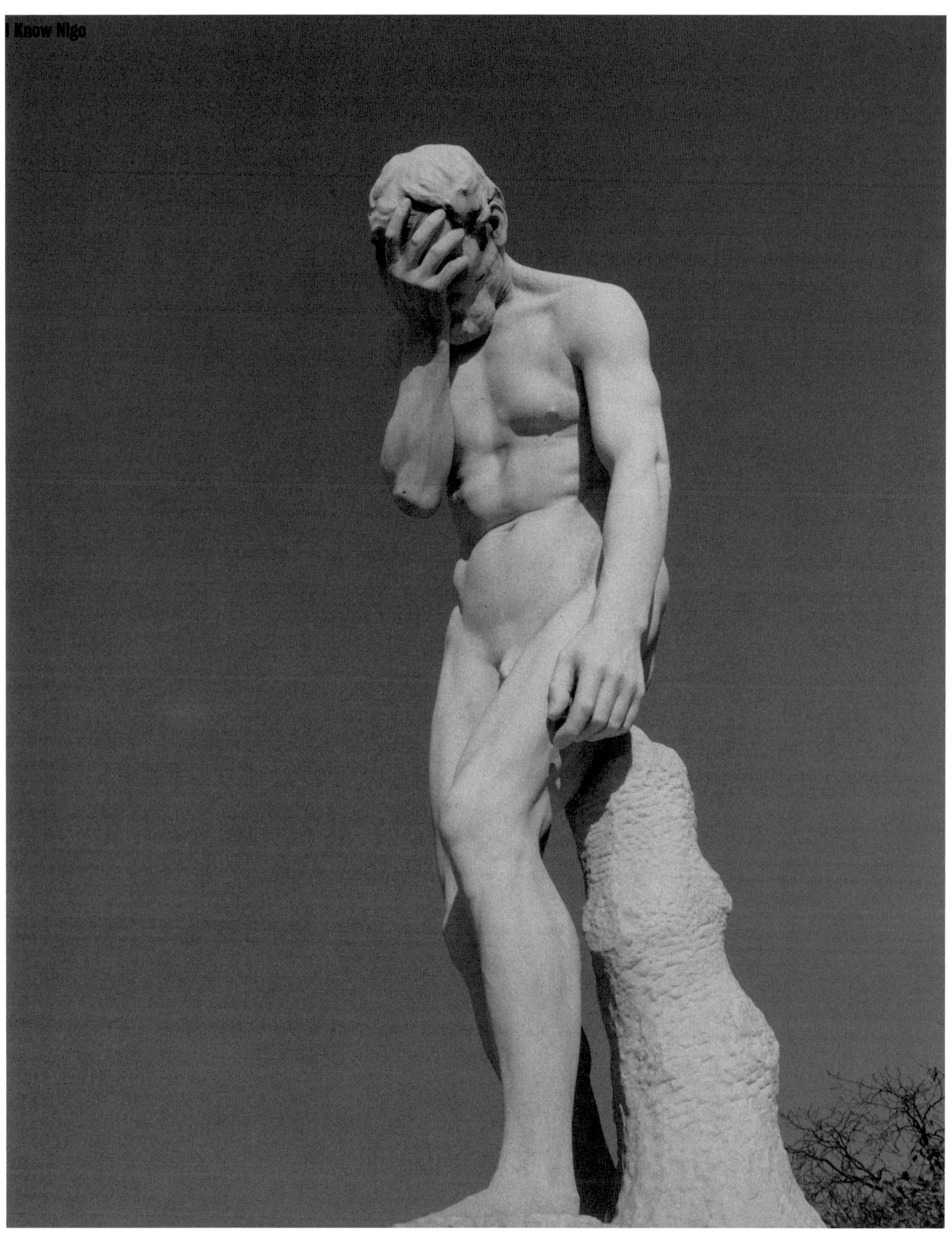

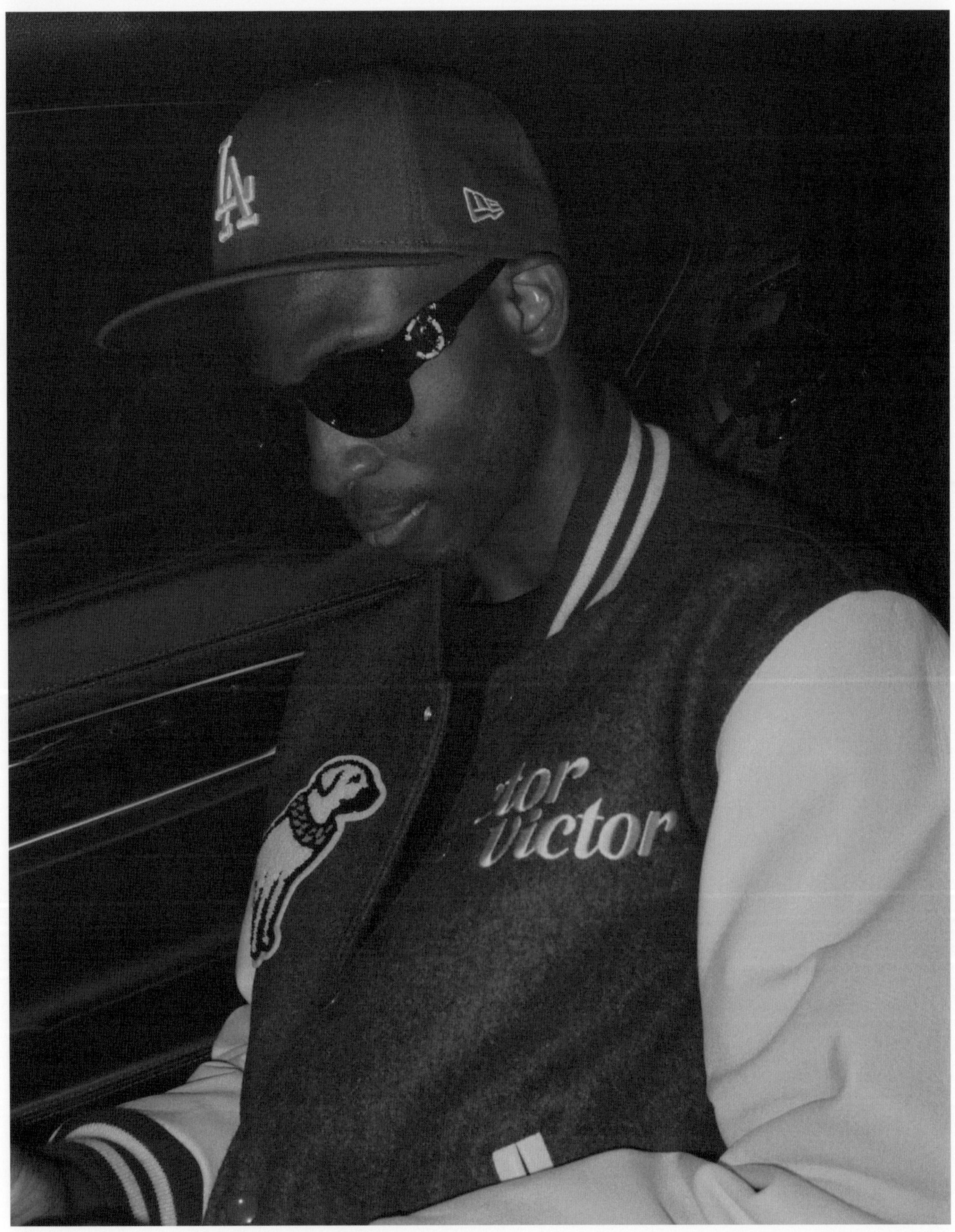

Steven Victor in Paris, December 2021

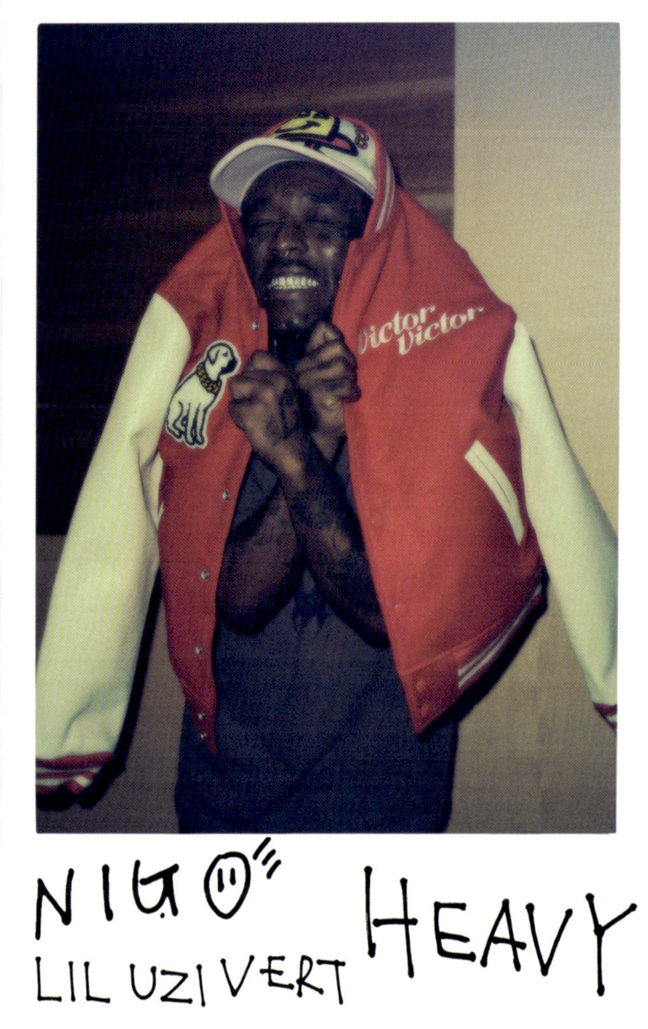

Lil Uzi Vert, “HEAVY” single cover, New York City, Released March 28, 2022

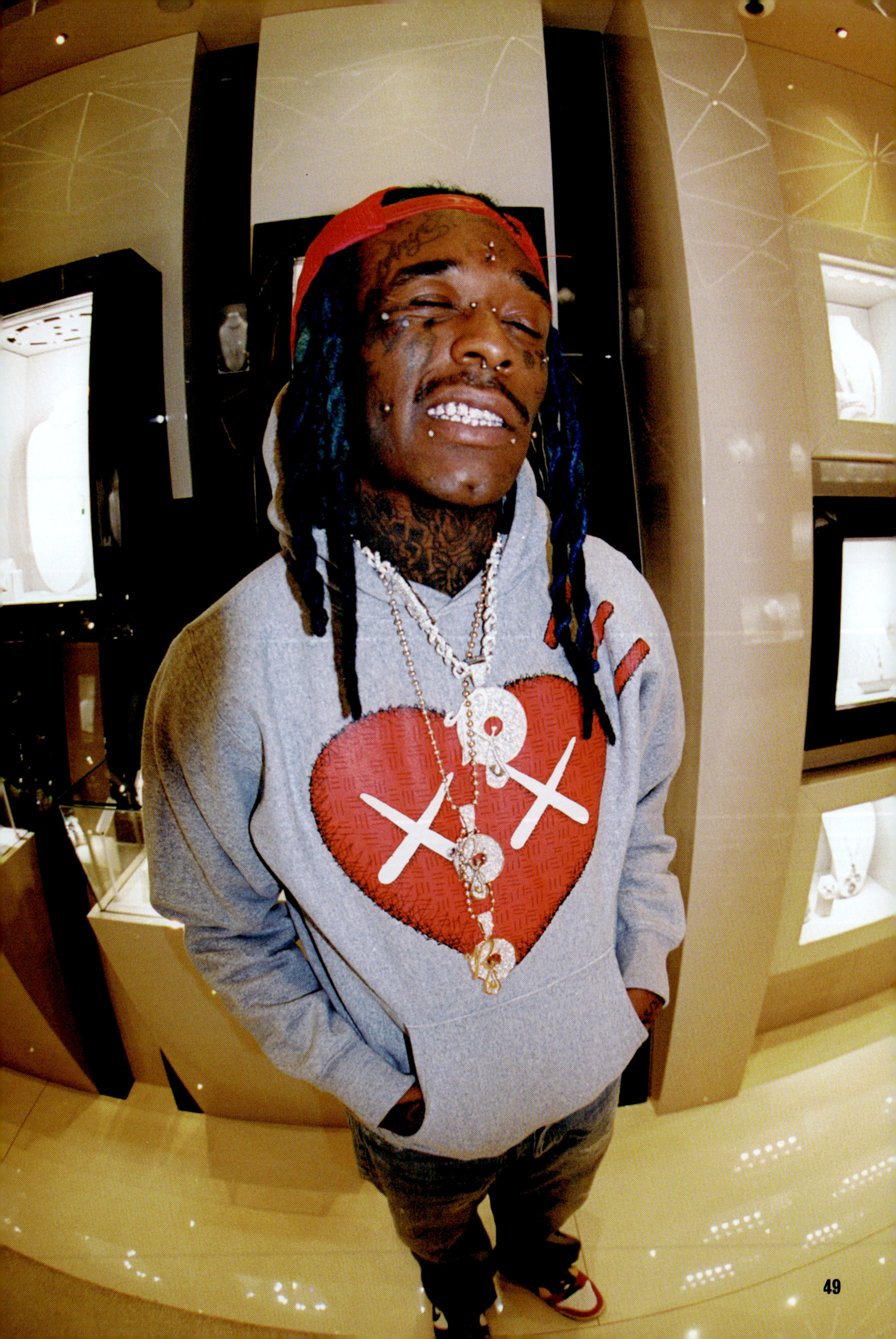

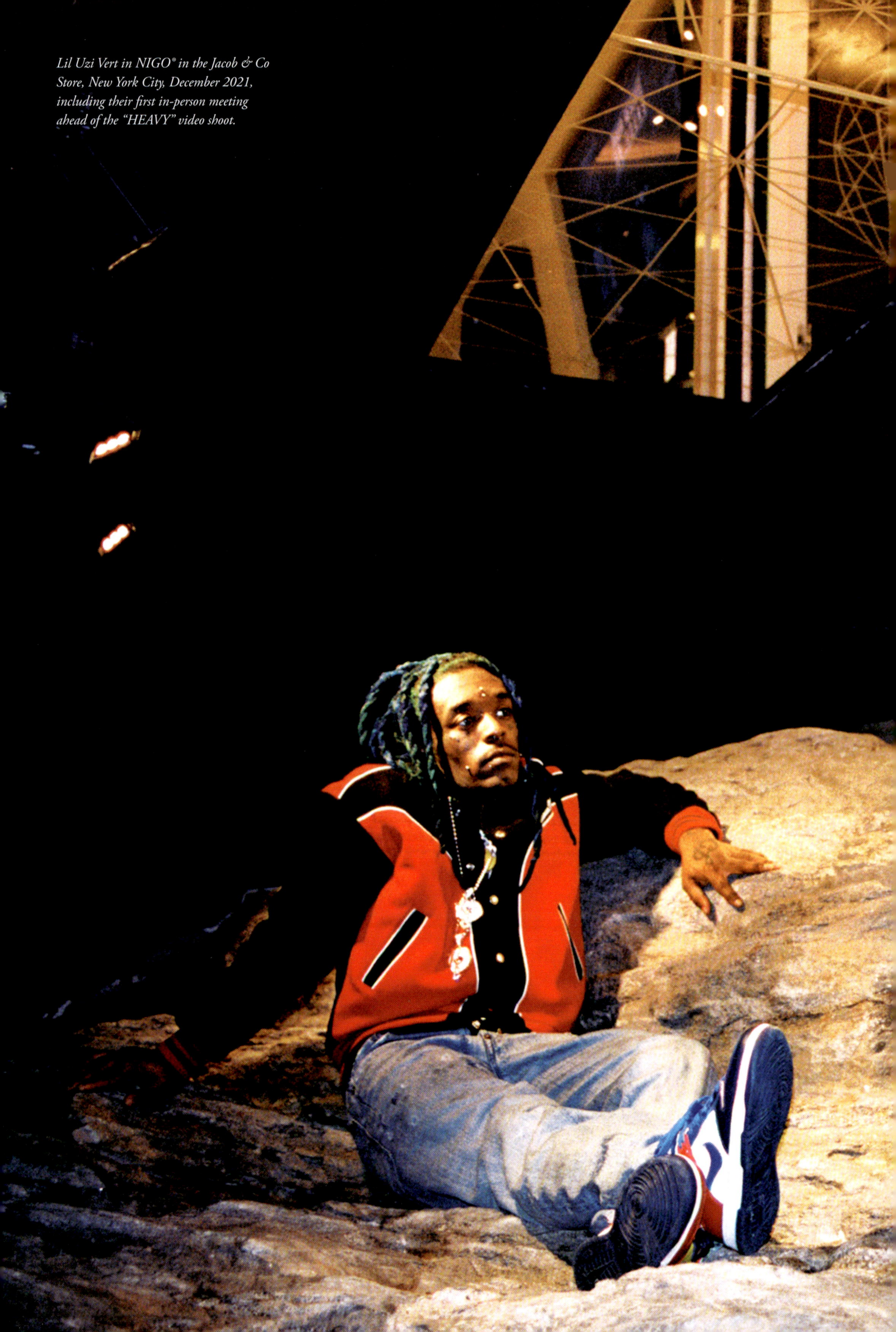

Lil Uzi Vert in NIGO® in the Jacob & Co Store, New York City, December 2021, including their first in-person meeting ahead of the "HEAVY" video shoot.

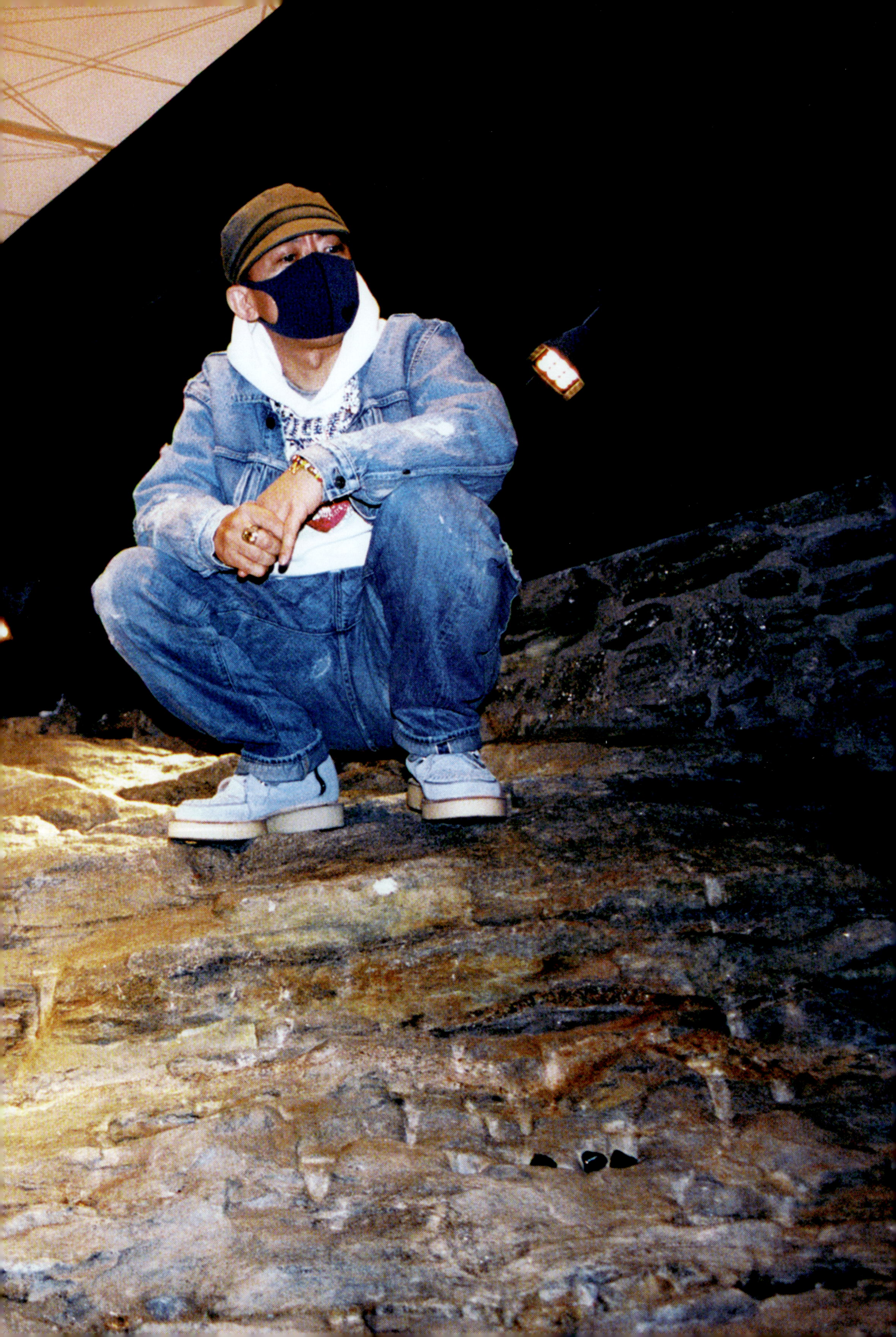

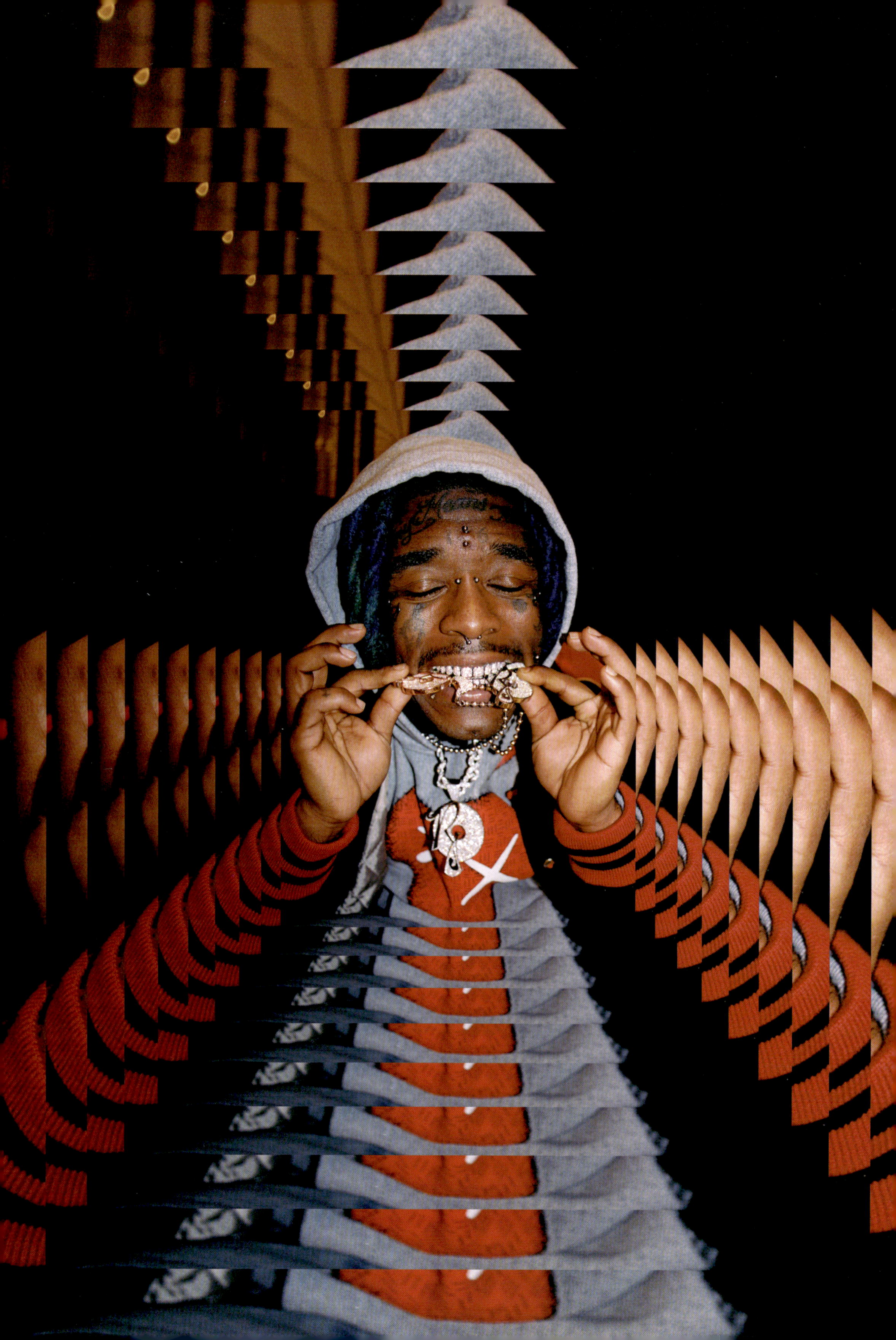

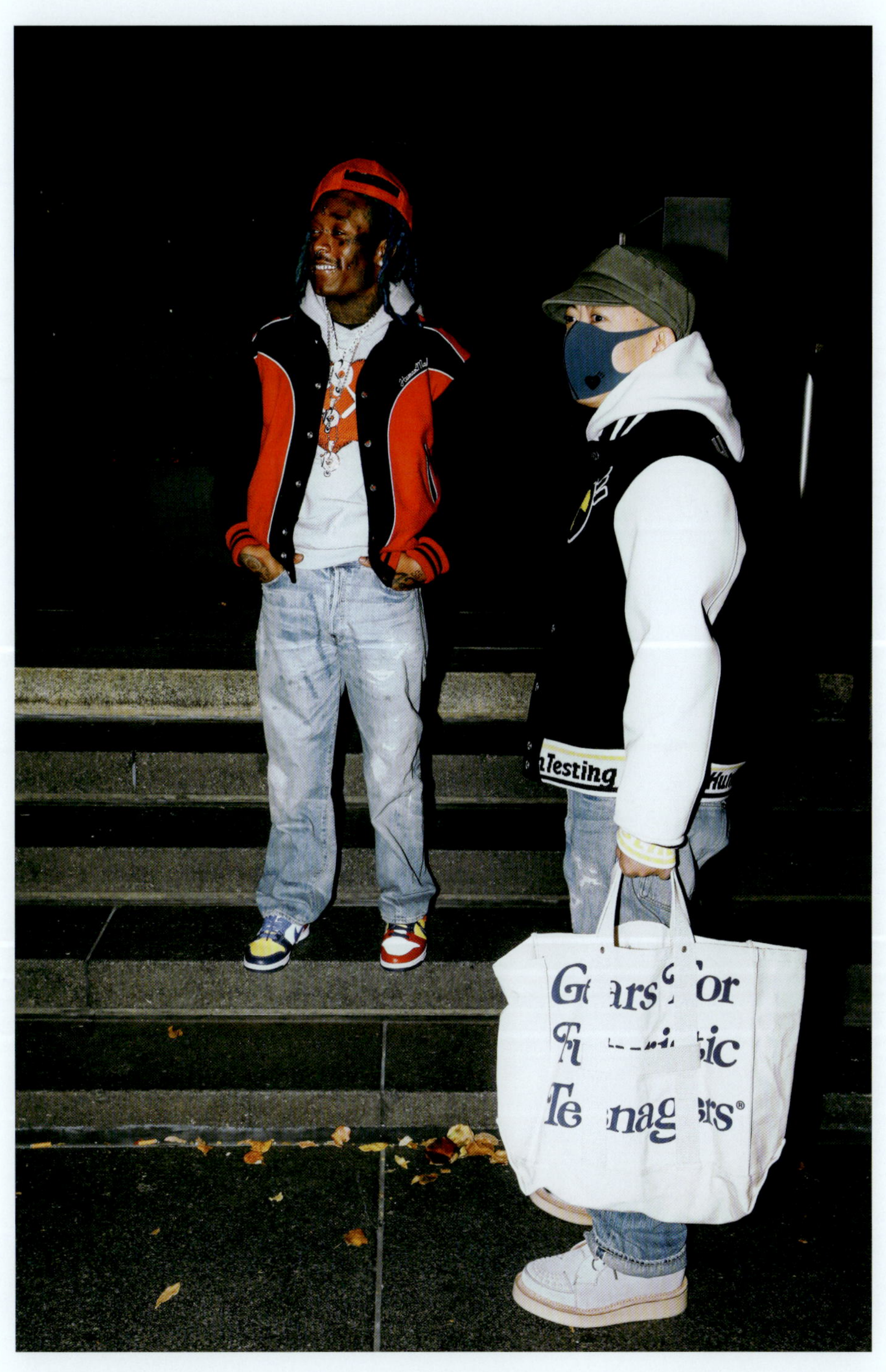
Testing

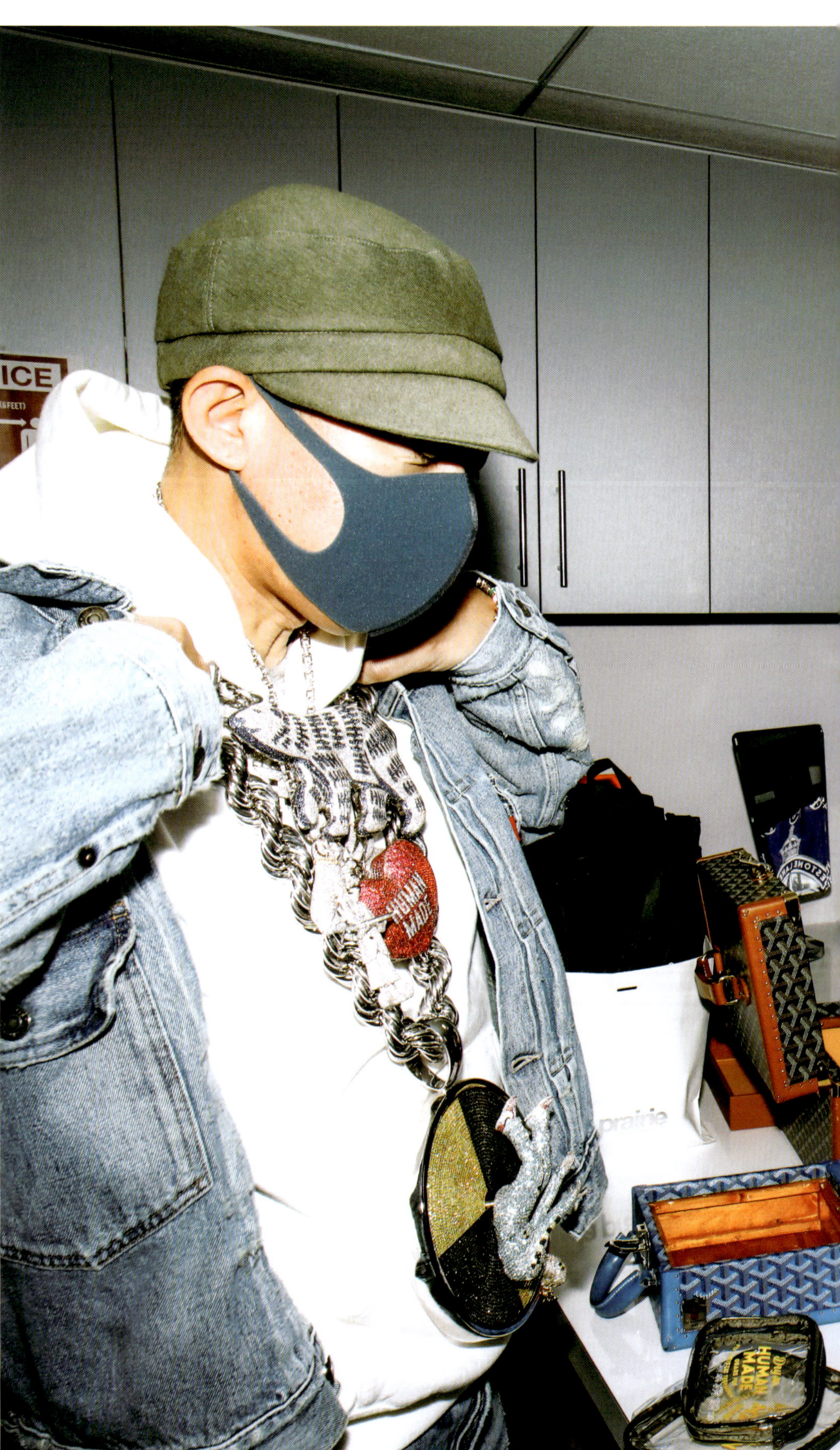

Pages 54-57: Lil Uzi Vert, NIGO® and A$AP Rocky talk jewelry in the Jacob & Co Store, New York City, December 2021

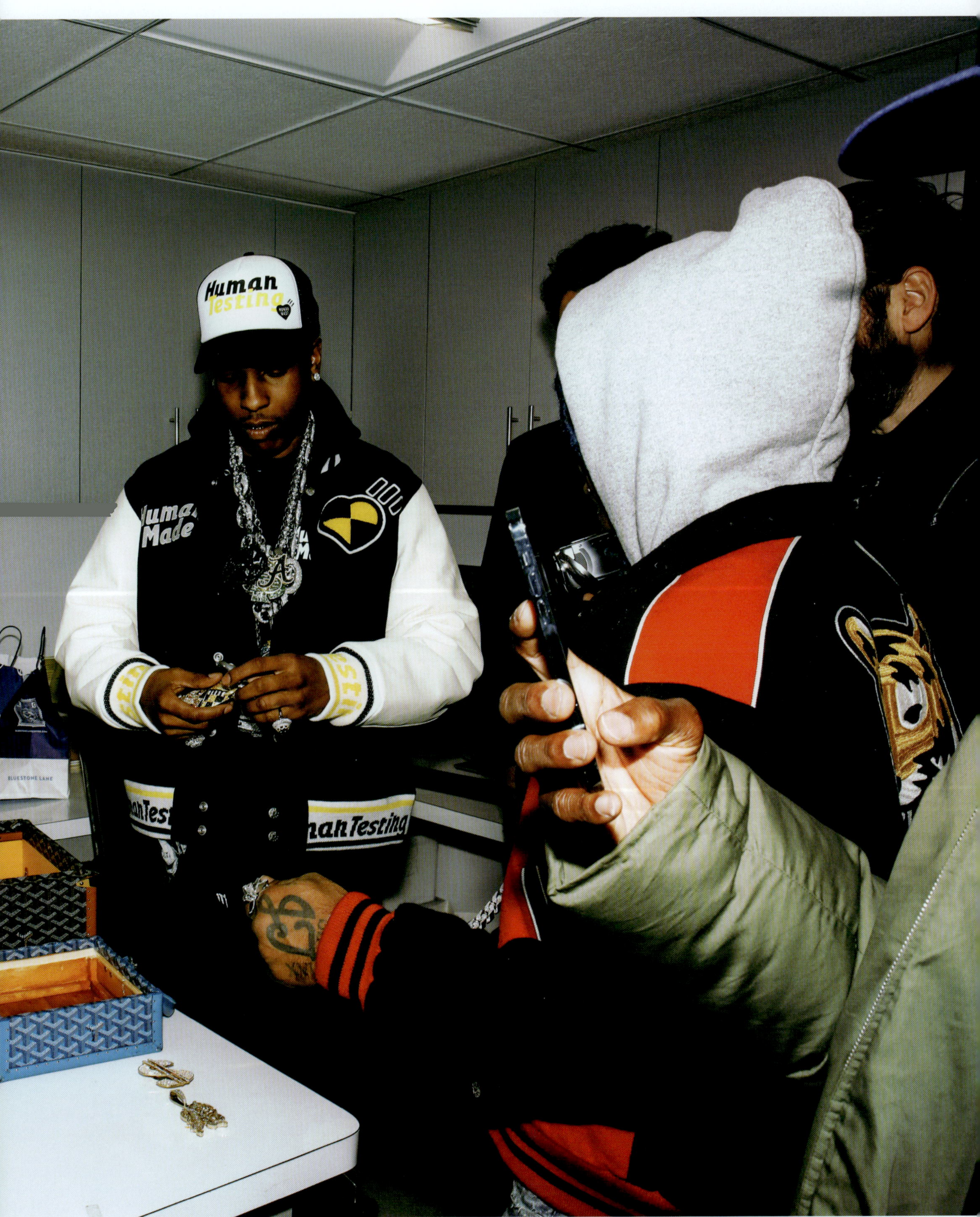
Human Testing
Human Made

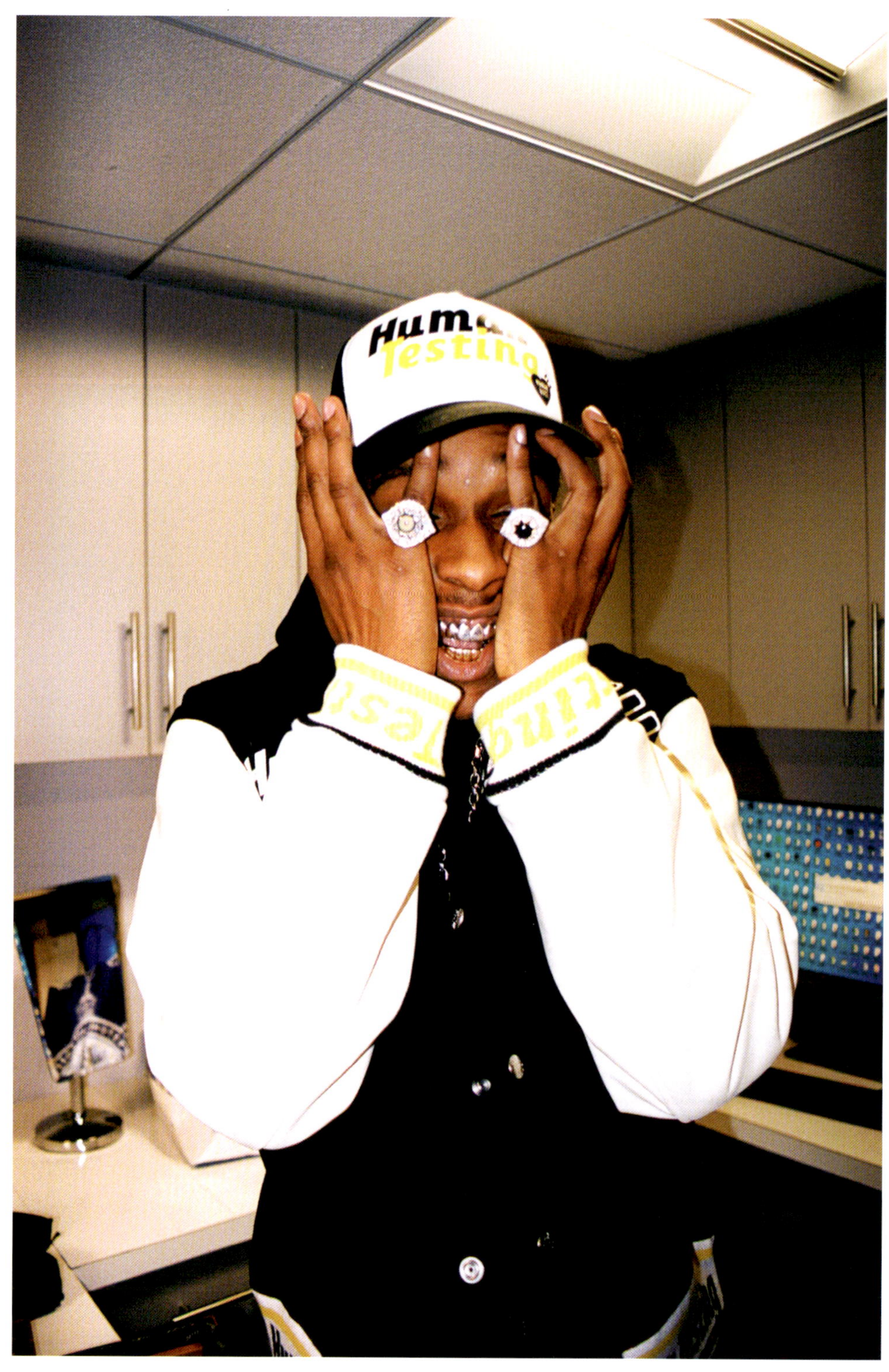
Testing

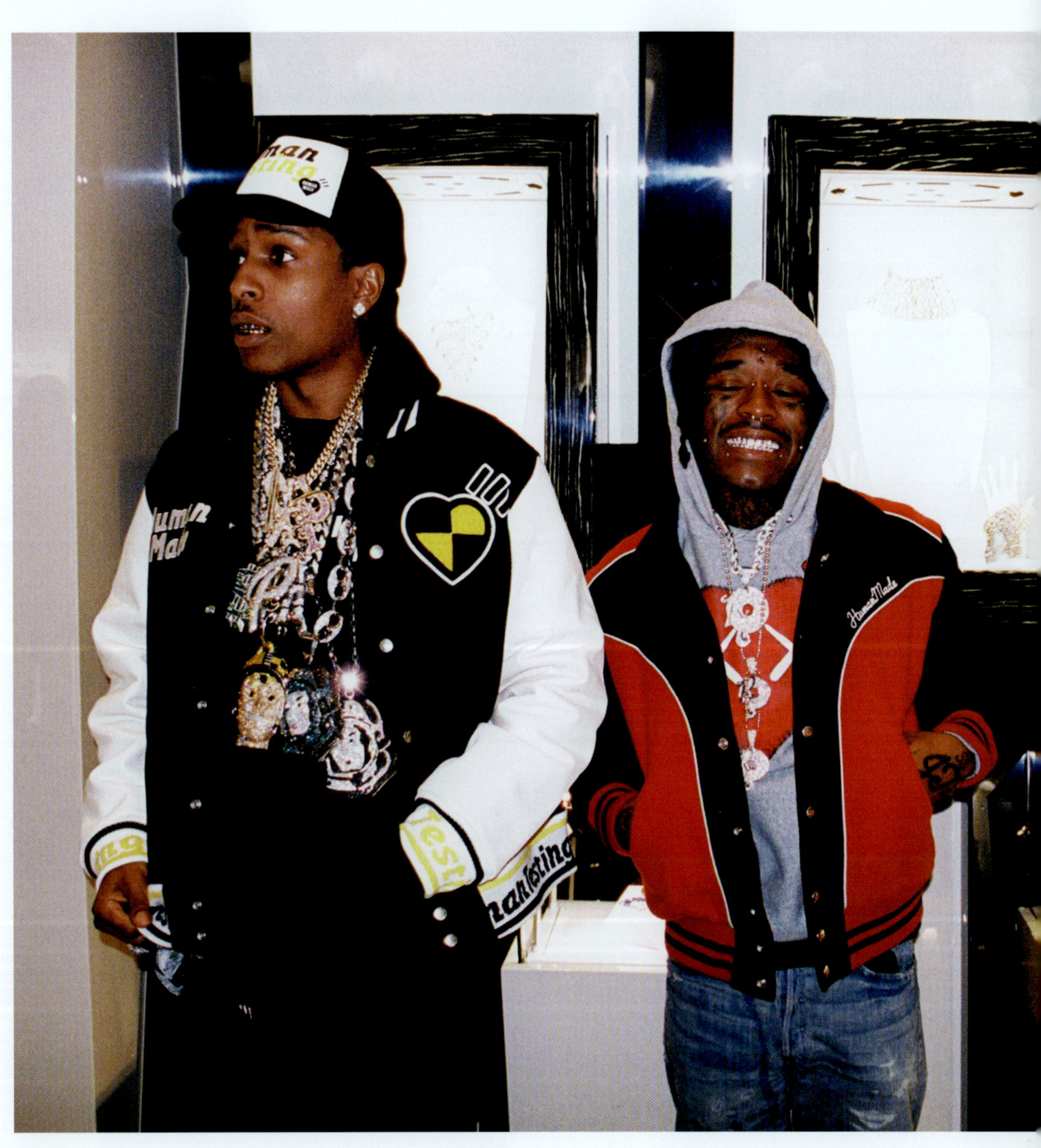

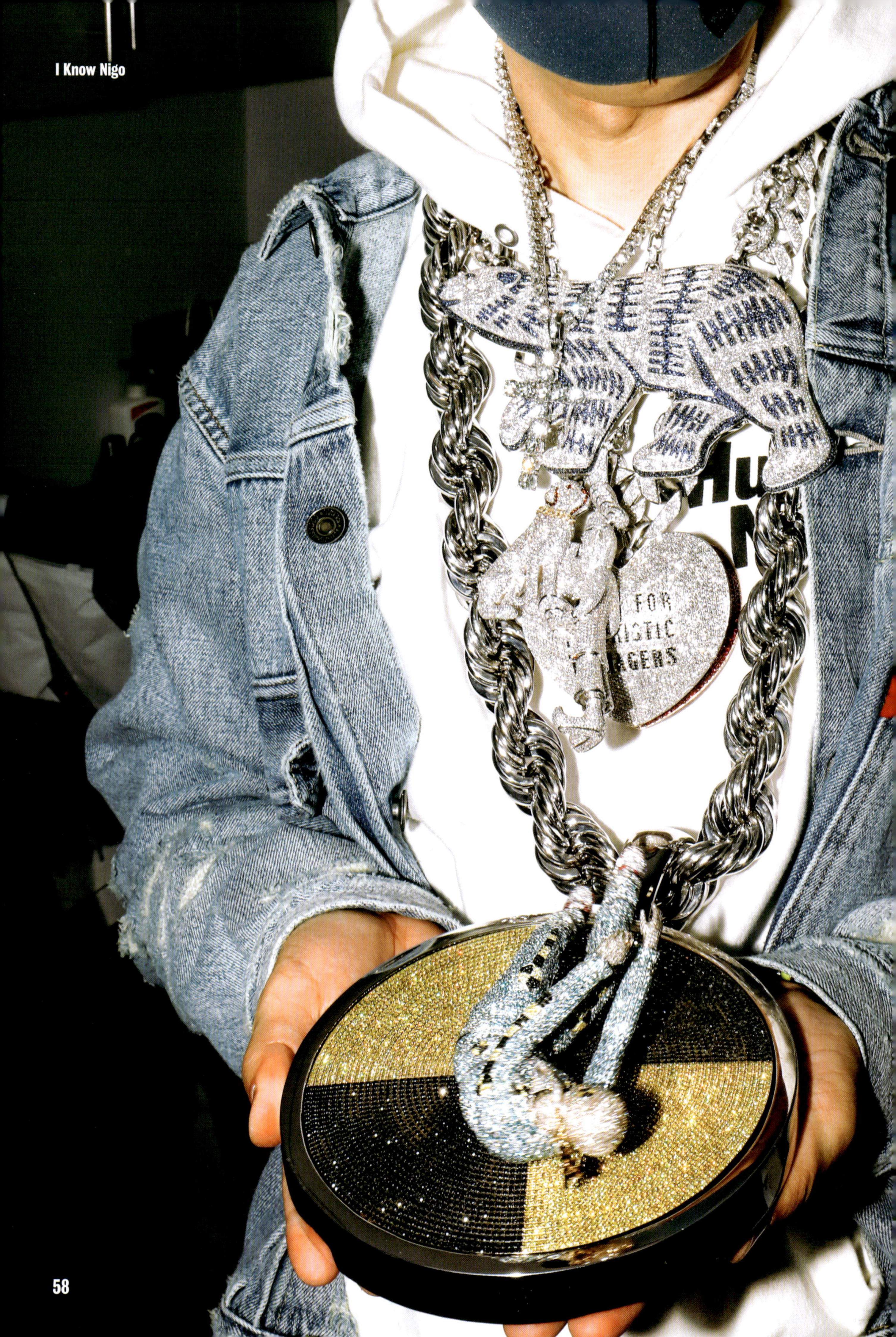

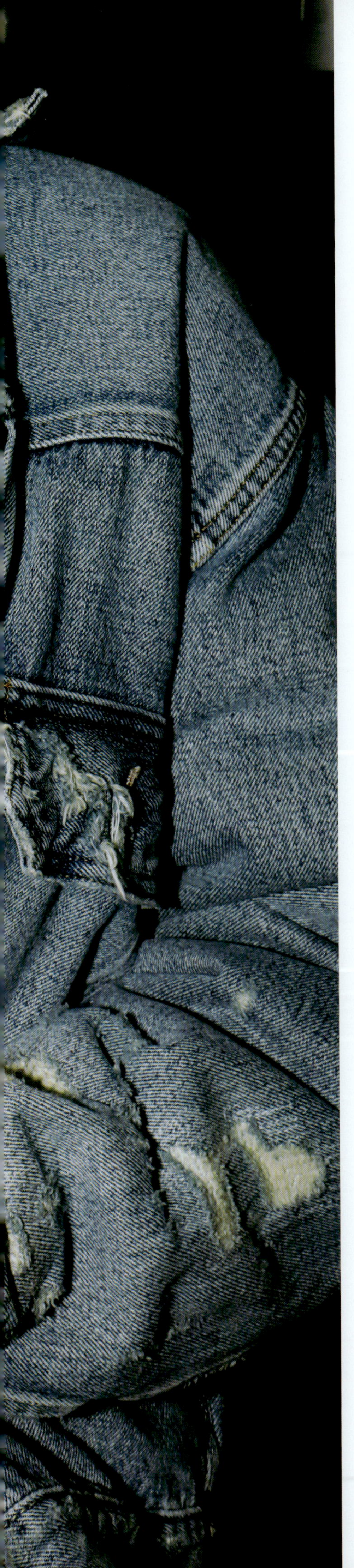

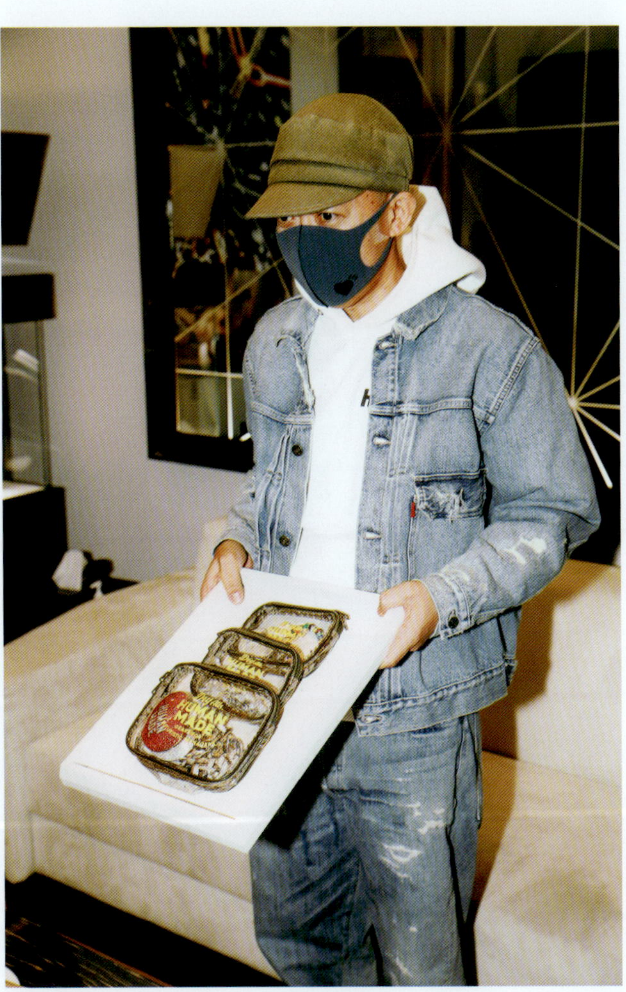

New pickups from Jacob & Co for NIGO®, with jewelry inspired by the crash-test logo that features prominently in the "HEAVY" single and the Human Made x A$AP Rocky "HUMAN TESTING" capsule collection.

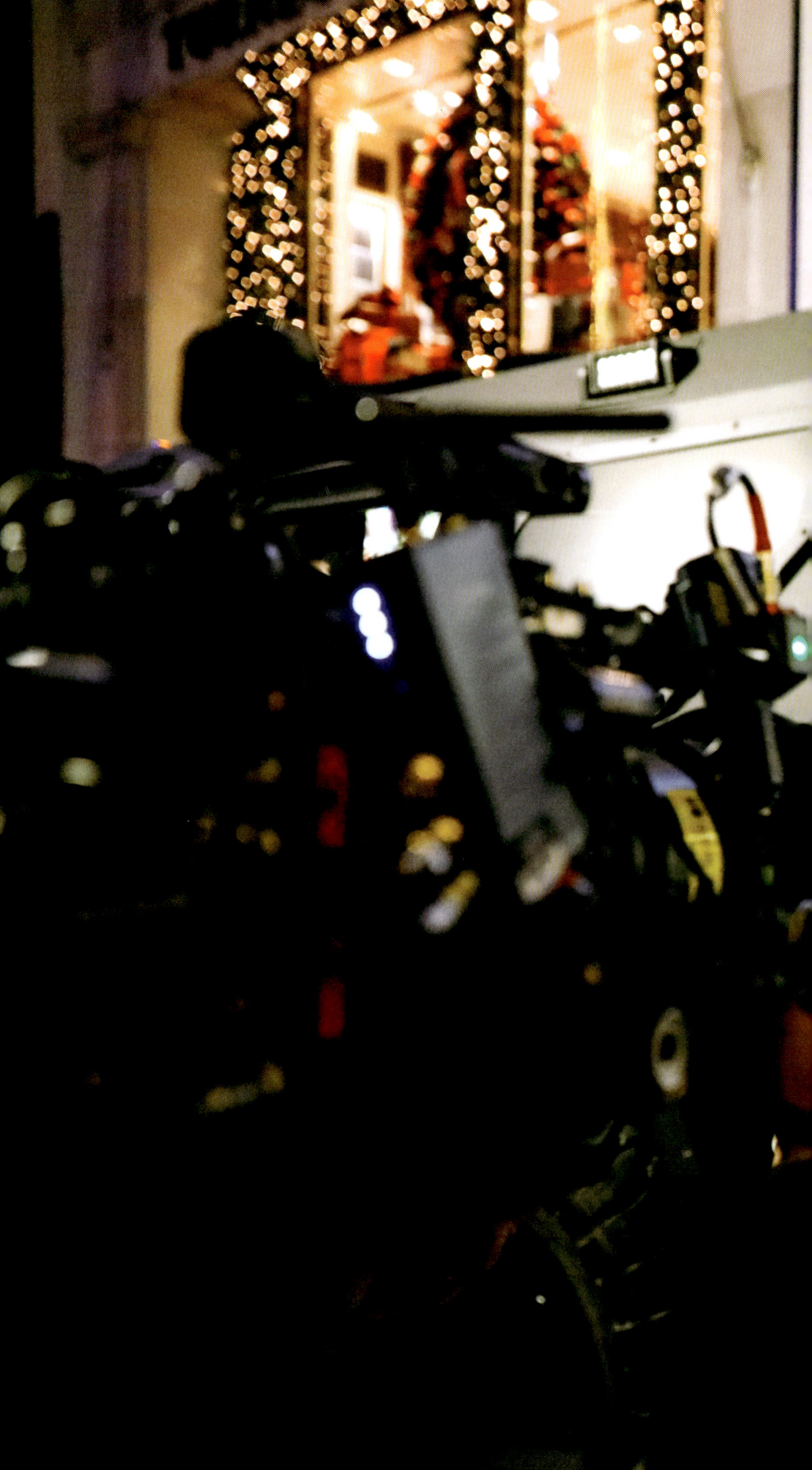

Impromptu presser with A$AP Rocky & Lil Uzi Vert in front of Jacob & Co, New York City, December 2021

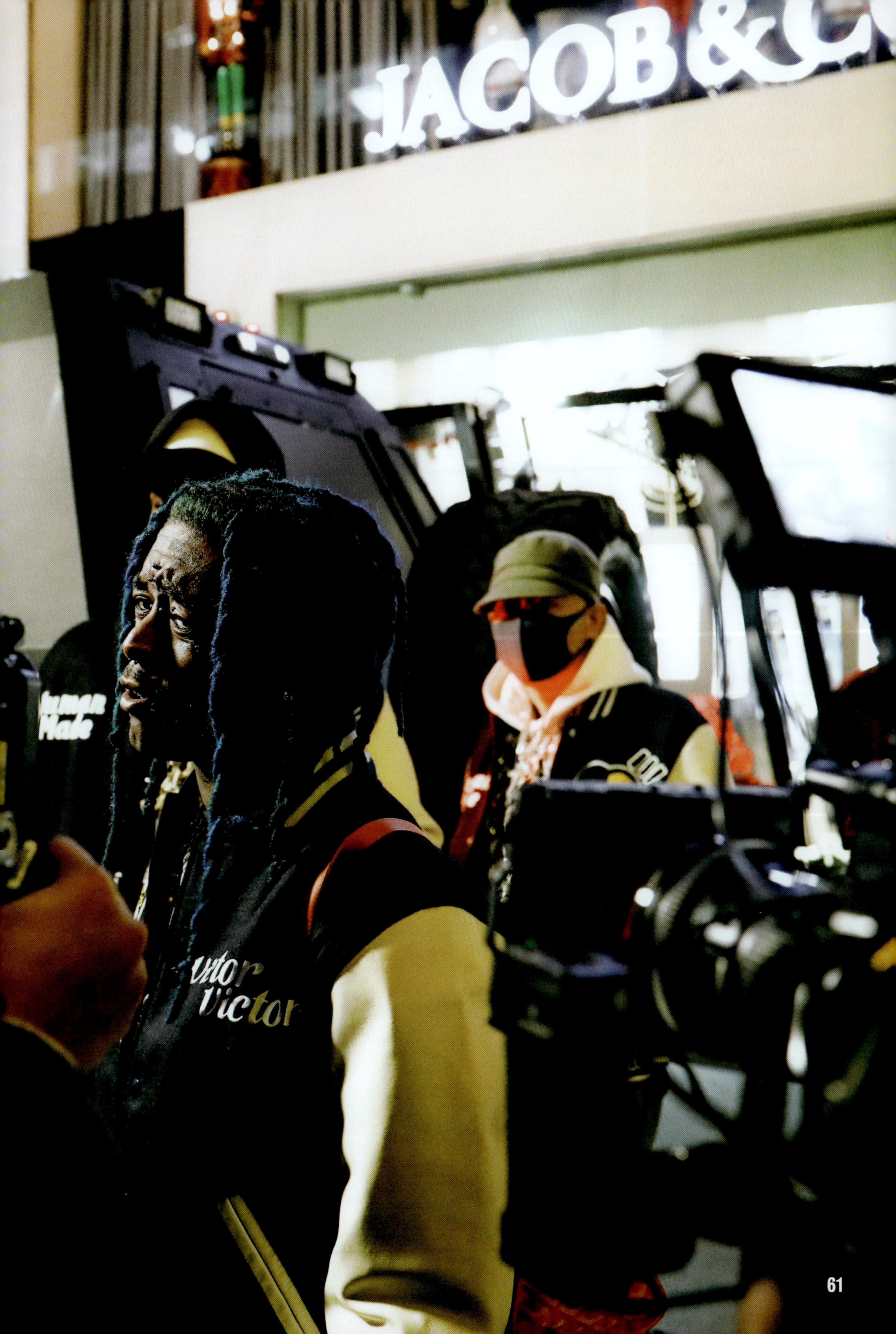
JACOB &
Human Made
Victor

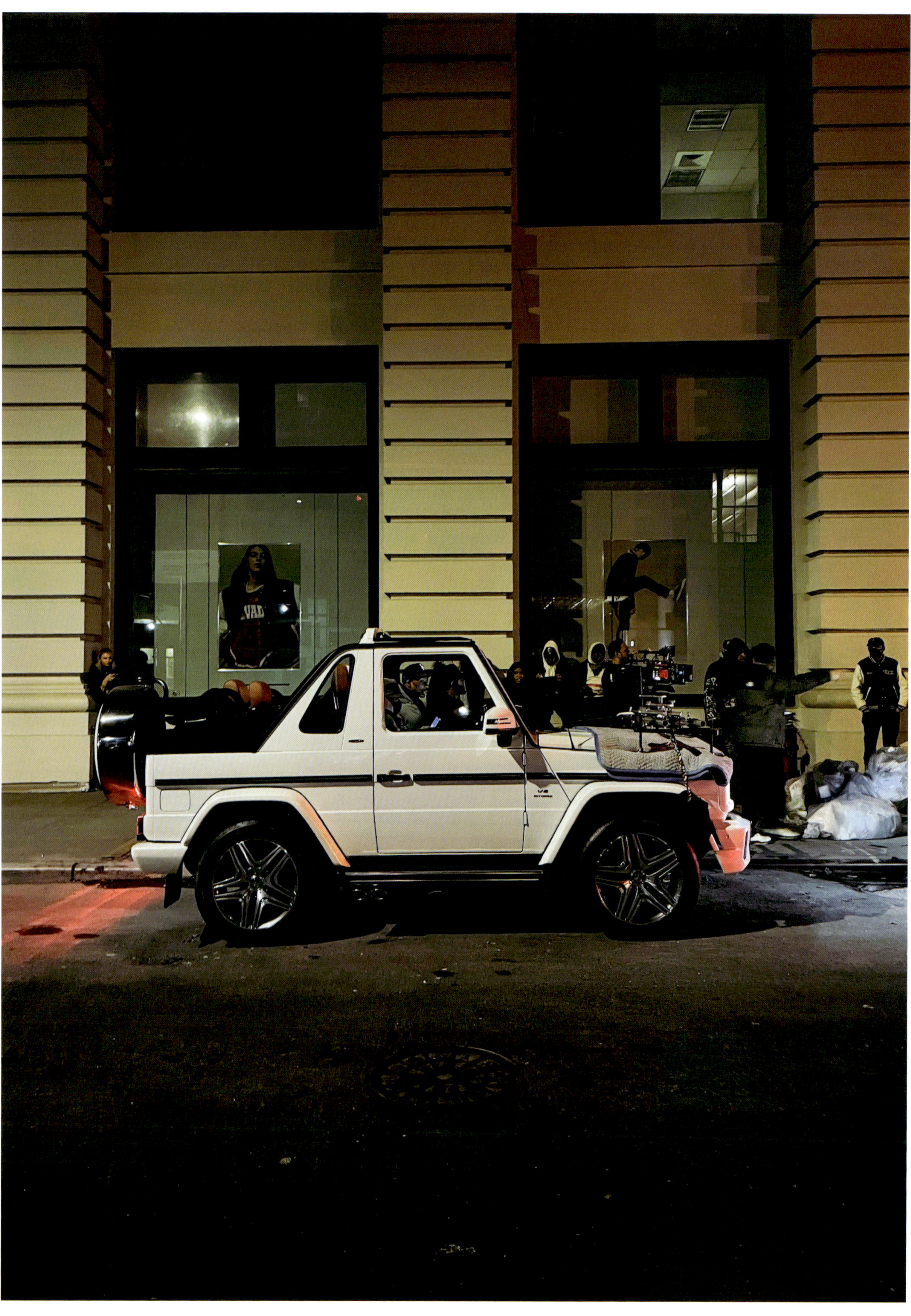

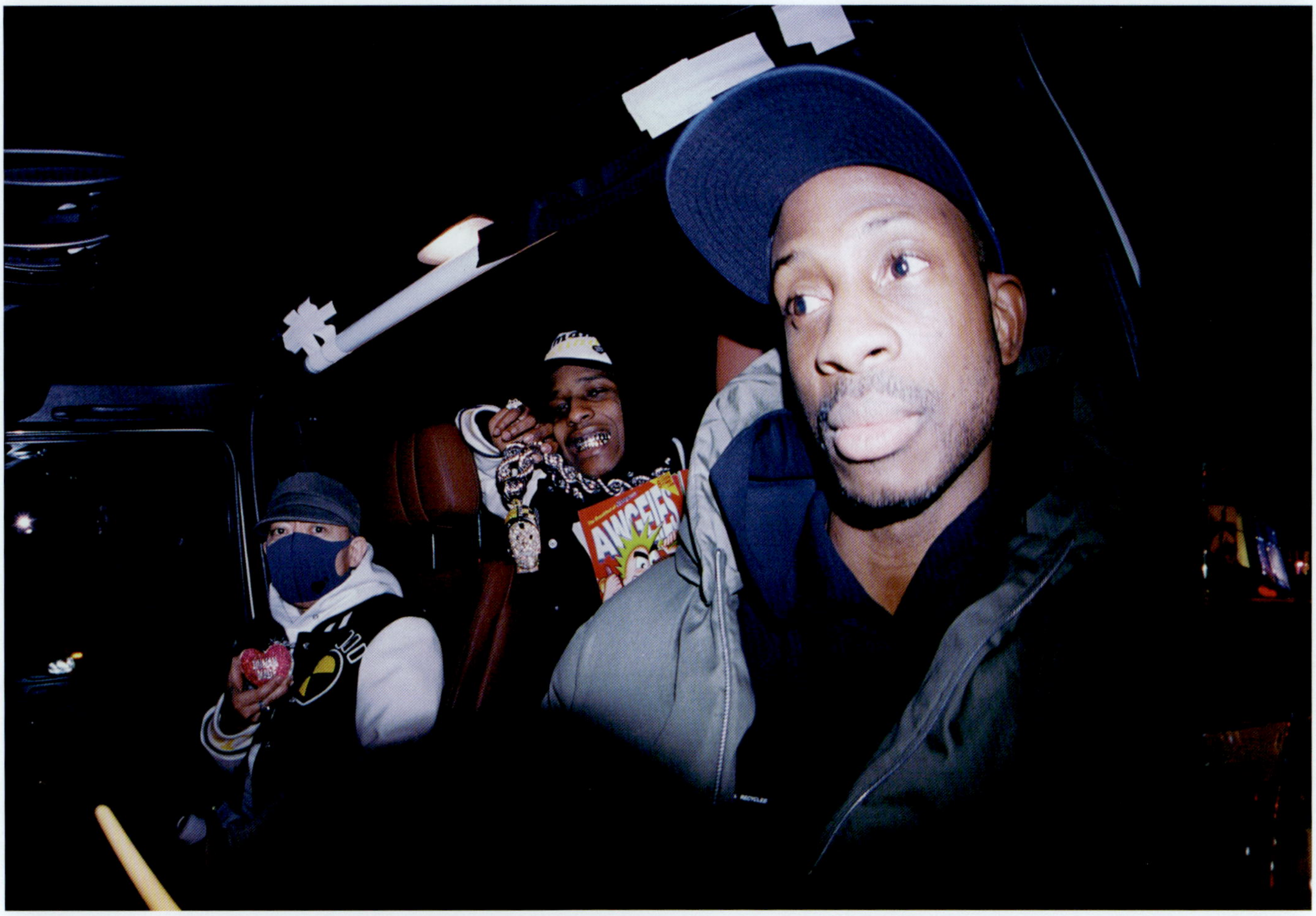

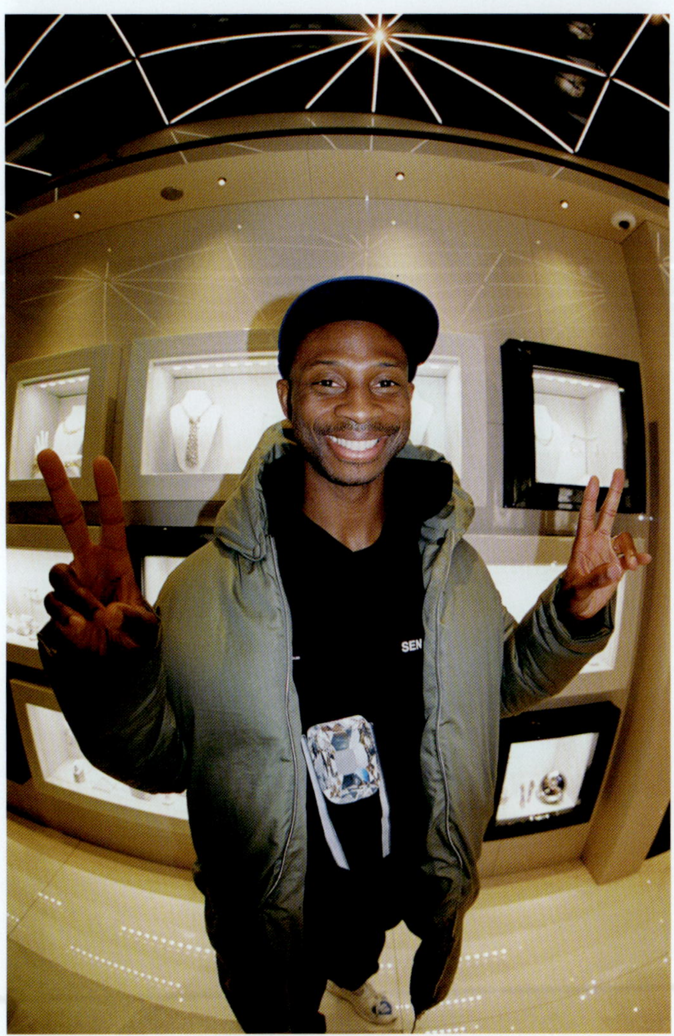

Behind-the-scenes at the "HEAVY" shoot, New York City, December 2021

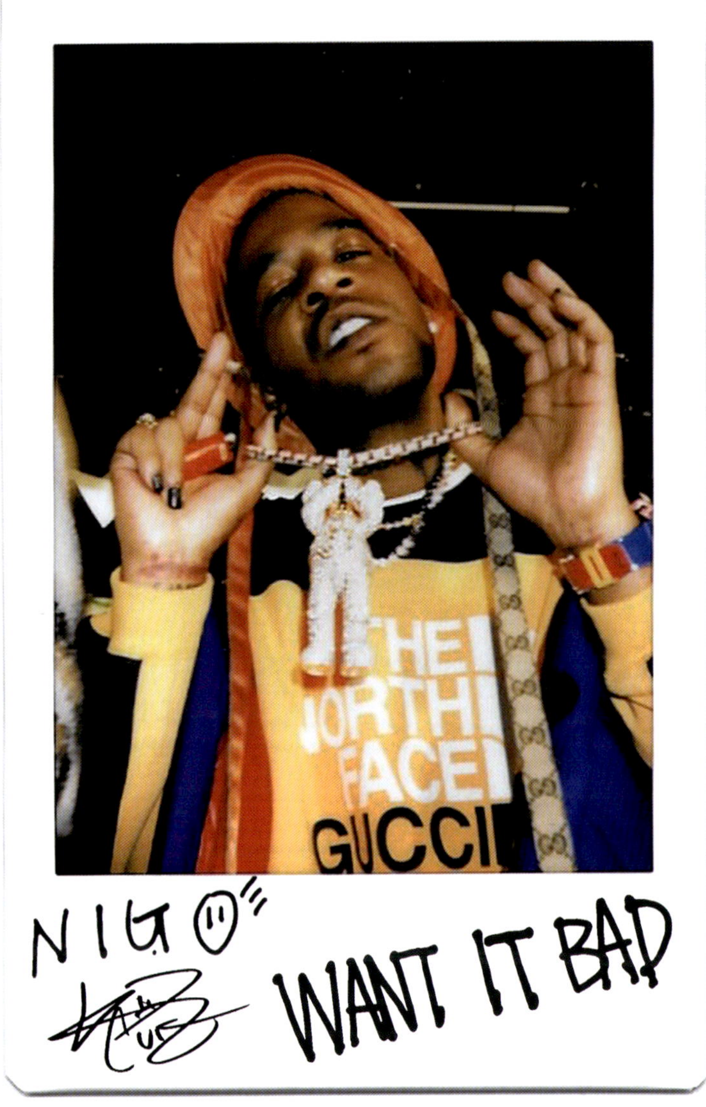

Kid Cudi, "WANT IT BAD" single cover, released February 18, 2022, New York City

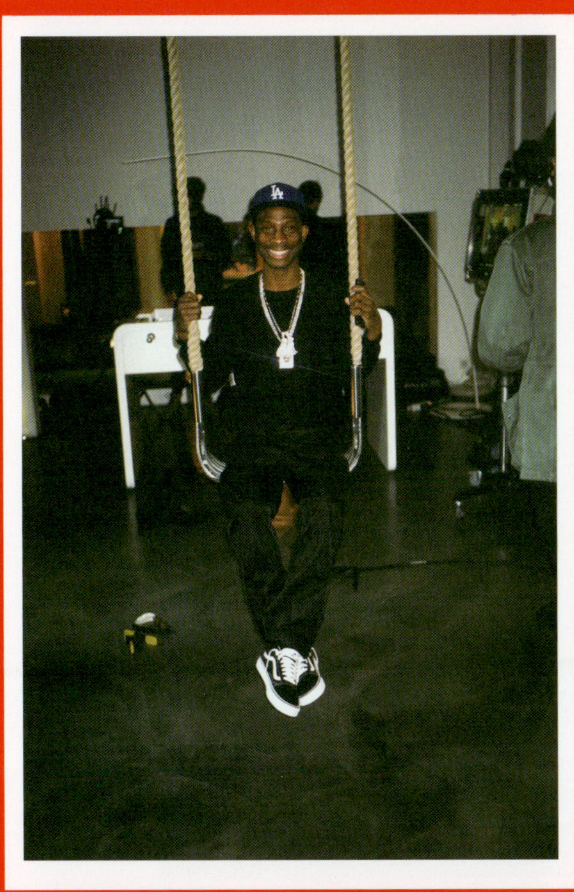

Behind-the-scenes at the "WANT IT BAD" video shoot, Paris November 2021

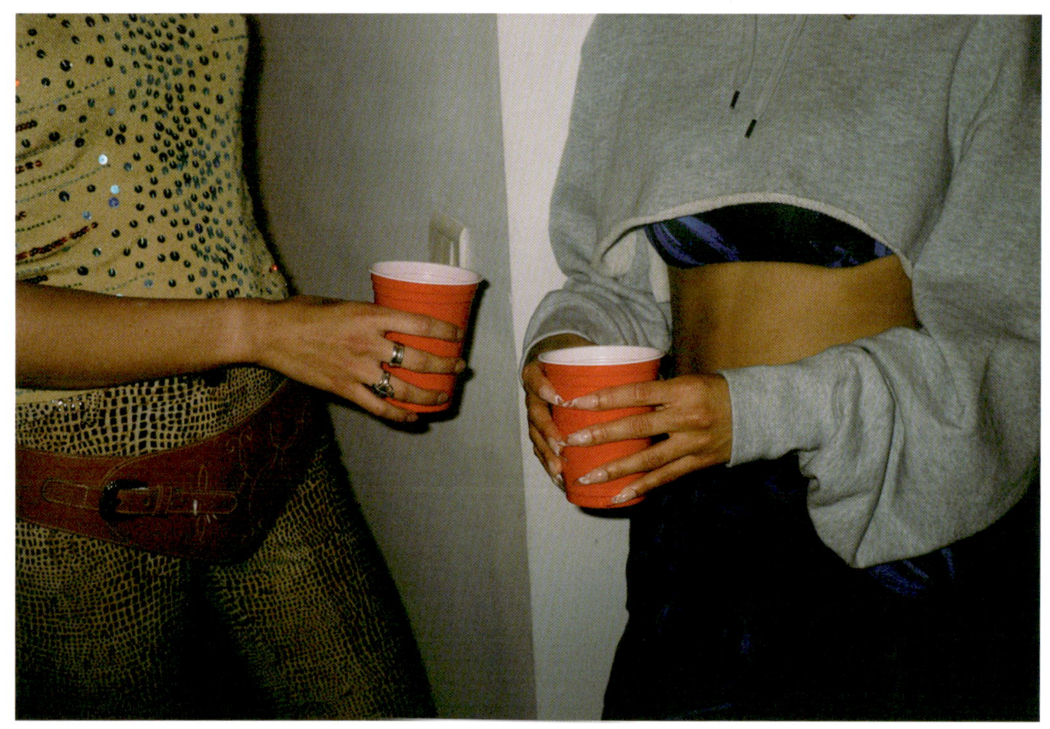

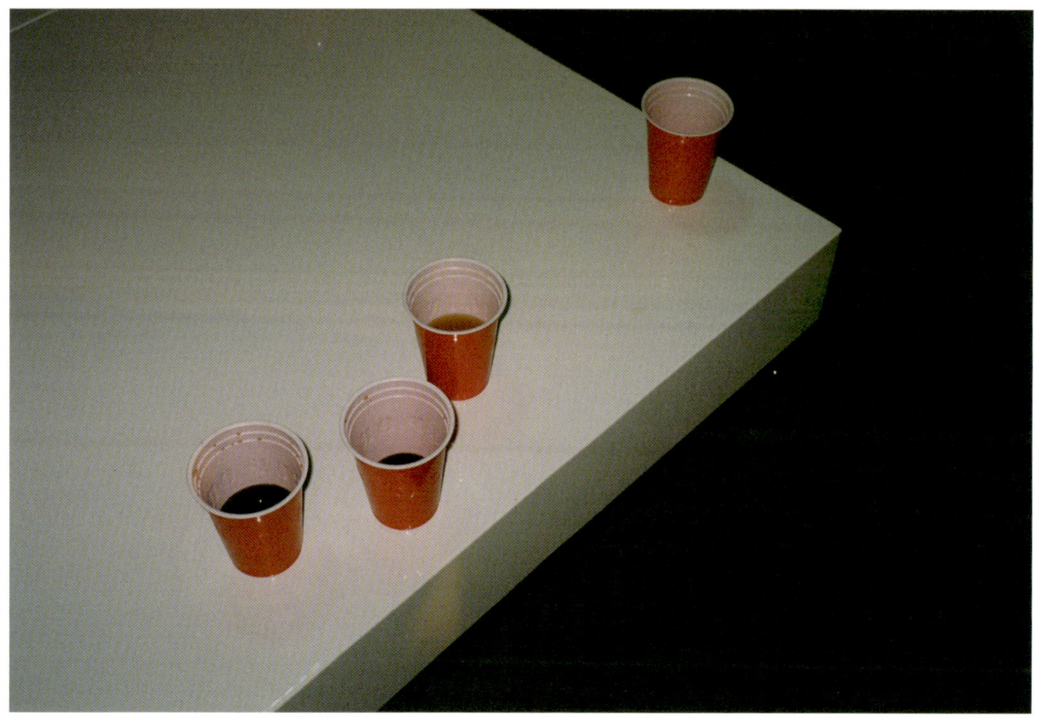

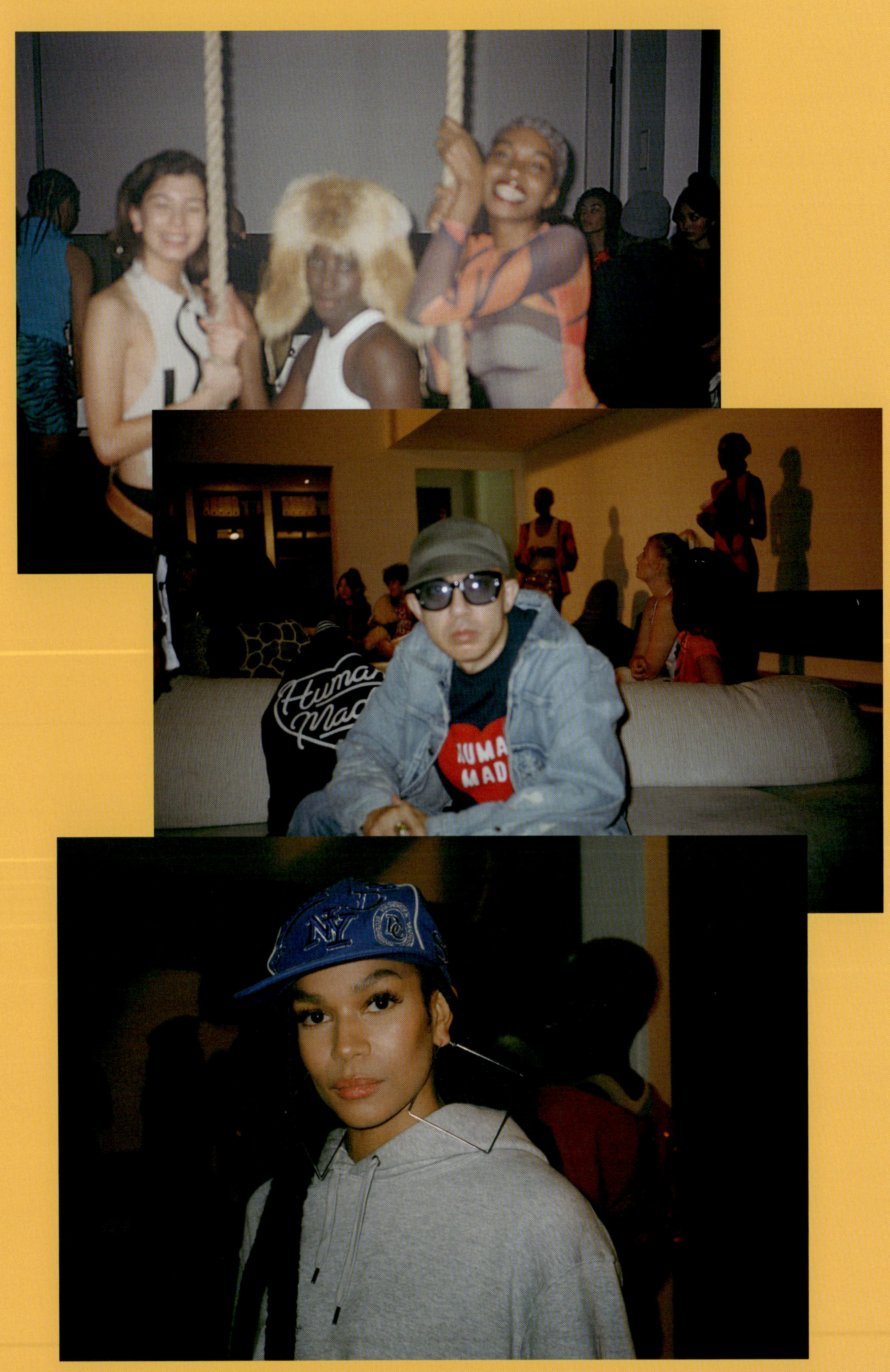
NY

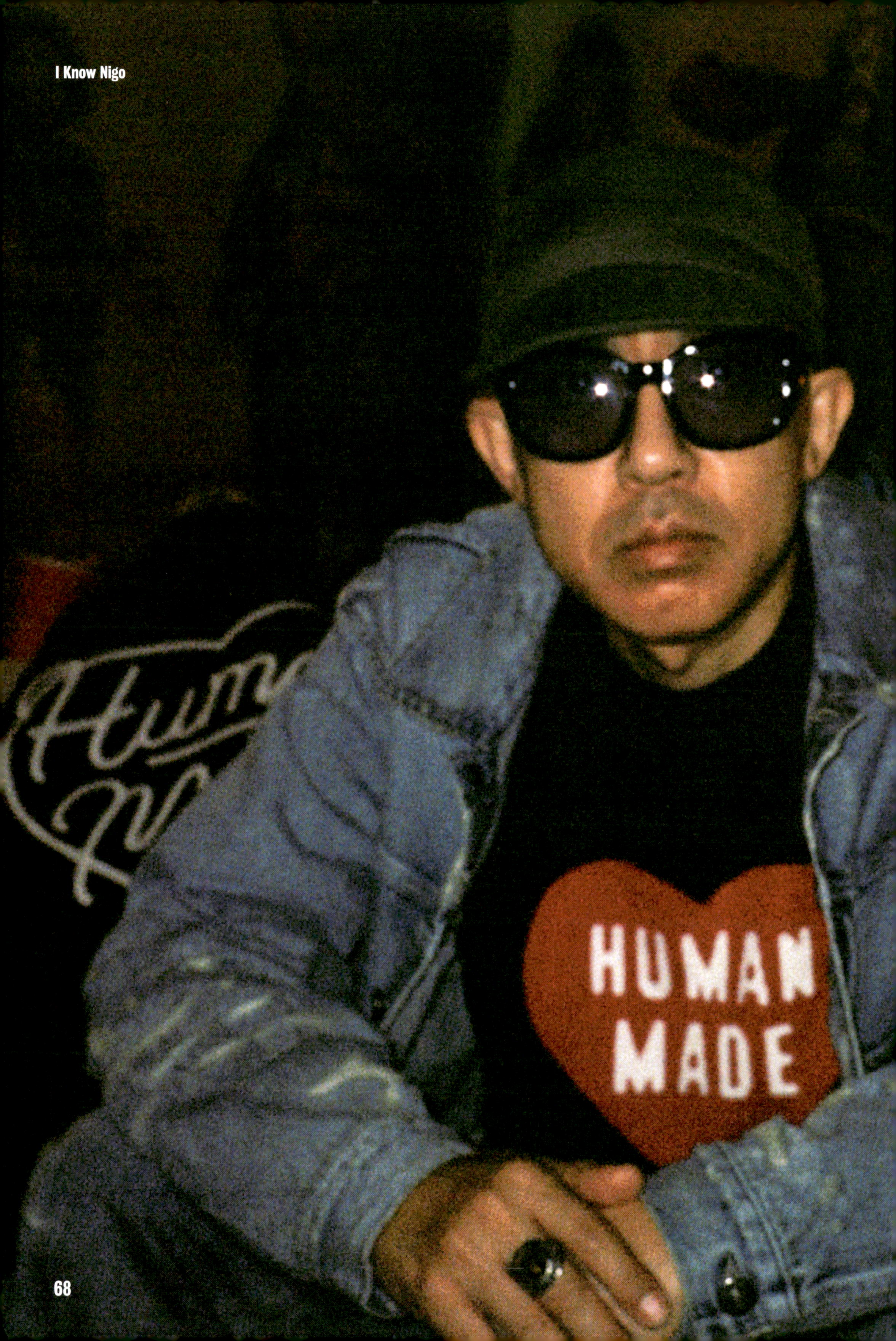
HUMAN
MADE

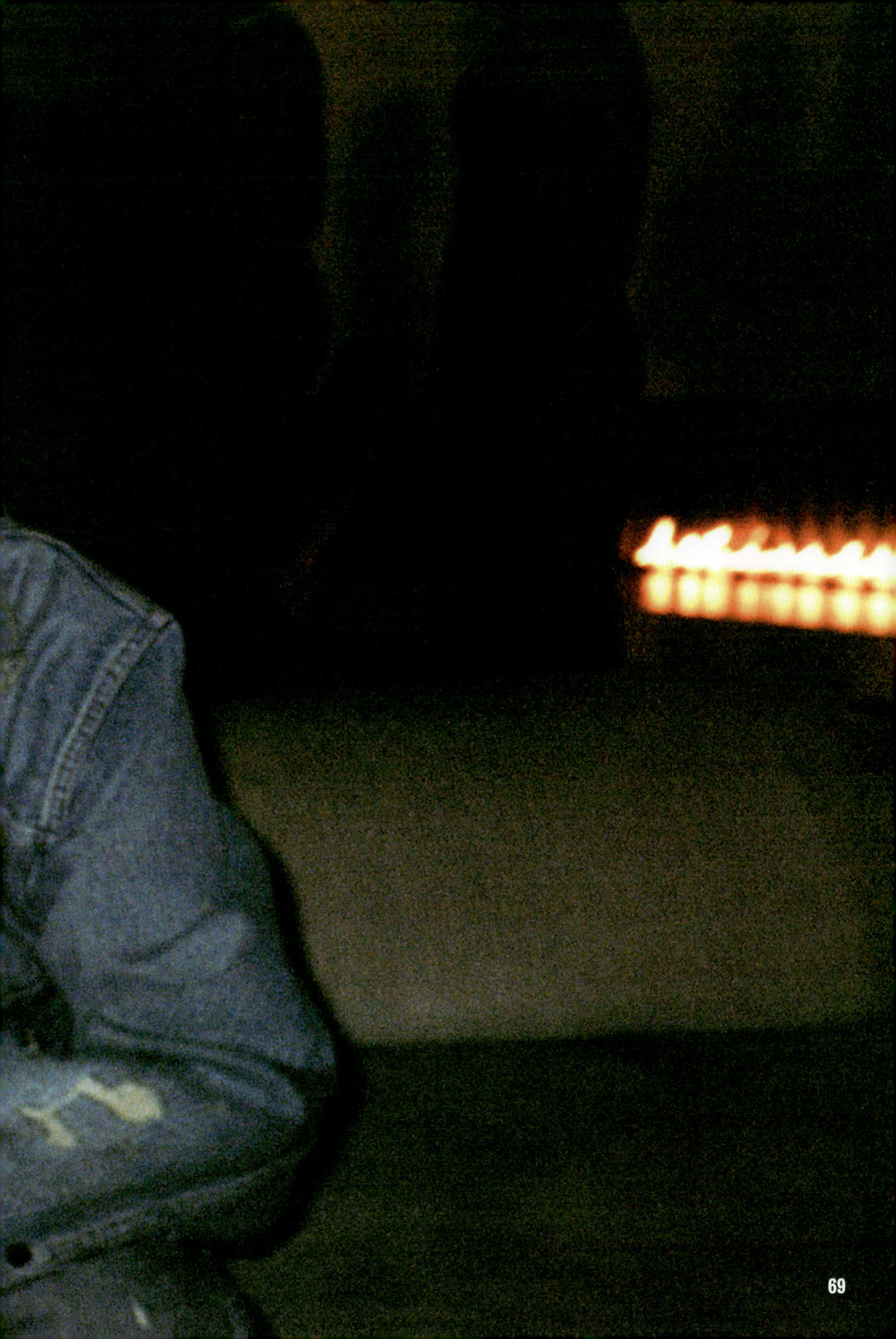

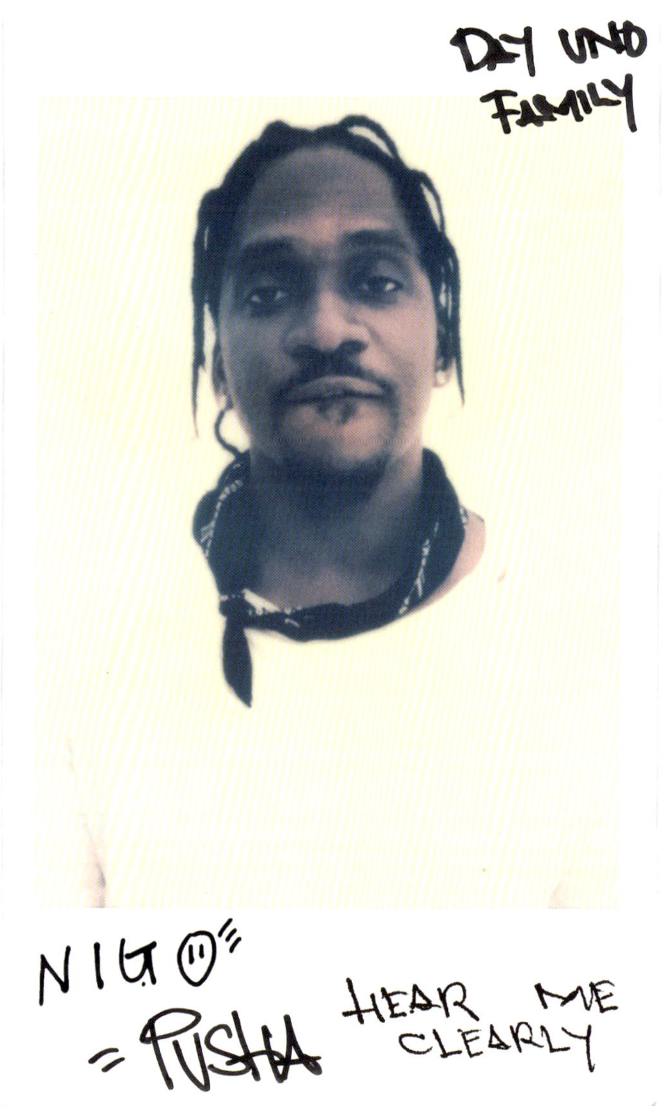

Pusha T, "HEAR ME CLEARLY" single cover, released March 4, 2022, Tokyo

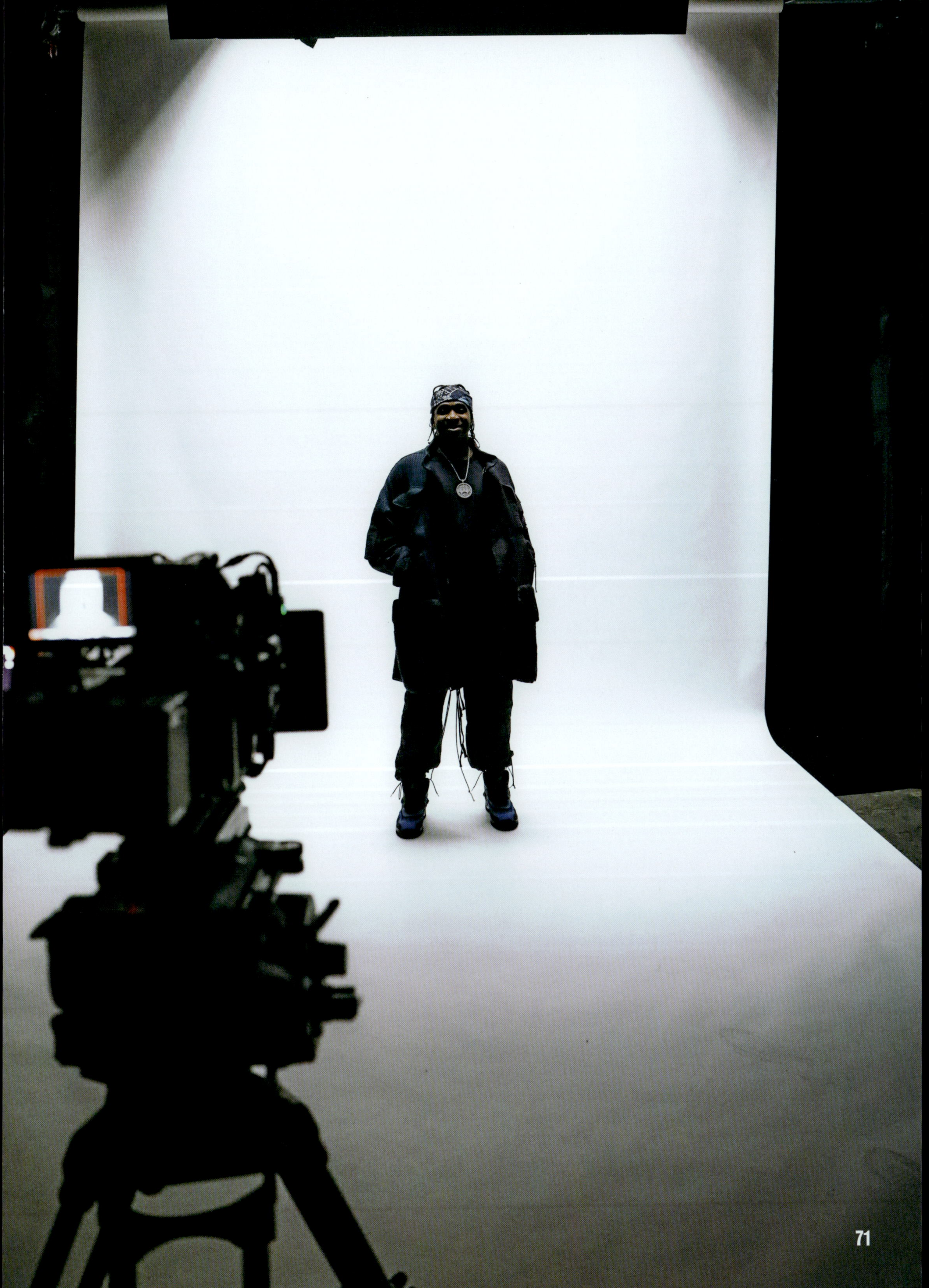

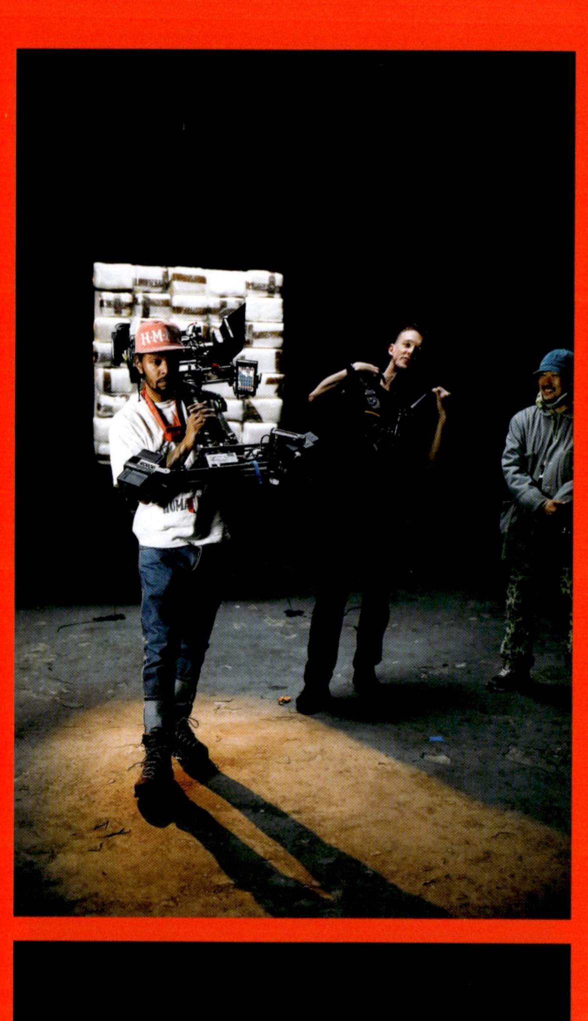
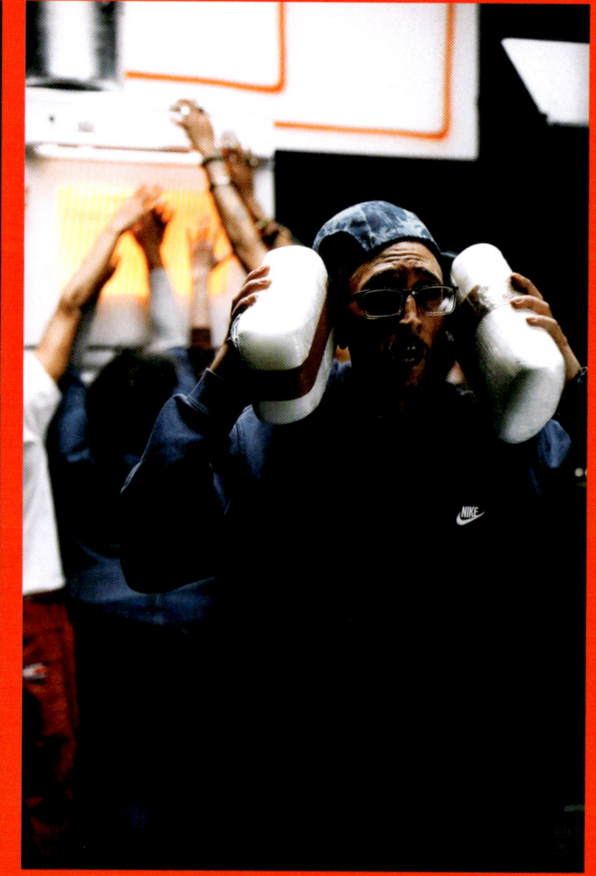
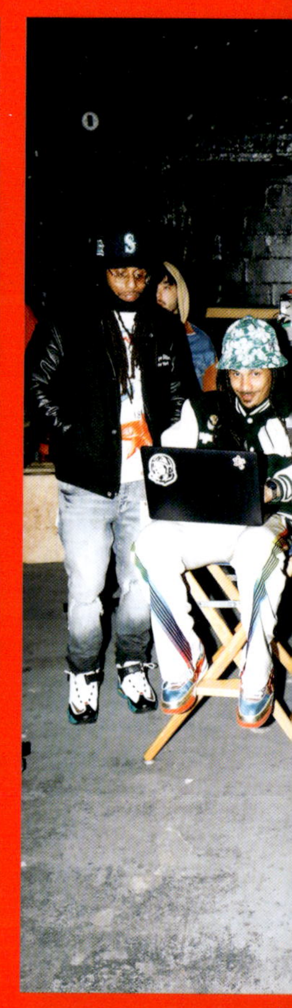
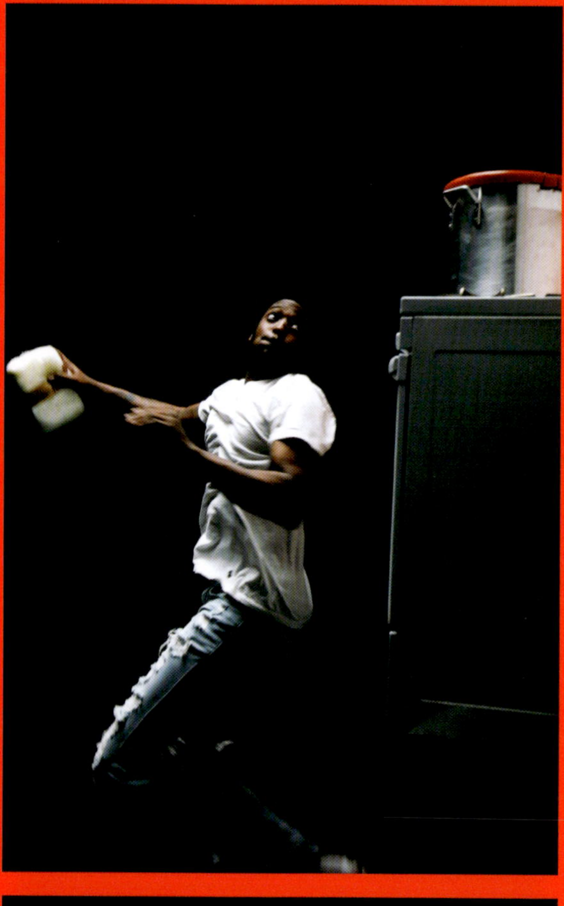
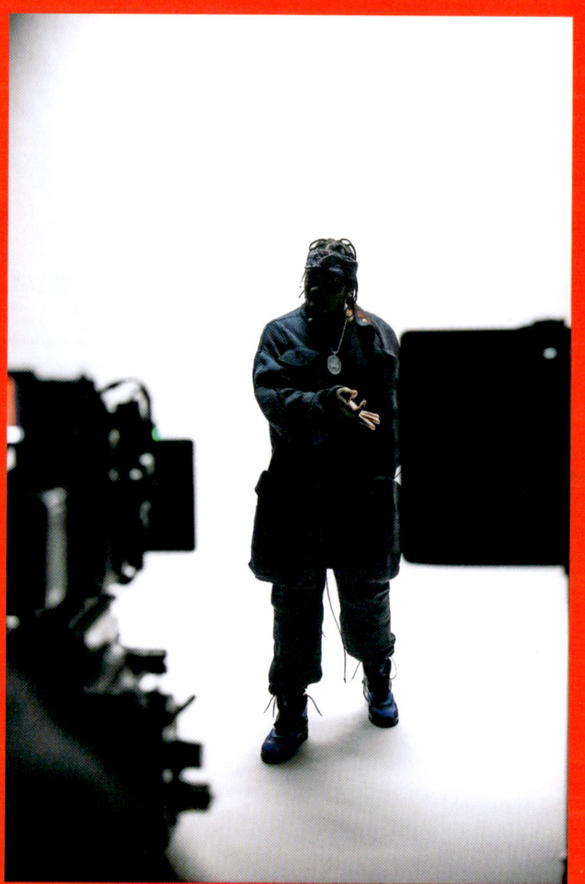
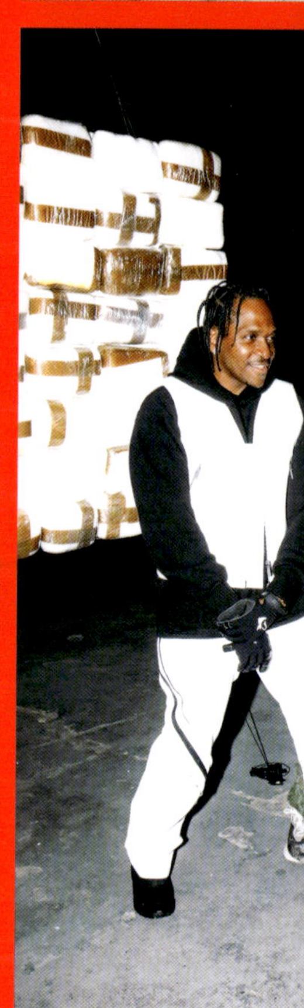
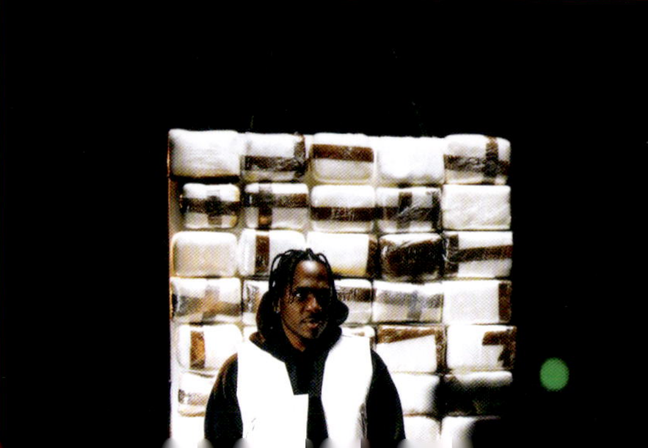
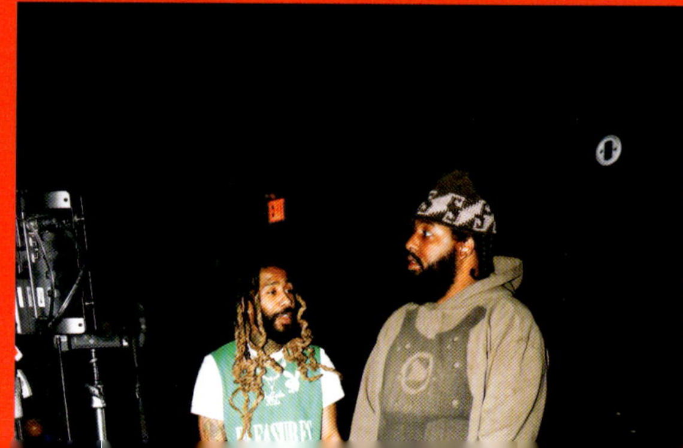
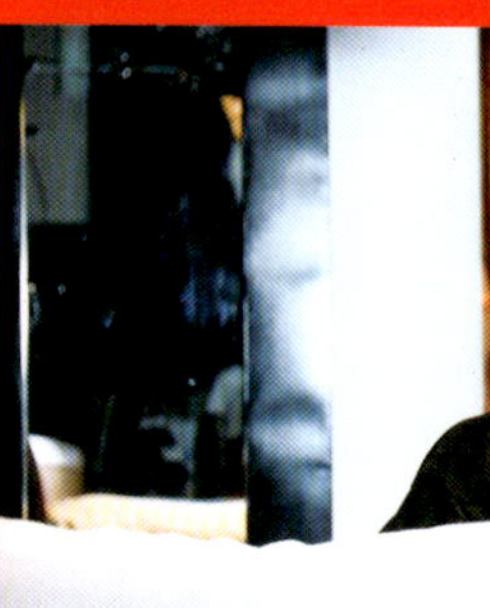

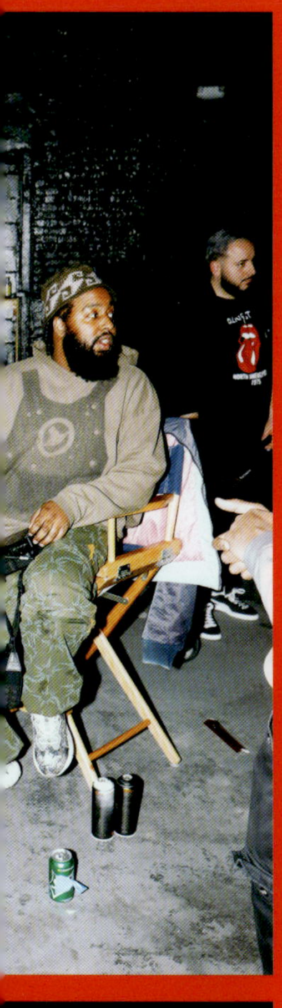
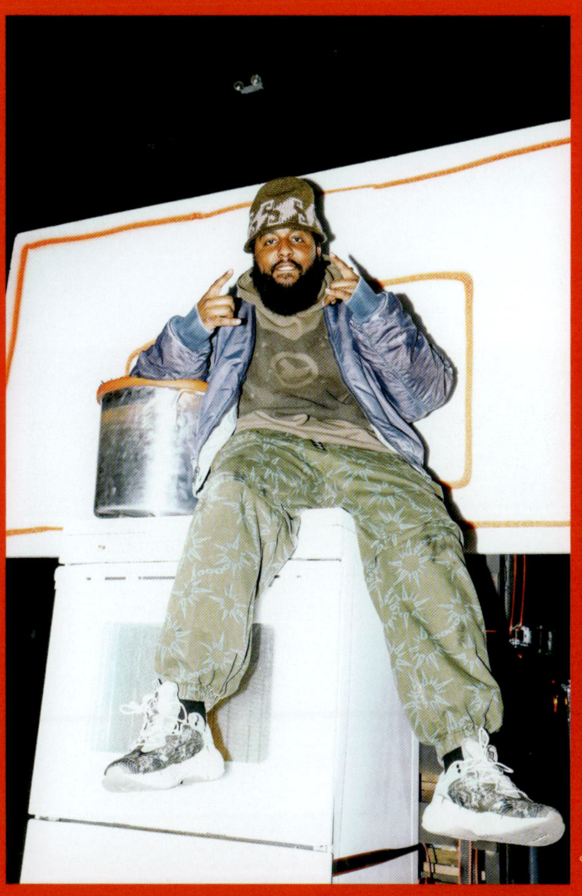
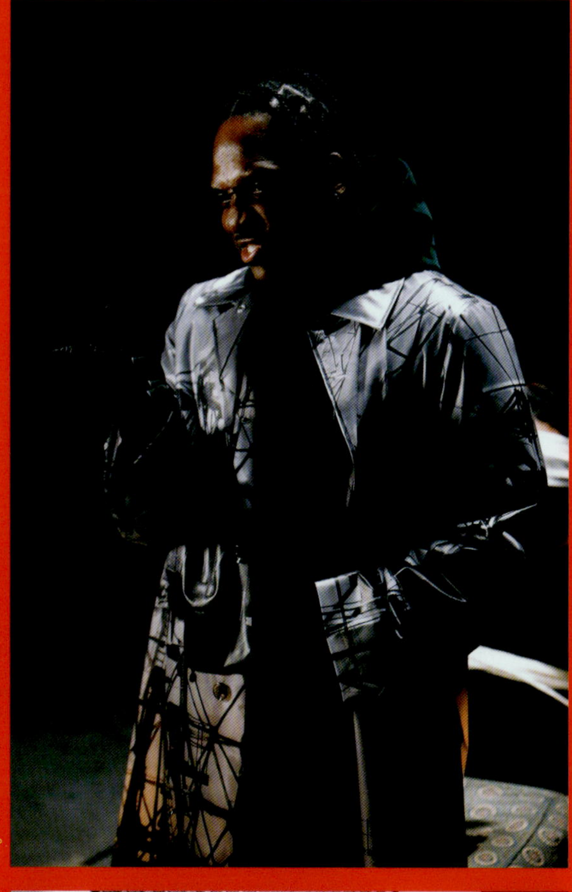
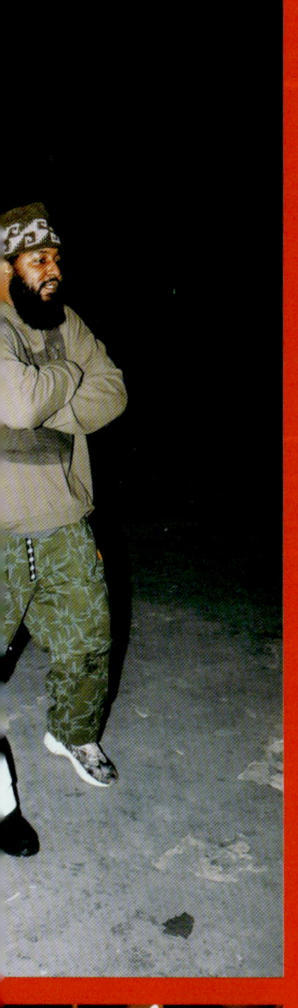
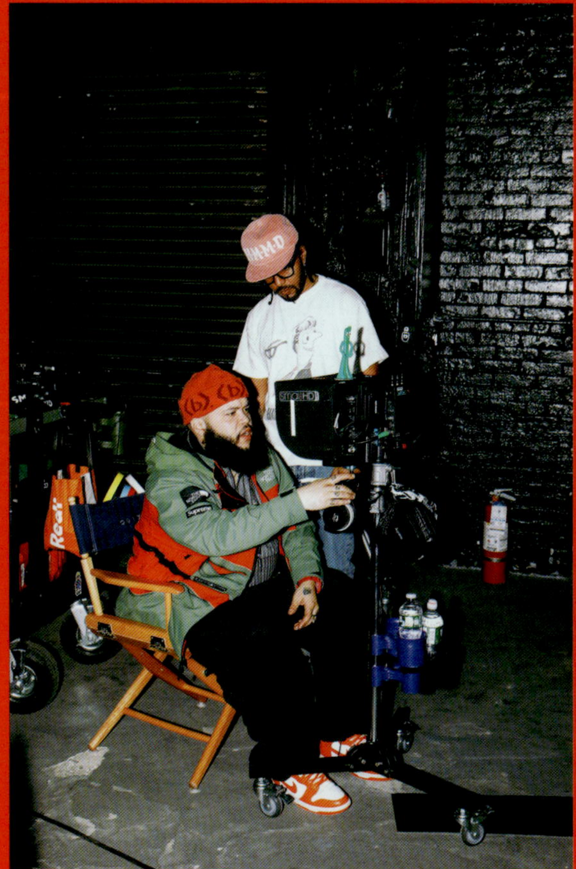
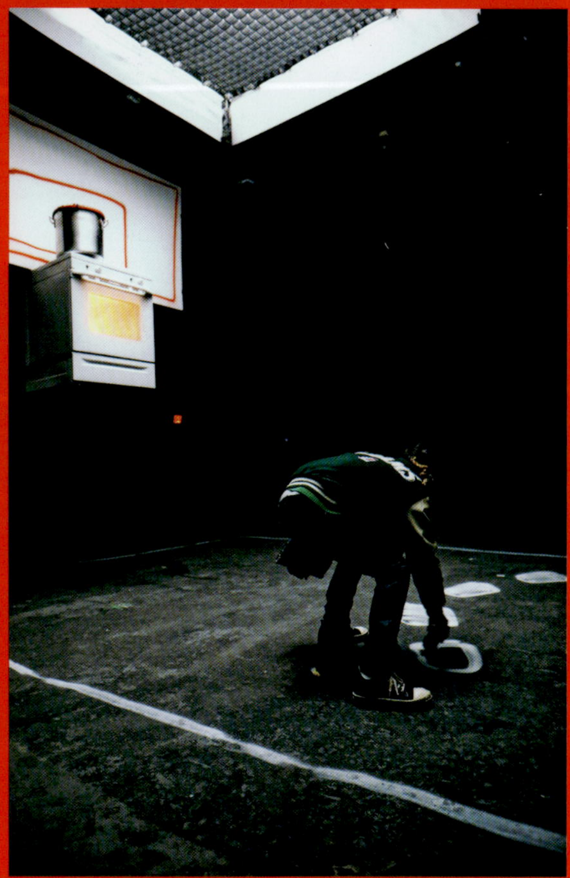
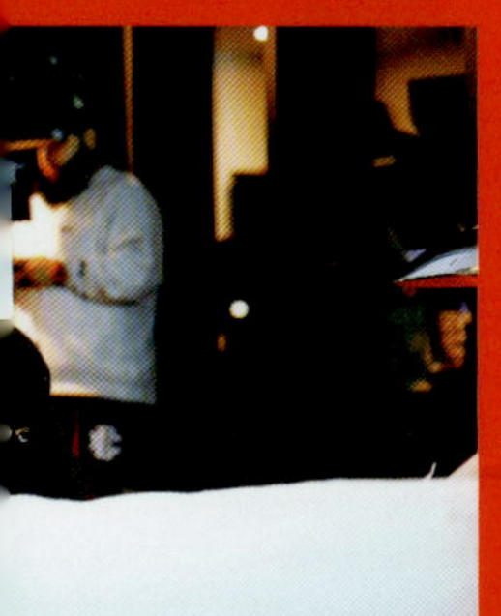
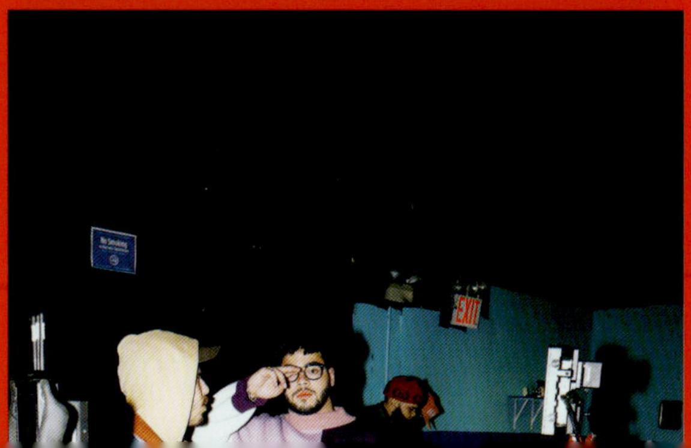
EXIT
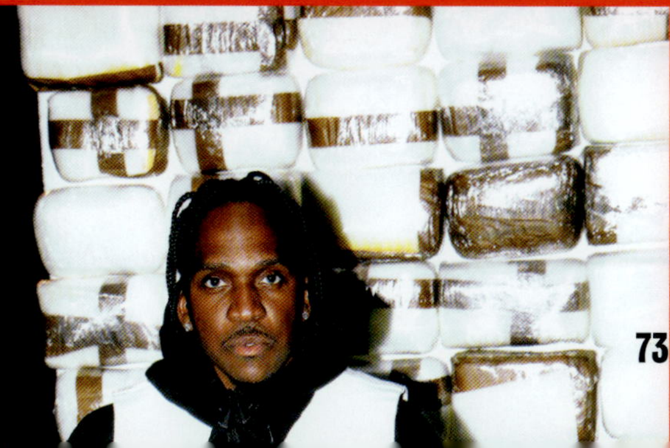

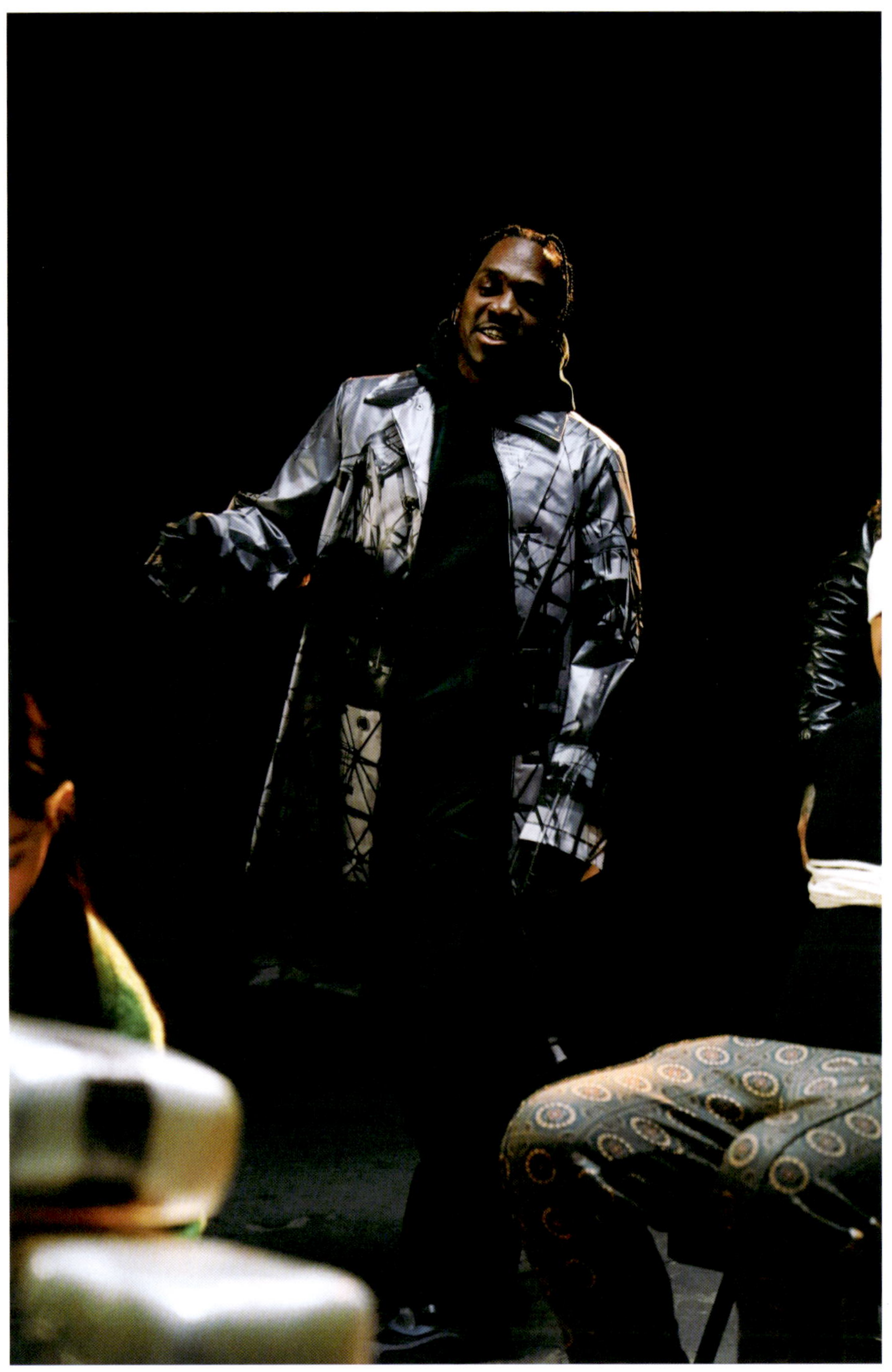

Behind-the-scenes at the "HEAR ME CLEARLY" video shoot, March 2022, New York City, directed by Hidji Films

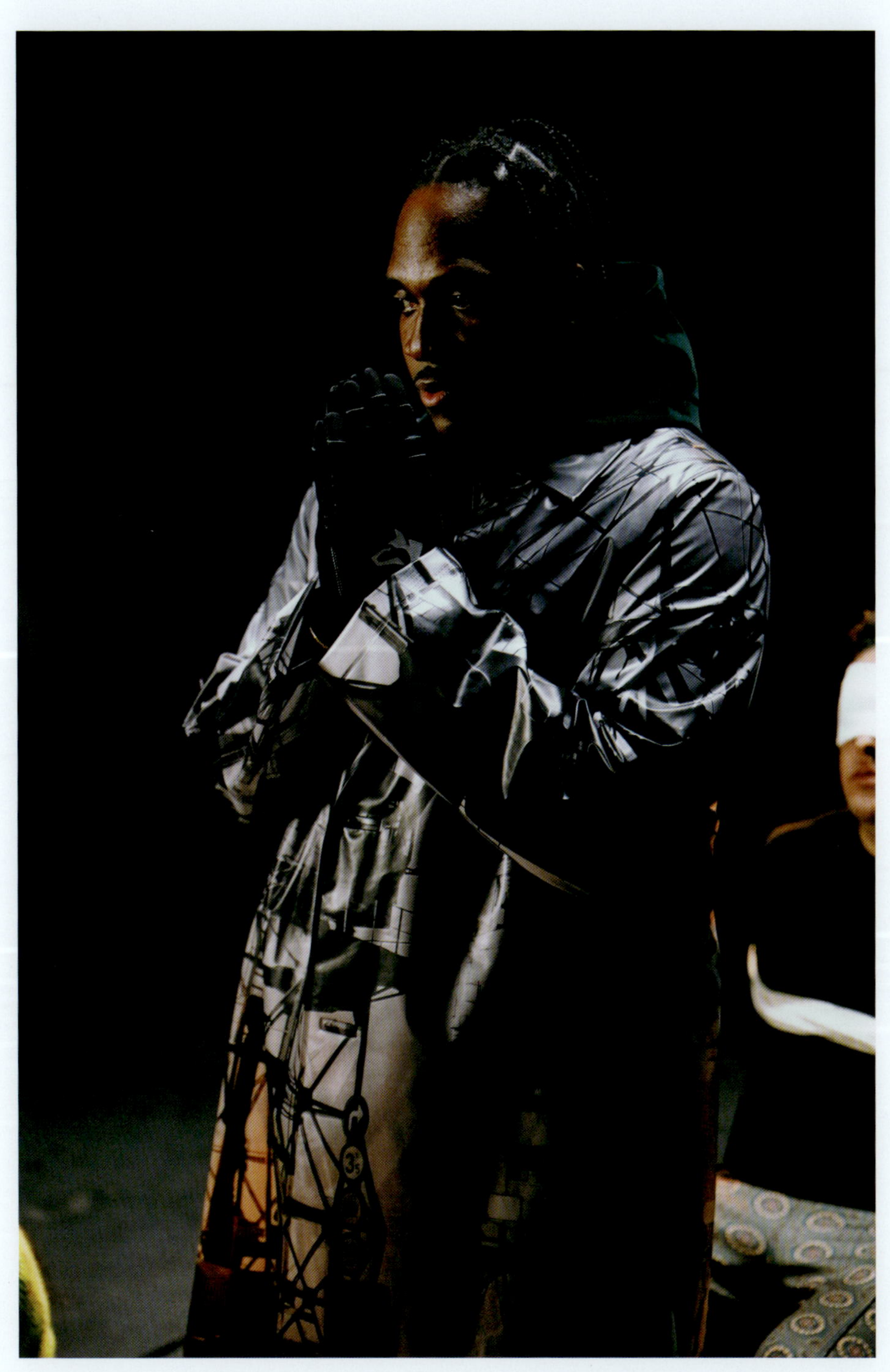

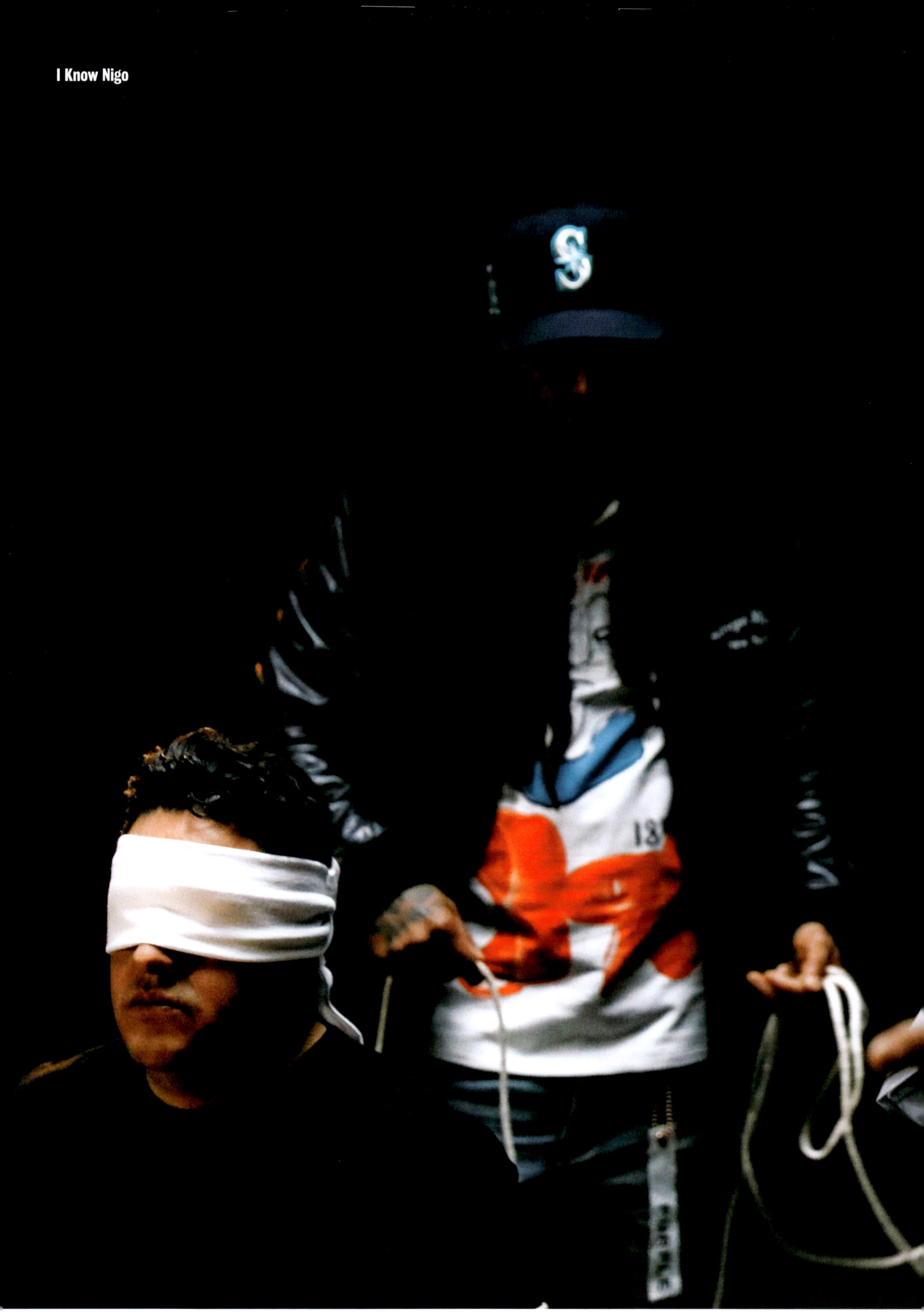

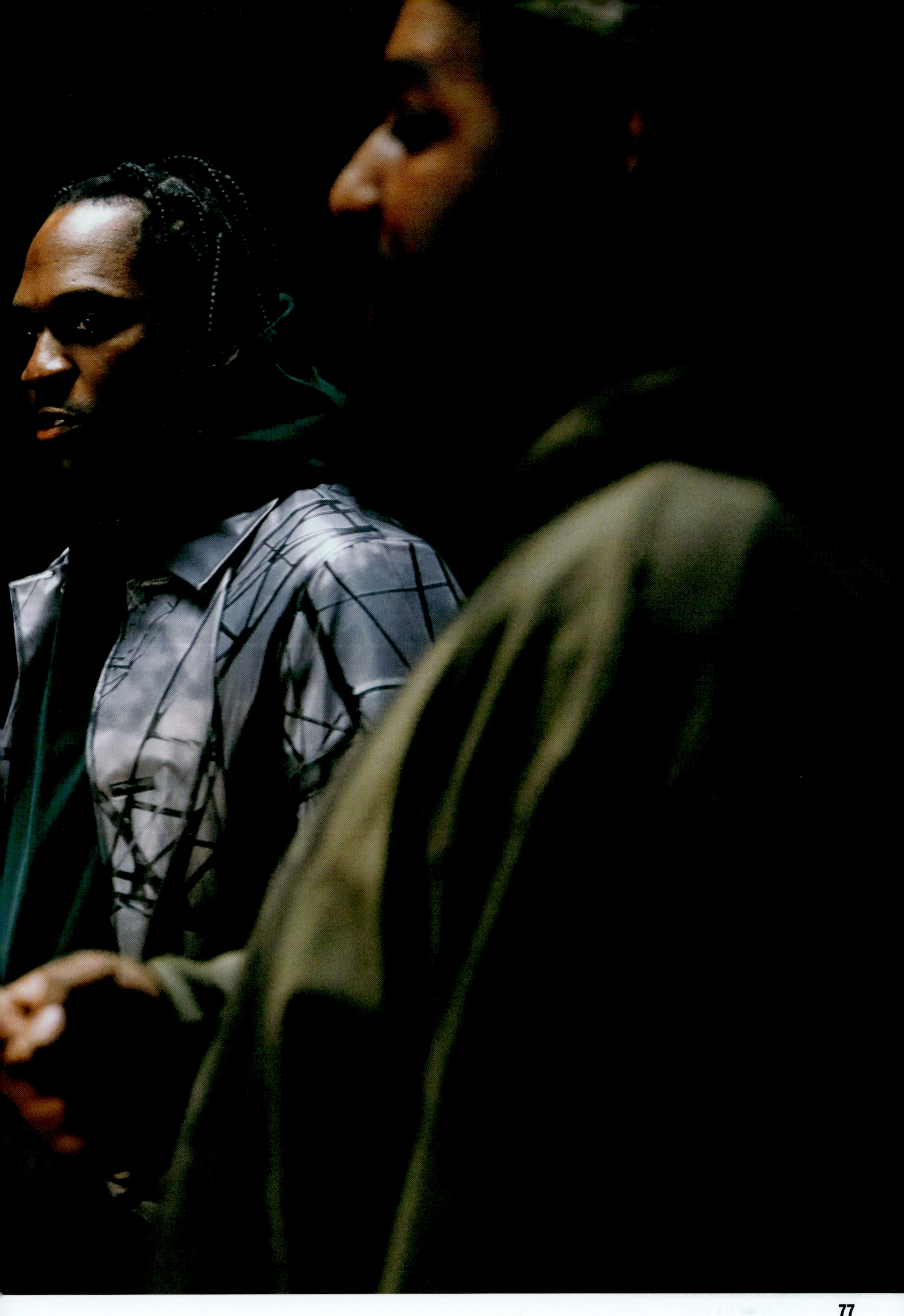

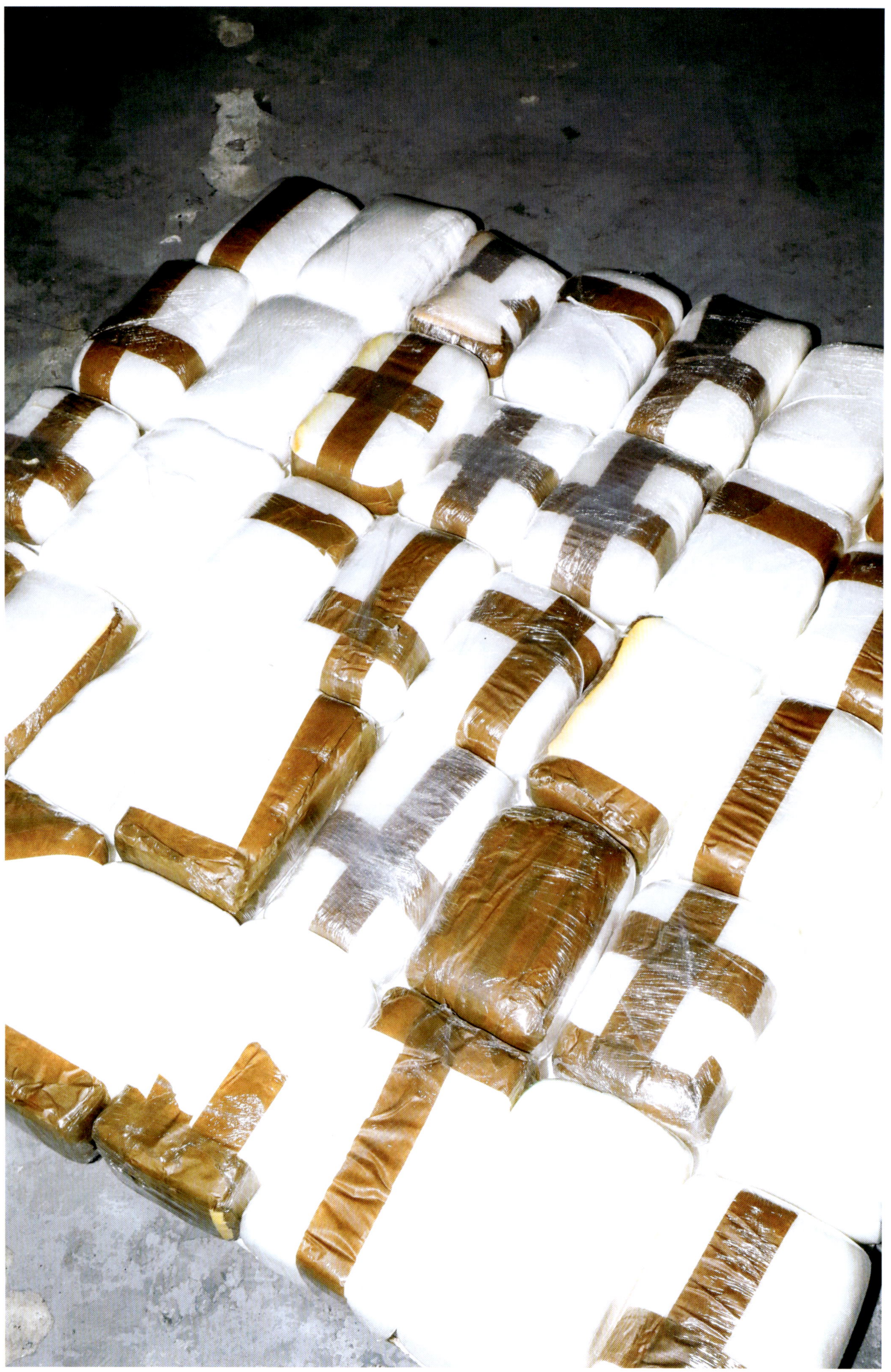

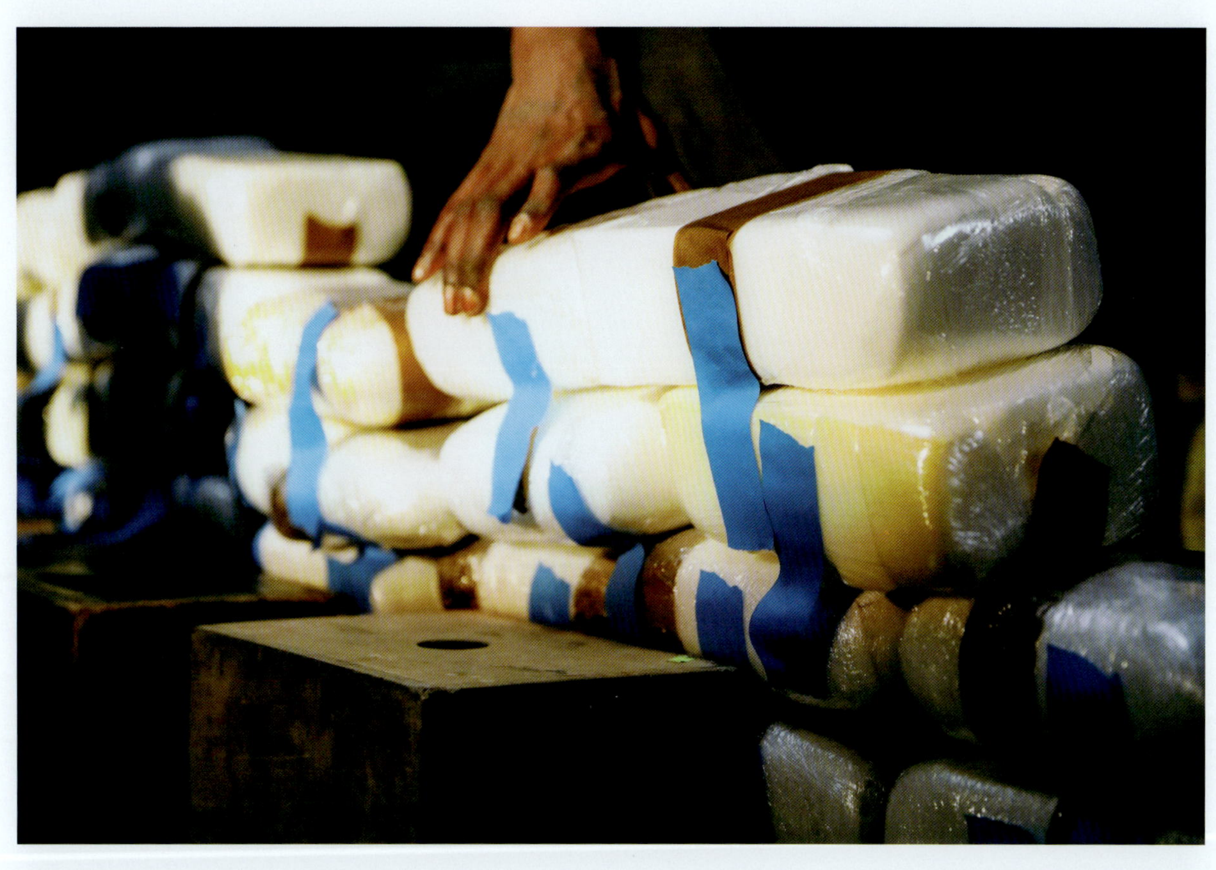

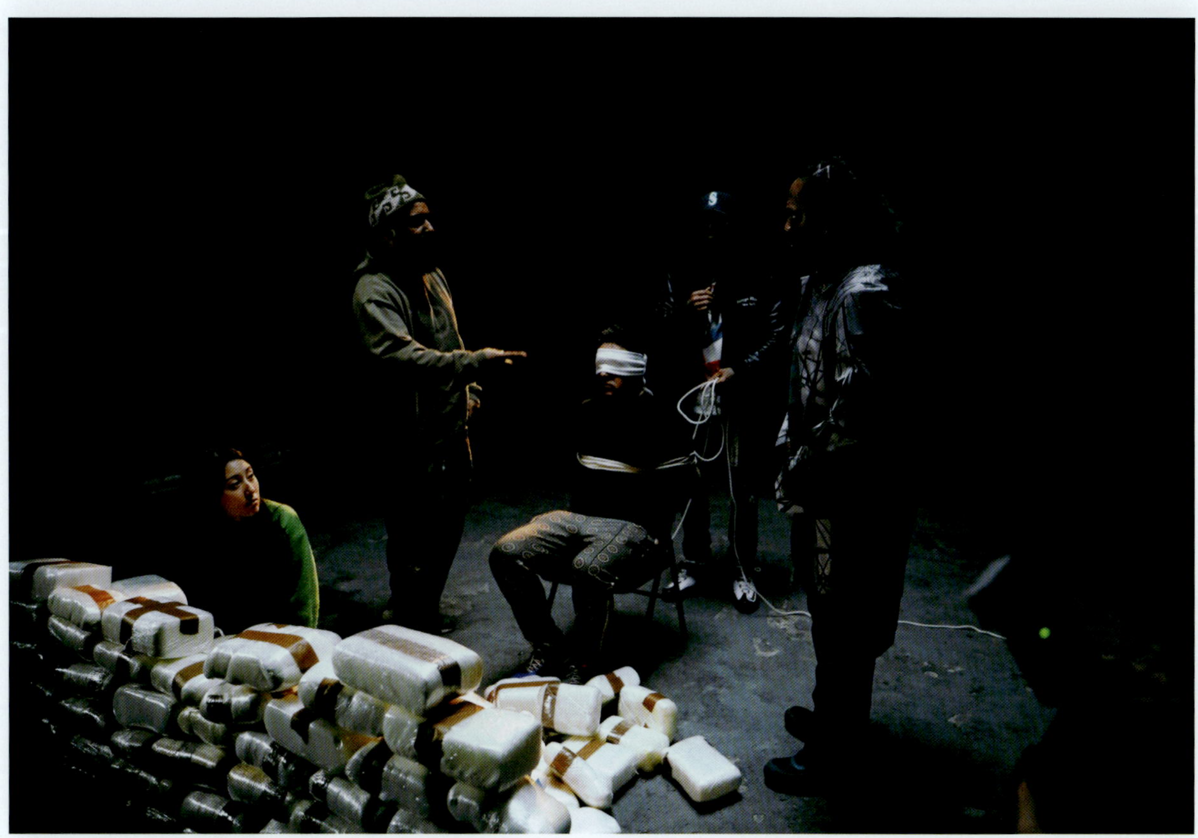

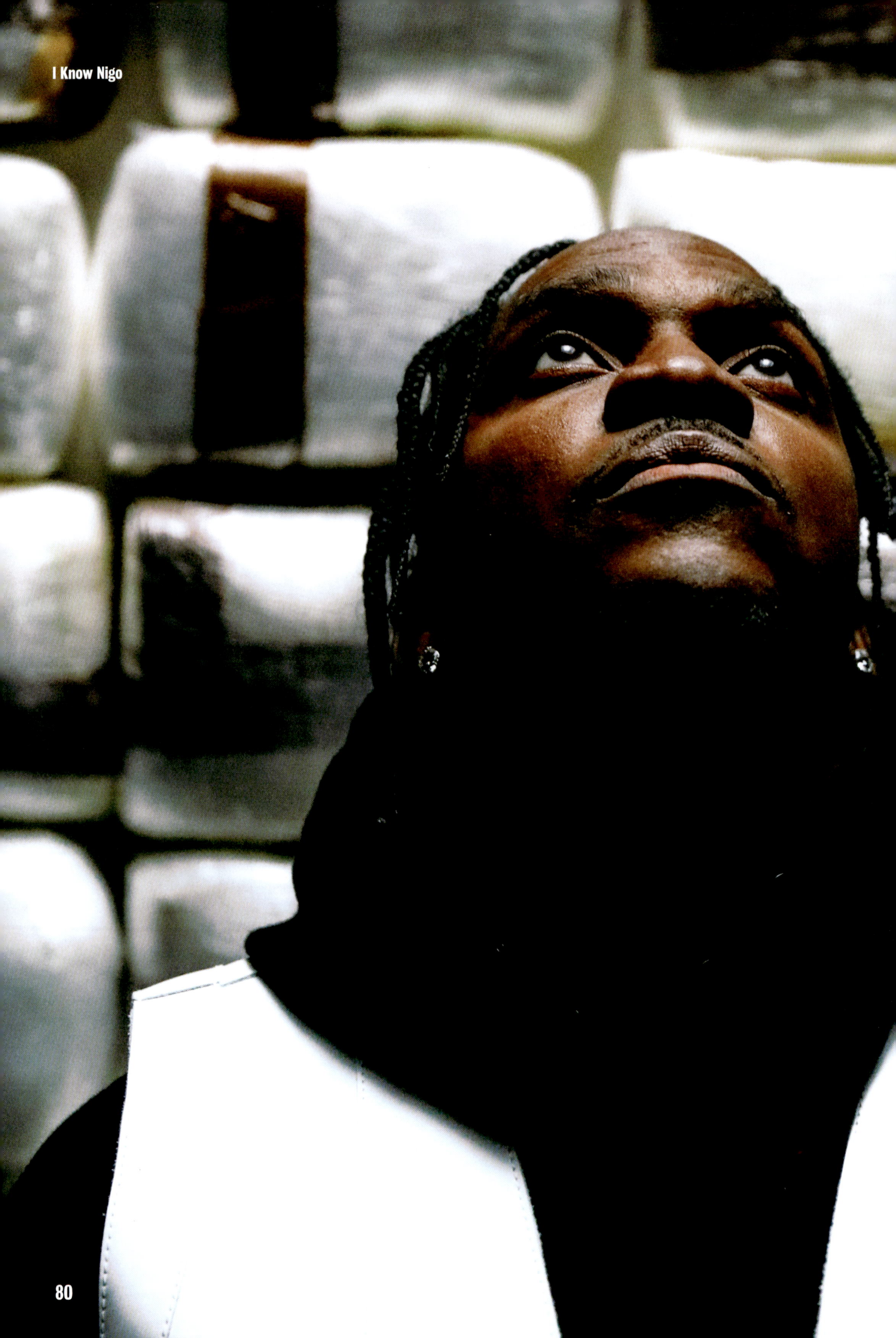

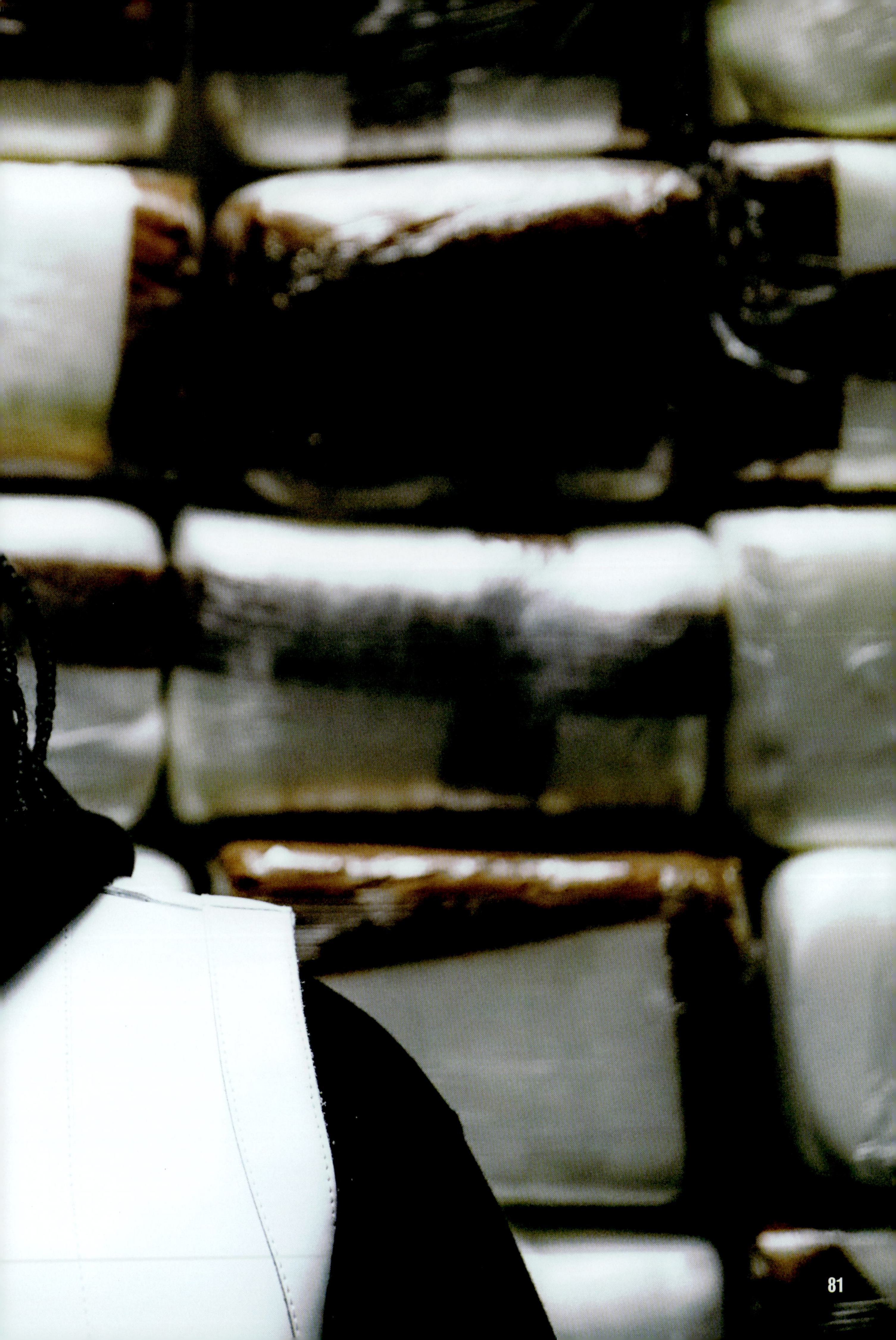

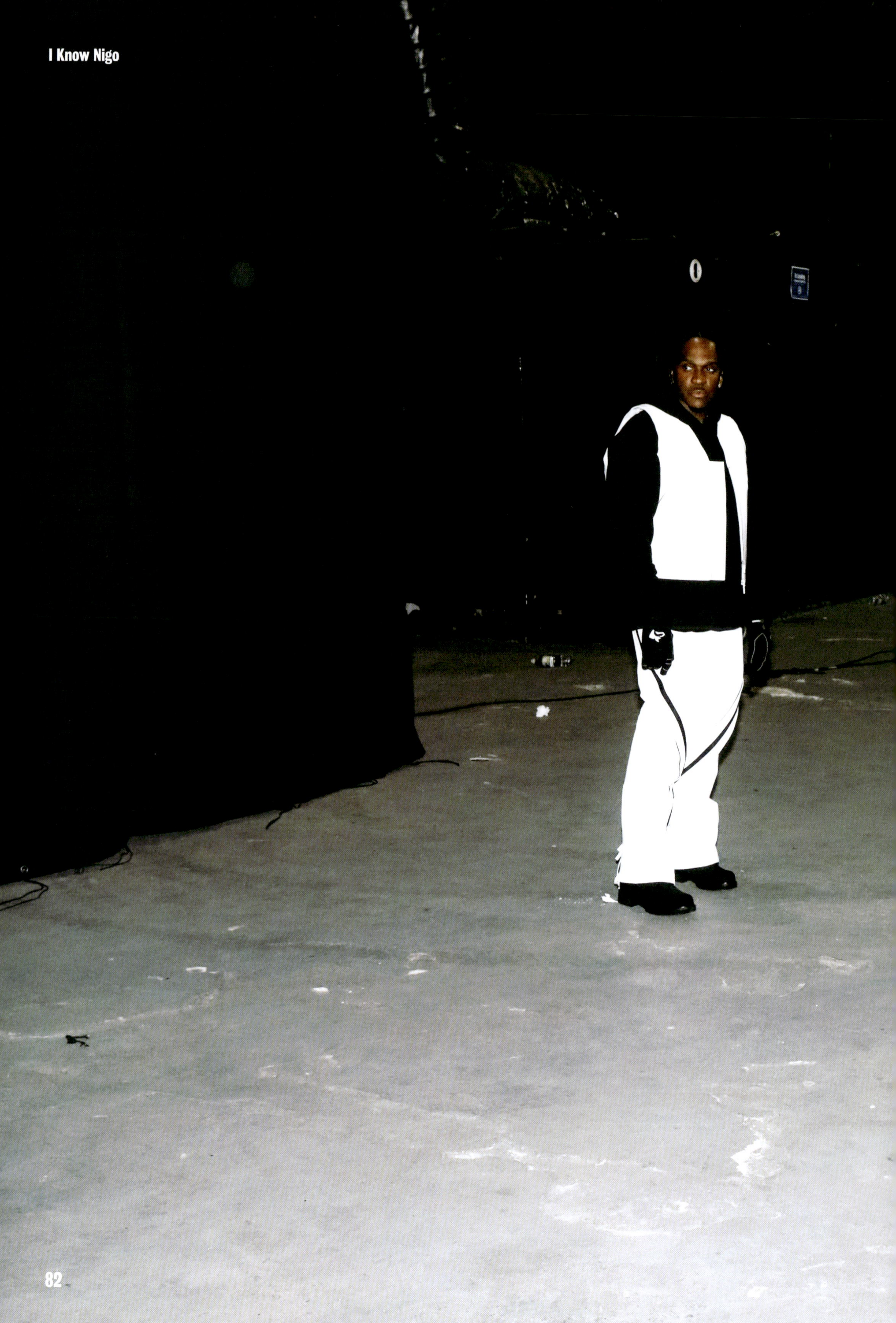

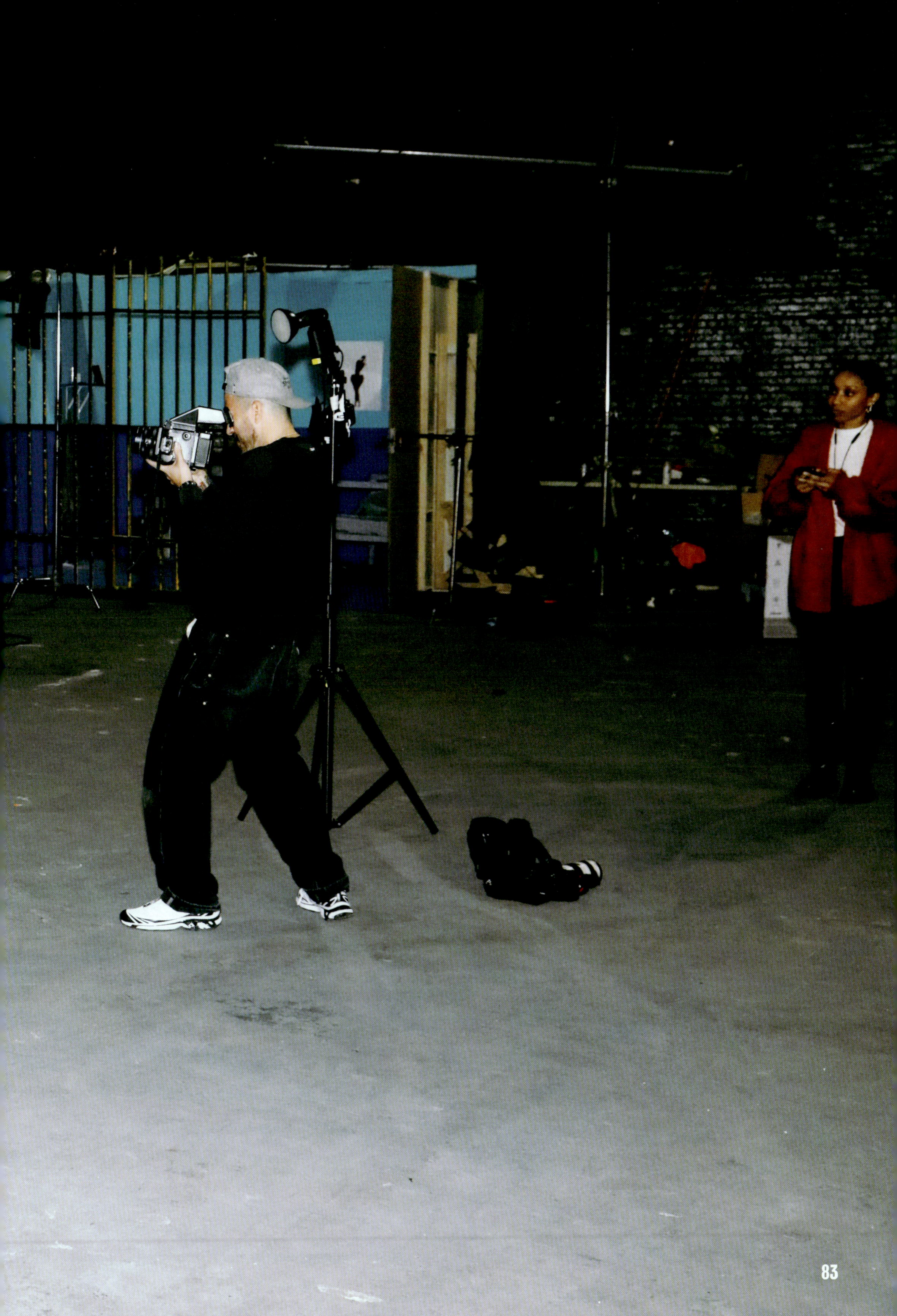

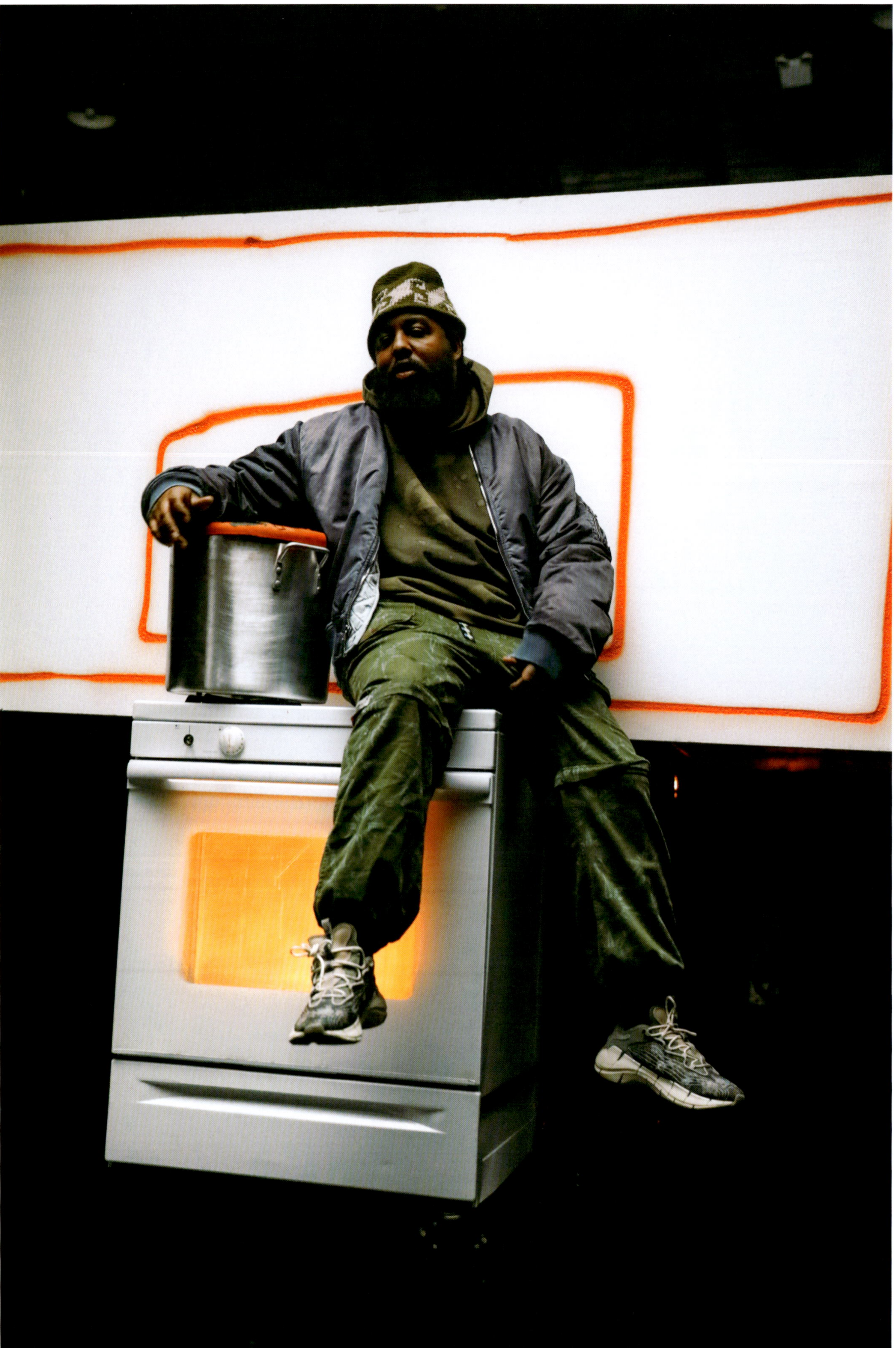

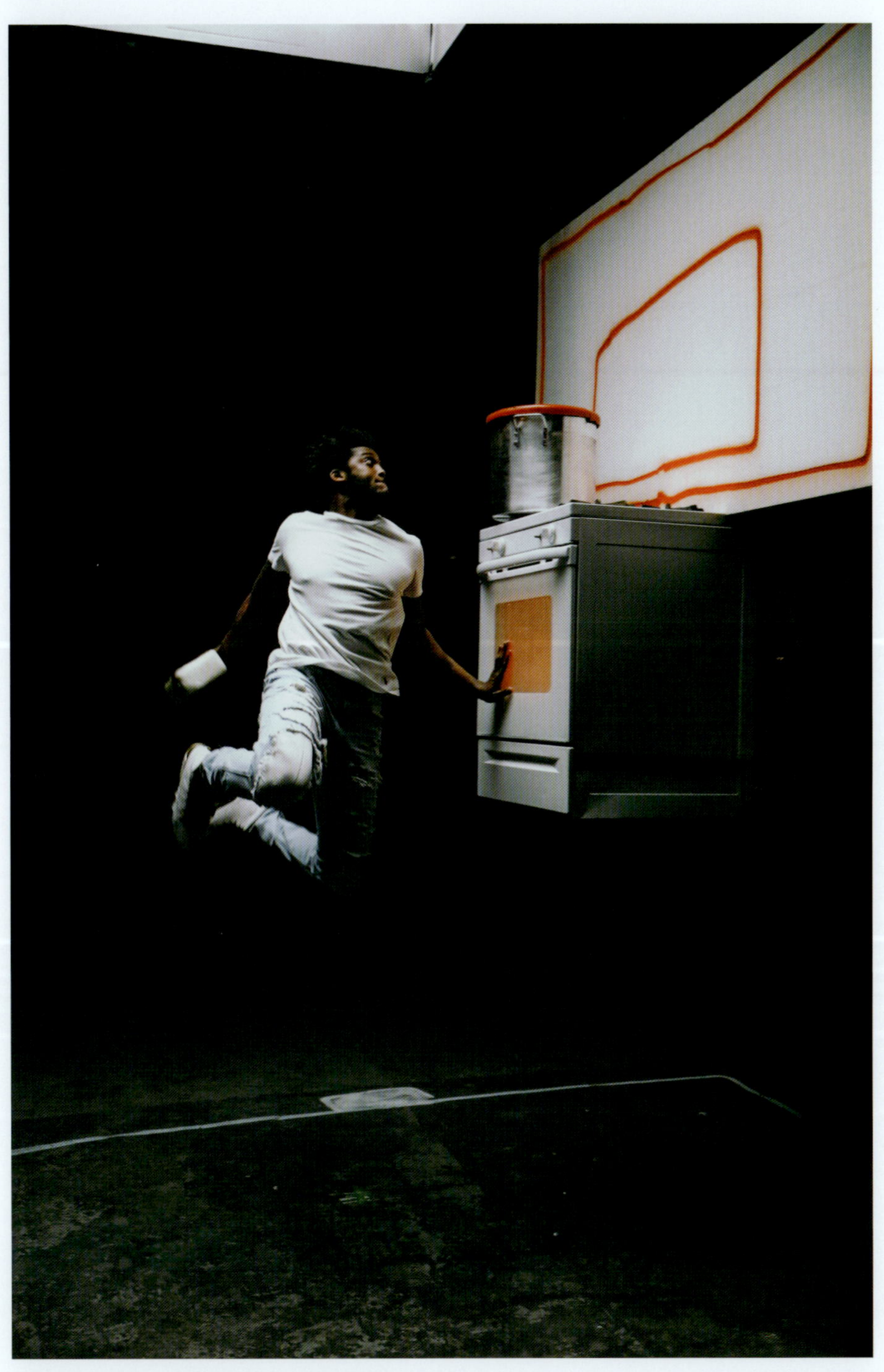

Camera tests featuring Hidji, director of the "HEAR ME CLEARLY" music video

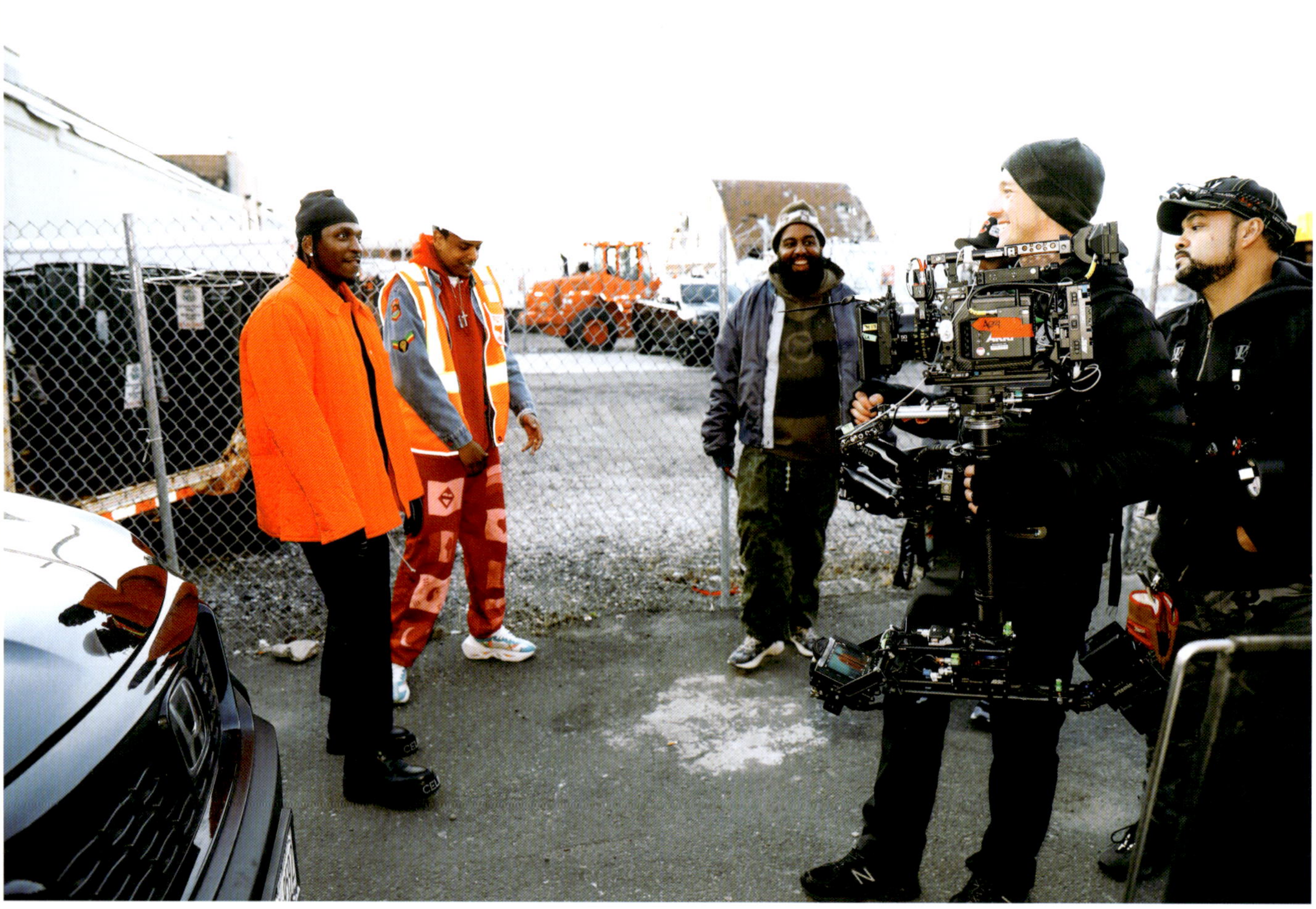

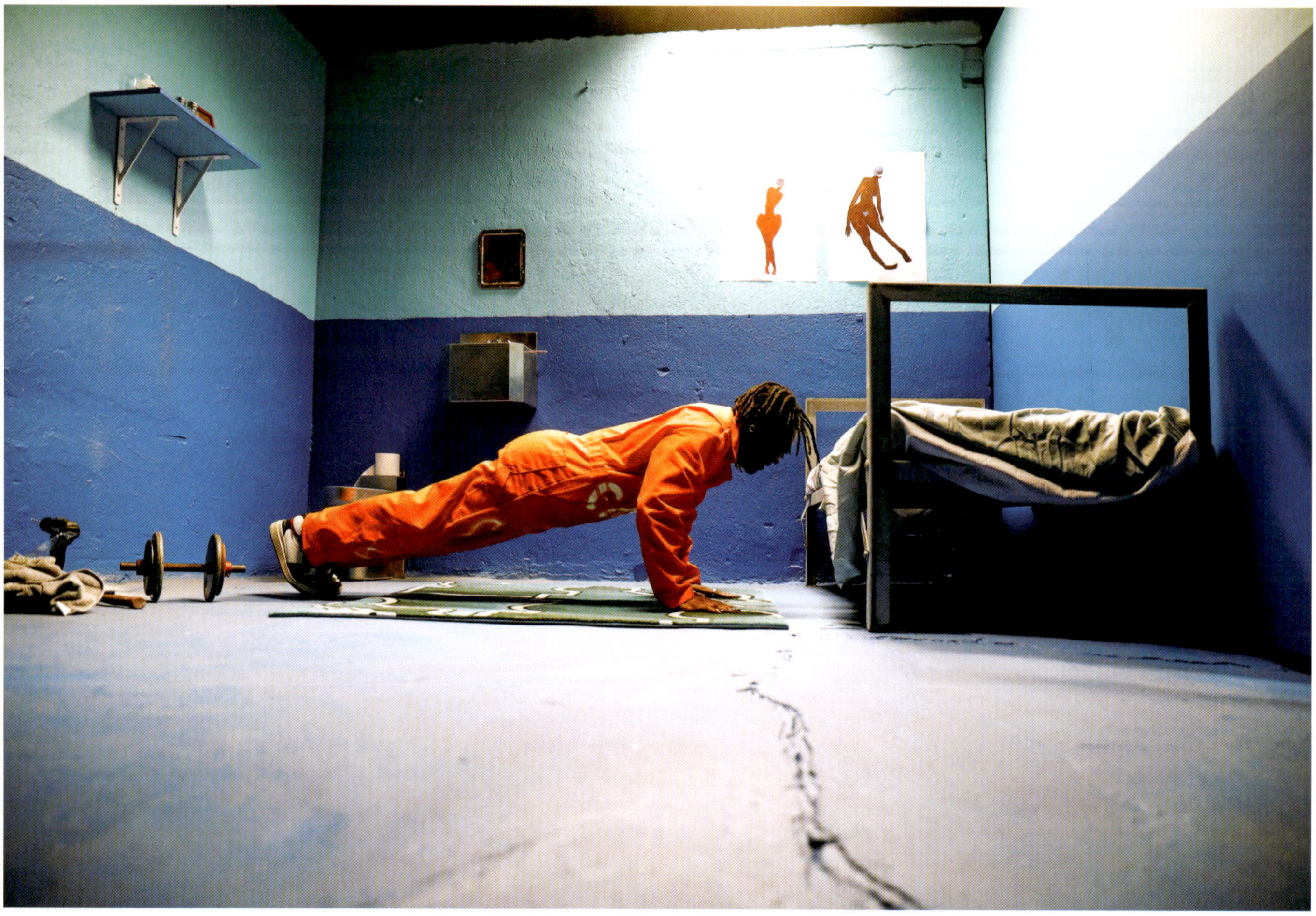

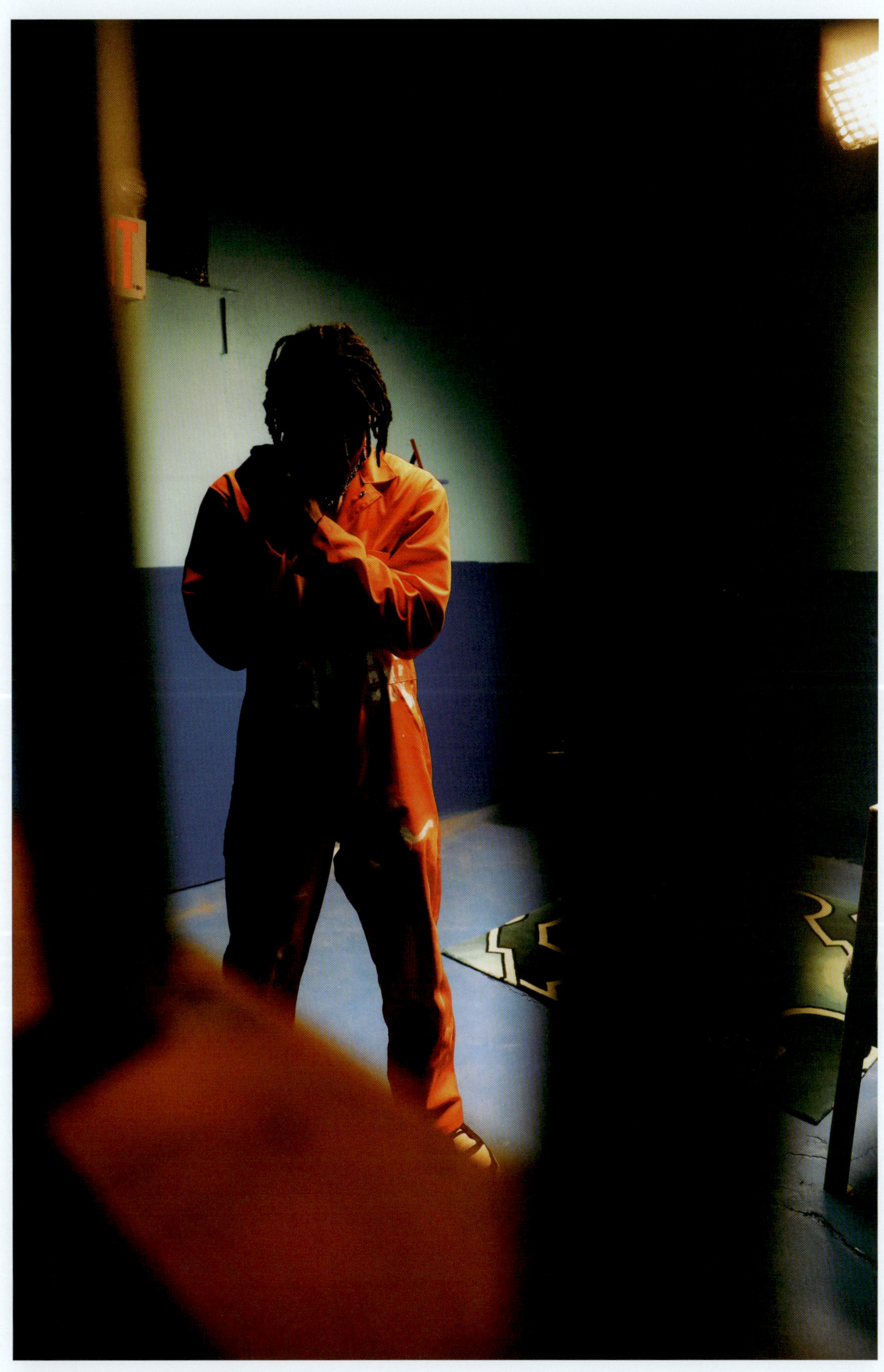

Behind-the-scenes at the "HEAR ME CLEARLY" video shoot, March 2022, New York City

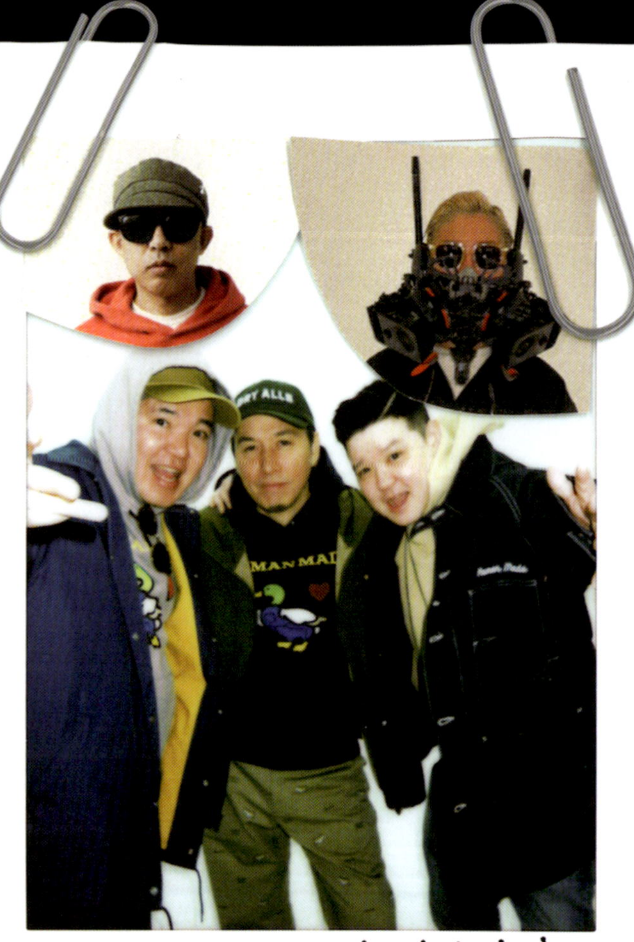

TERIYAKI BOYZ®, "MORË TONIGHT" single, released March 14, 2022, Tokyo

An Appreciation: by VERBAL

I met NIGO® for the first time in a recording studio in 2002. We had just freshly named the group TERIYAKI BOYZ®, after doing our verses for a track on NIGO®'s music project, which later went on to become "KAMIKAZE 108."

In the early 2000s when the Japanese music industry's focus was 99% domestic, it was very difficult to make all the stars align to execute a successful international music collaboration, let alone a full album. But as with anything he did, NIGO®'s venture into music was experimental and ambitious; pulling together A-list foreign producers with Japanese MC's, adding his magic to position the record as a covetable premium product.

Growing up in Tokyo listening to American hip-hop, I was always an advocate for cross-culture/genre/platform collaboration, so I was thrilled to participate in the rule-bending enterprise. TERIYAKI BOYZ® went on to release *Beef or Chicken* in 2005 and *Serious Japanese* in 2009, during which time I got to witness NIGO®'s unique curatorial executions firsthand.

During this period, YOON and I launched the brand AMBUSH® in 2008. Much of the fashion industry was still very traditional, and there was a lack of understanding for the synergy between luxury and streetwear. But NIGO® understood our ethos and we immediately clicked, leading to multiple series of jewelry, apparel, and sneaker collaborations.

It's safe to say, that ever since his days with the genesis of NOWHERE, NIGO®'s influence on culture and inspiration to the youth is an essential part of the Japanese fashion history, inventing a new playbook for the up-and-coming creatives.

— Tokyo, October 2023

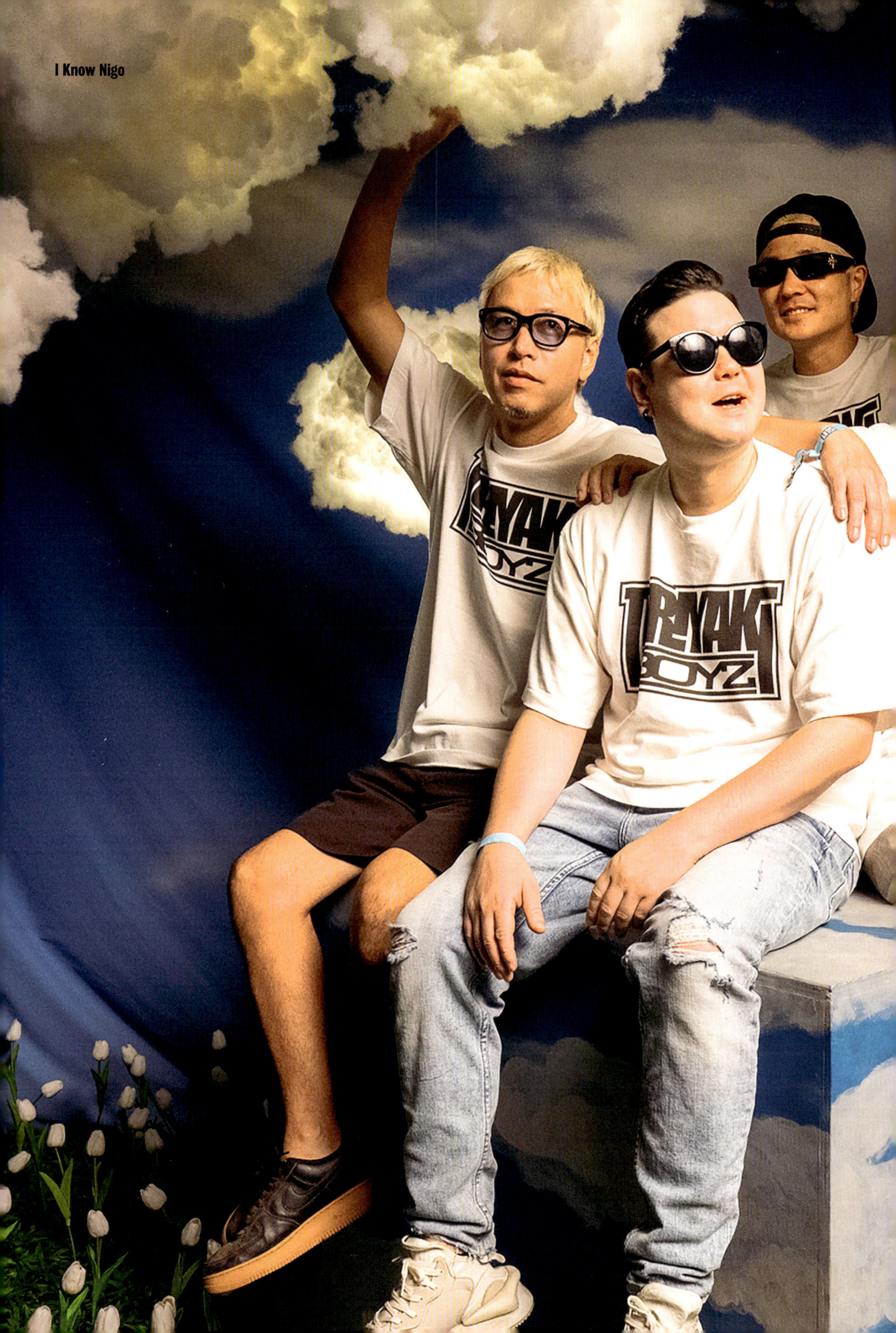
BOYZ

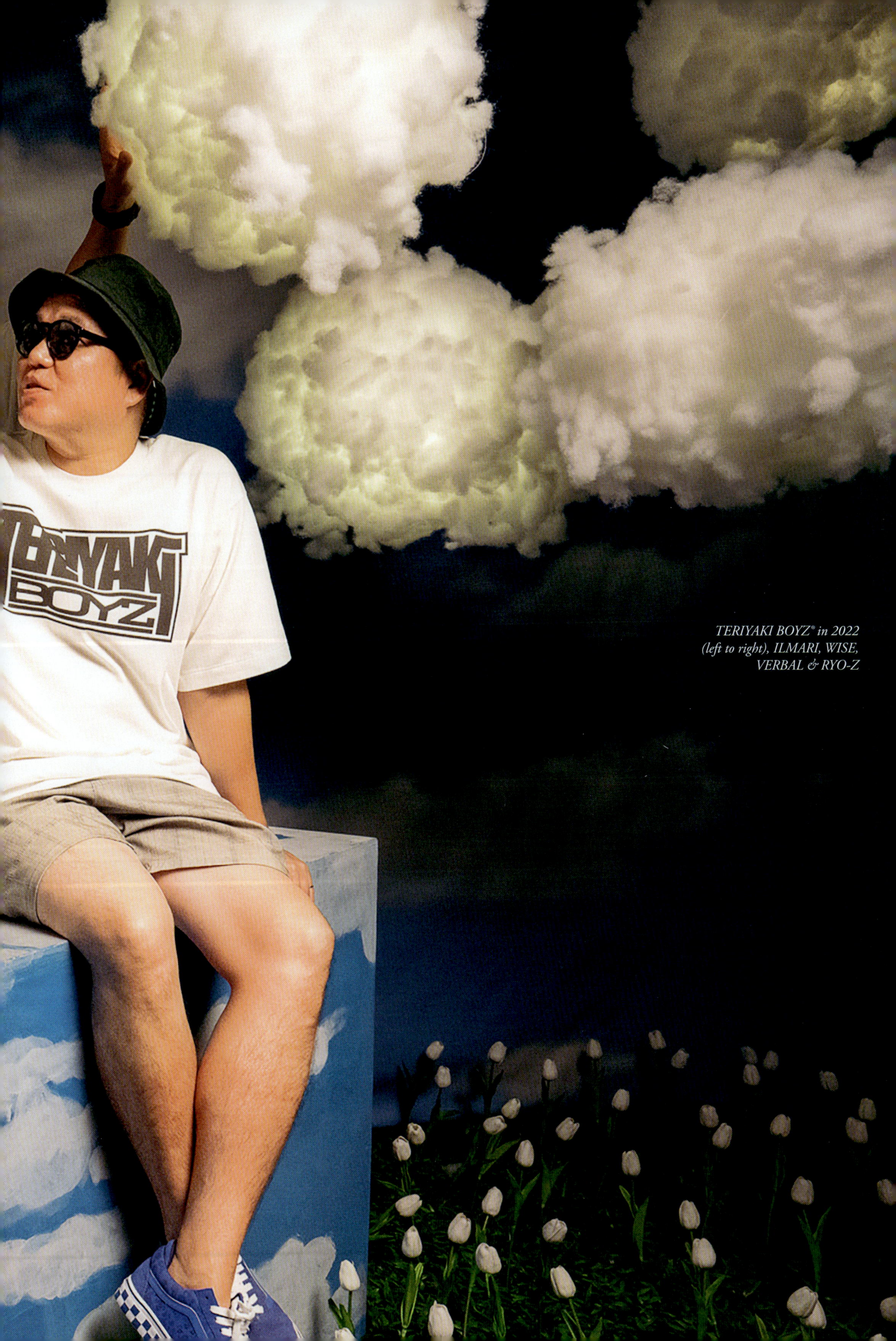

TERIYAKI BOYZ® in 2022 (left to right), ILMARI, WISE, VERBAL & RYO-Z

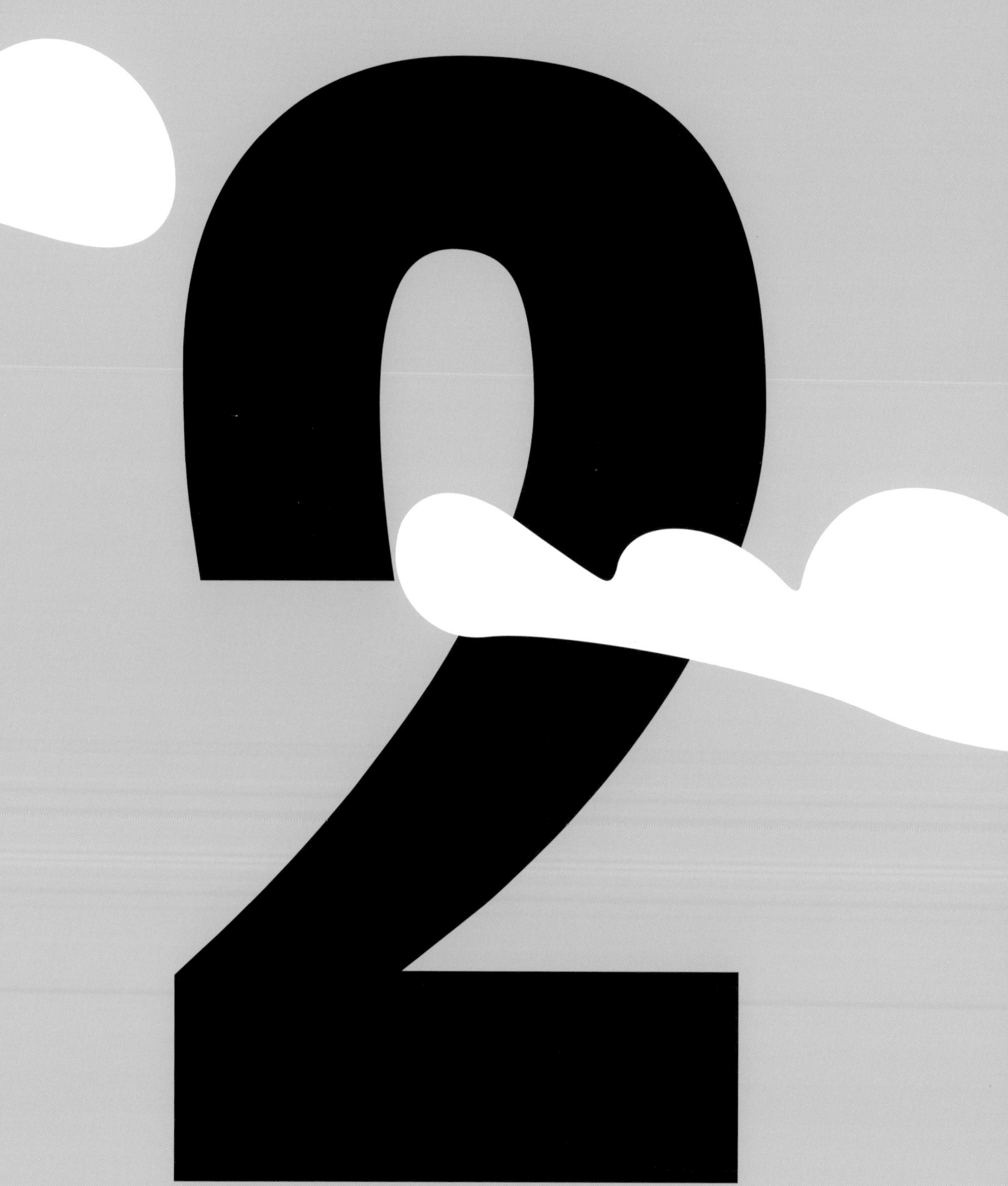

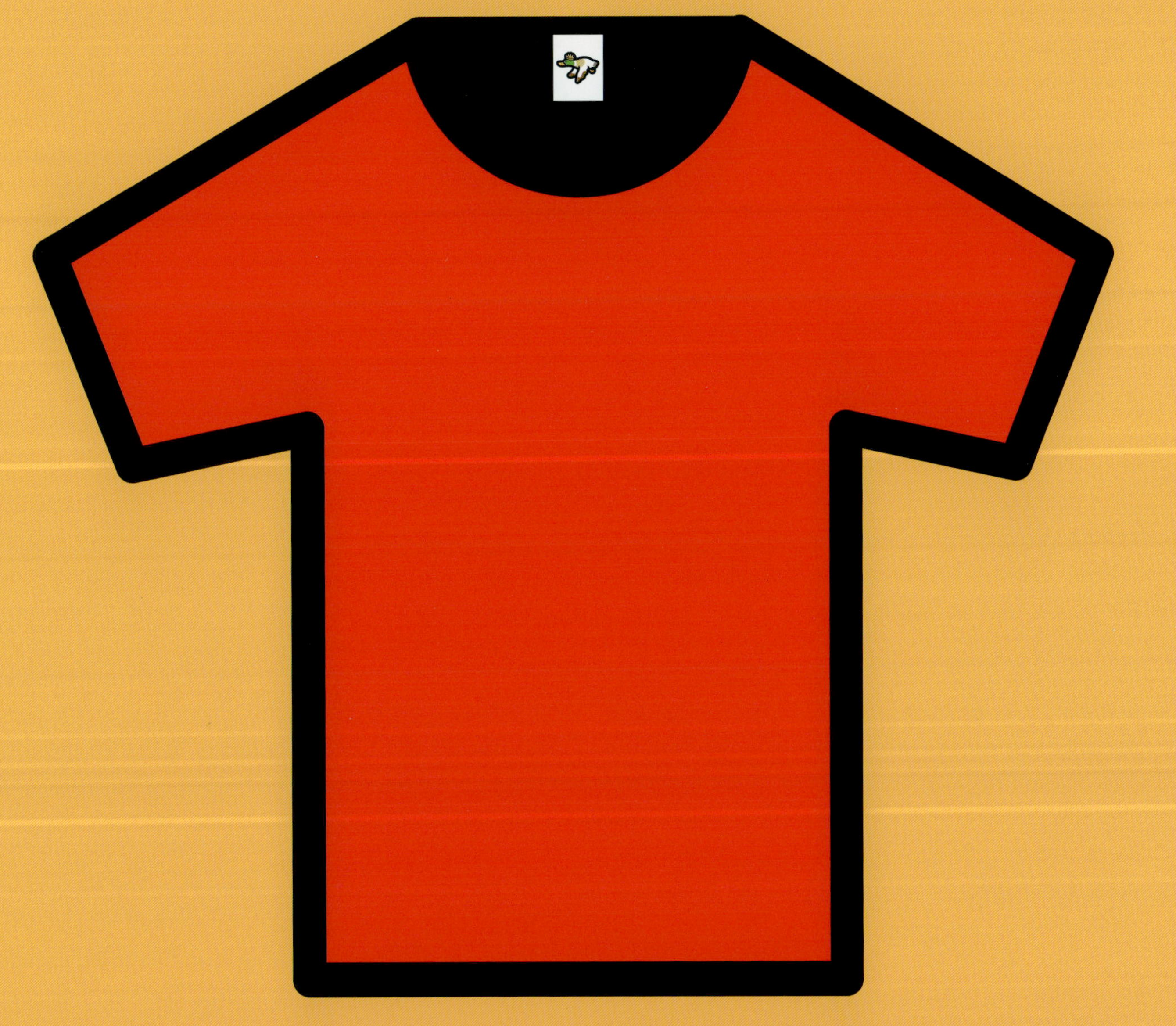

An Appreciation: by KAWS

As an artist and designer, I have had the privilege of meeting and collaborating with many talented individuals throughout my career. Few have had as significant an impact on my life and work as NIGO®.

I was first made aware of NIGO®'s work through two artist friends back in New York, Stash and Futura. It wasn't until I made a trip to Tokyo in the late 1990s that I had the opportunity to meet him. A friend of mine, Yoshifumi Egawa, took me to visit NIGO®'s office and shop in Shibuya. NIGO® was already a well-established figure in the Japanese streetwear culture, having founded BAPE in 1993.

Our friendship was initially based on an appreciation of design and pop culture. It was fascinating visiting his home and viewing his collection. In NIGO®, I found a kindred spirit who didn't subscribe to the typical hierarchies like "high" versus "low." He collects across genres and follows his intuition by going after things that spark his interest. How he would arrange his spaces elevated everything in the room. NIGO® applies this thoughtful curation and philosophy to everything he does.

I've always valued my early trips to Tokyo. NIGO® was a big part of what made those trips influential. What he was doing with his company *A Bathing Ape® was unlike anything anyone else in the world was doing. It was so far ahead of its time in so many ways. The level of quality in his product and store design was miles beyond what you saw happening in "streetwear."

In 2000, I was working on an exhibition to be held at Parco Gallery in Tokyo that would open in early 2001. One of the works I was interested in creating was a series of paintings titled *The Kimpsons* that I envisioned being displayed in toy packaging, known as blister packs. I asked NIGO® for advice on how to get the packaging made, and not only did he give advice, but he actually went and produced the packaging for me. At that same time, we decided to make a cushion together to be sold at the exhibition. This first collaboration was the beginning of a long partnership between NIGO® and myself. Over the years, we've continued to work together on various projects across different disciplines.

More than just our professional achievements, our friendship has been a source of inspiration over the years. It's been encouraging to watch NIGO® grow and maneuver over the last twenty-plus years. I remember designing album art for CHERIE®, one of the artists on his music label Ape Sounds in 2002—fast forward to today and I designed a cover for his 2022 album release *I Know NIGO®* on the Victor Victor label. We've come full circle, and while a lot has changed, NIGO® has steadfastly remained the same.

His passion for authenticity and getting to the core of an object, understanding its history, and creating new ways to rework it through his lens has never wavered. His entrepreneurial spirit and his determined commitment to excellence have taught me valuable lessons and pushed me to be a better artist and designer. But it is his generosity that has made him such an important figure in my life.

Perhaps more than anything else, working together all these years has been a lesson in the importance of human connection. When you see a finished product on a shelf, it's easy to forget that there are real people behind it, giving their care and energy to get it there. In a world that often focuses on individual achievement and success, it is easy to overlook the importance of relationships and community that are always there behind the scenes. NIGO® has been supportive of my career on so many levels over the years, and I am always happy to work with him on his latest projects. What really stands out about NIGO® is the community he has built around him, and it has been a privilege to be a part of that community for a good part of my career.

— New York, October 2023

Exclusive limited-edition vinyl records: designed by KAWS & NIGO®

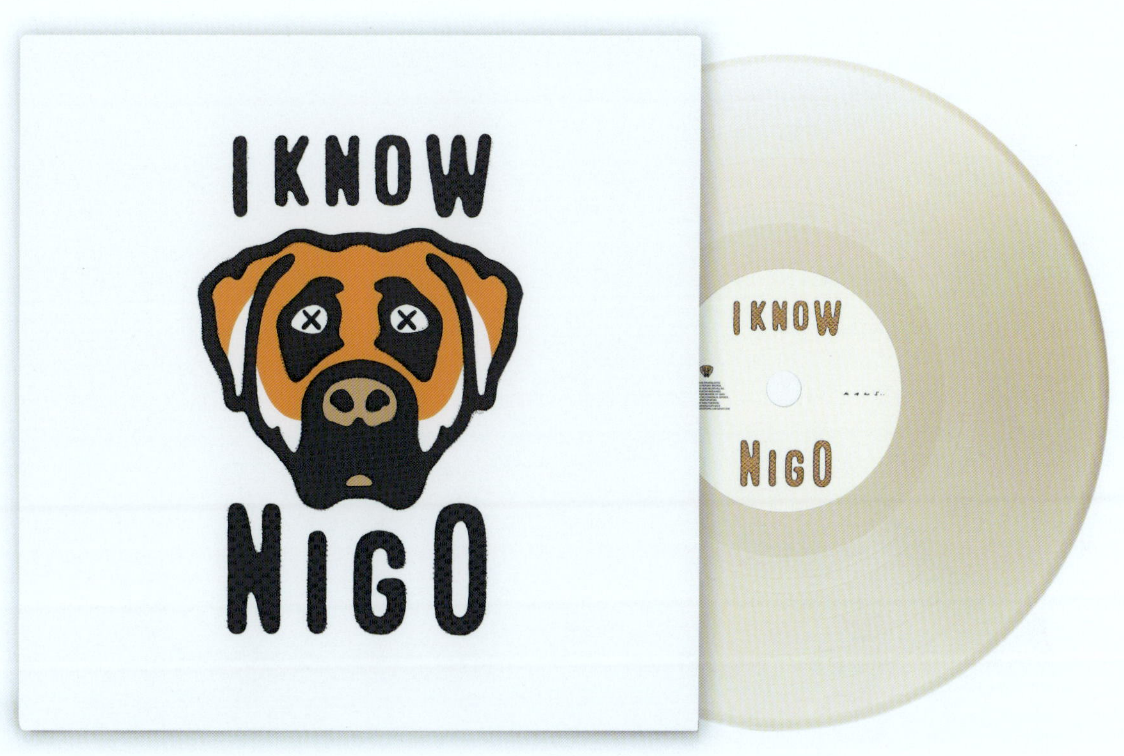
I KNOW
NIGO
I KNOW
NIGO

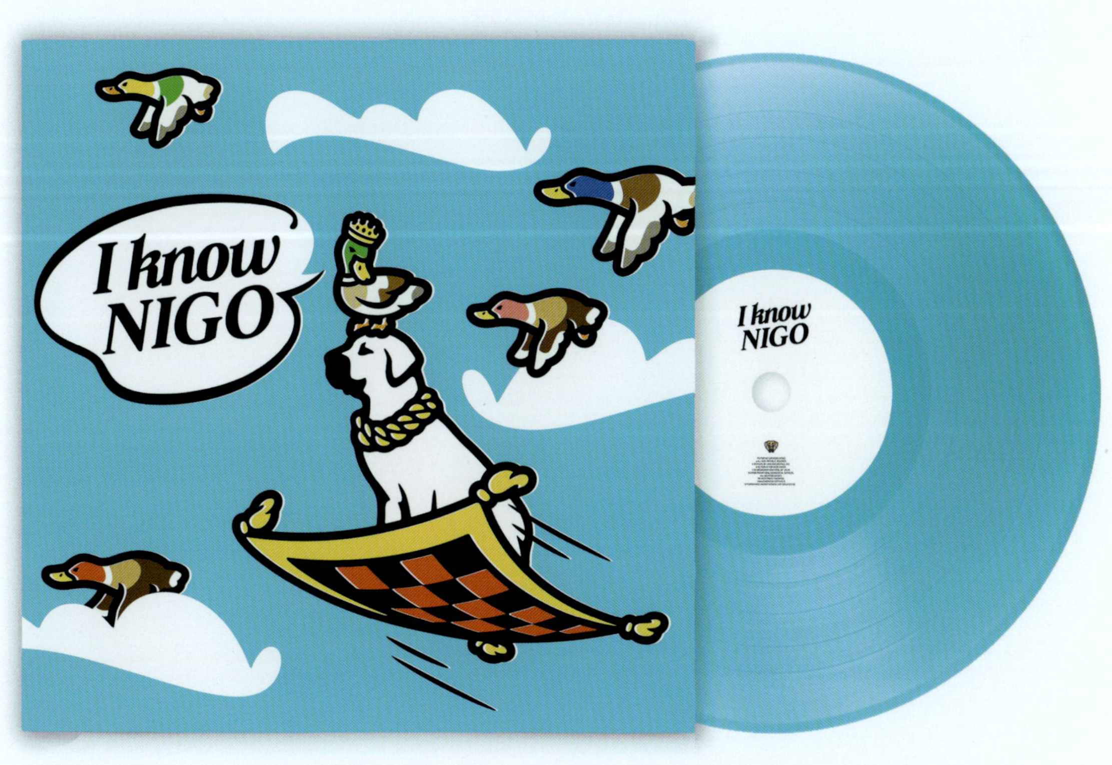
I know
NIGO
I know
NIGO

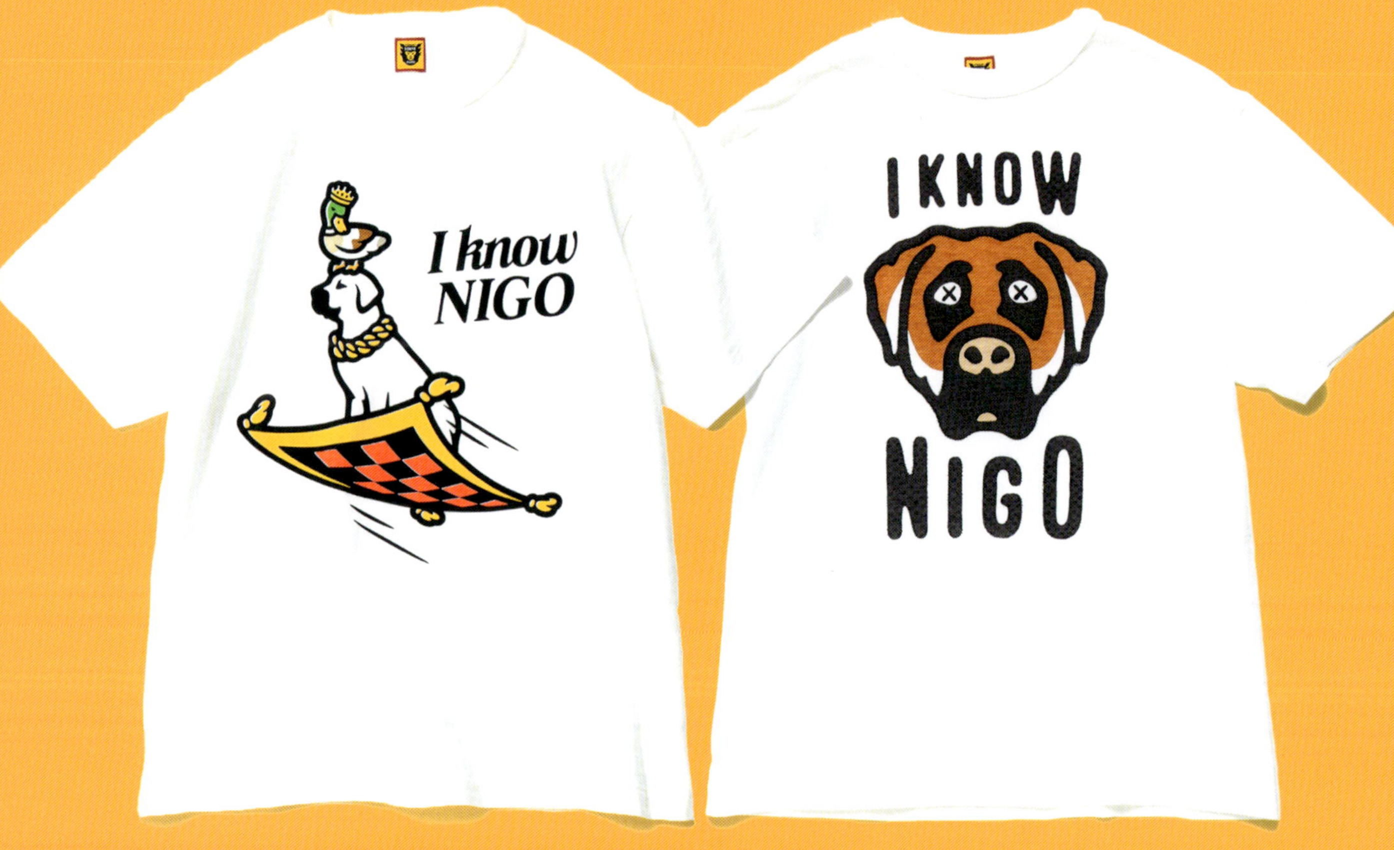

I Know NIGO® x Human Made (left), and I Know NIGO® x Human Made x KAWS (right), limited-edition t-shirts, only available online the week of the album release; Reverse

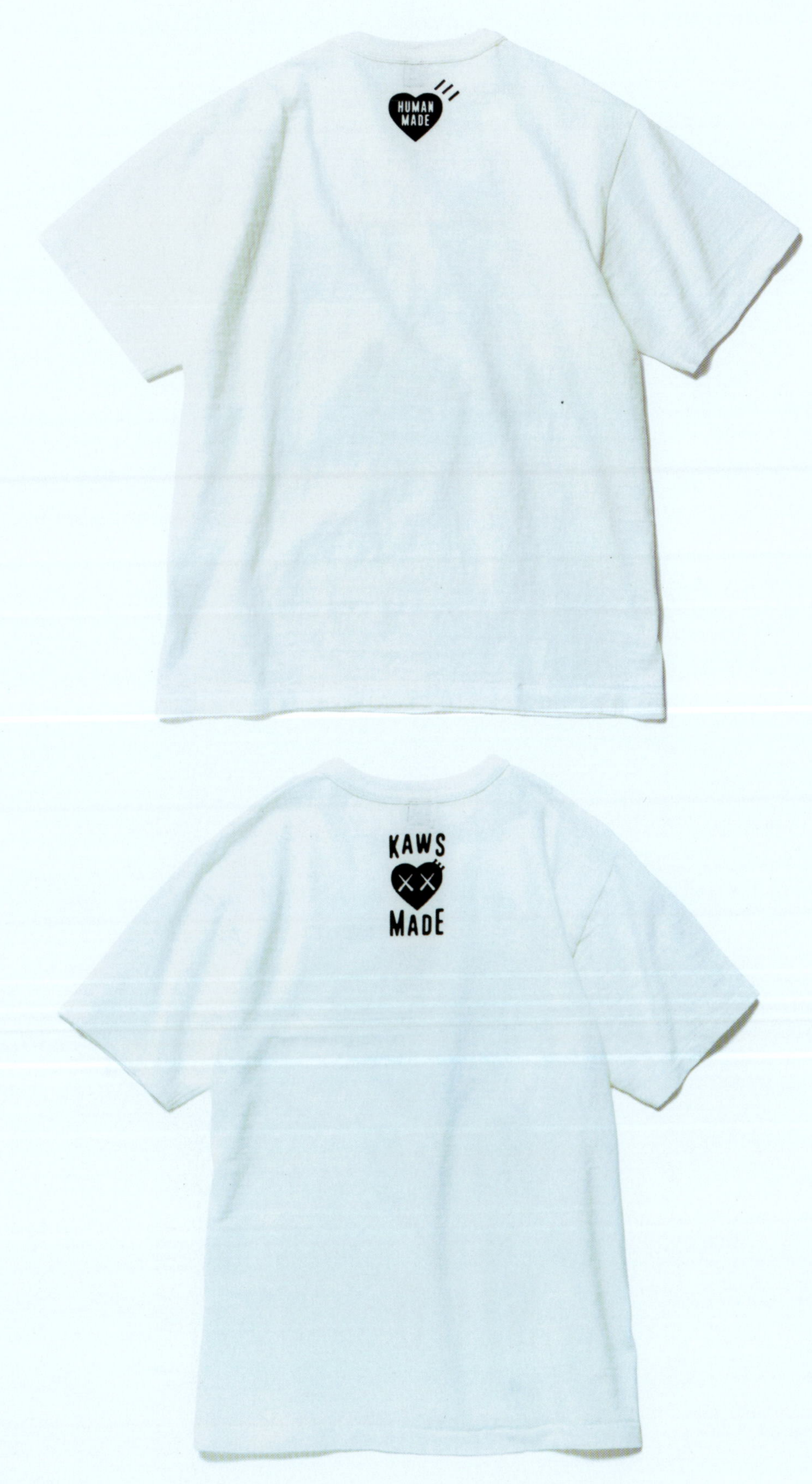
HUMAN
MADE
KAWS
MADE

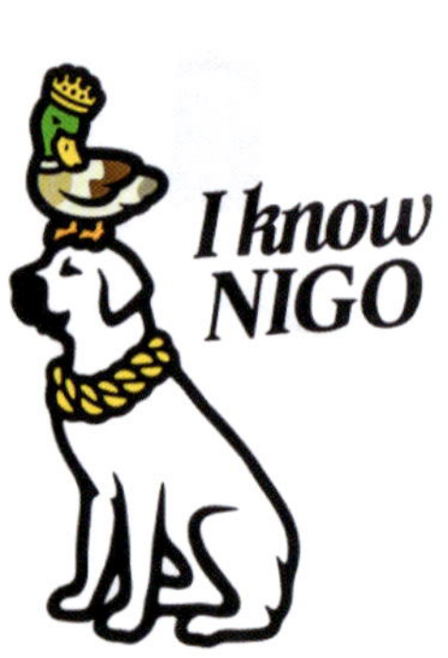

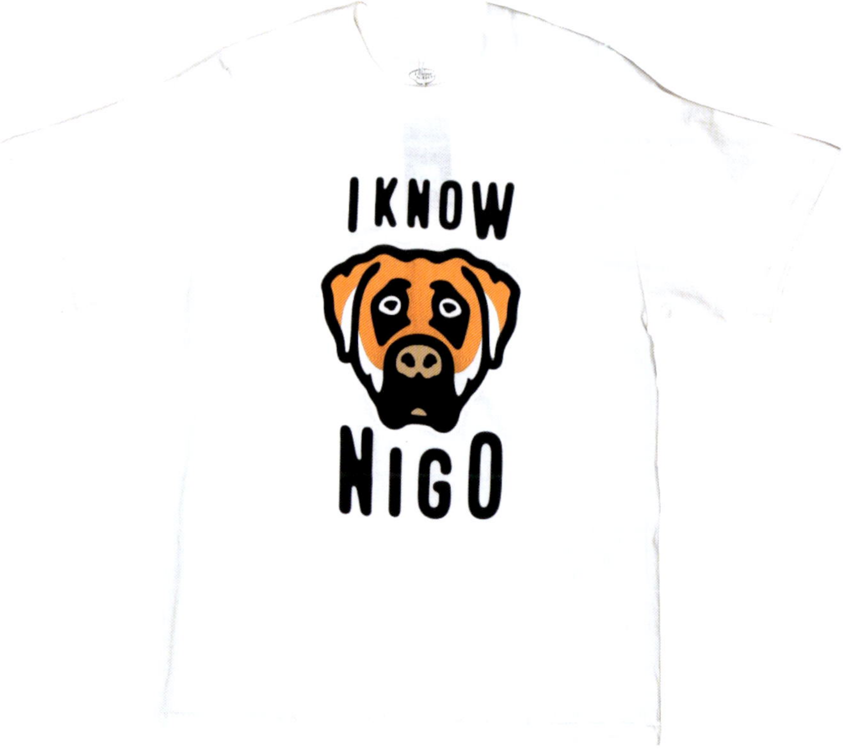

I KNOW

NIGO

I Know NIGO® x
VICTOR VICTOR
limited-edition
t-shirts.

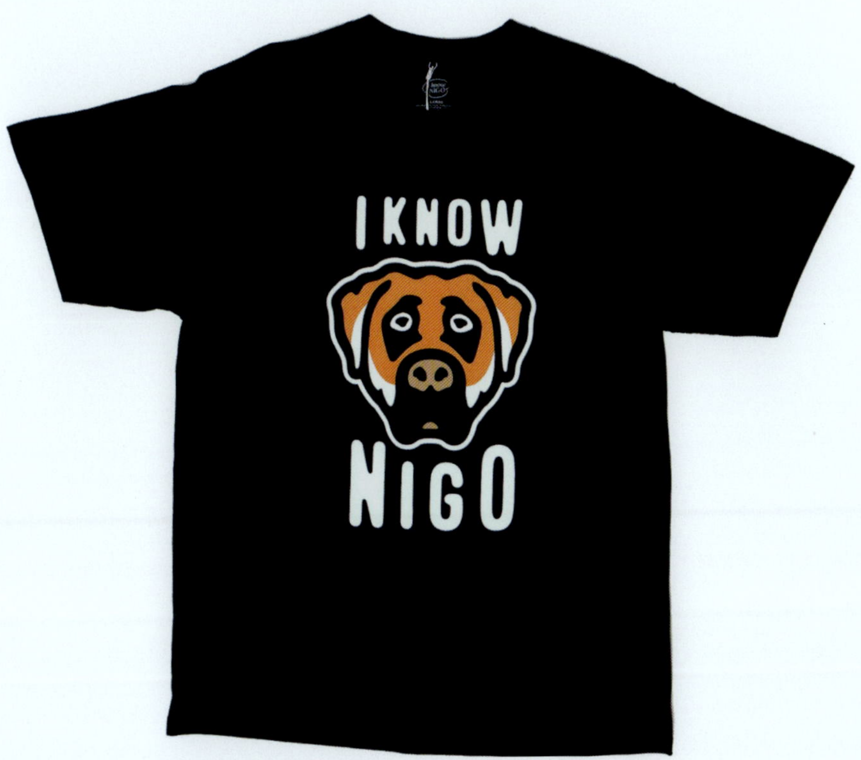

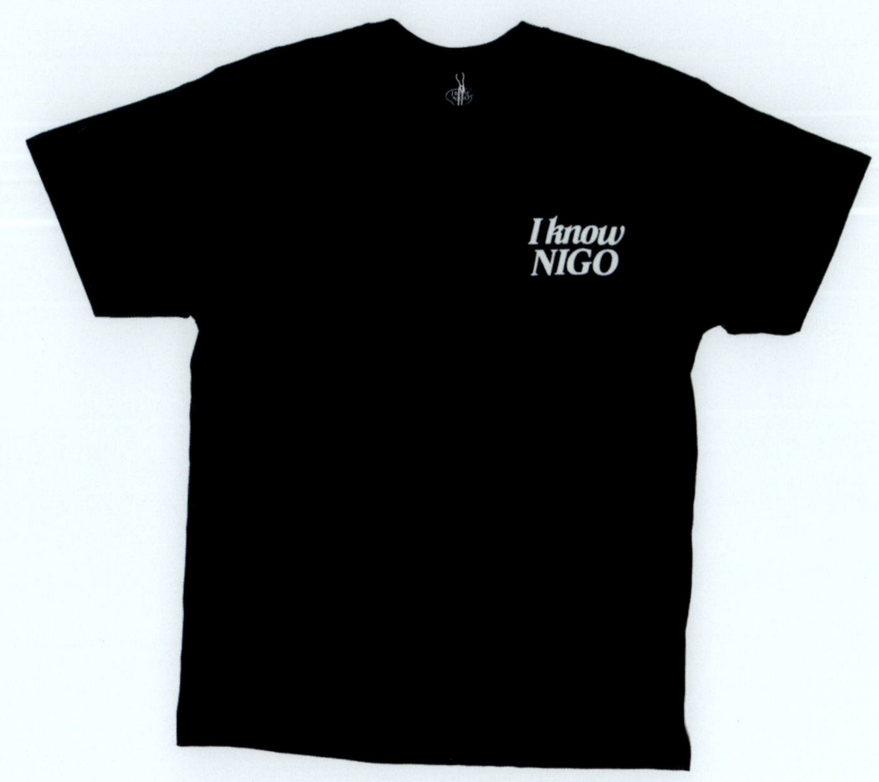

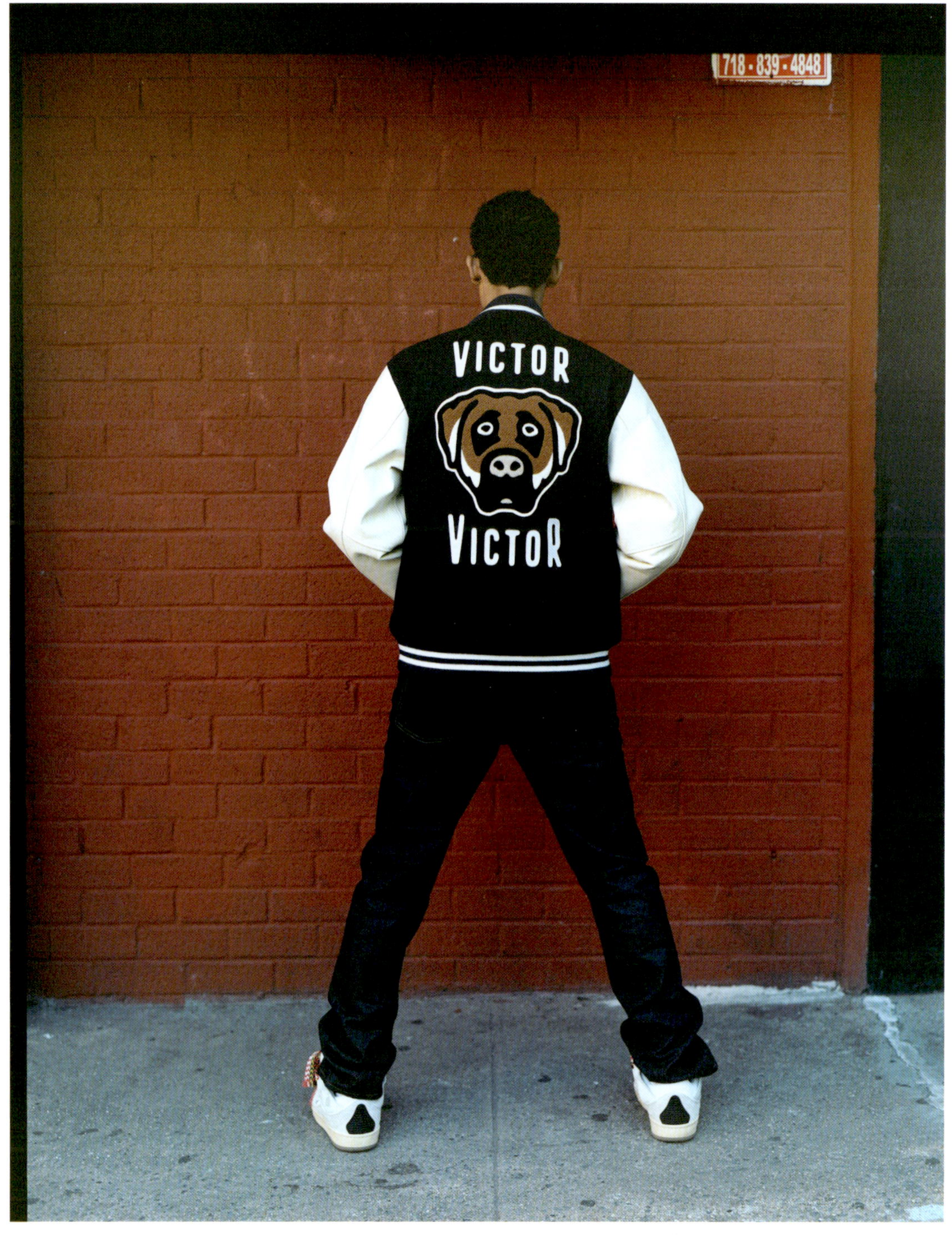
718-839-4848
VICTOR
VICTOR

Lil Jupiter in the VICTOR VICTOR varsity jacket produced by Human Made

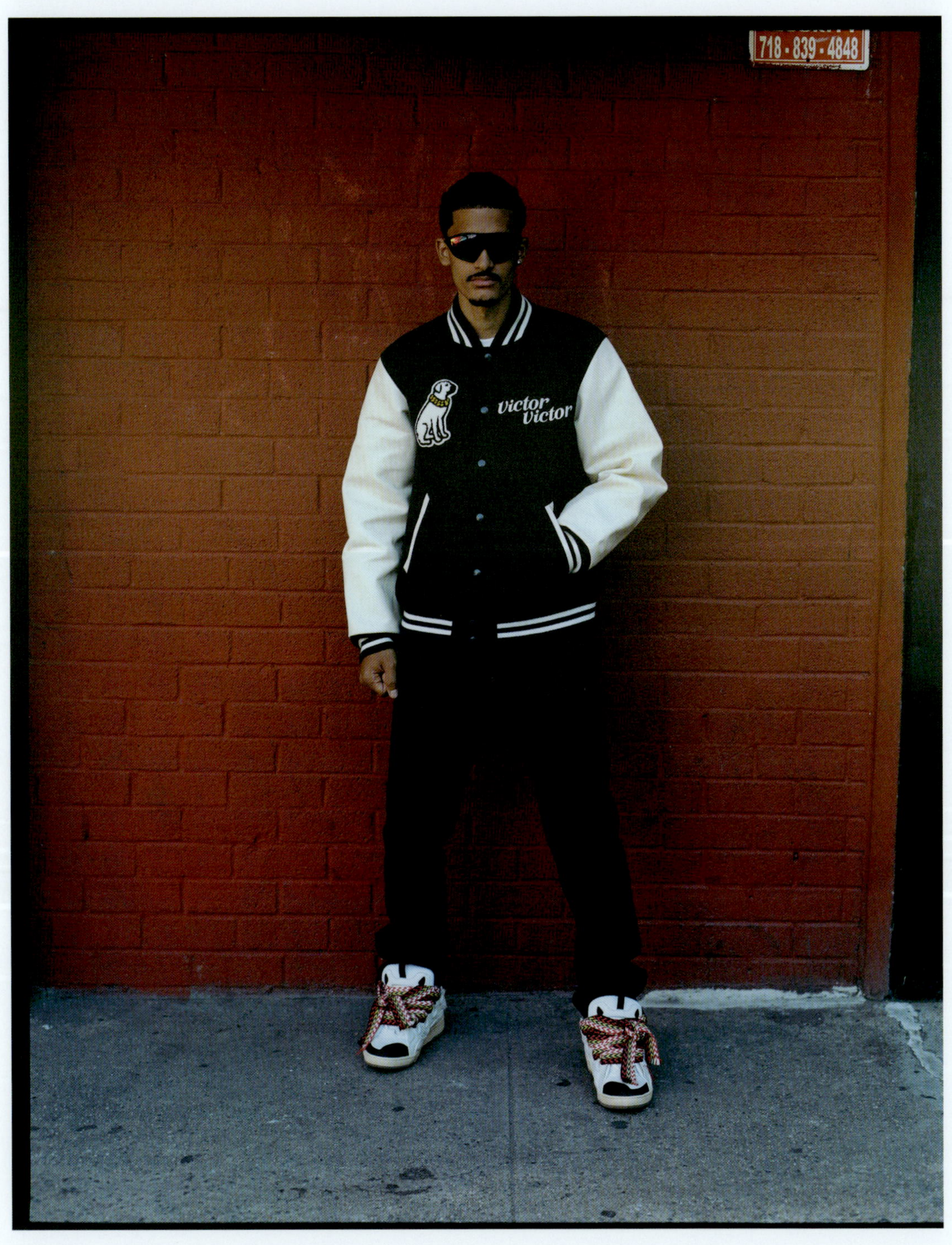

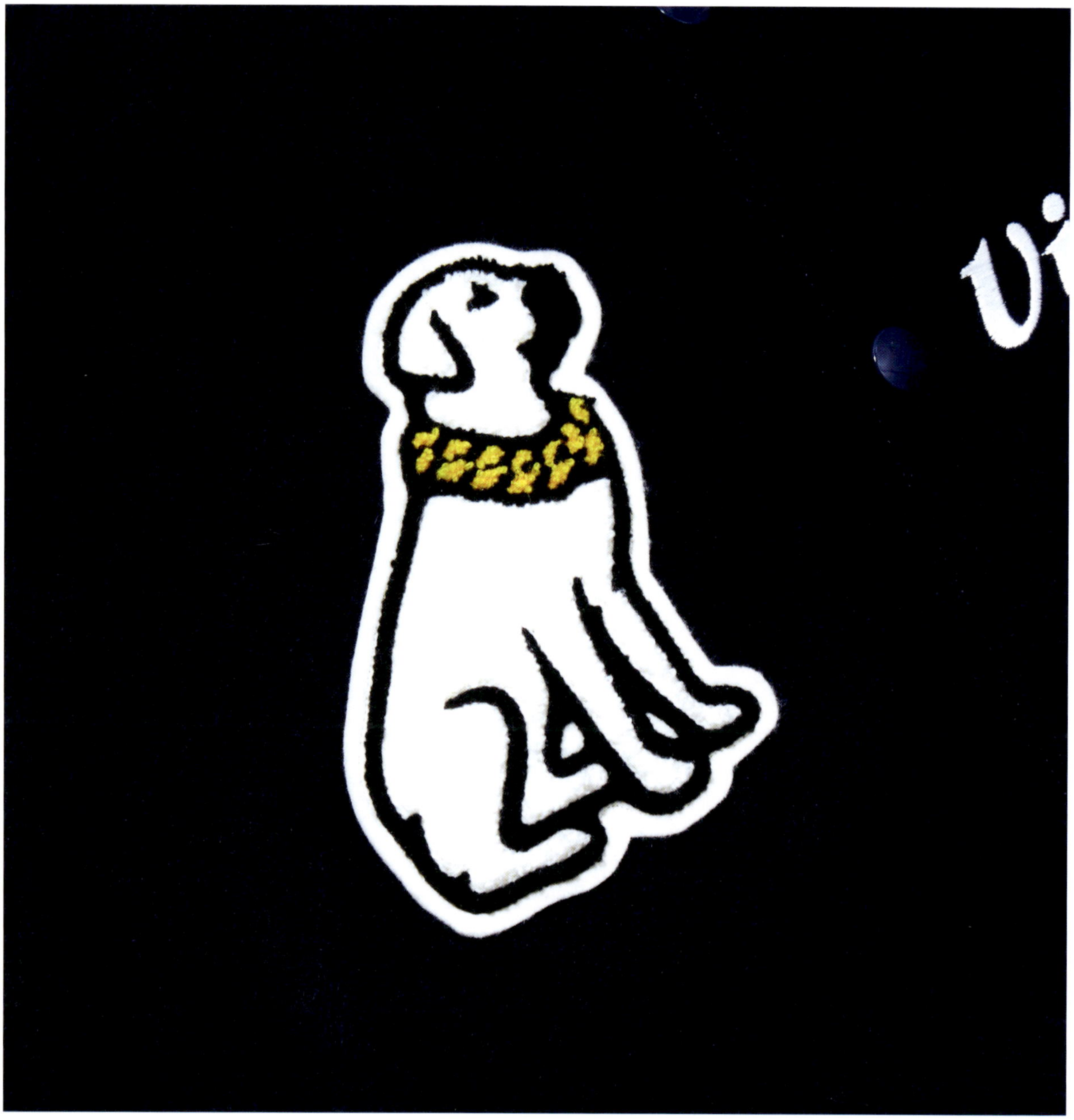

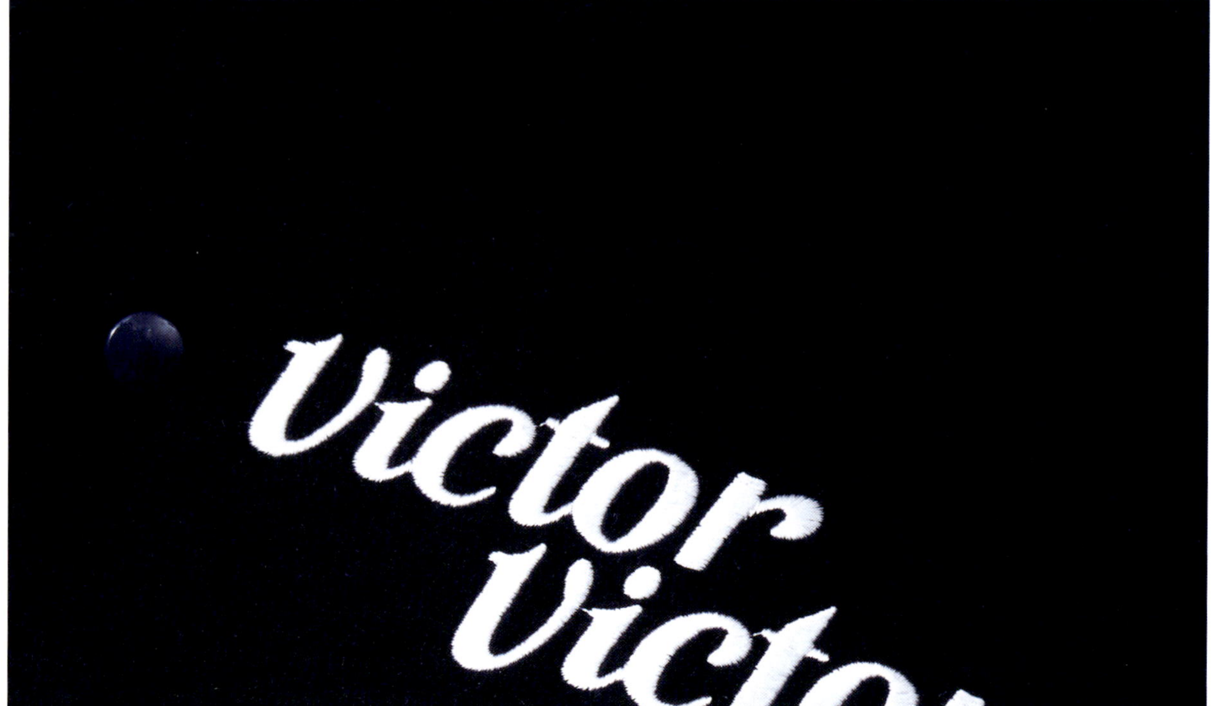
Victor

VICTOR VICTOR varsity jacket details produced by Human Made, designed by NIGO®

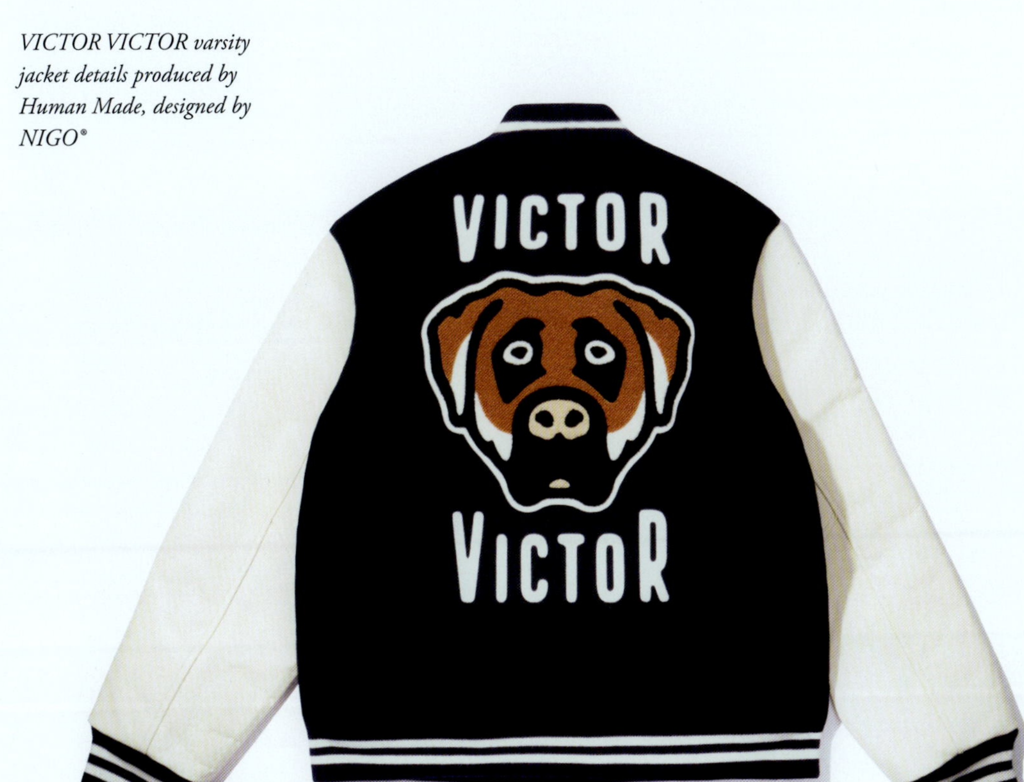

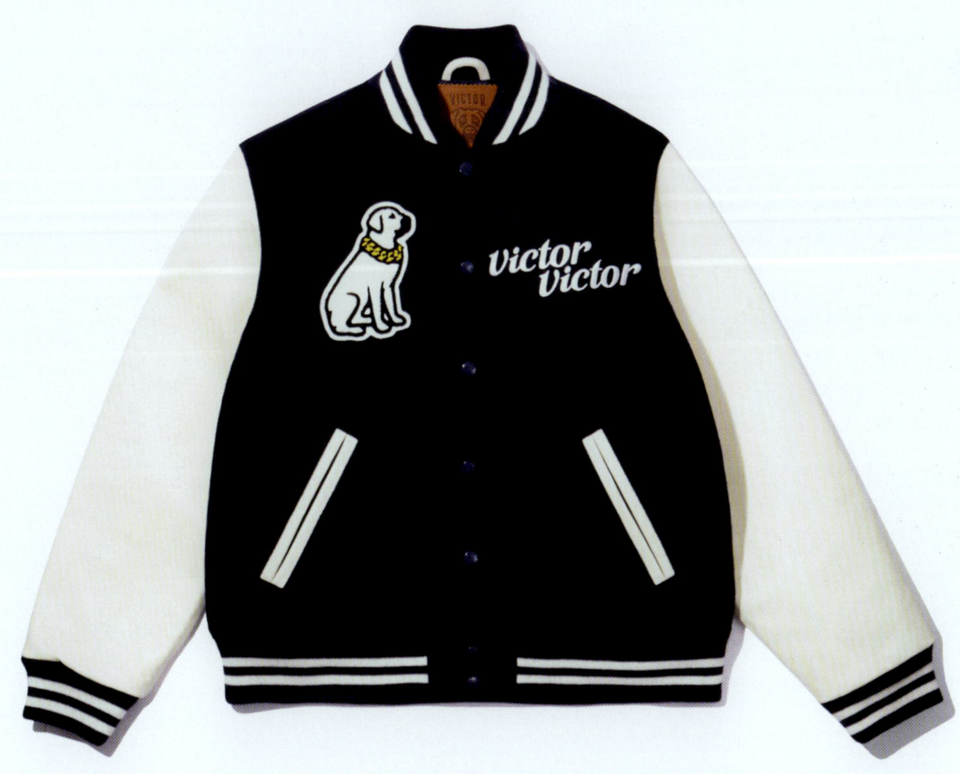

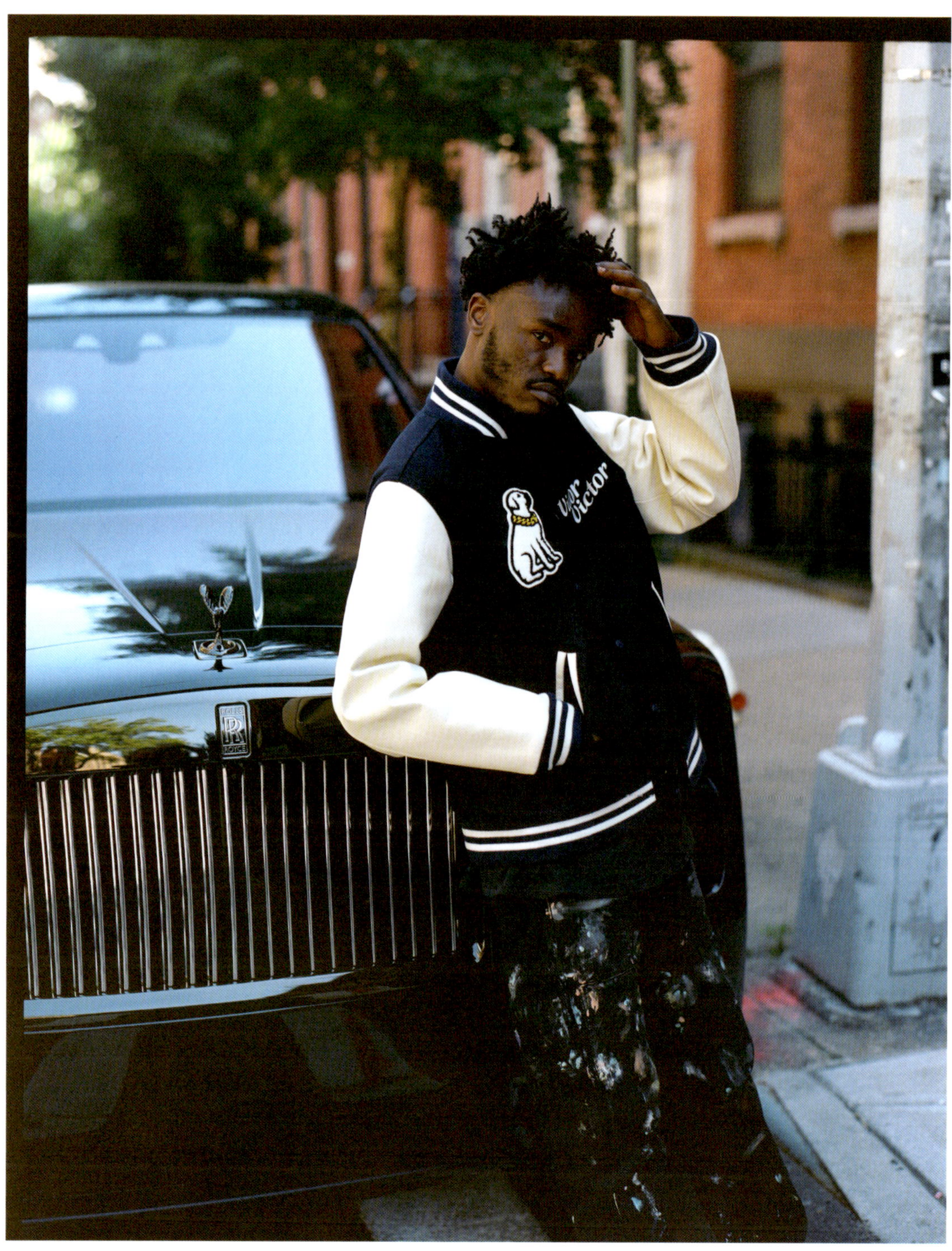
Victor

Ade & Lil Uzi Vert sporting the VICTOR VICTOR varsity jacket. Uzi (right) sports a rare version, only two examples were made.

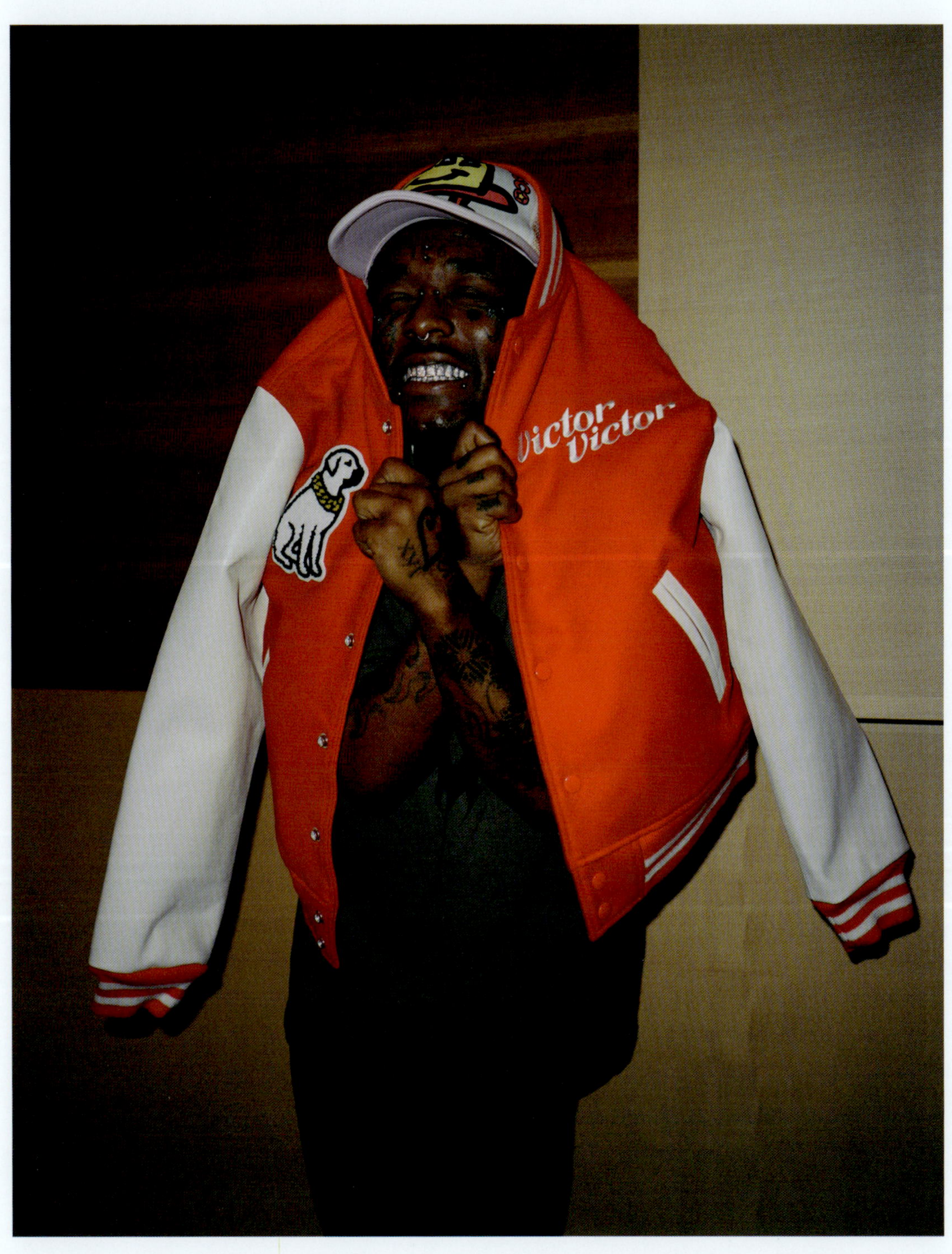

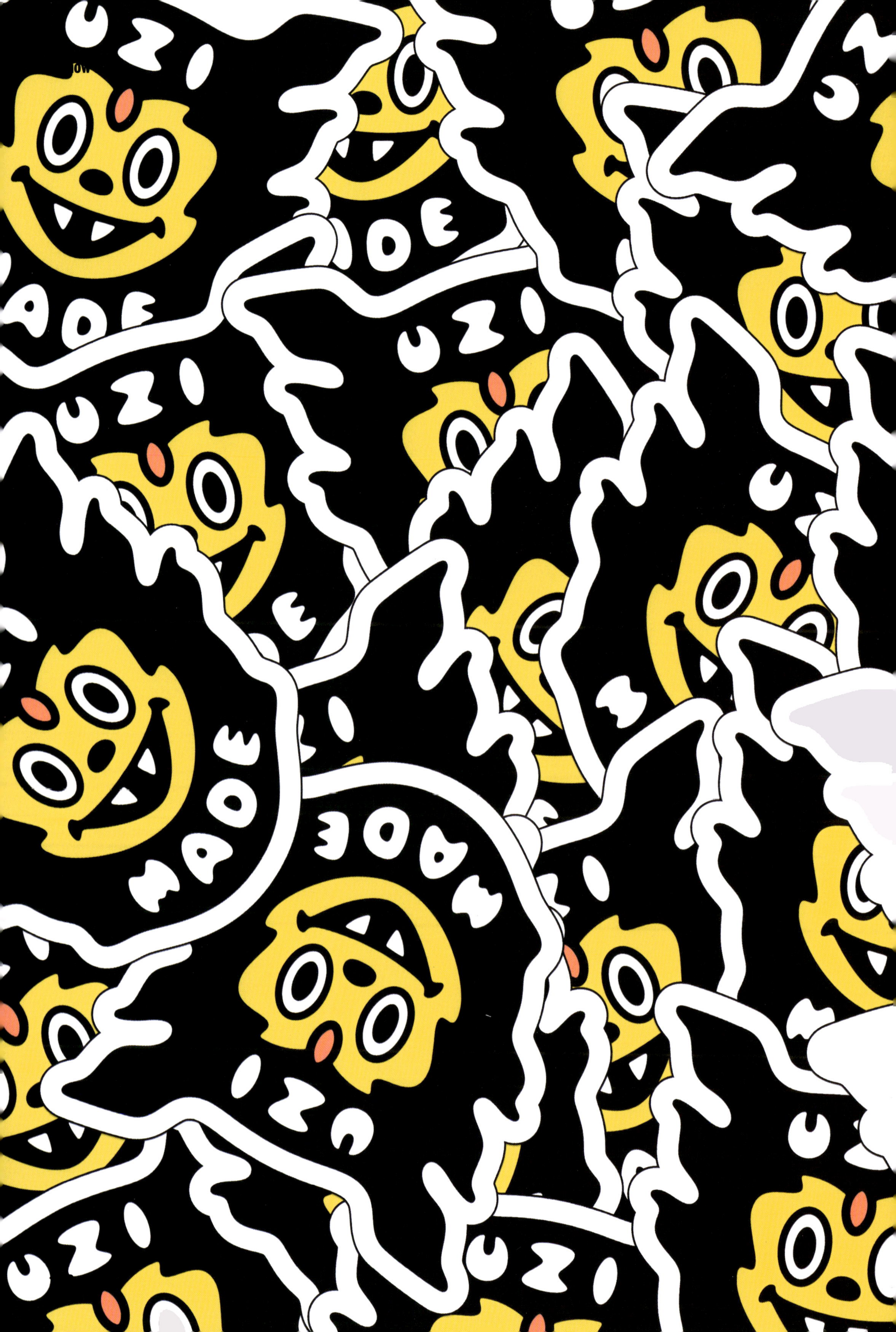
UZI
MADE

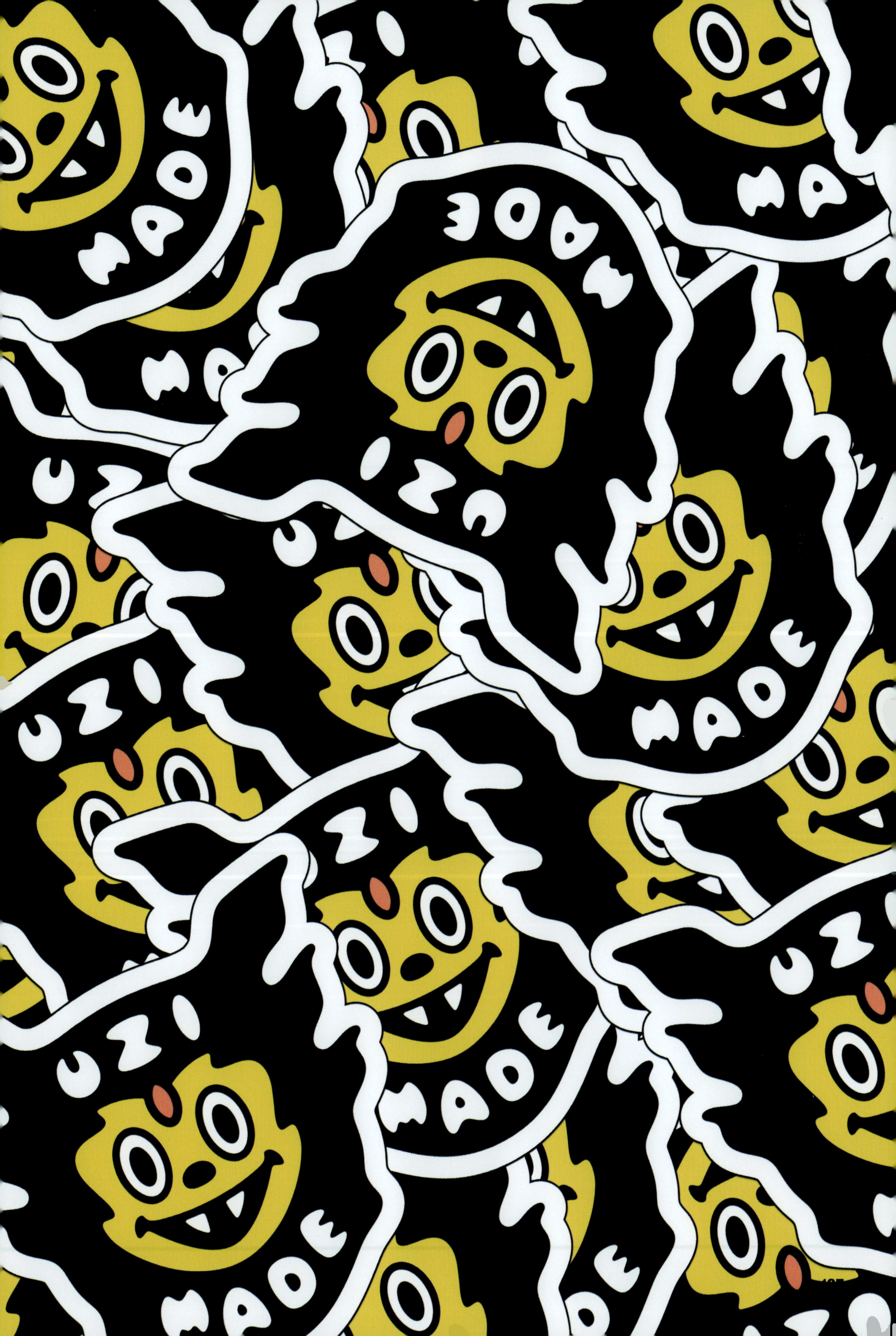
UZI
MADE

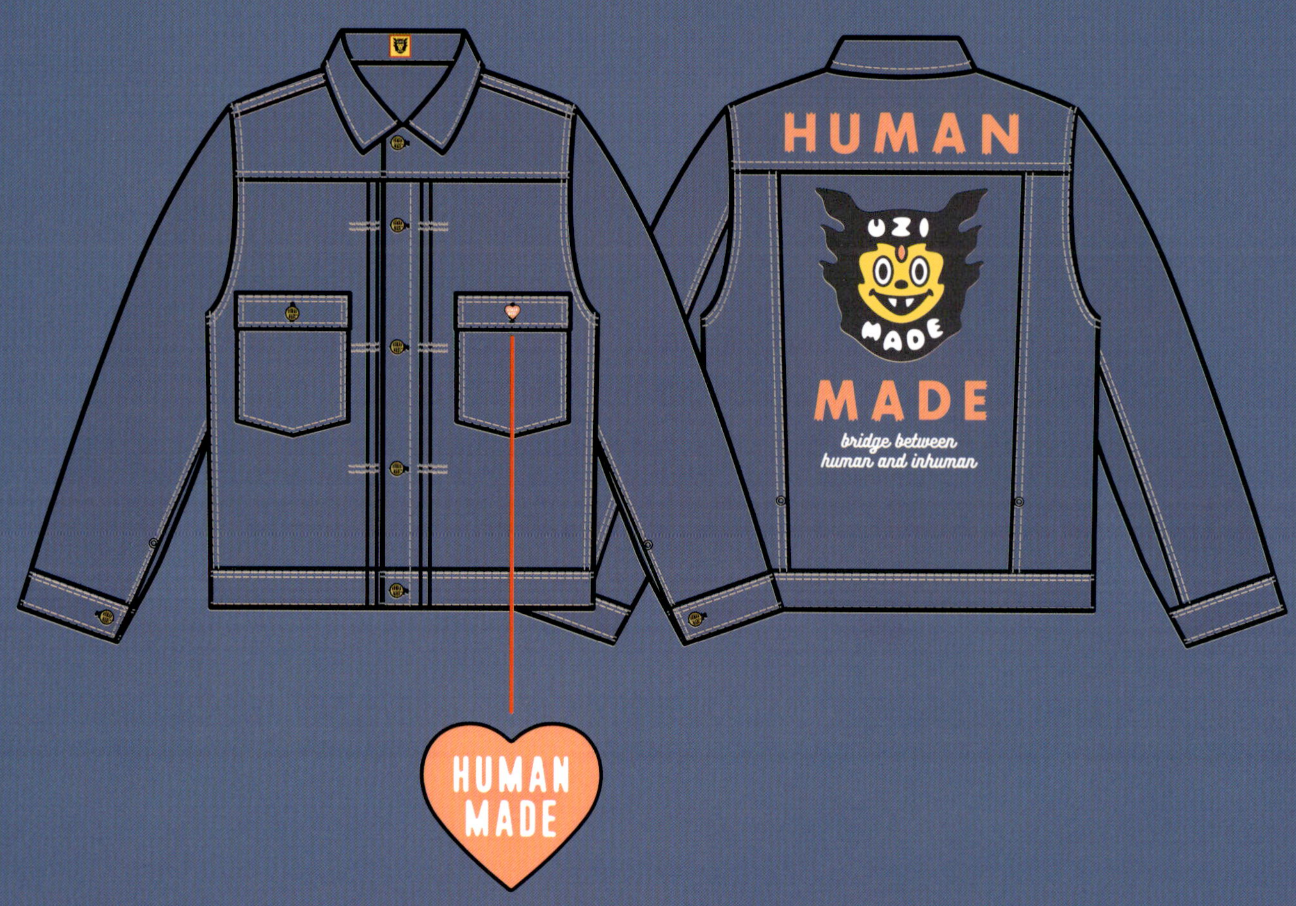
HUMAN
UZI
MADE
MADE
bridge between
human and inhuman
HUMAN
MADE

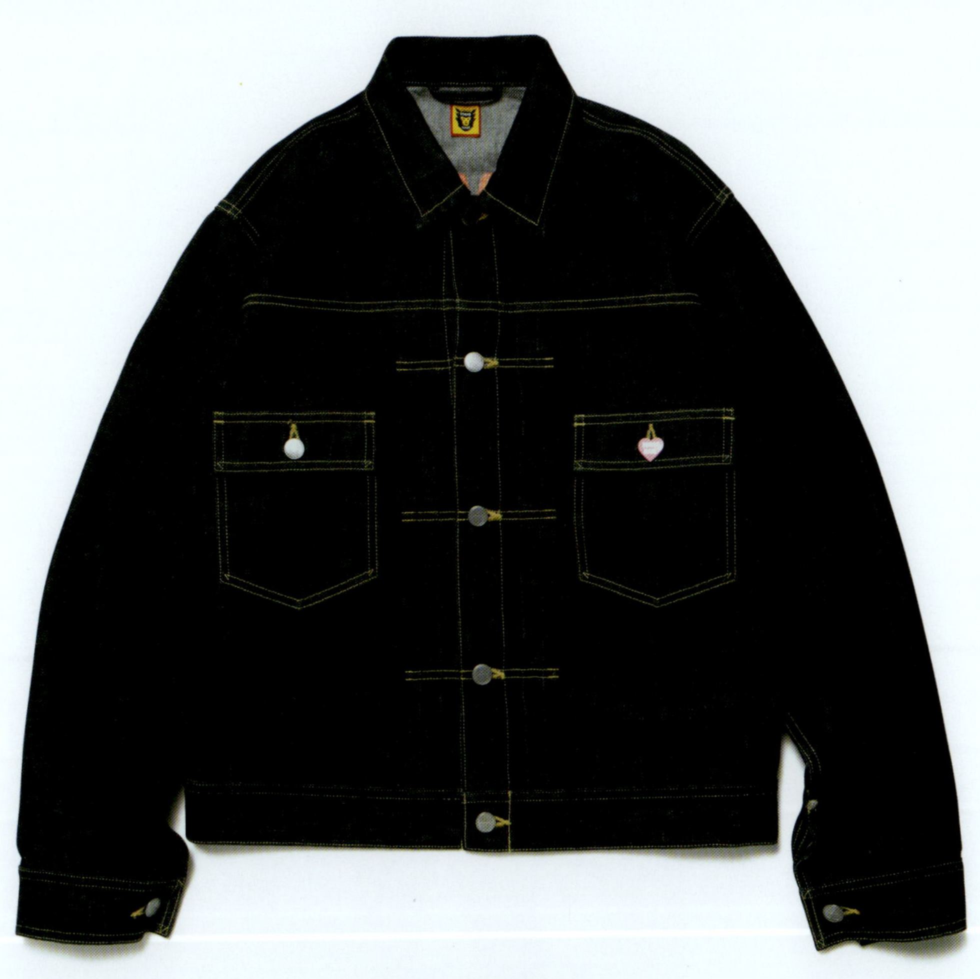

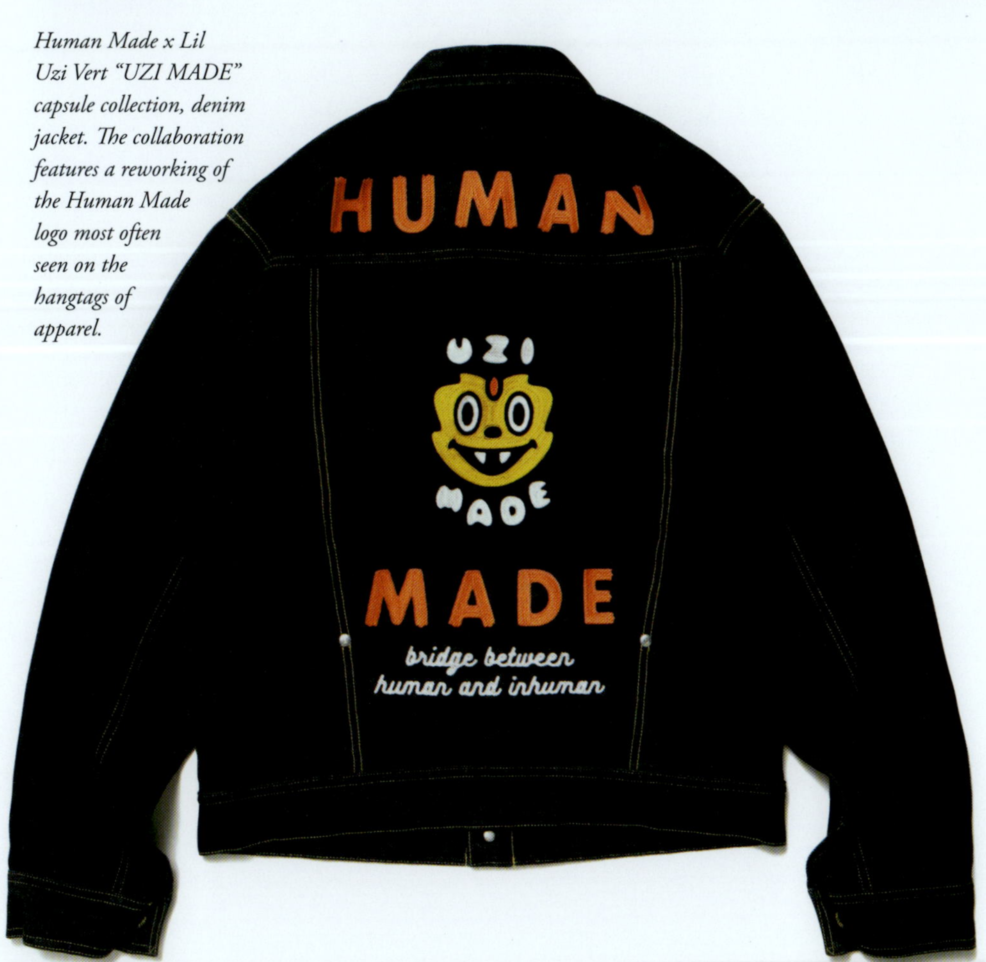

Human Made x Lil Uzi Vert "UZI MADE" capsule collection, denim jacket. The collaboration features a reworking of the Human Made logo most often seen on the hangtags of apparel.

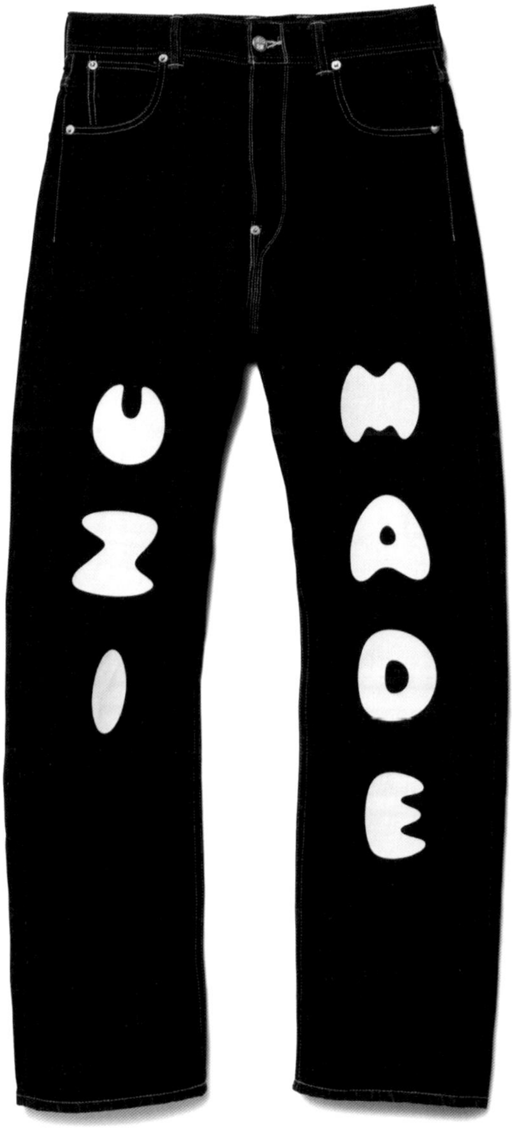

Human Made x Lil Uzi Vert "UZI MADE" capsule collection, denim pants

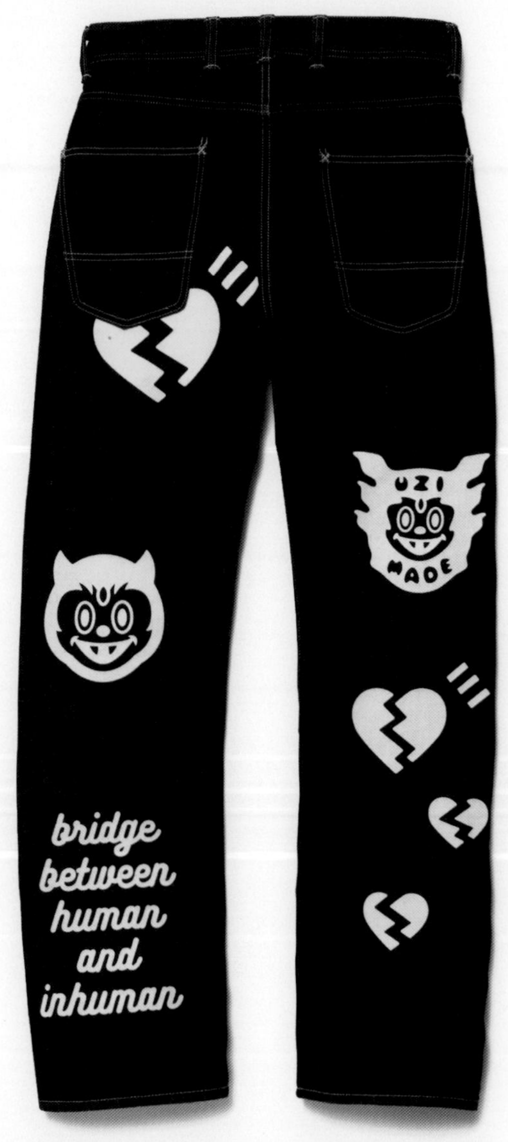
UZI
MADE
bridge
between
human
and
inhuman

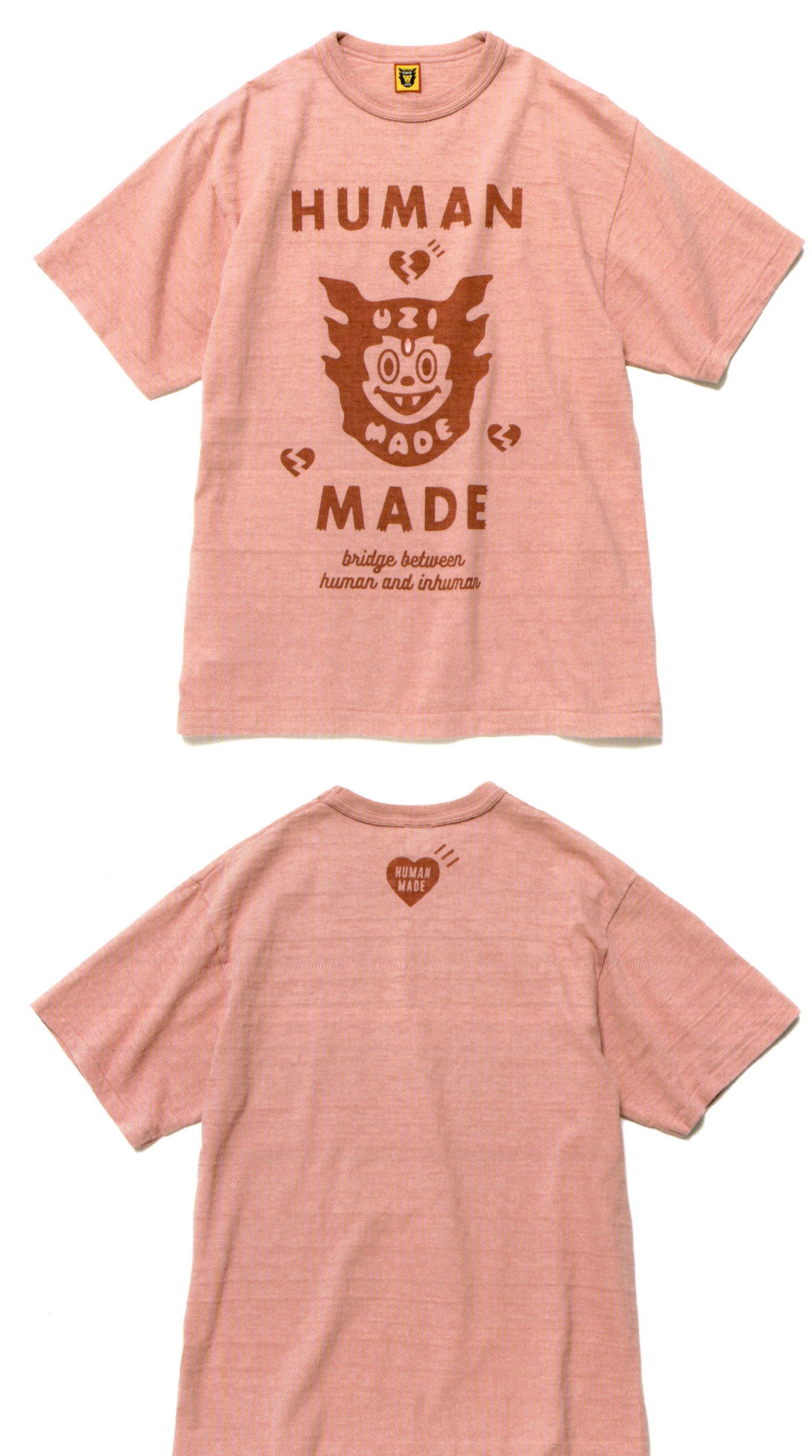

Human Made x Lil Uzi Vert "UZI MADE" capsule collection, t-shirts.

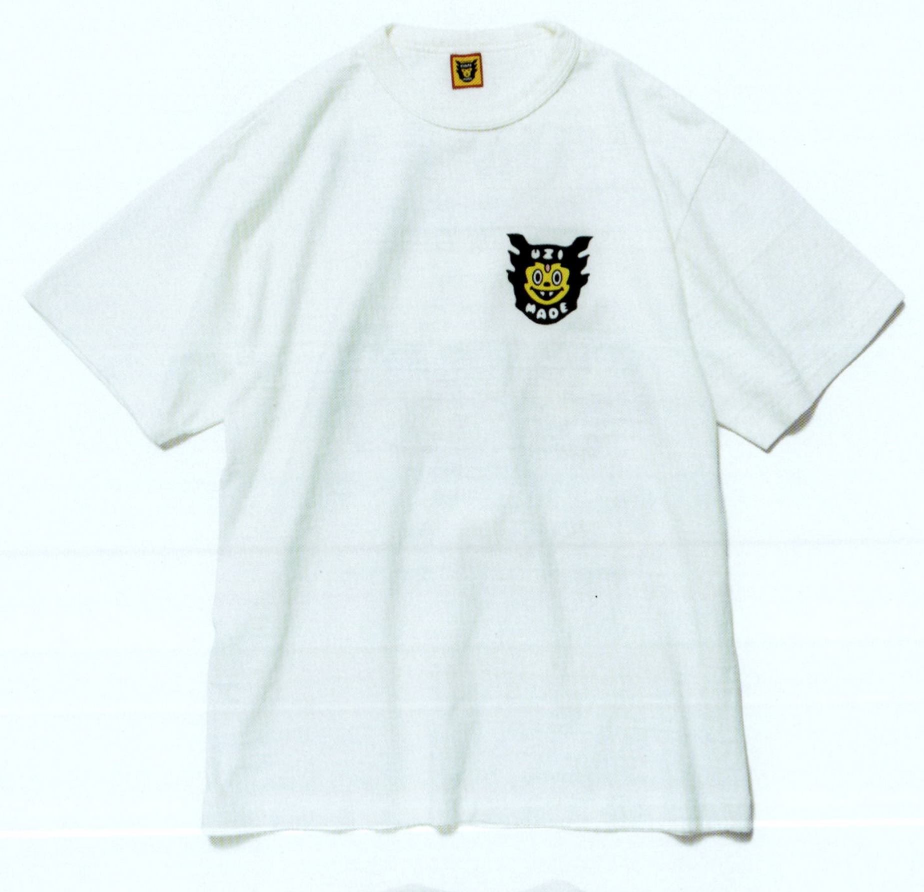

HUMAN
MADE

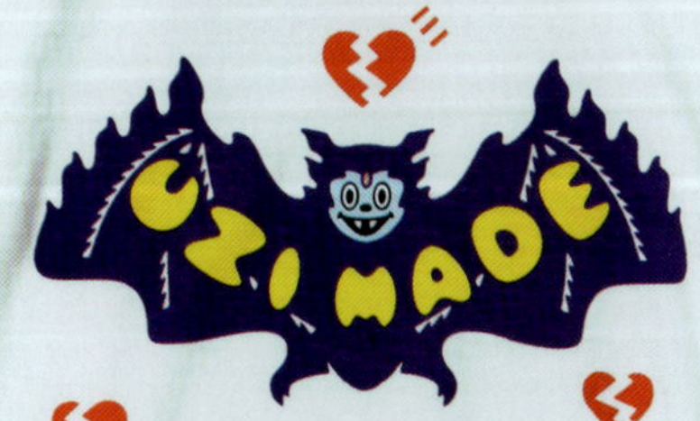

bridge between
human and inhuman

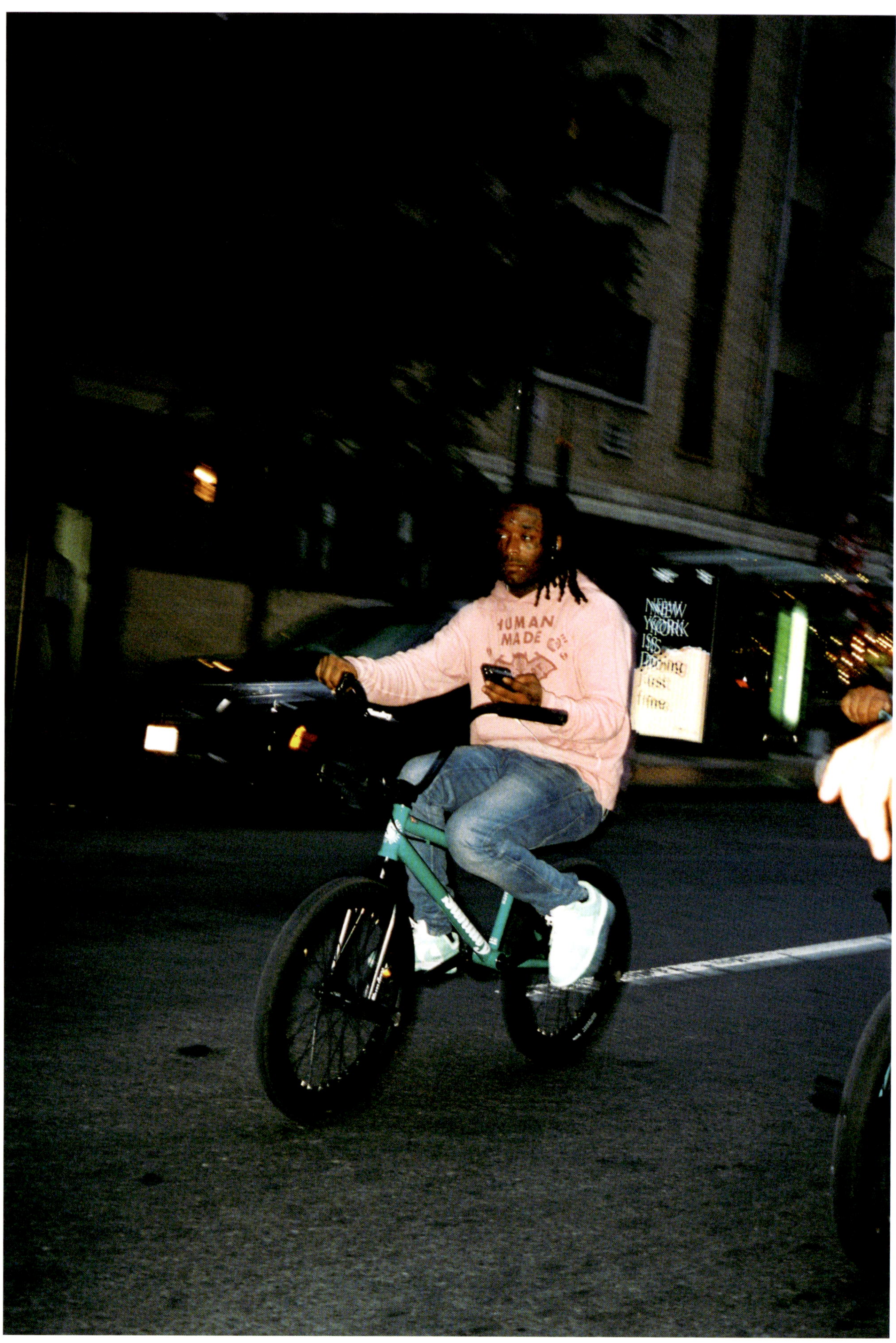
HUMAN
MADE
NEW
YORK
IS

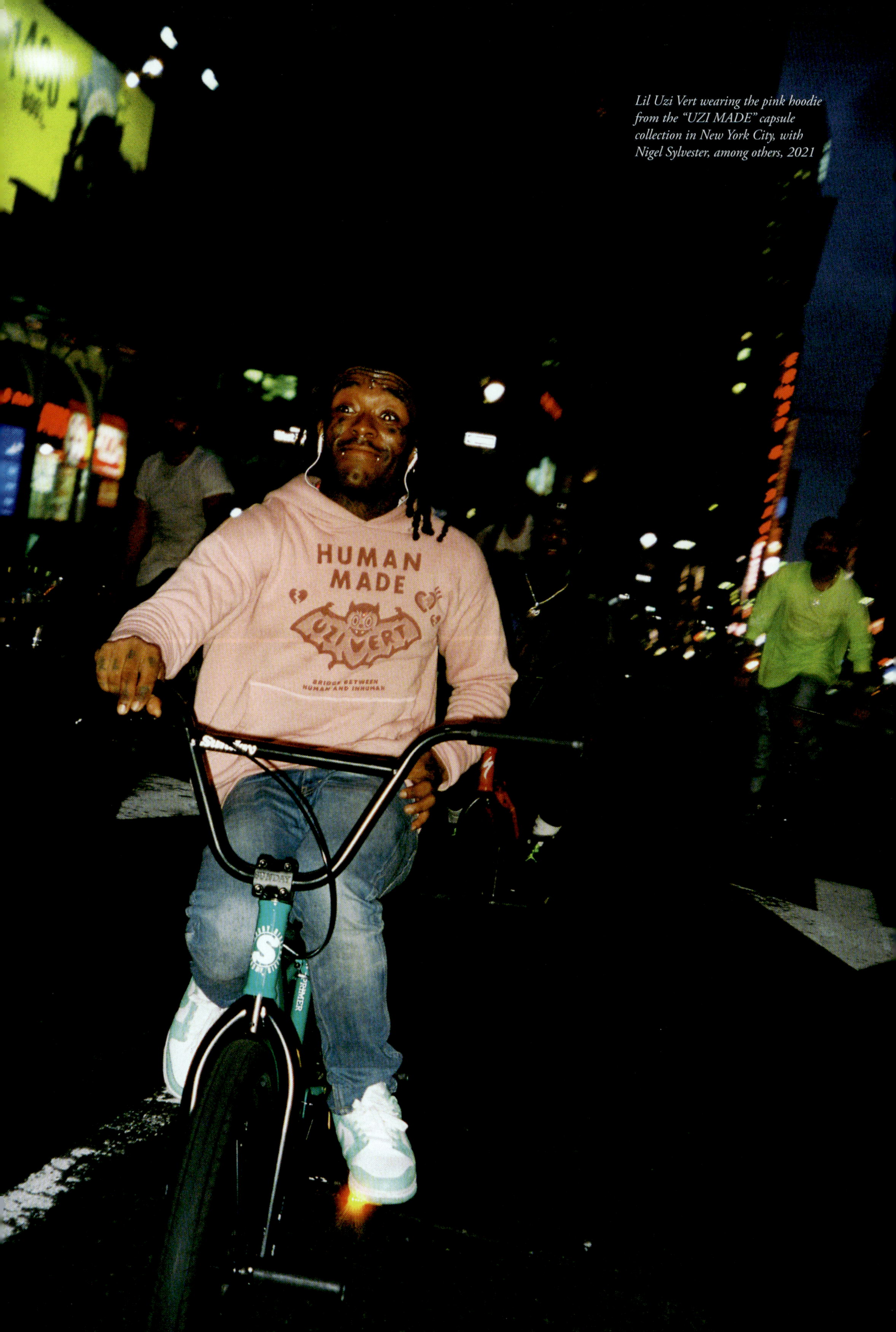

Lil Uzi Vert wearing the pink hoodie from the "UZI MADE" capsule collection in New York City, with Nigel Sylvester, among others, 2021

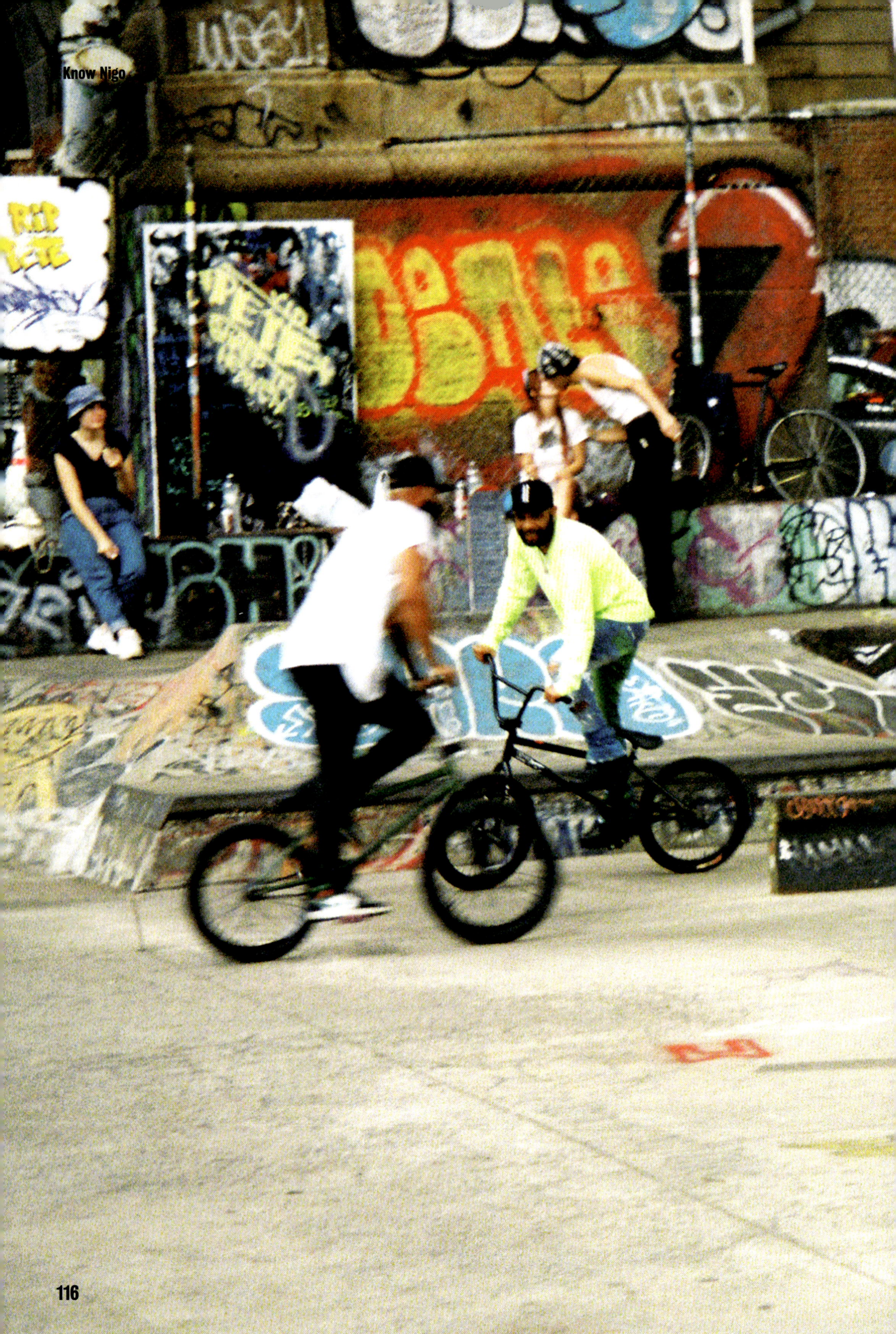

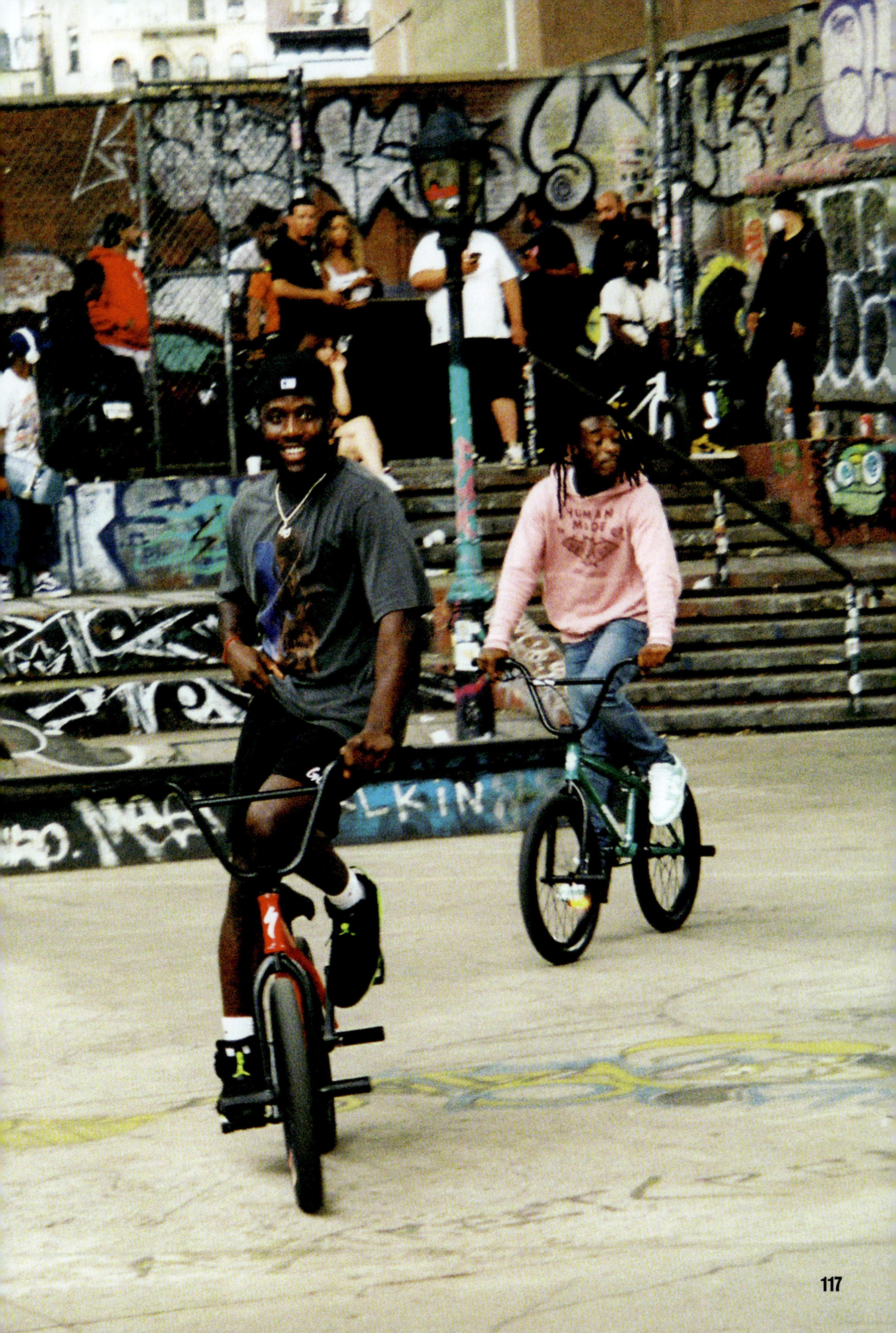

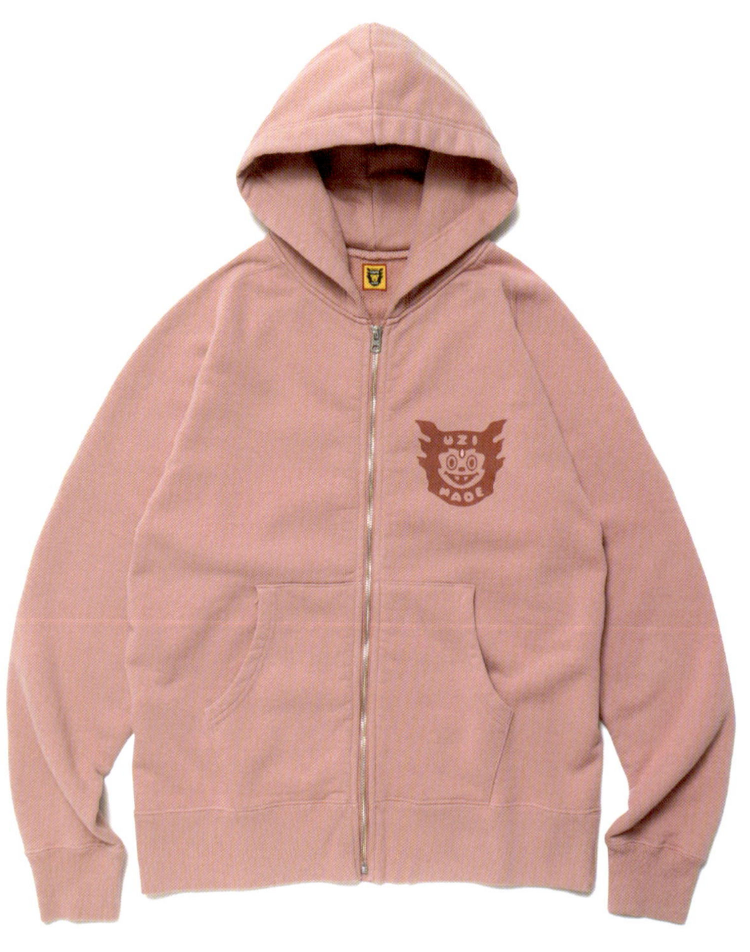

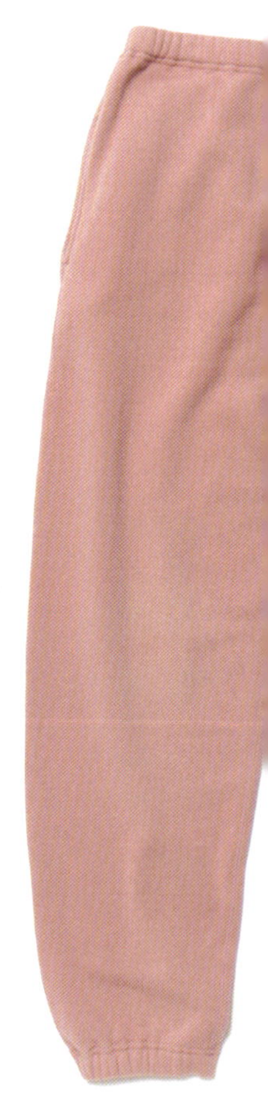

Human Made x Lil Uzi Vert "UZI MADE" capsule collection, zip-up hoodies and sweatpants

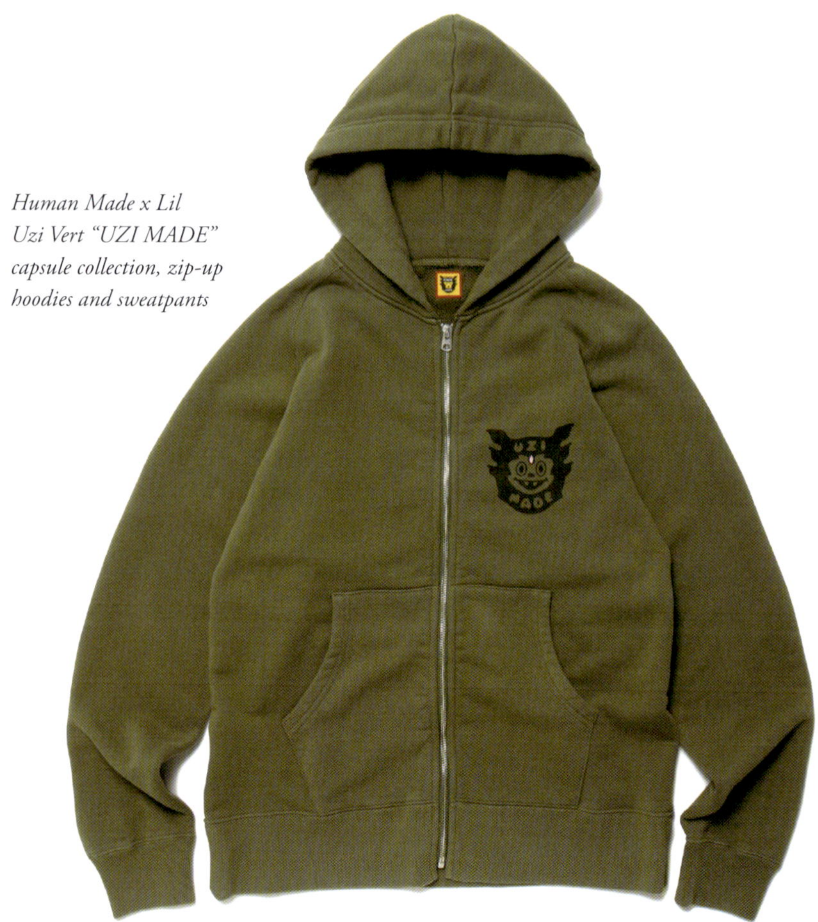

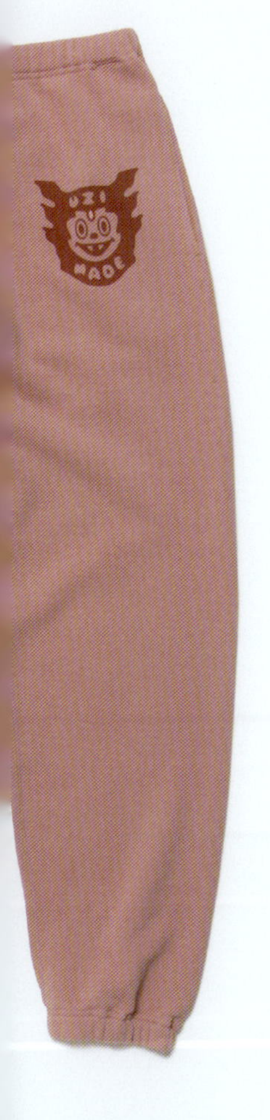
UZI
MADE

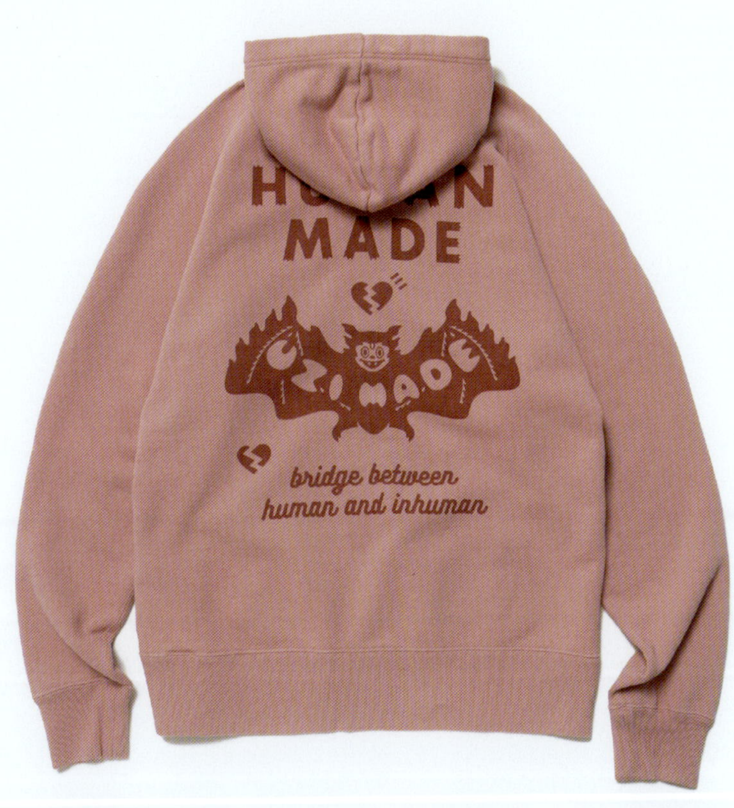
MADE
bridge between
human and inhuman

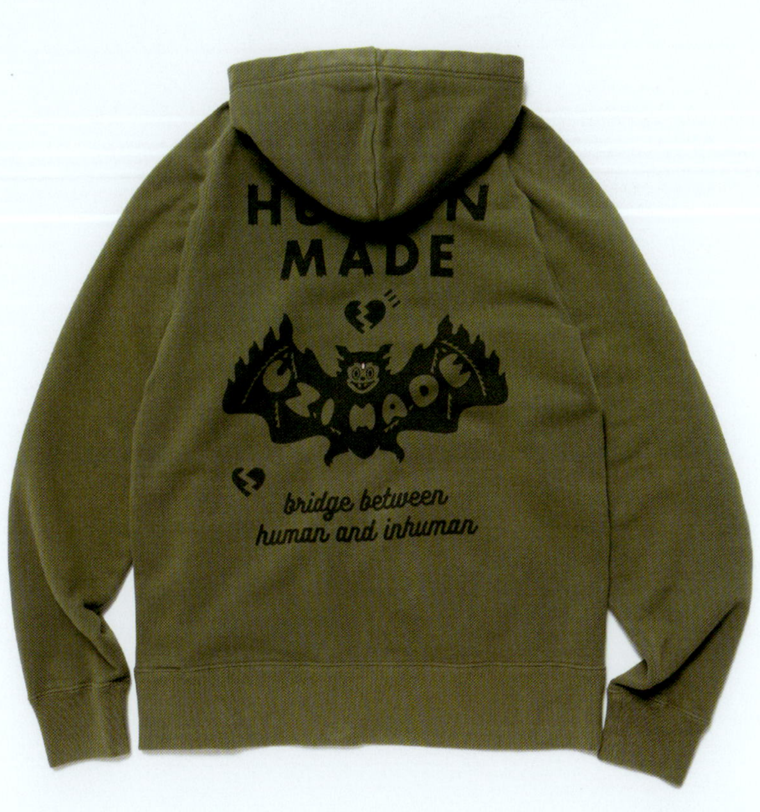
MADE
bridge between
human and inhuman

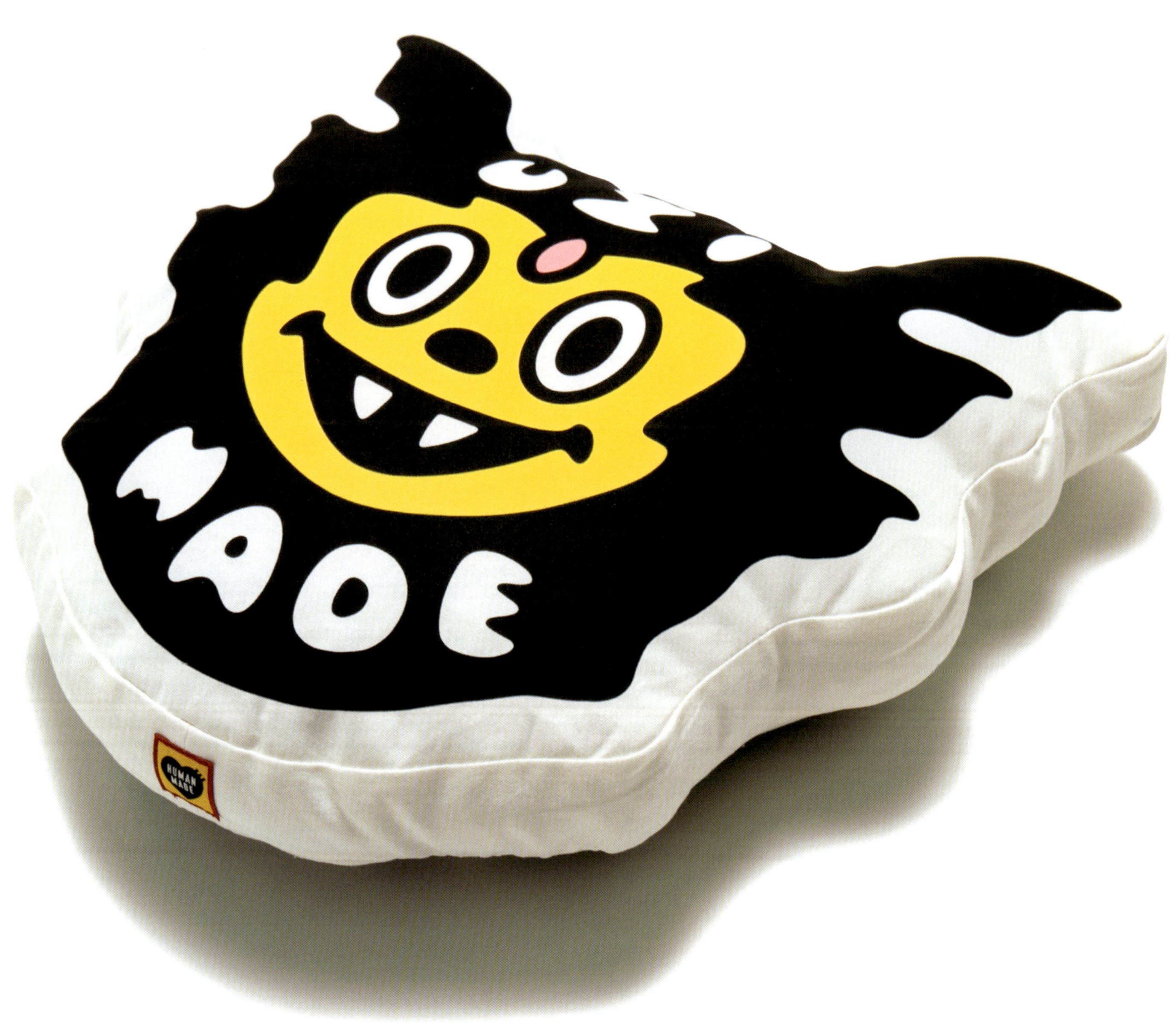
MADE

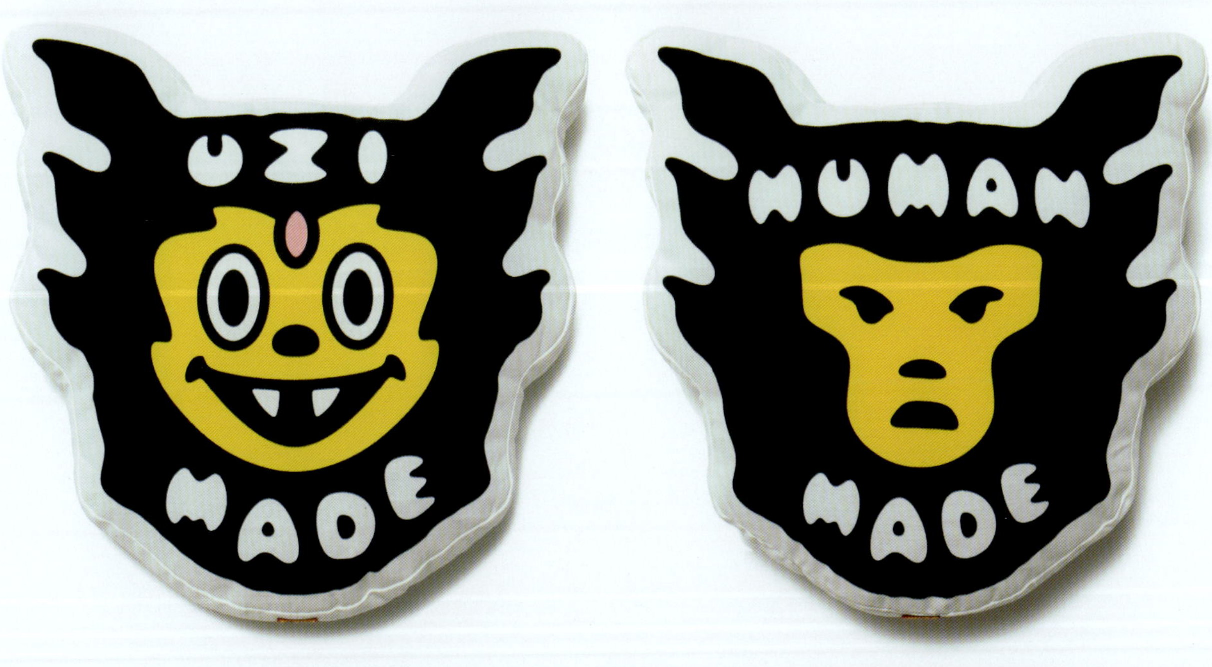

Human Made x Lil Uzi Vert "UZI MADE" capsule collection, plush cushion

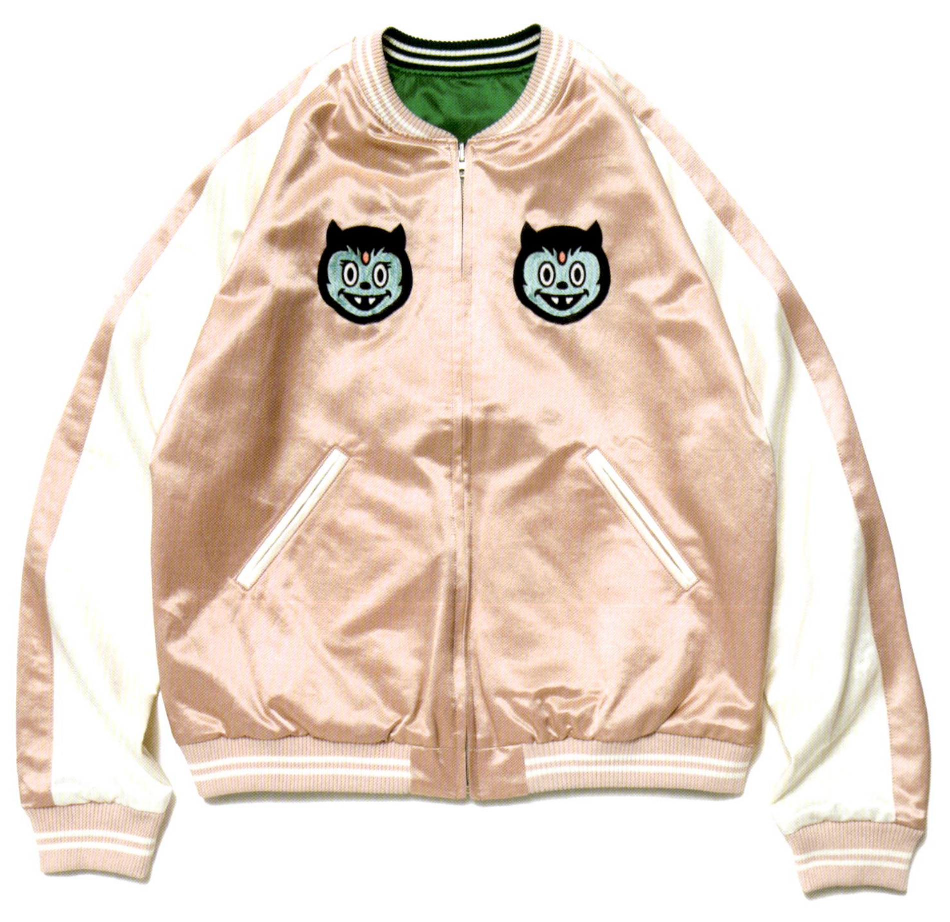

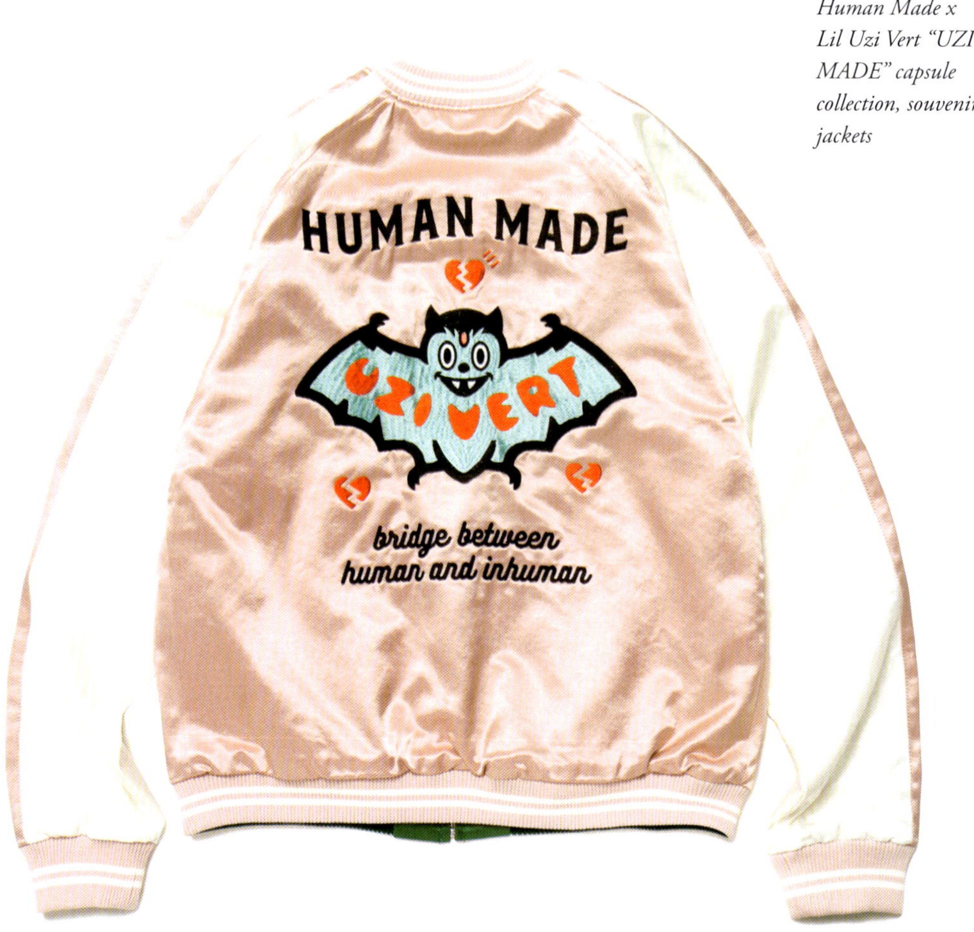

Human Made x Lil Uzi Vert "UZI MADE" capsule collection, souvenir jackets

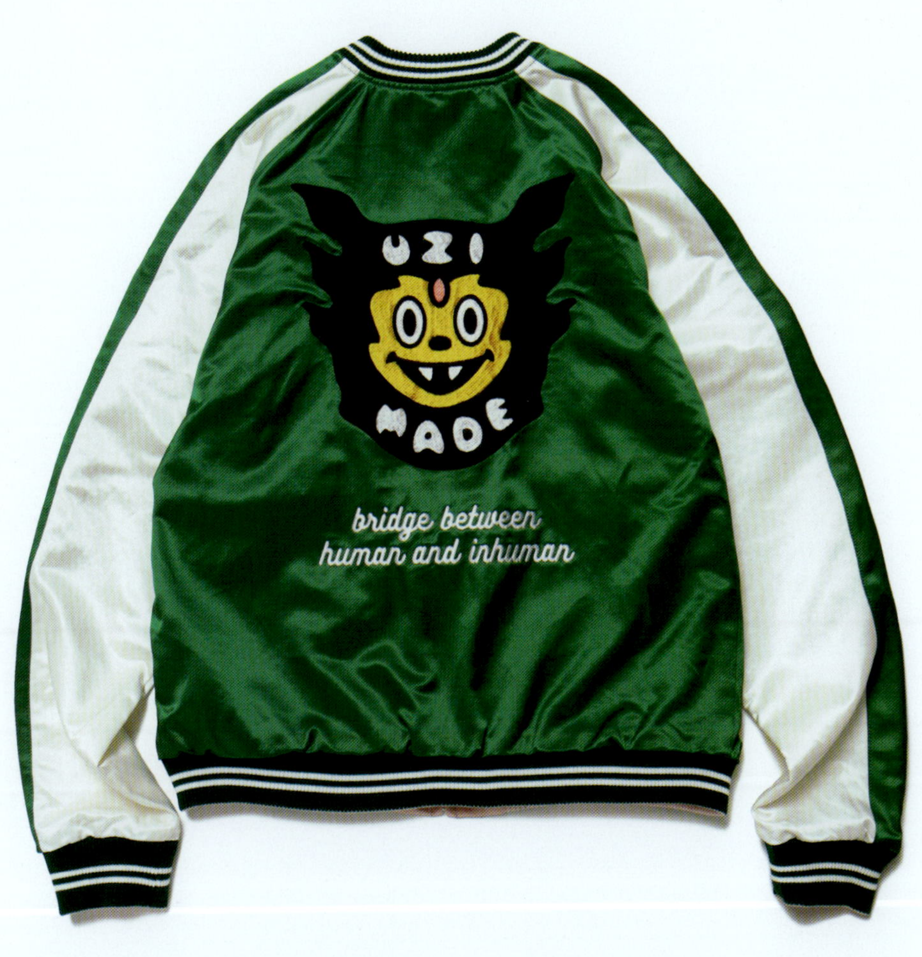
UZI
MADE
bridge between
human and inhuman

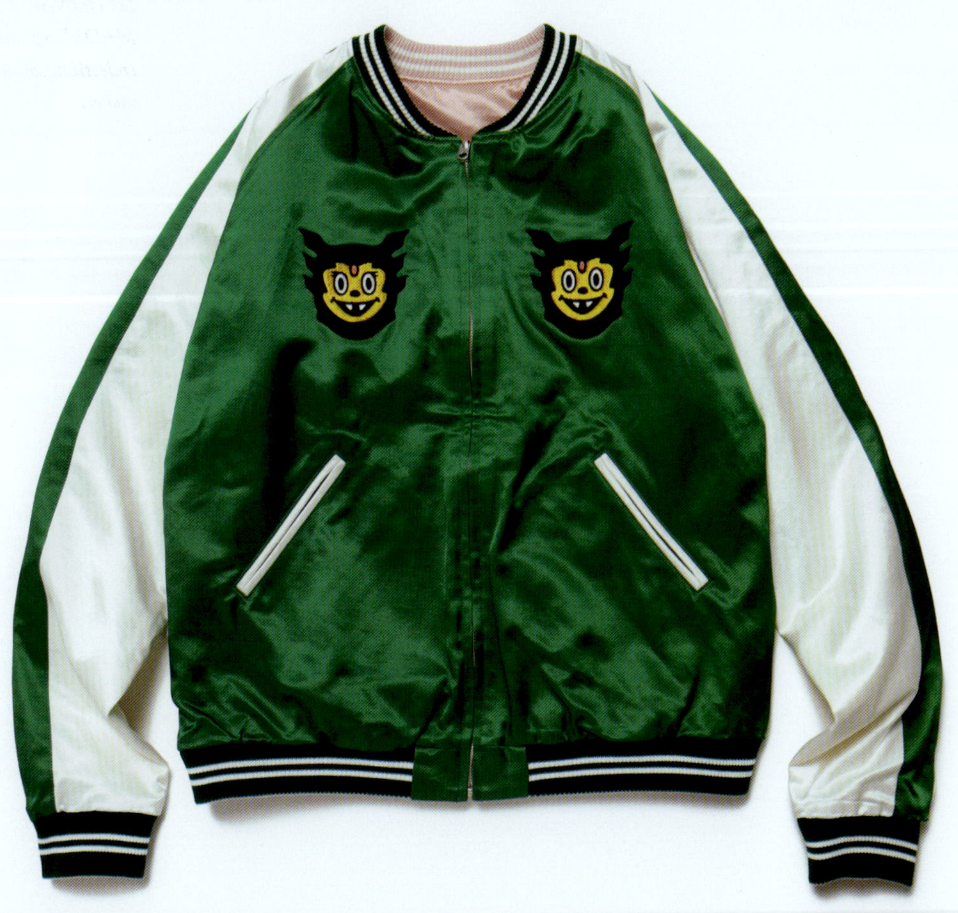

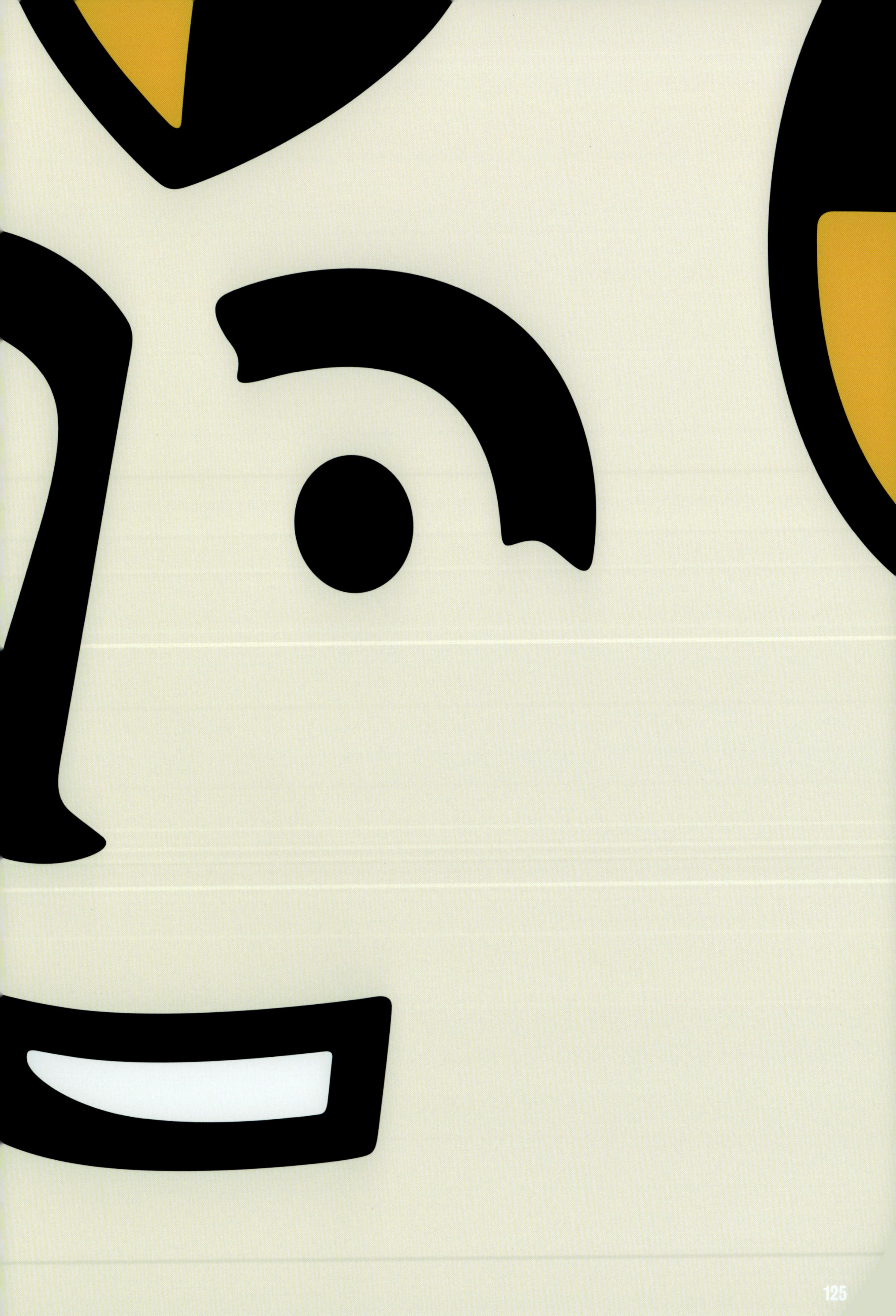

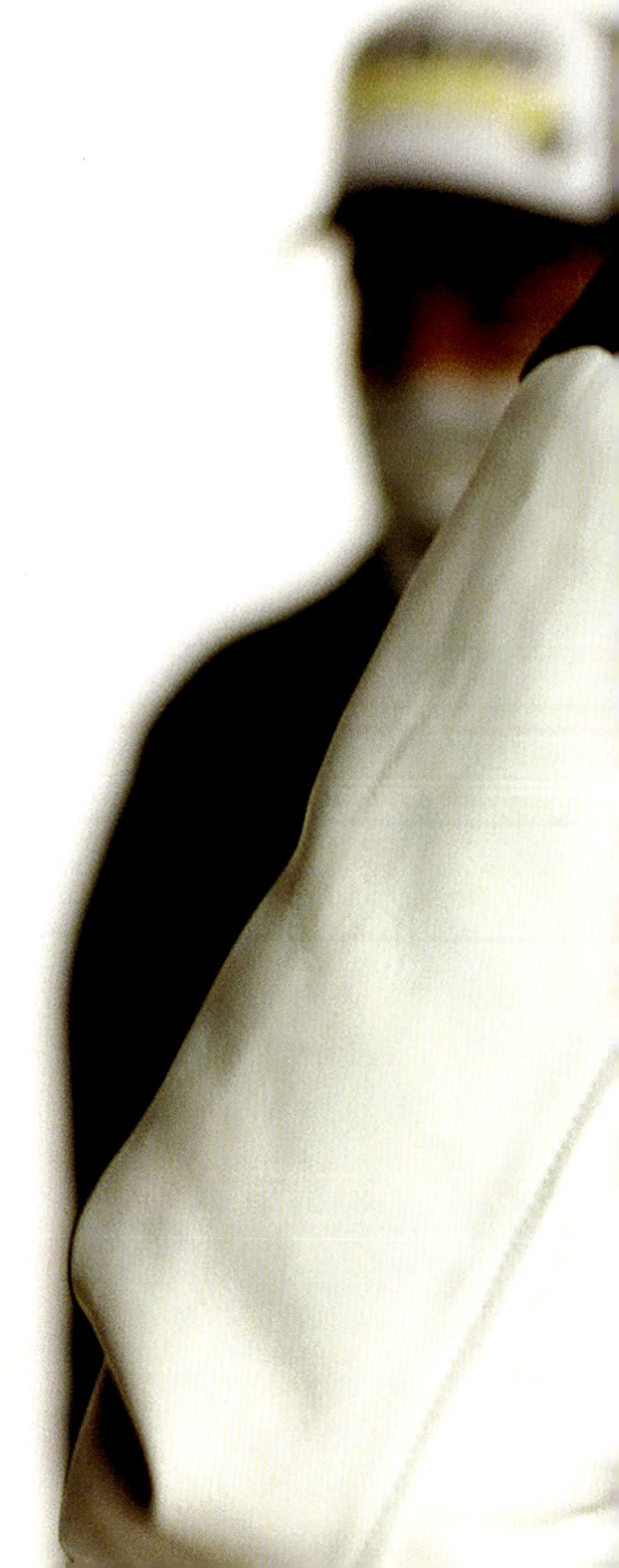

Human Made x A$AP Rocky
"HUMAN TESTING"
capsule collection, varsity jacket

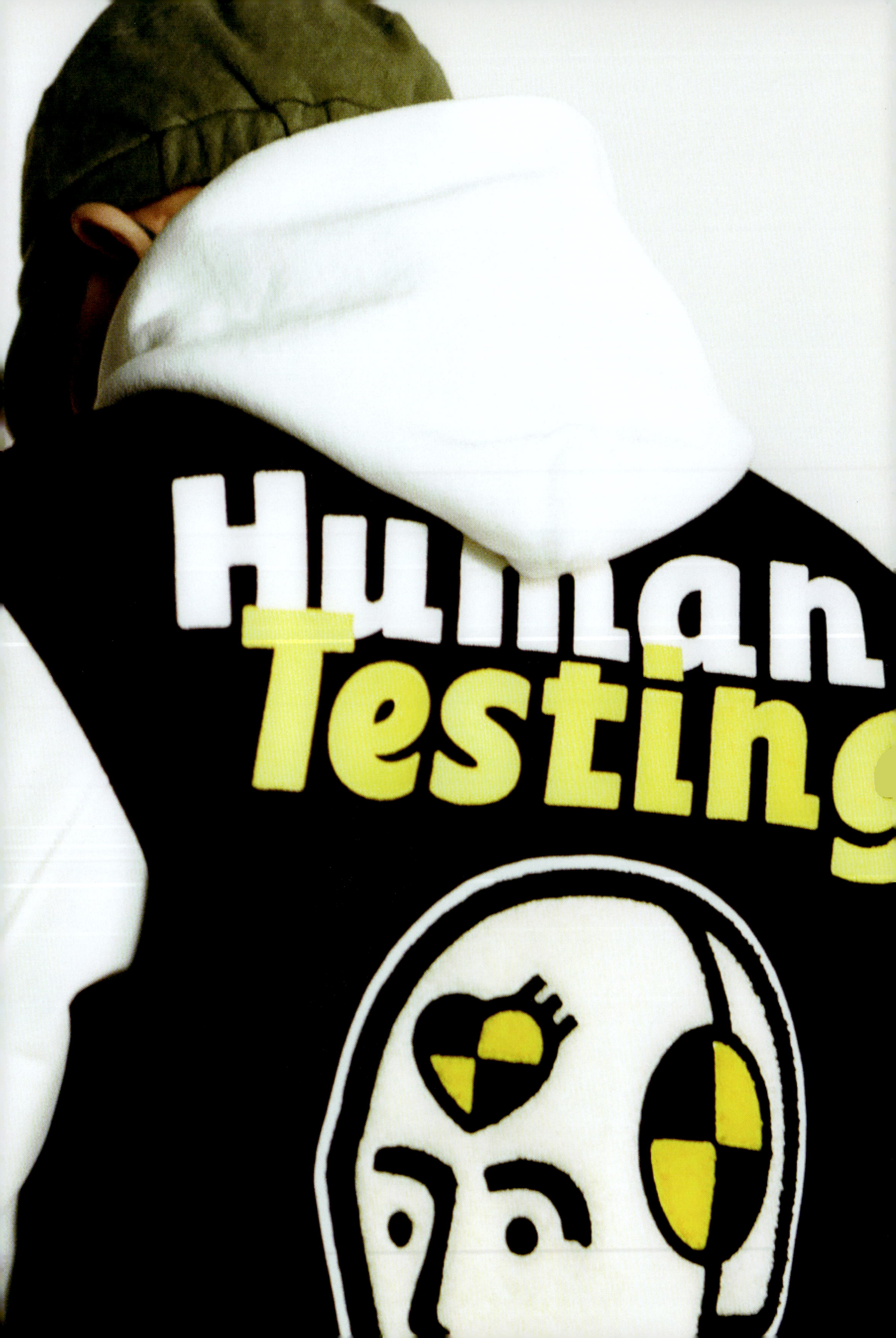
Human

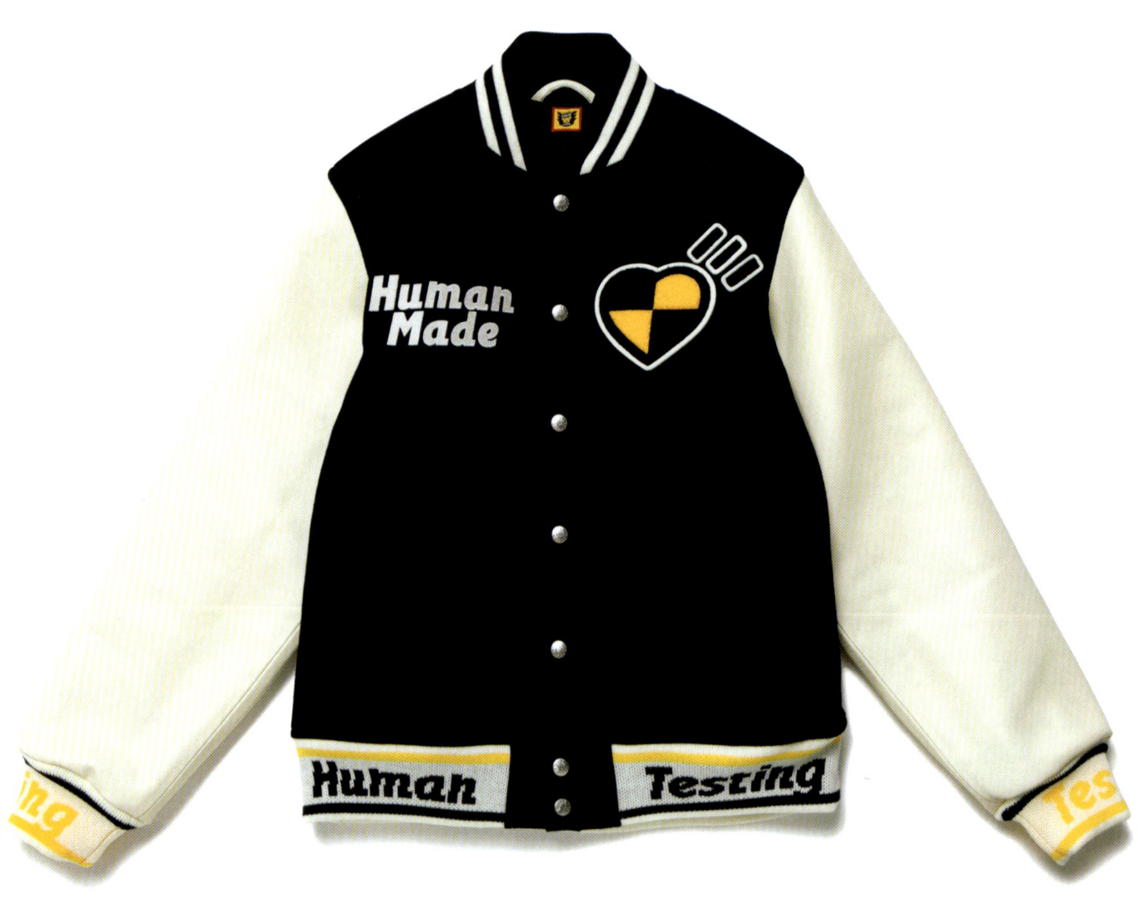
Human
Made
Human
Testing

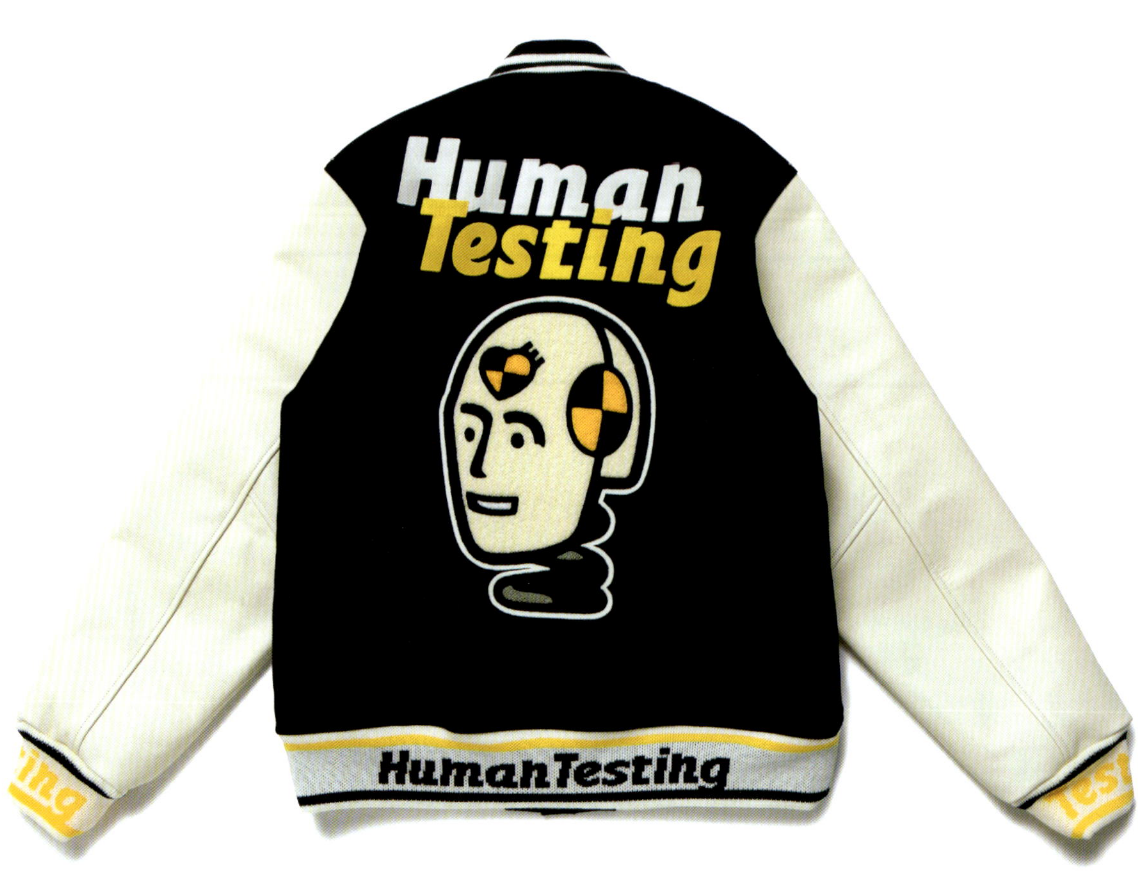
Human
Testing
HumanTesting

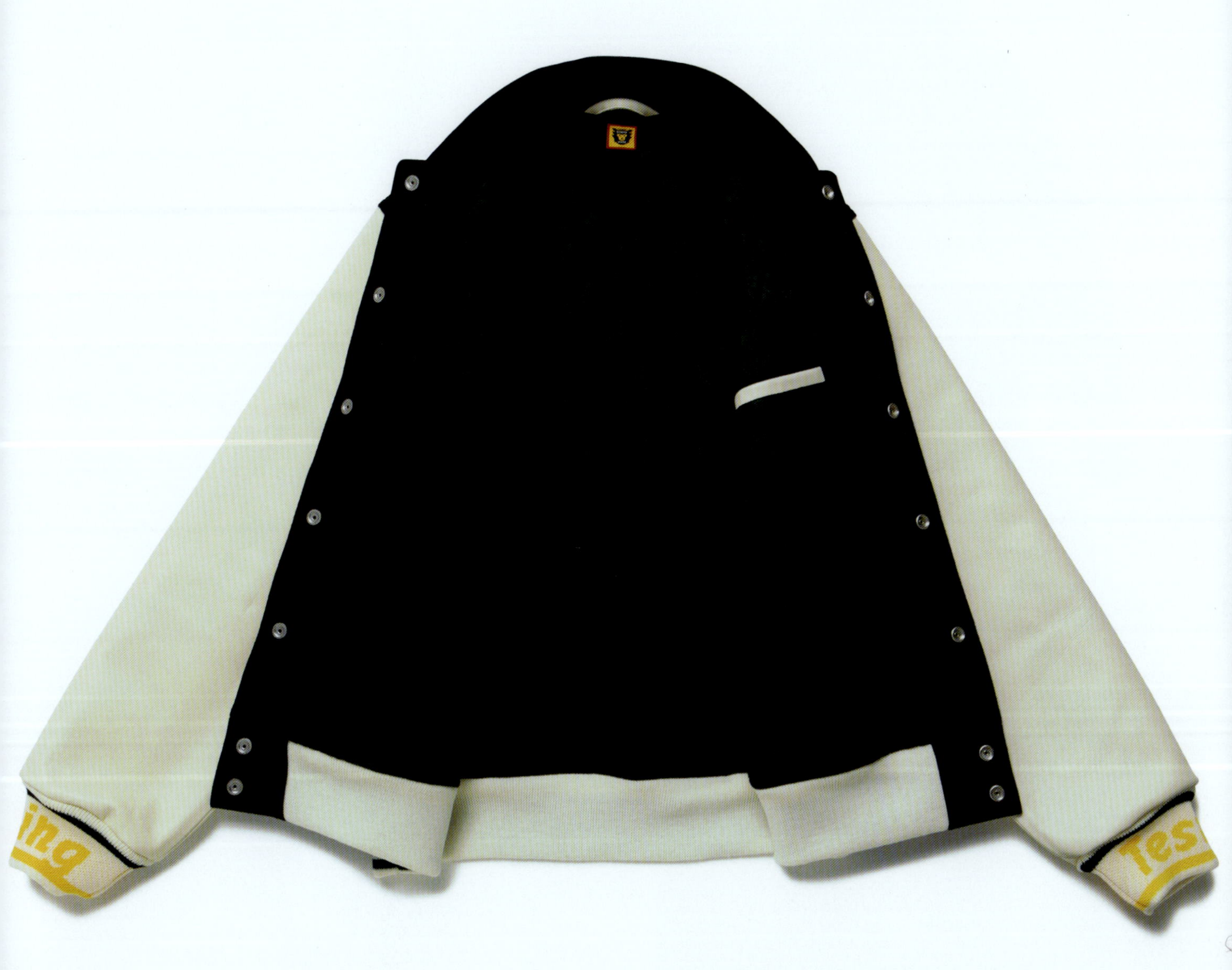

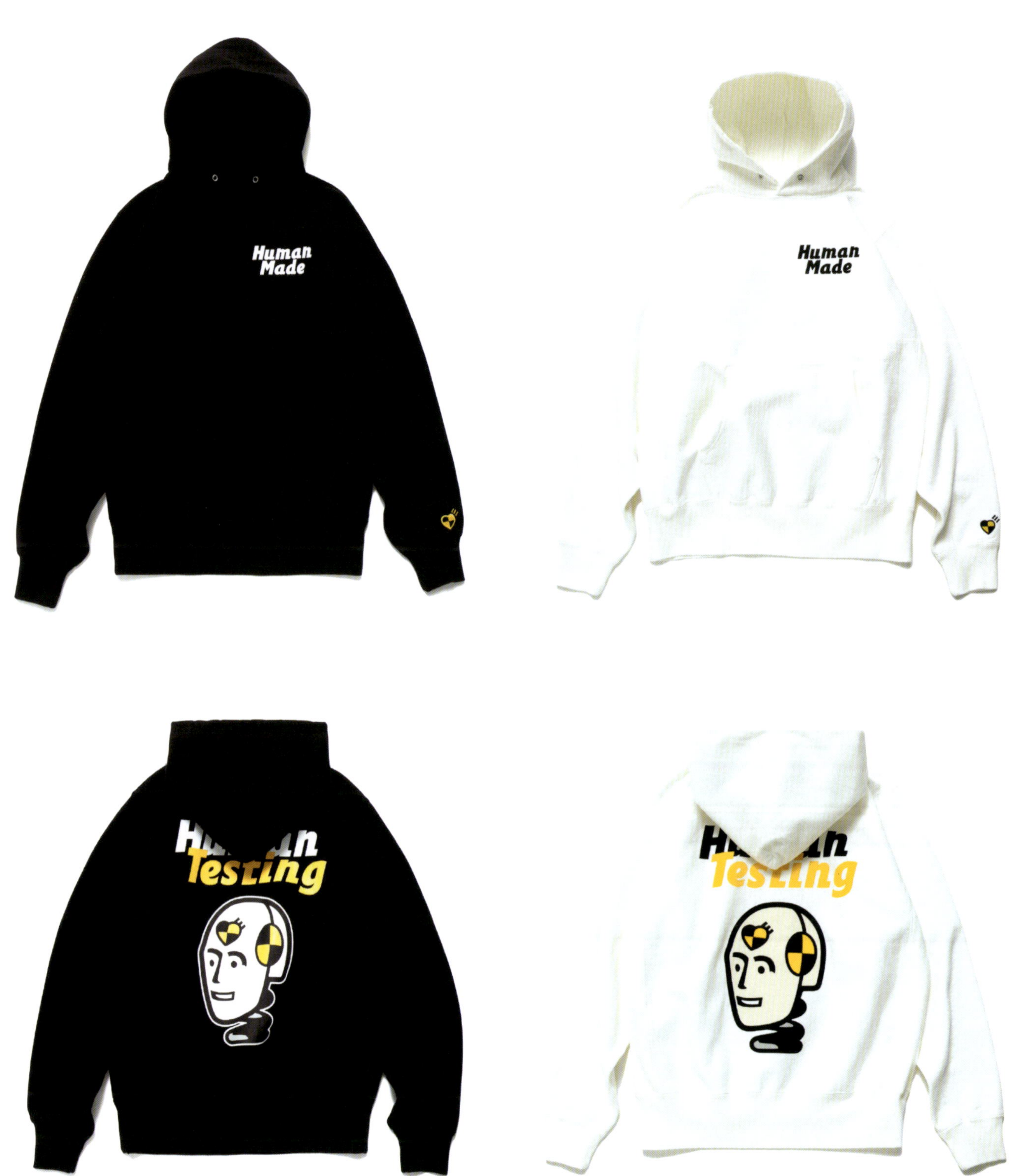

Human Made x A$AP Rocky "HUMAN TESTING" capsule collection, hoodies and trucker cap

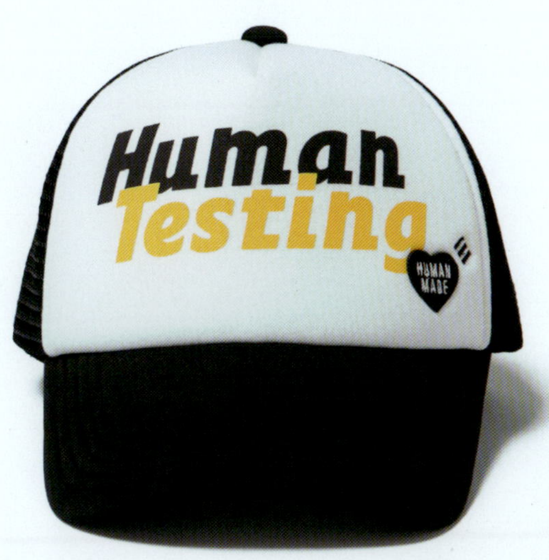
Human
Testing
HUMAN
MADE

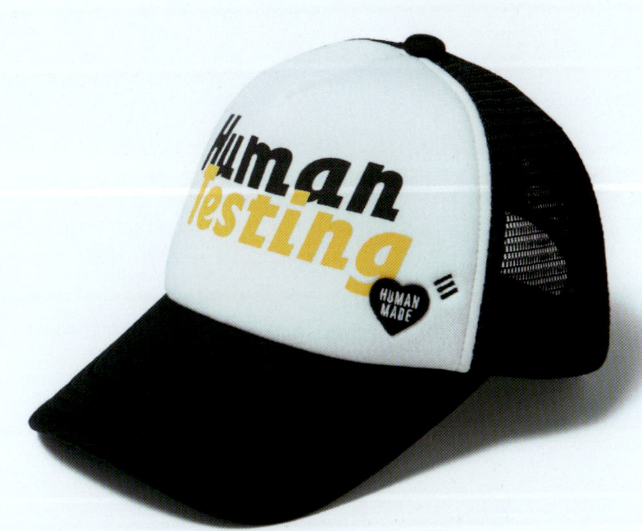
Human
Testing
HUMAN
MADE

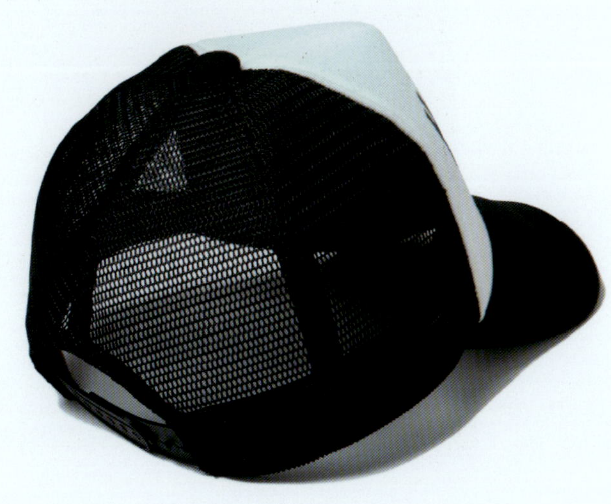

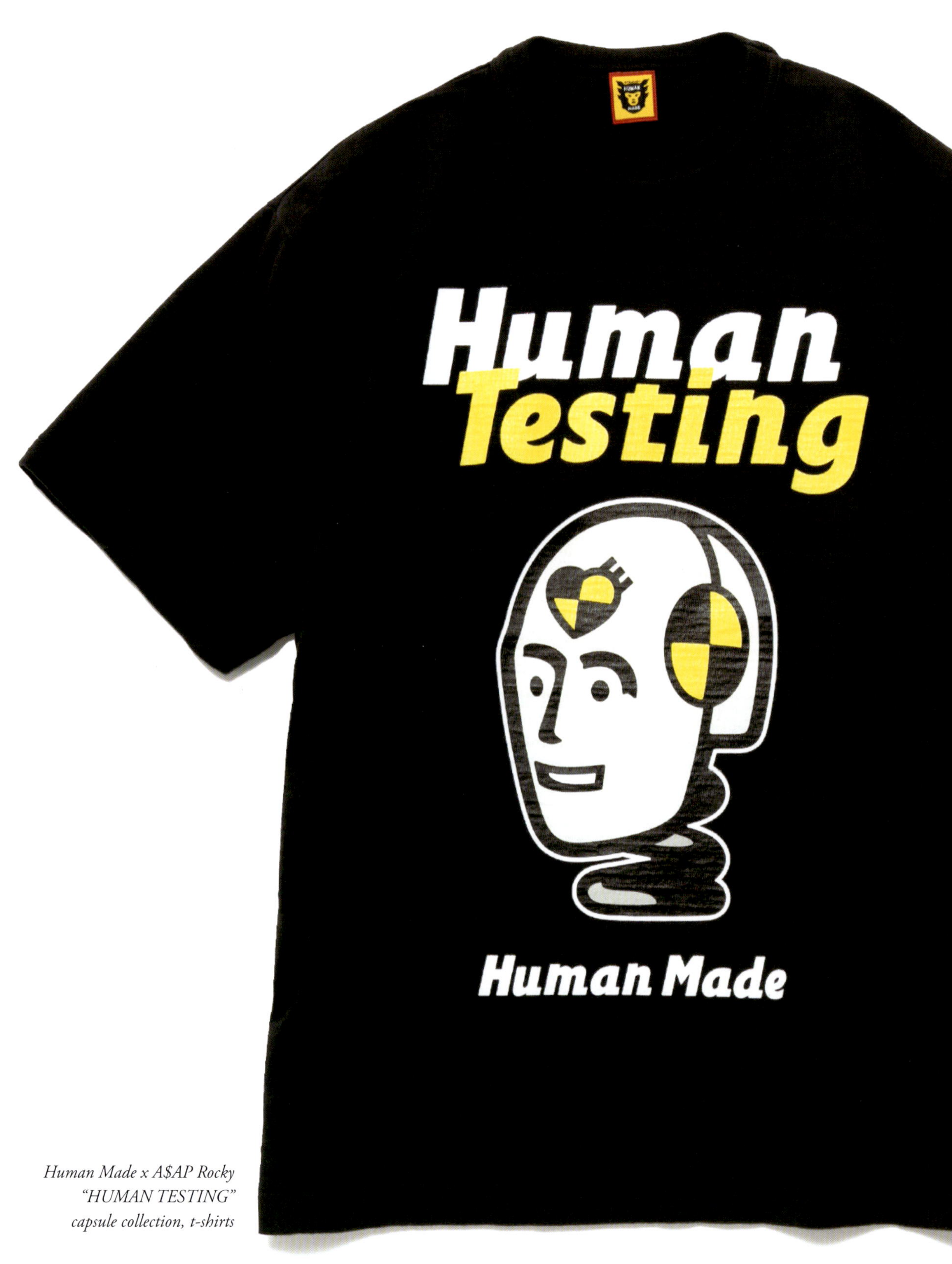

Human Made x A$AP Rocky
"HUMAN TESTING"
capsule collection, t-shirts

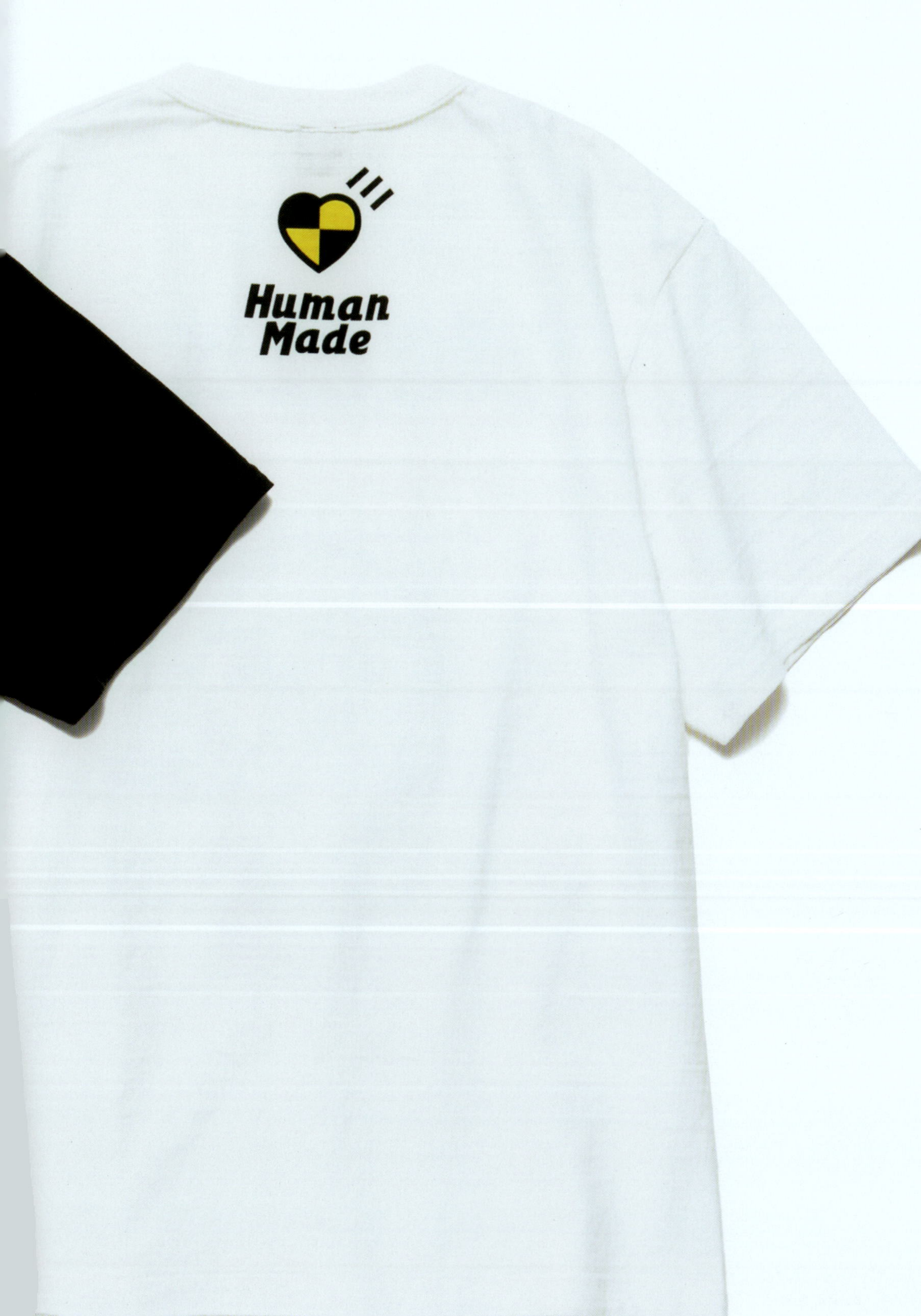
Human
Made

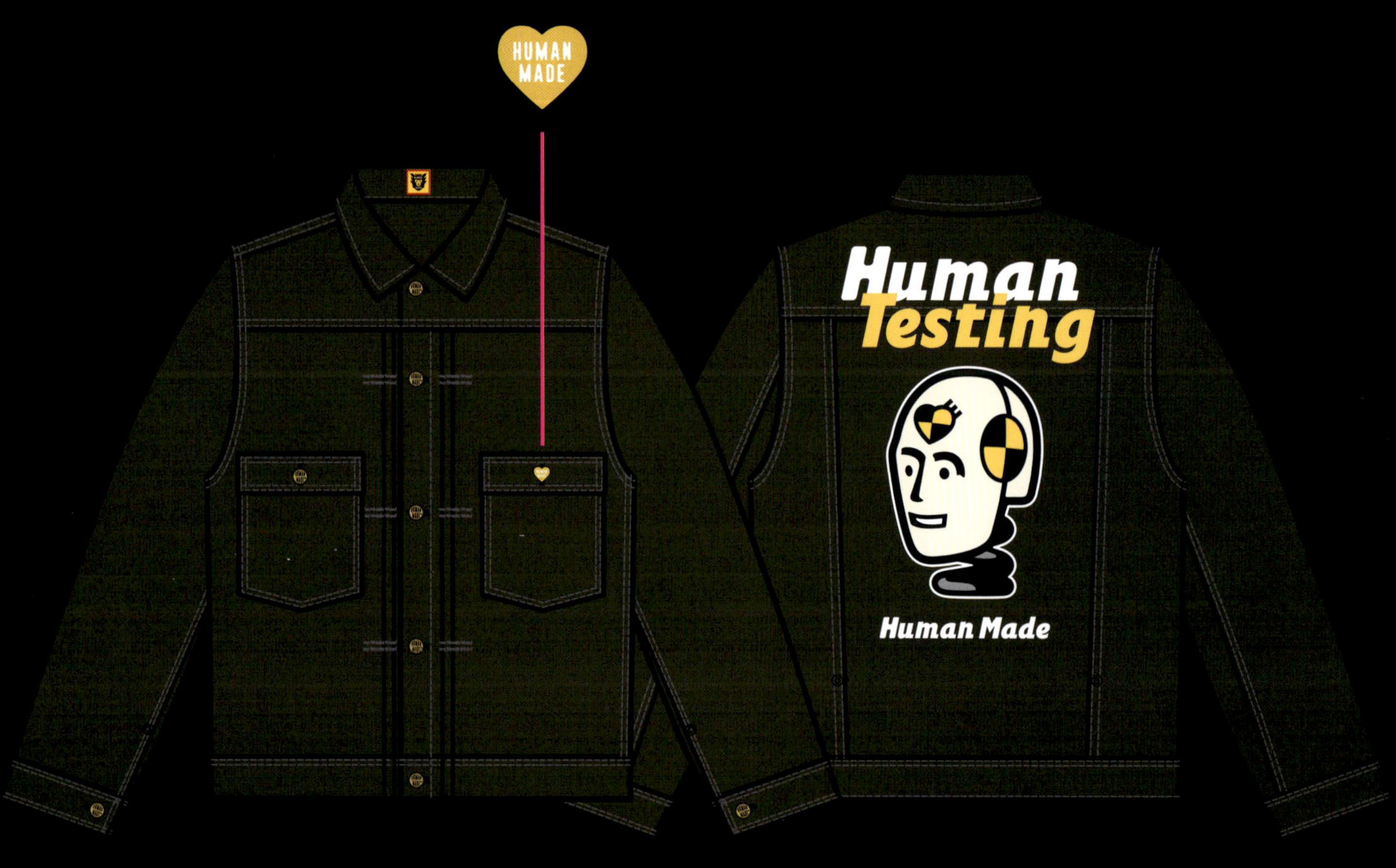

Human Made x A$AP Rocky
"HUMAN TESTING"
capsule collection, denim jacket

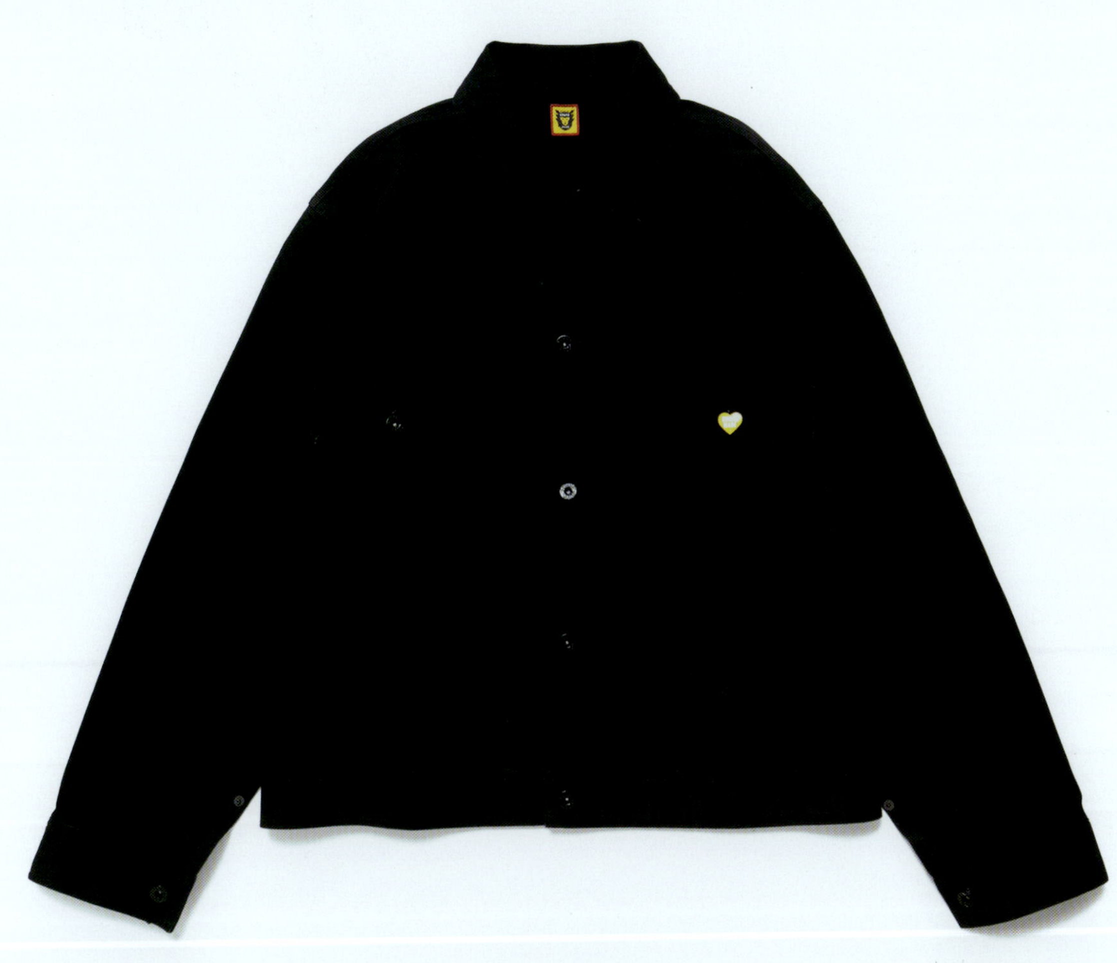

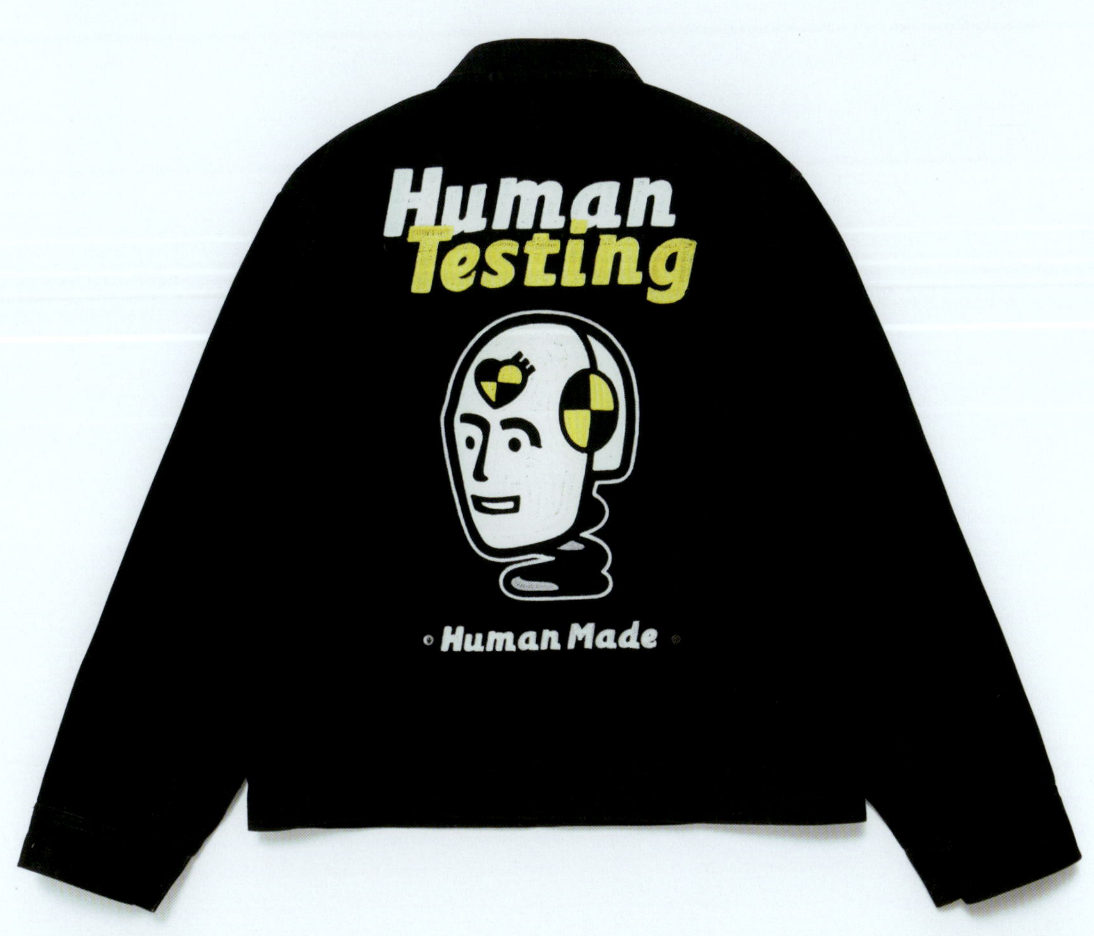
Human
Testing
Human Made

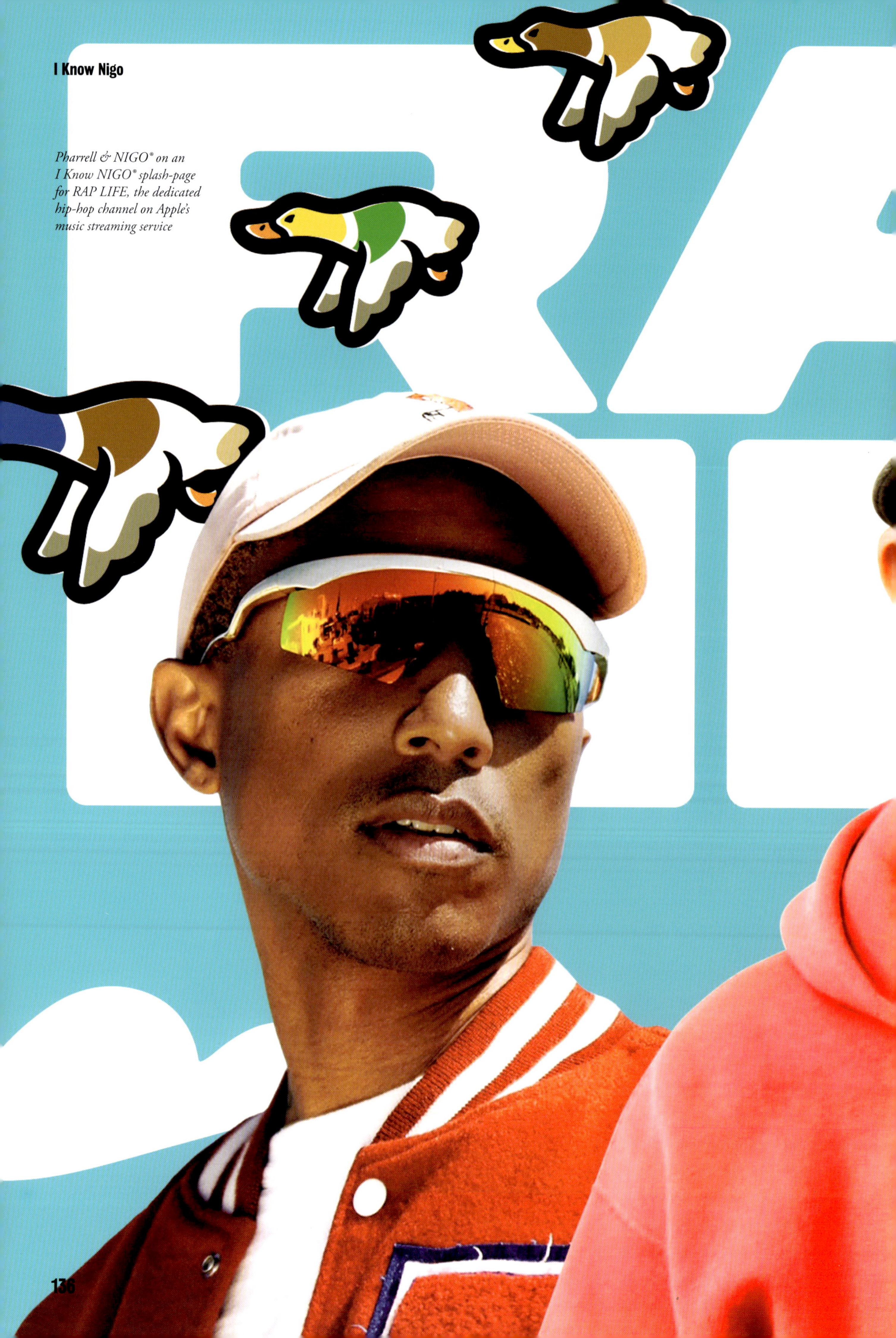

Pharrell & NIGO® on an I Know NIGO® splash-page for RAP LIFE, the dedicated hip-hop channel on Apple's music streaming service

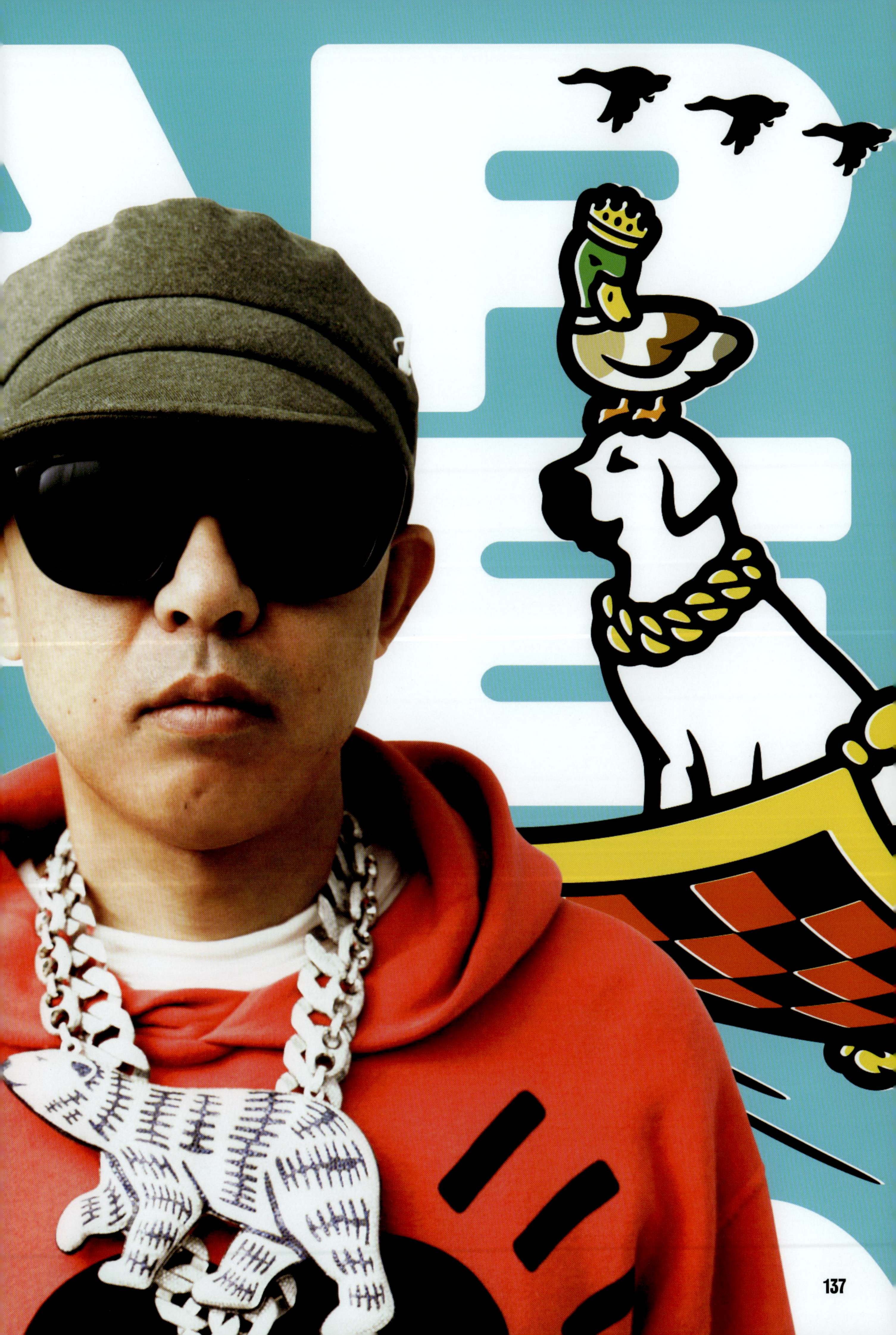

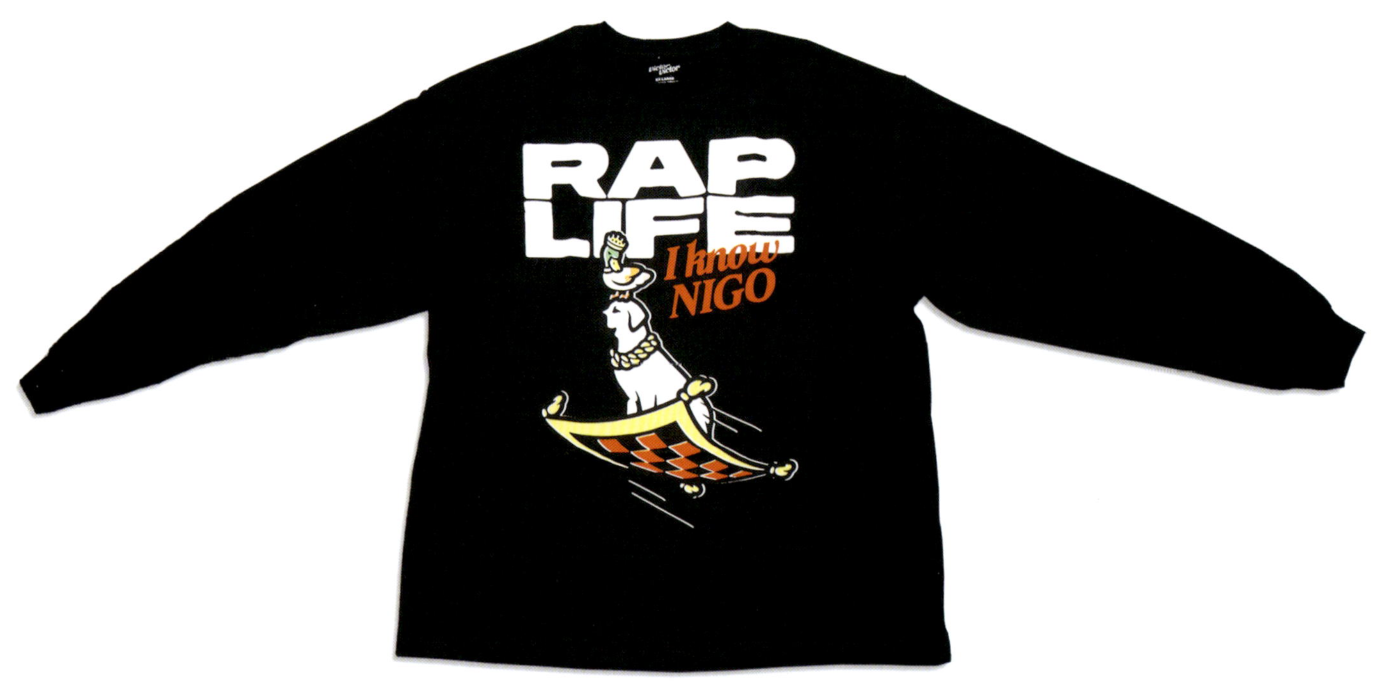
RAP
LIFE
I know
NIGO

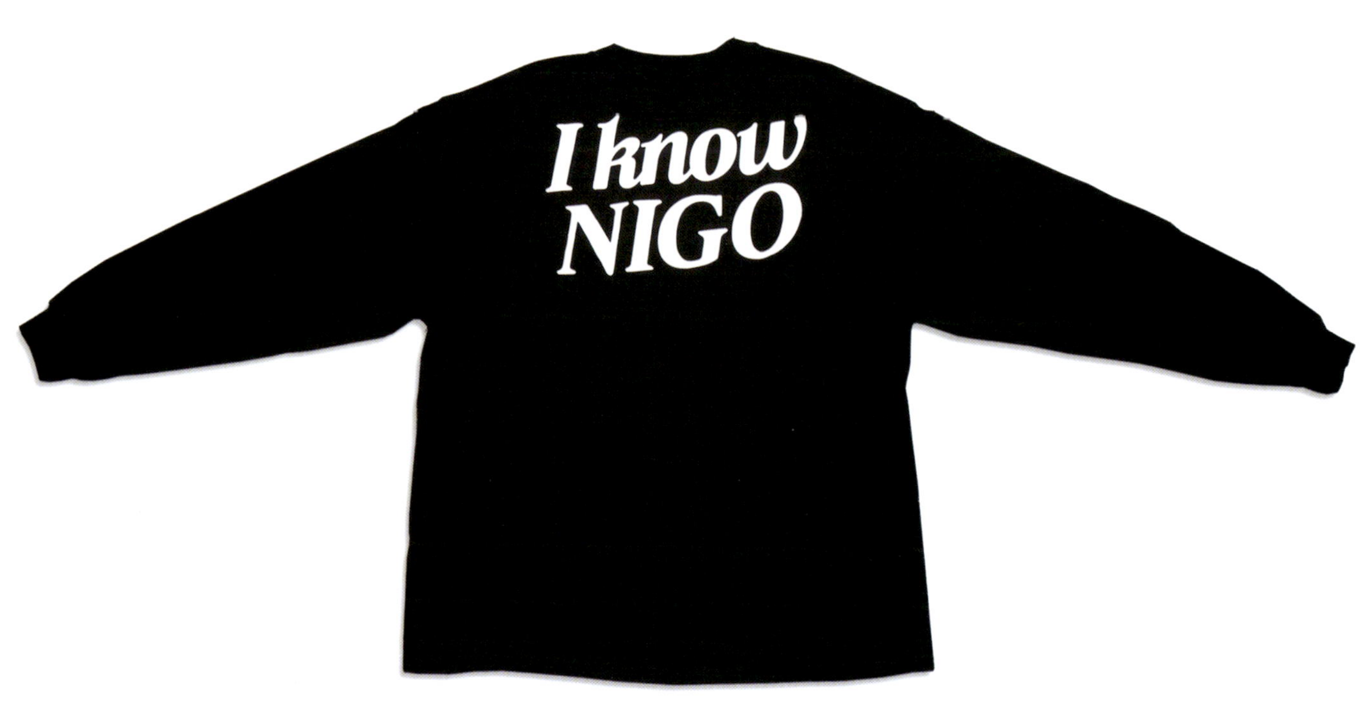
I know
NIGO

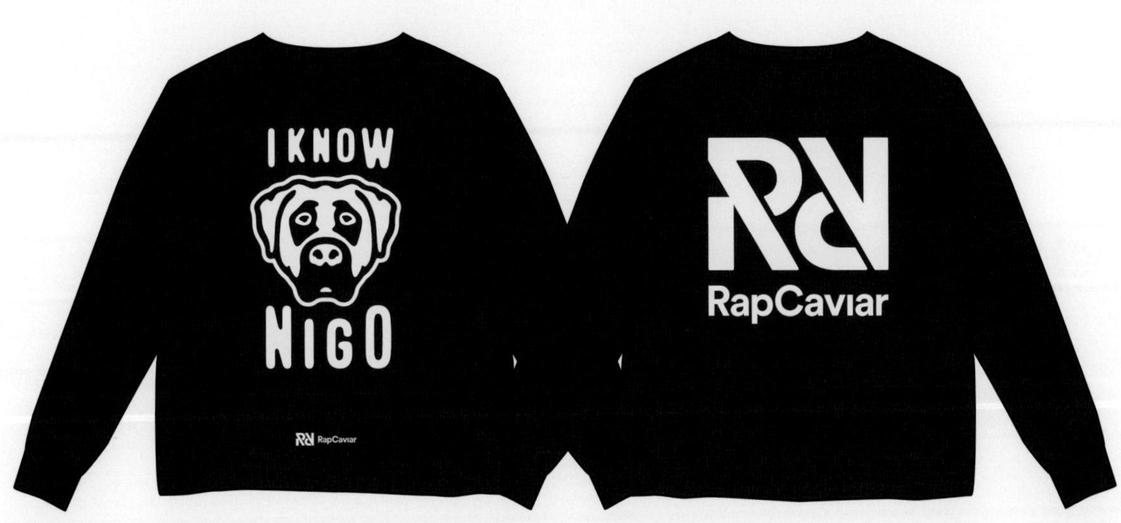

I Know NIGO® x RAP LIFE (Apple) and RapCaviar (Spotify) t-shirt collaborations

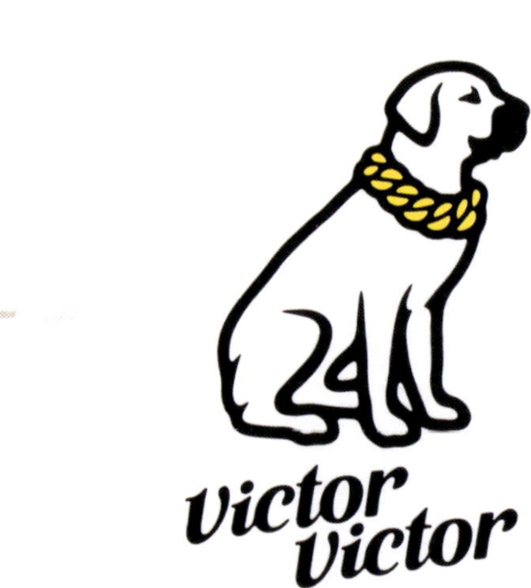
Victor
Victor

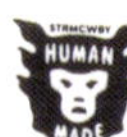
HUMAN
MADE

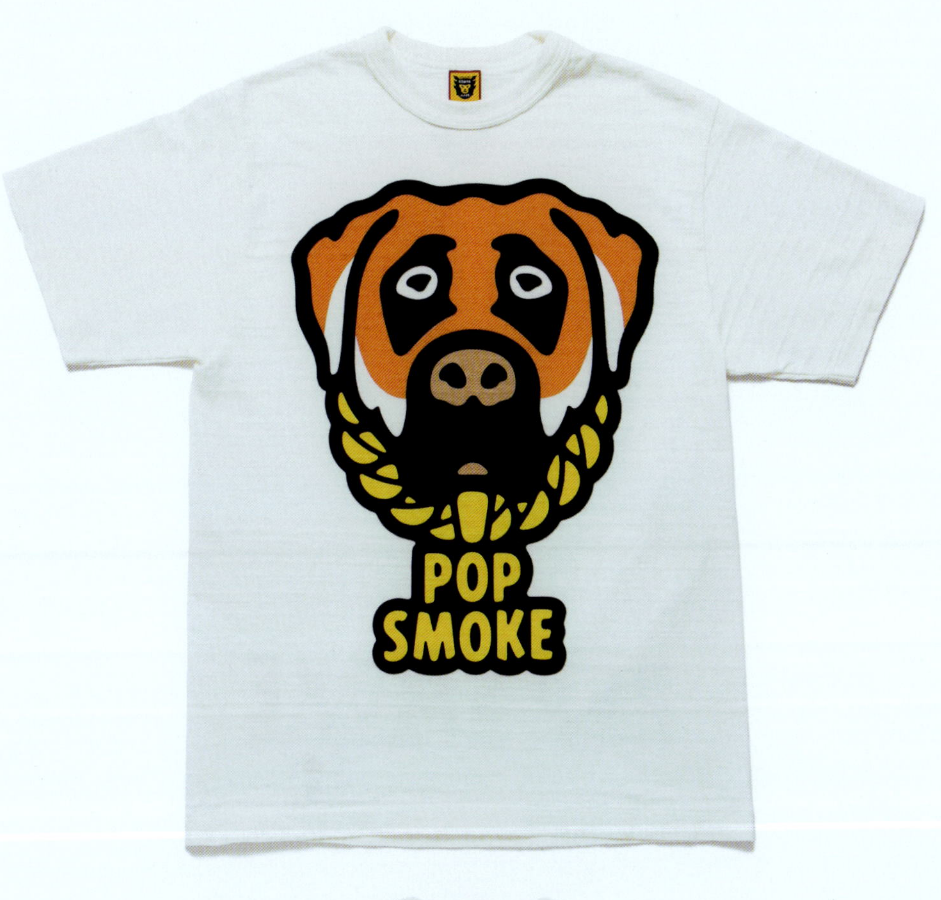

I Know NIGO® x
Human Made x Pop
Smoke t-shirts

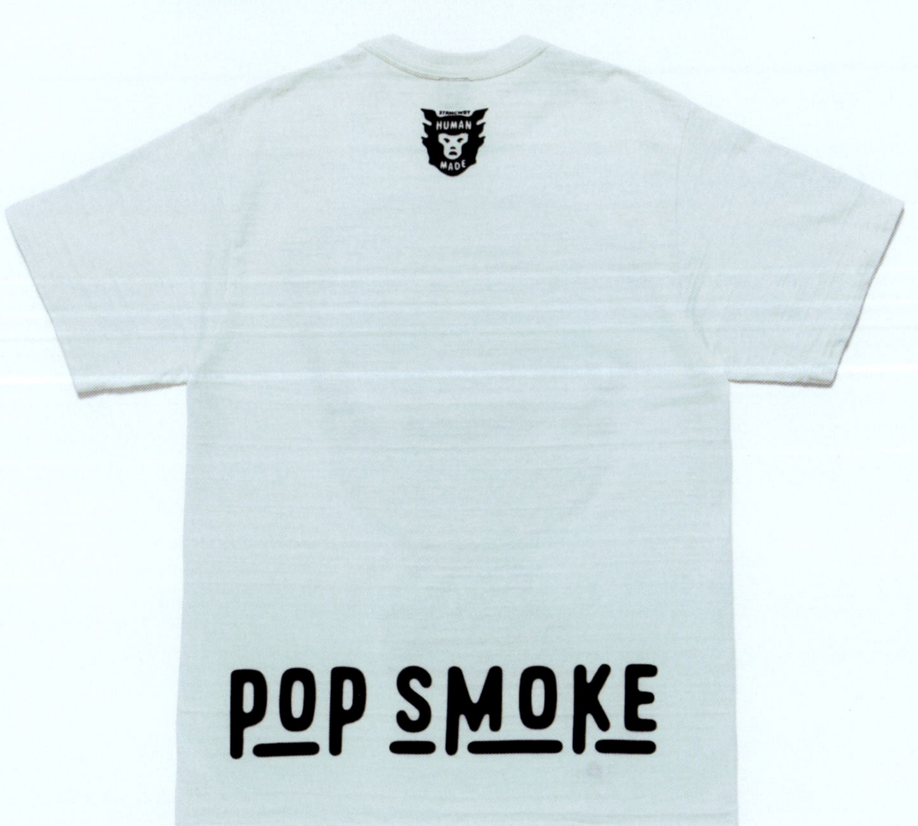

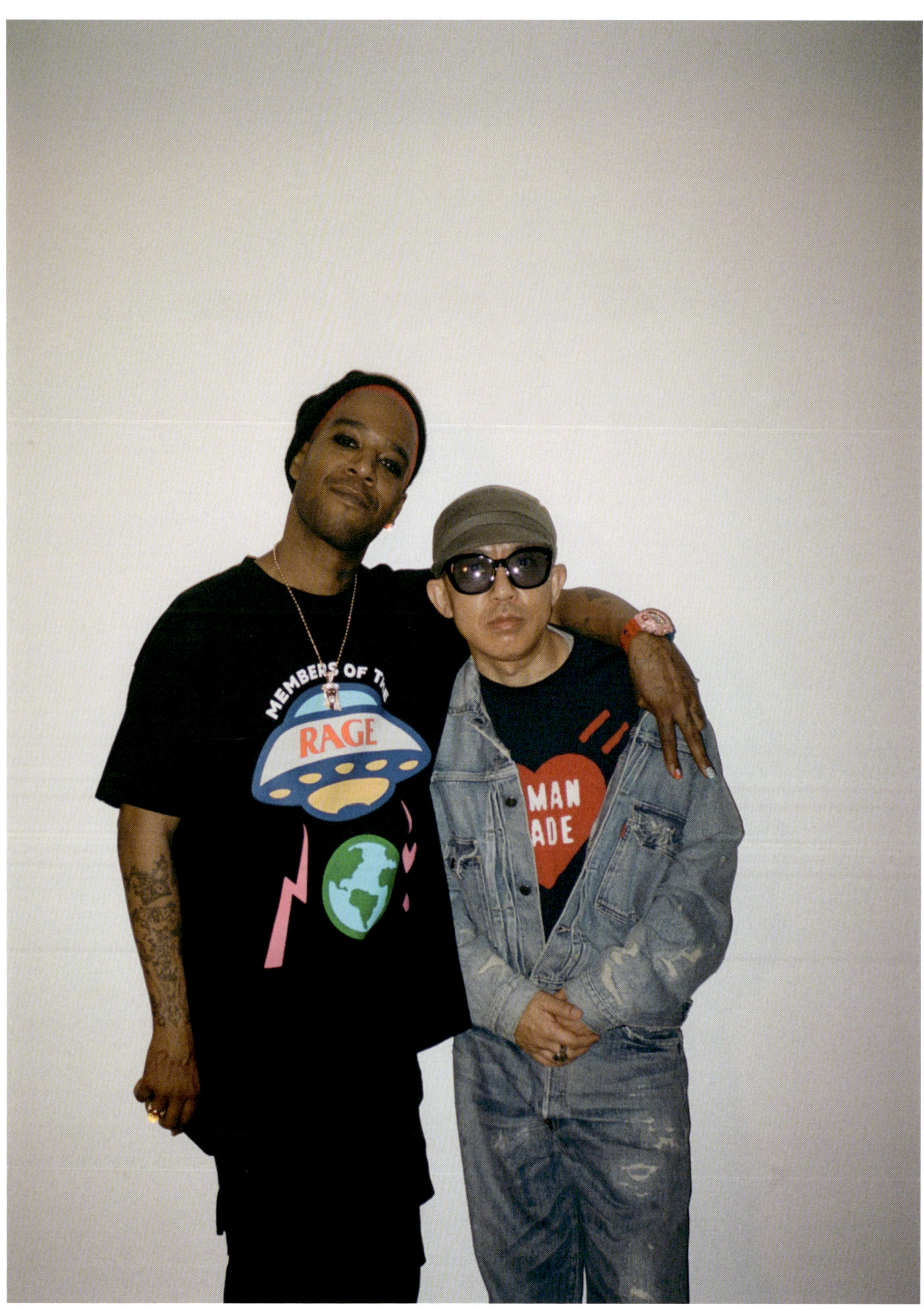
MEMBERS OF TH
RAGE

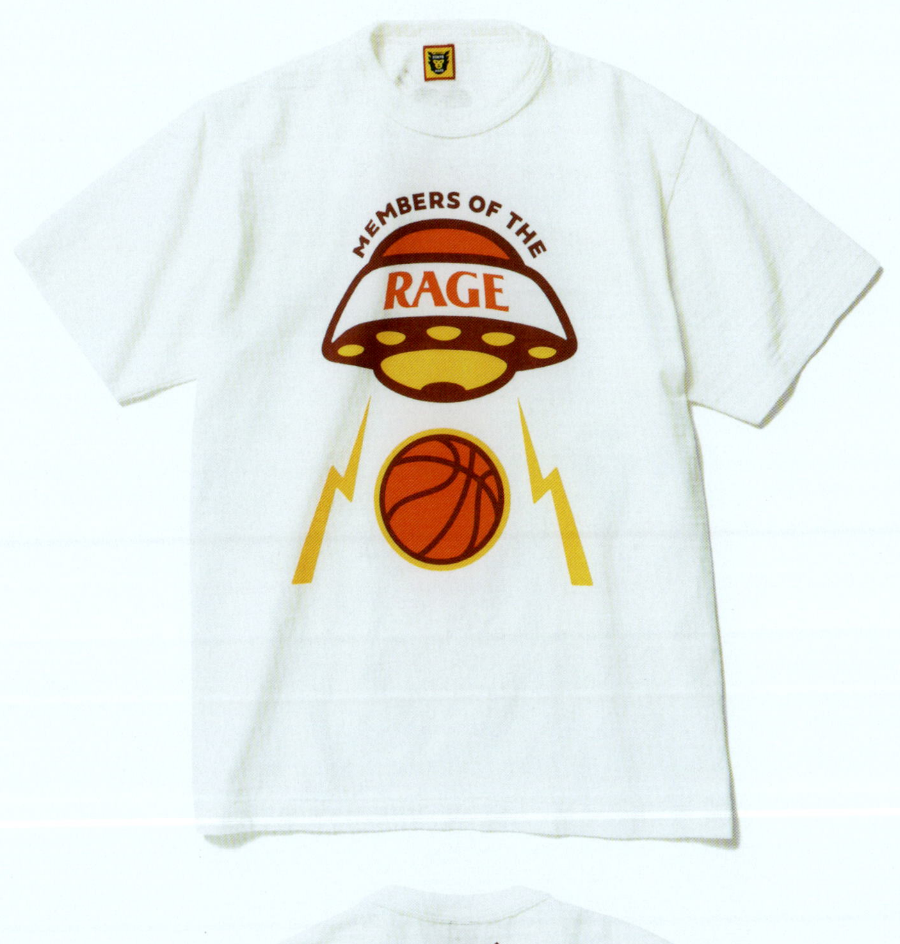

I Know NIGO® x Kid Cudi x Human Made "Members of the Rage" t-shirts, featuring a rare basketball-themed release for the 2022 NBA All-Star Weekend

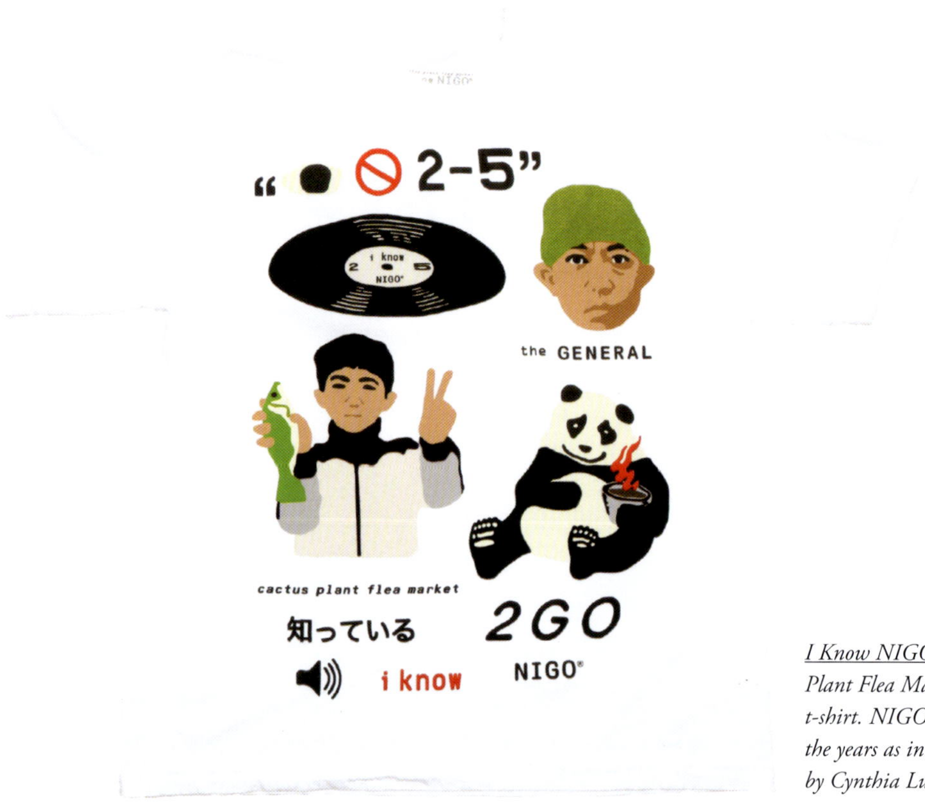

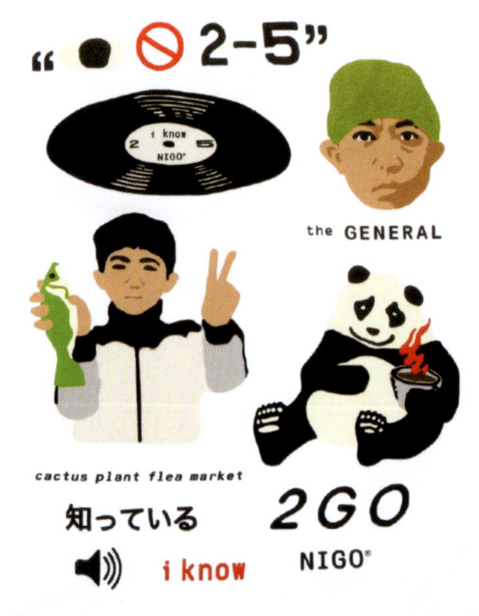

I Know NIGO® x Cactus Plant Flea Market t-shirt. NIGO® through the years as interpreted by Cynthia Lu

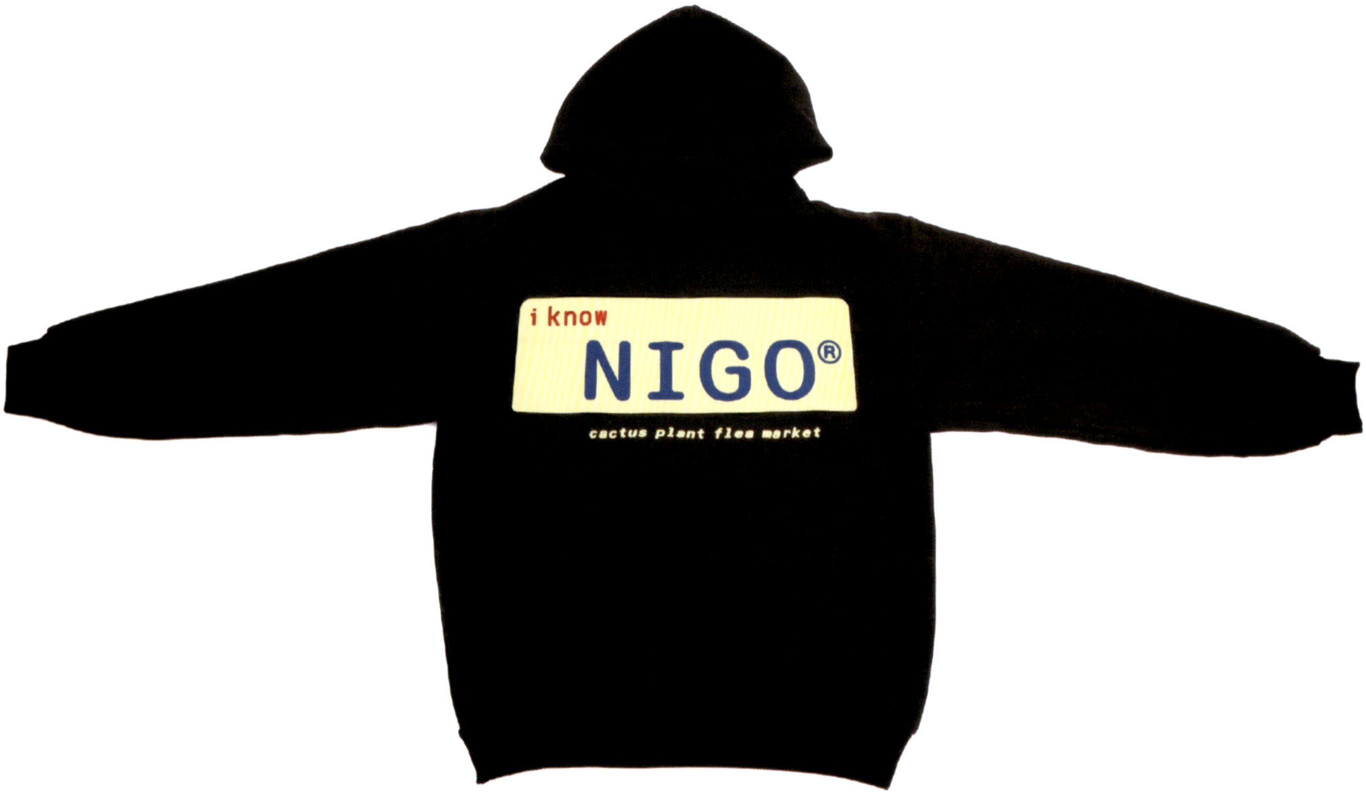

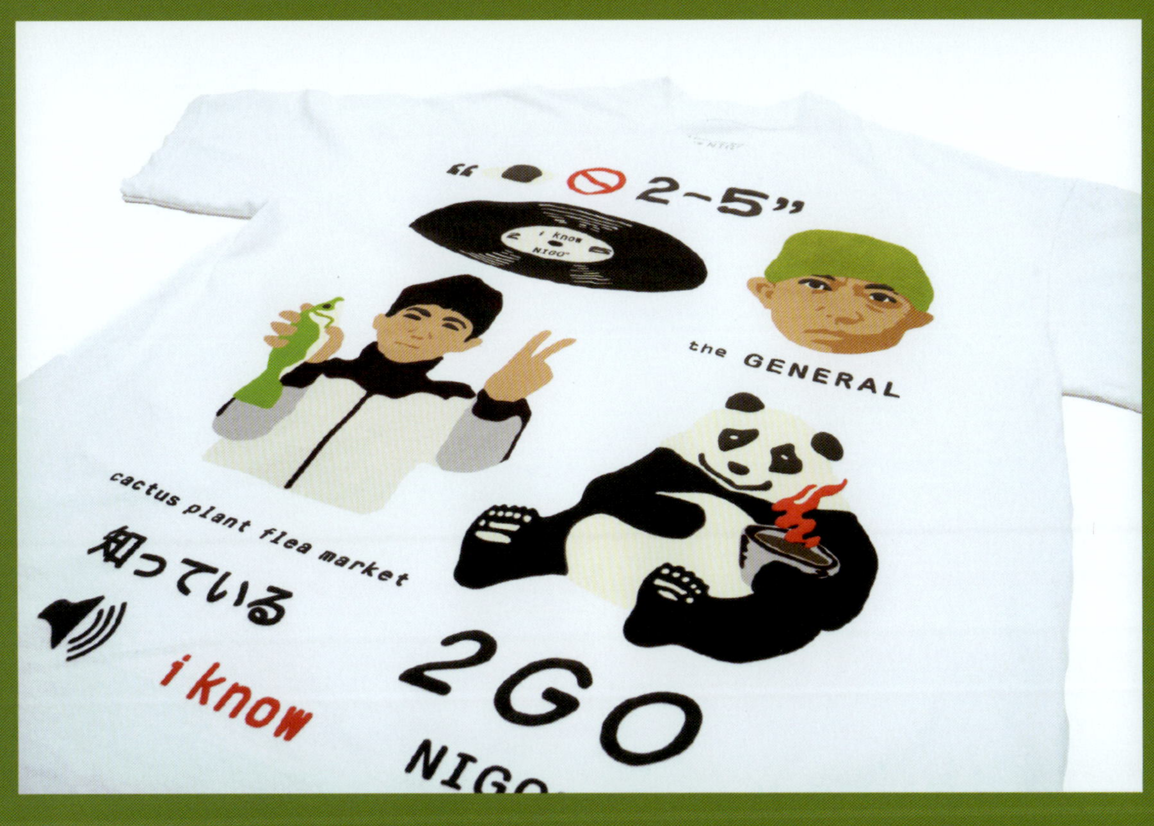
"2-5"
i know
NIGO®
the GENERAL
cactus plant flea market
知っている
i know
2GO

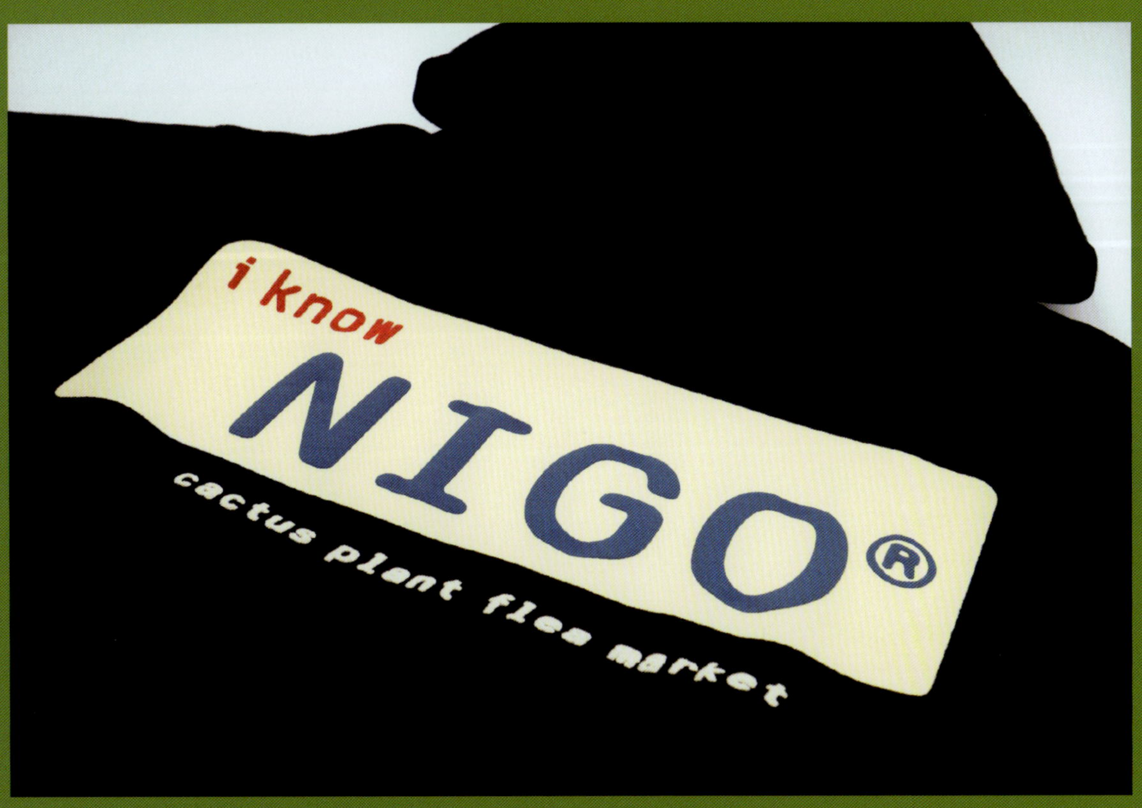
i know
NIGO®
cactus plant flea market

I Know NIGO® x Human Made x Verdy Friends & Family varsity jacket, designed for ComplexCon 2022, November 20, 2022, in Long Beach, California

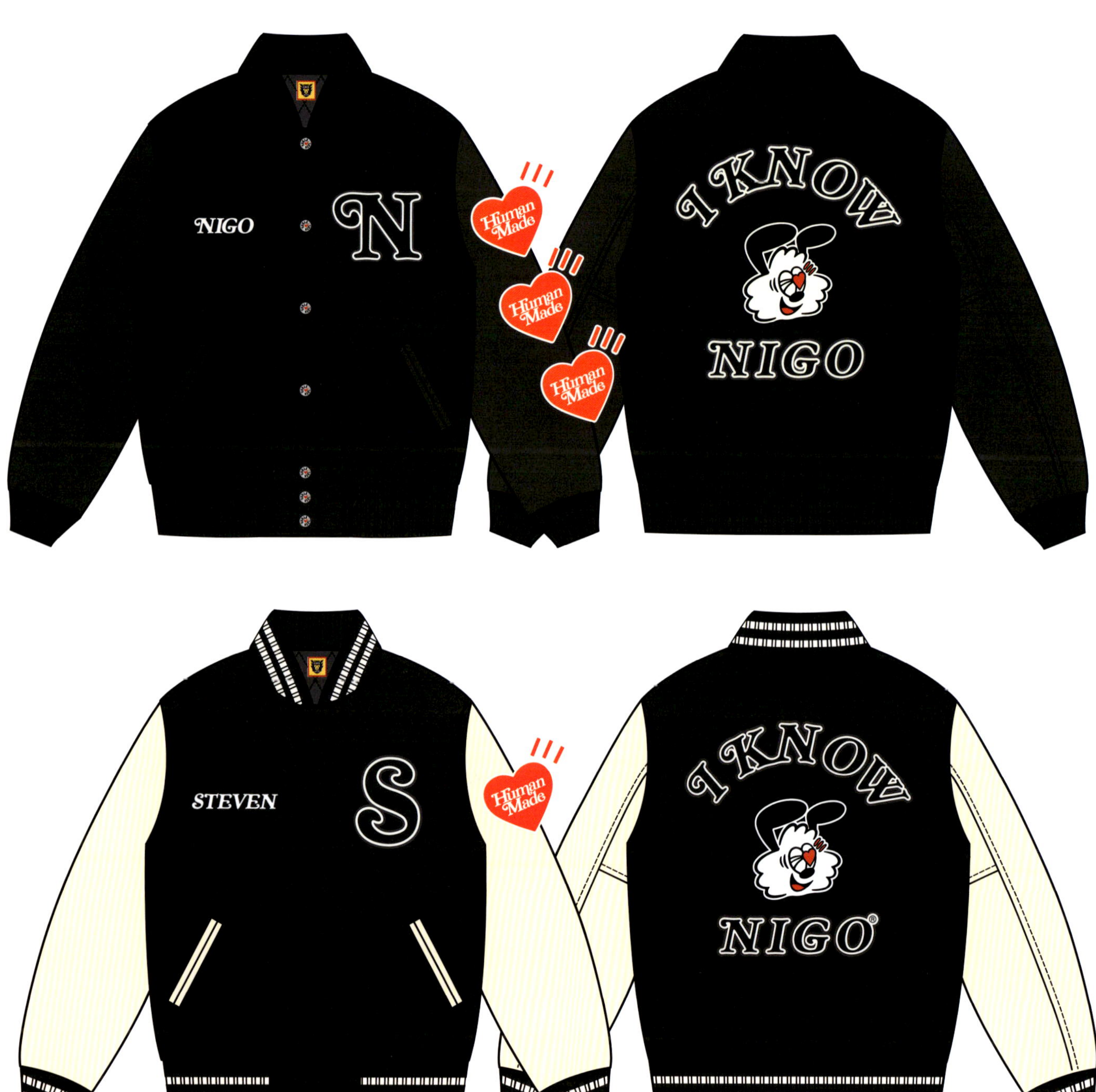

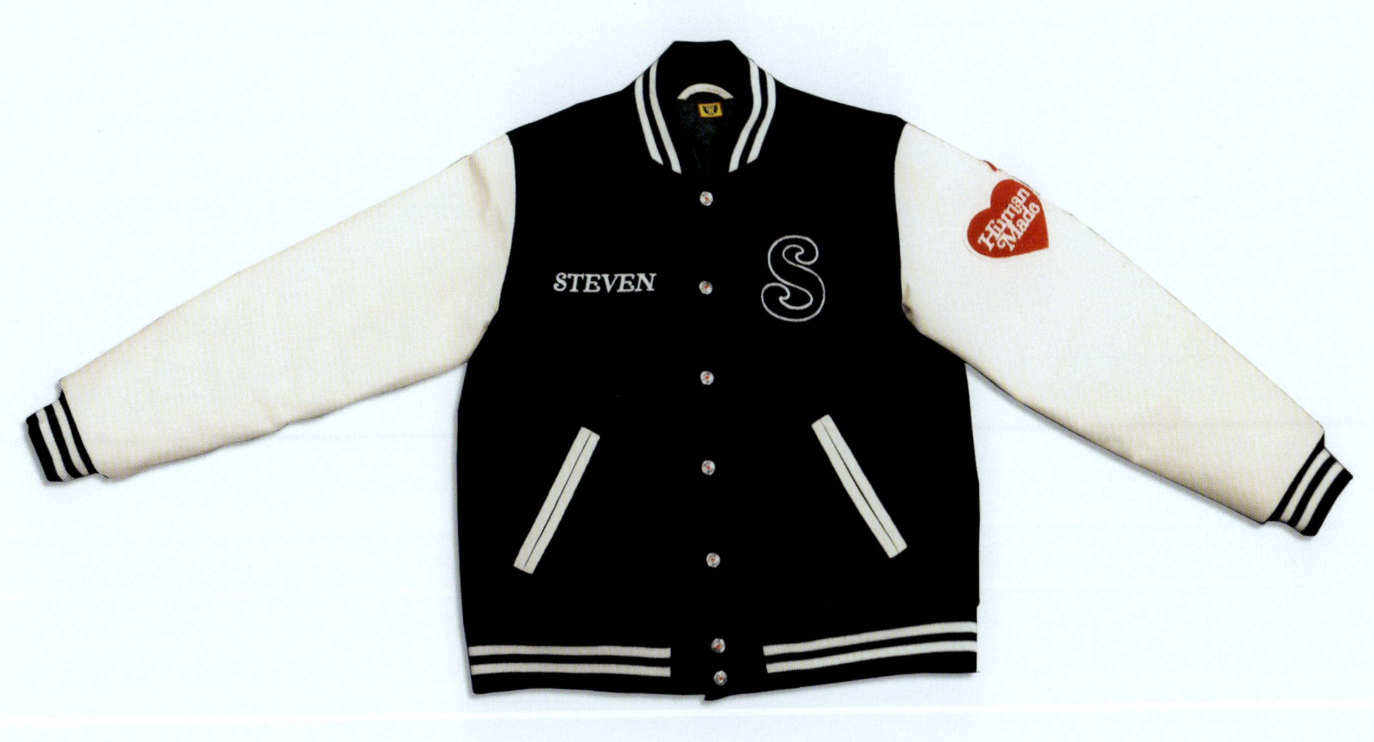
STEVEN
S
Human Made

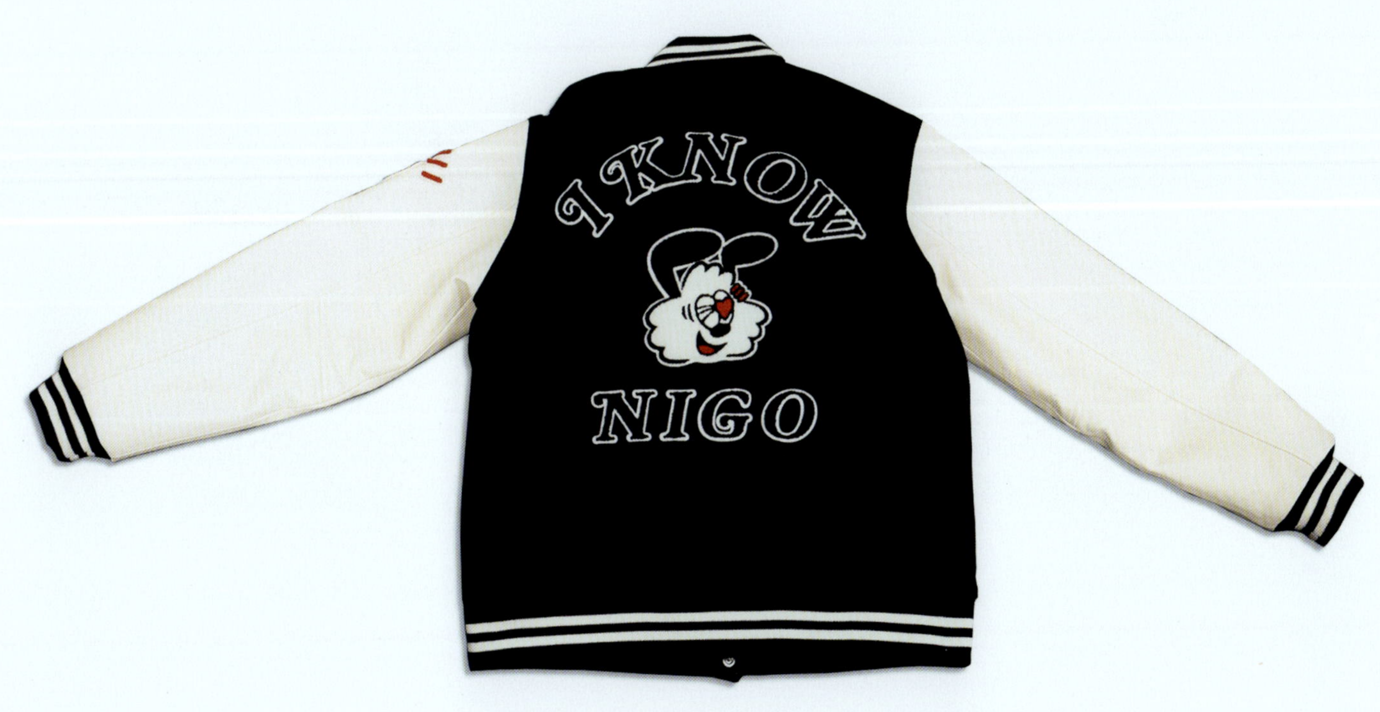
I KNOW
NIGO

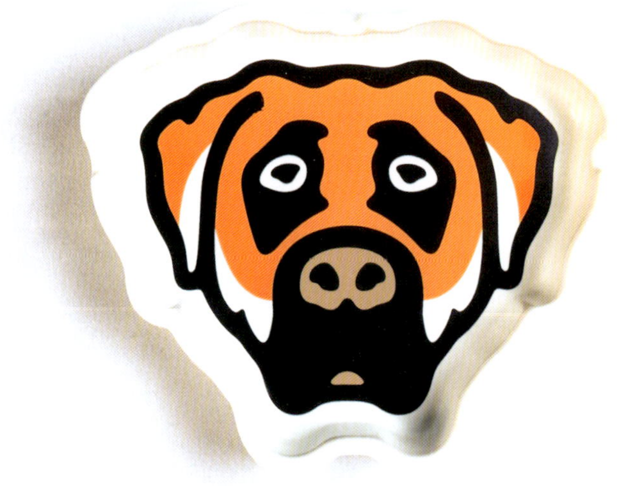

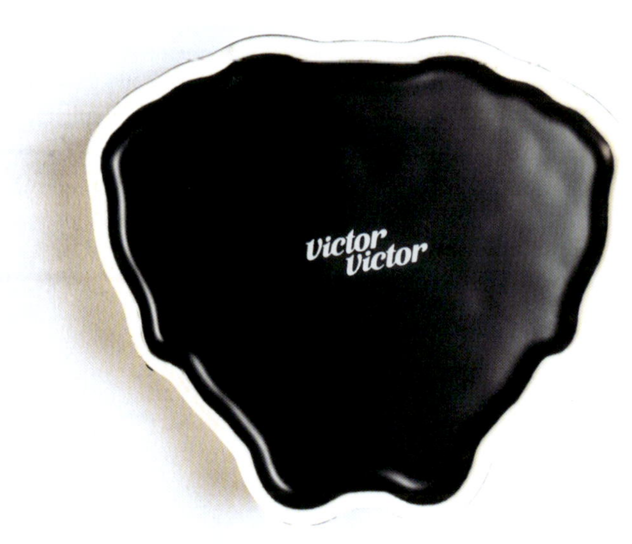

The full range of limited-edition VICTOR VICTOR home goods and other collectibles released at the I Know NIGO® pop-up (in partnership with Shopify) which opened in Soho, New York City on March 26, 2022.

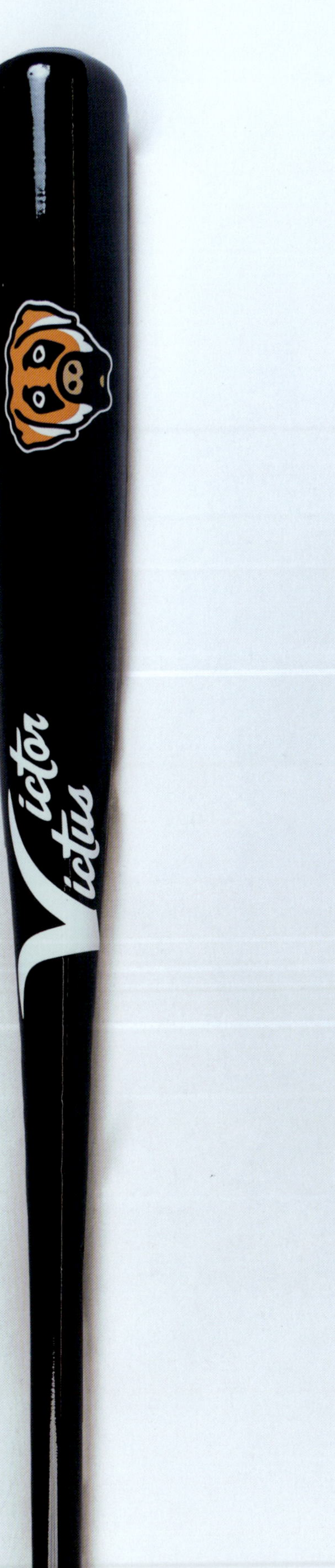
Victor Victus
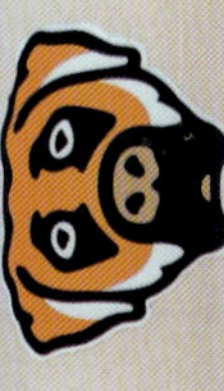
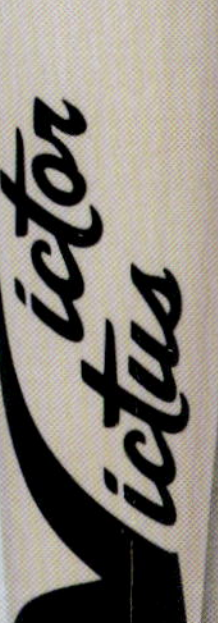
Victor Victus

The products included ash trays, dog dishes and leashes, skate decks and baseball bats in partnership with Victus

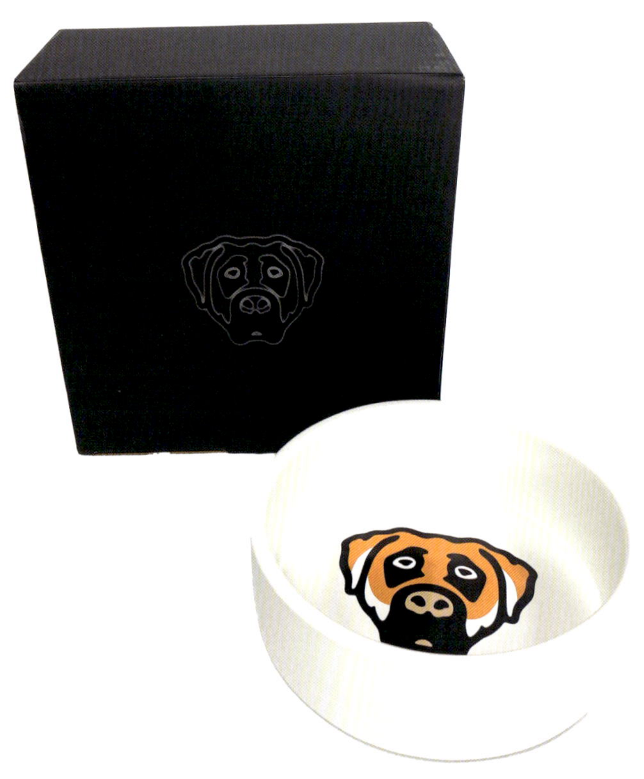

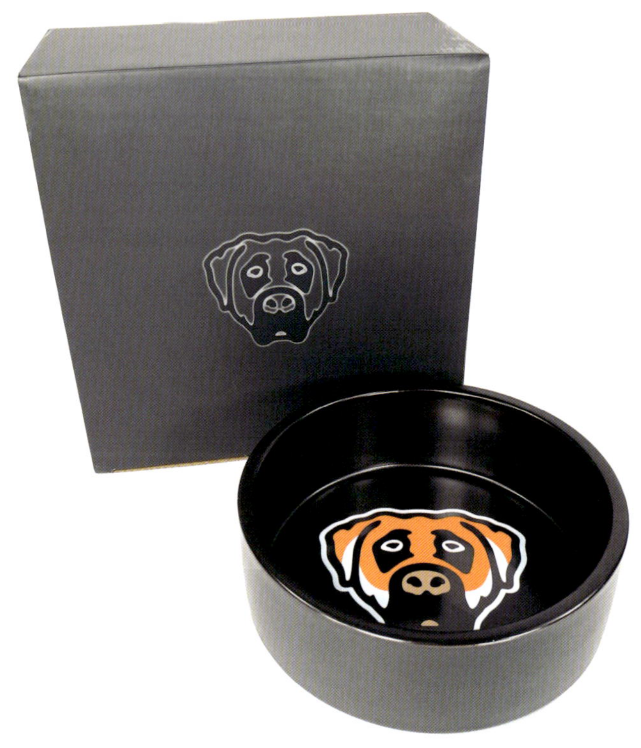

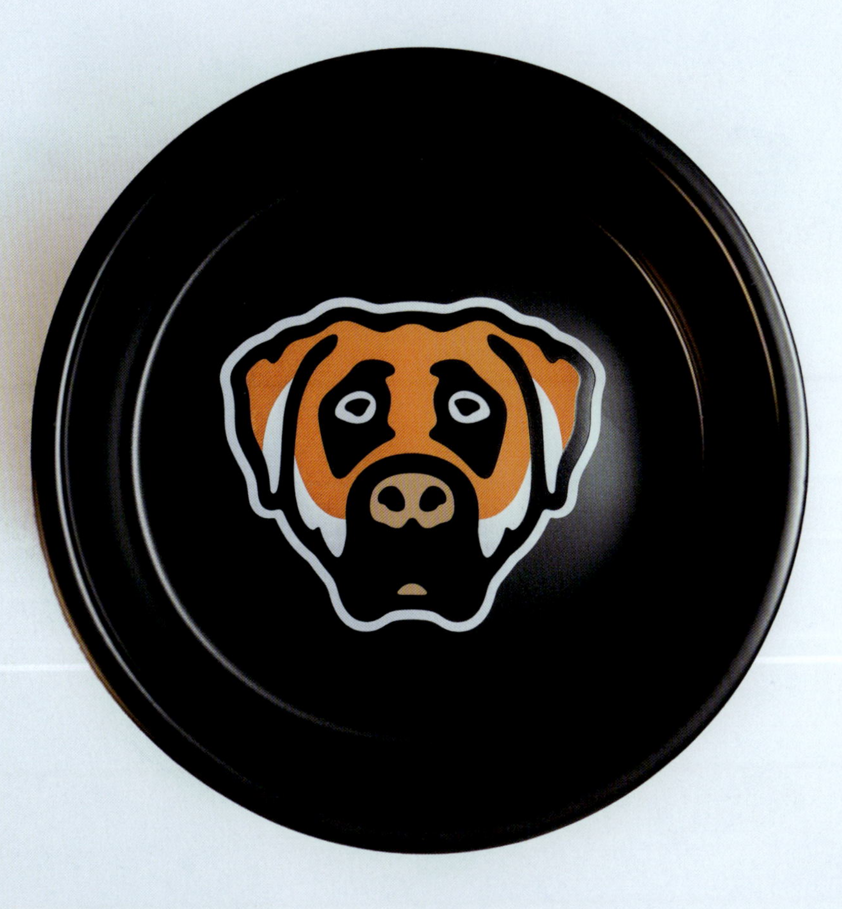

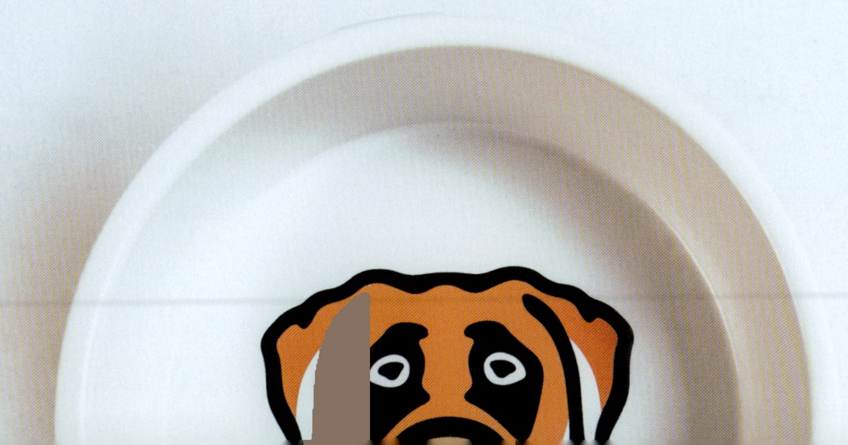

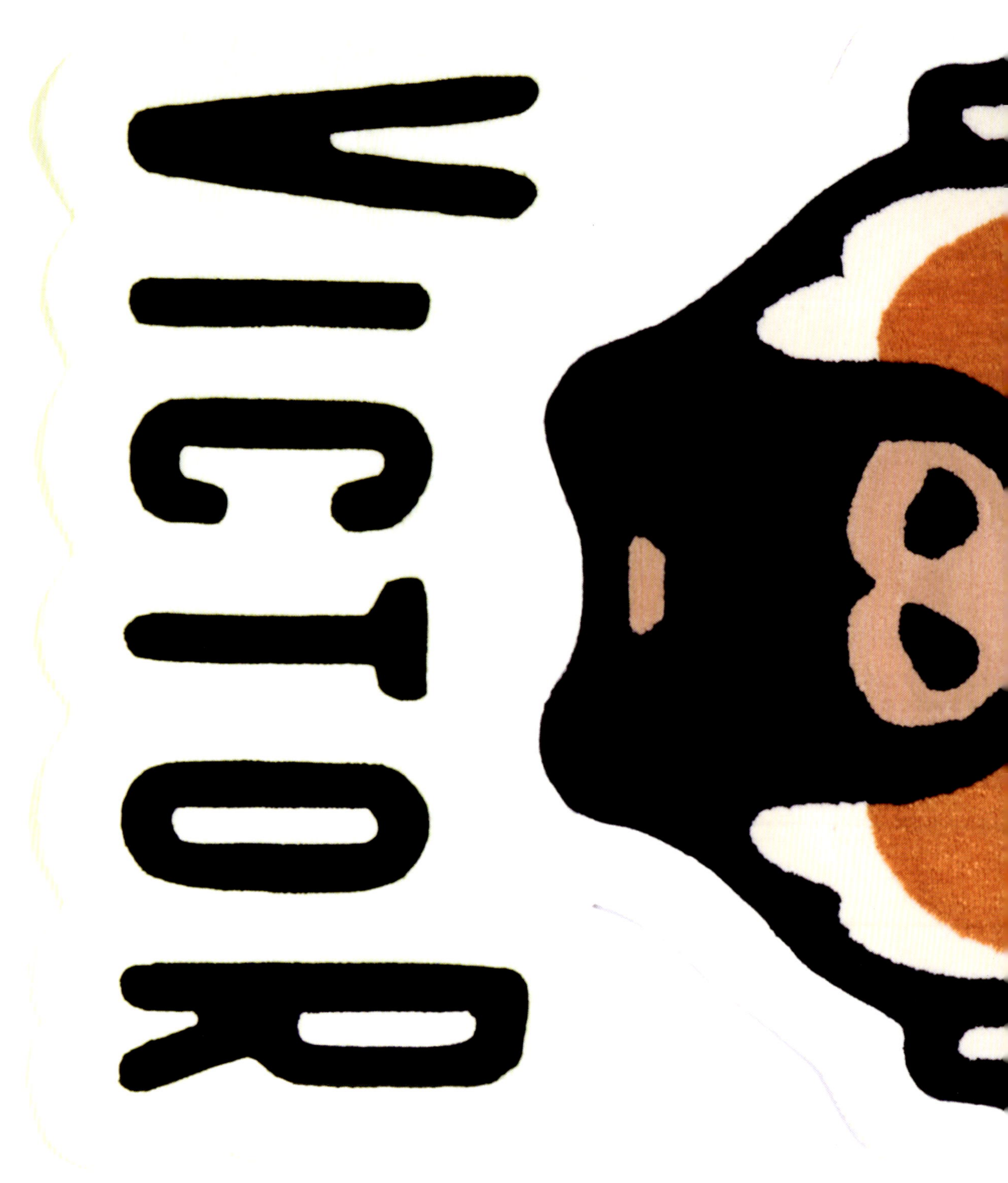
VICTOR

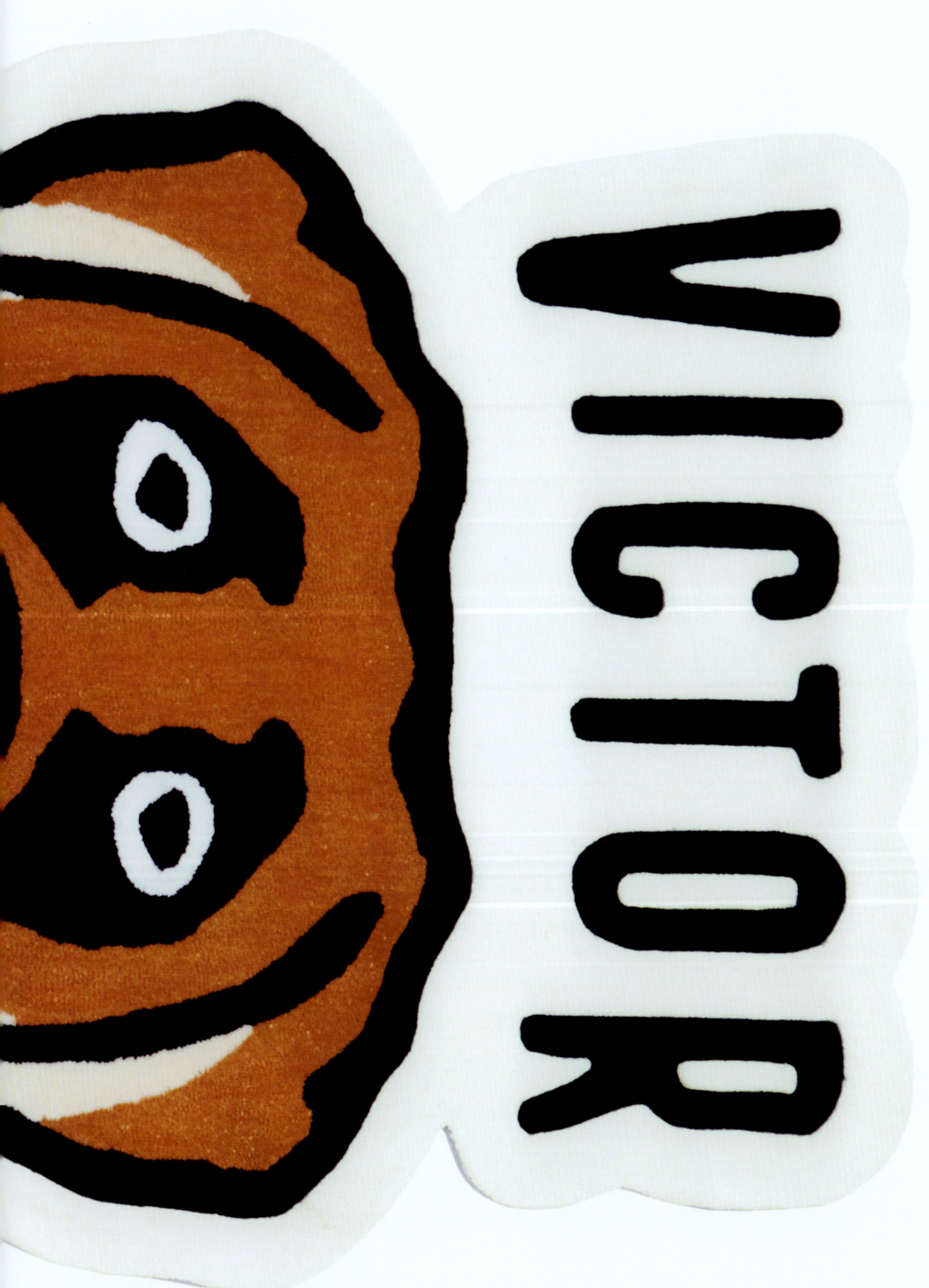
VICTOR

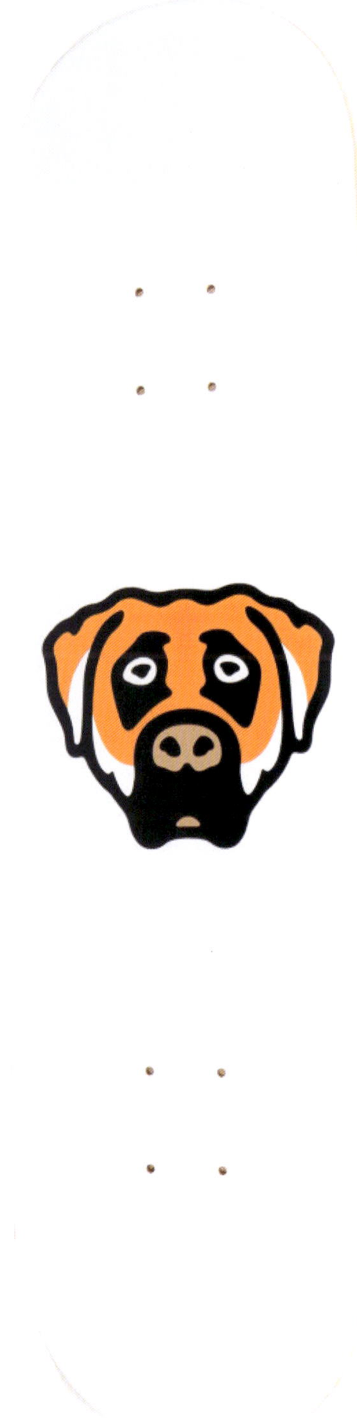

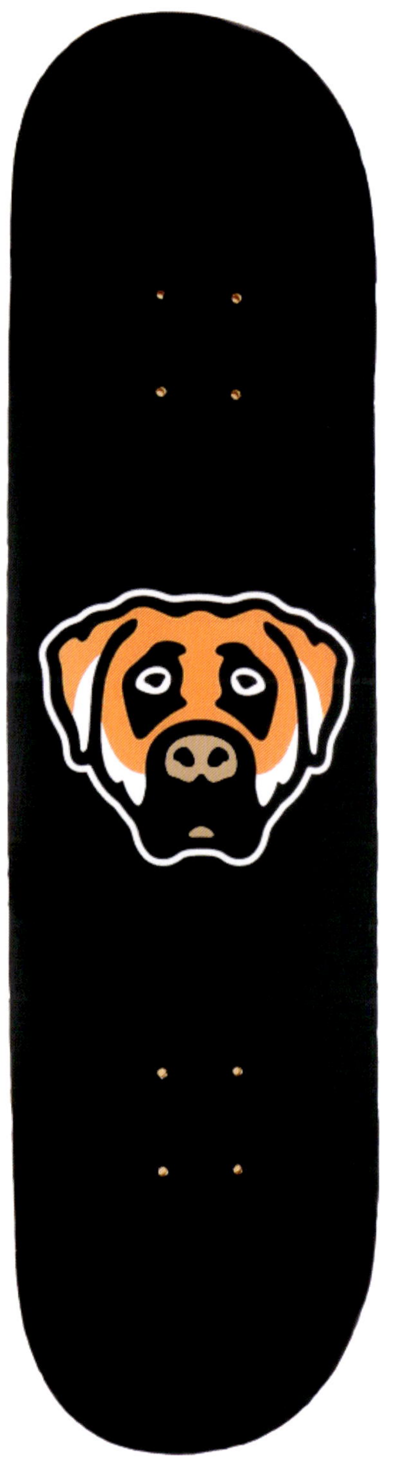

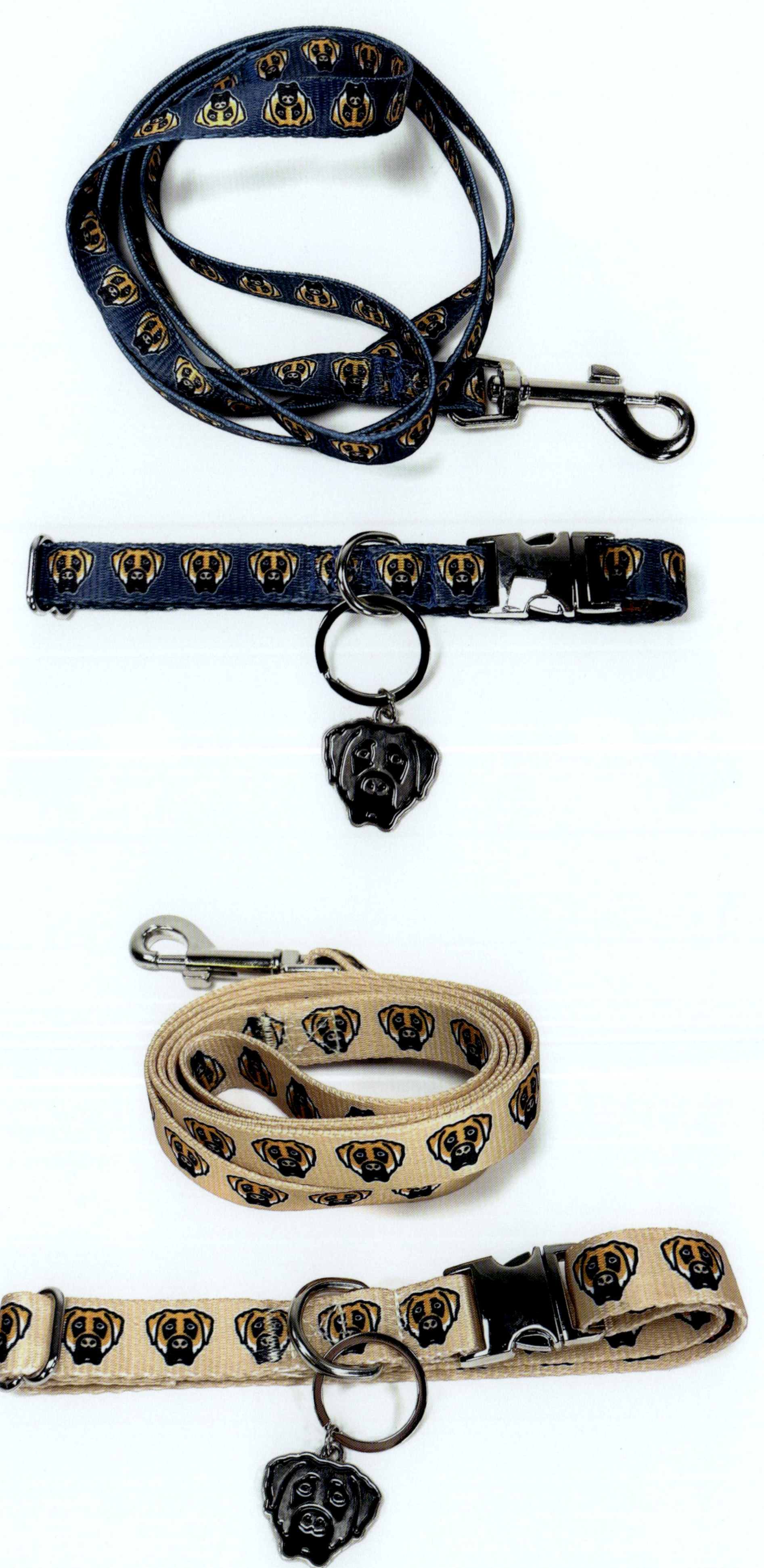

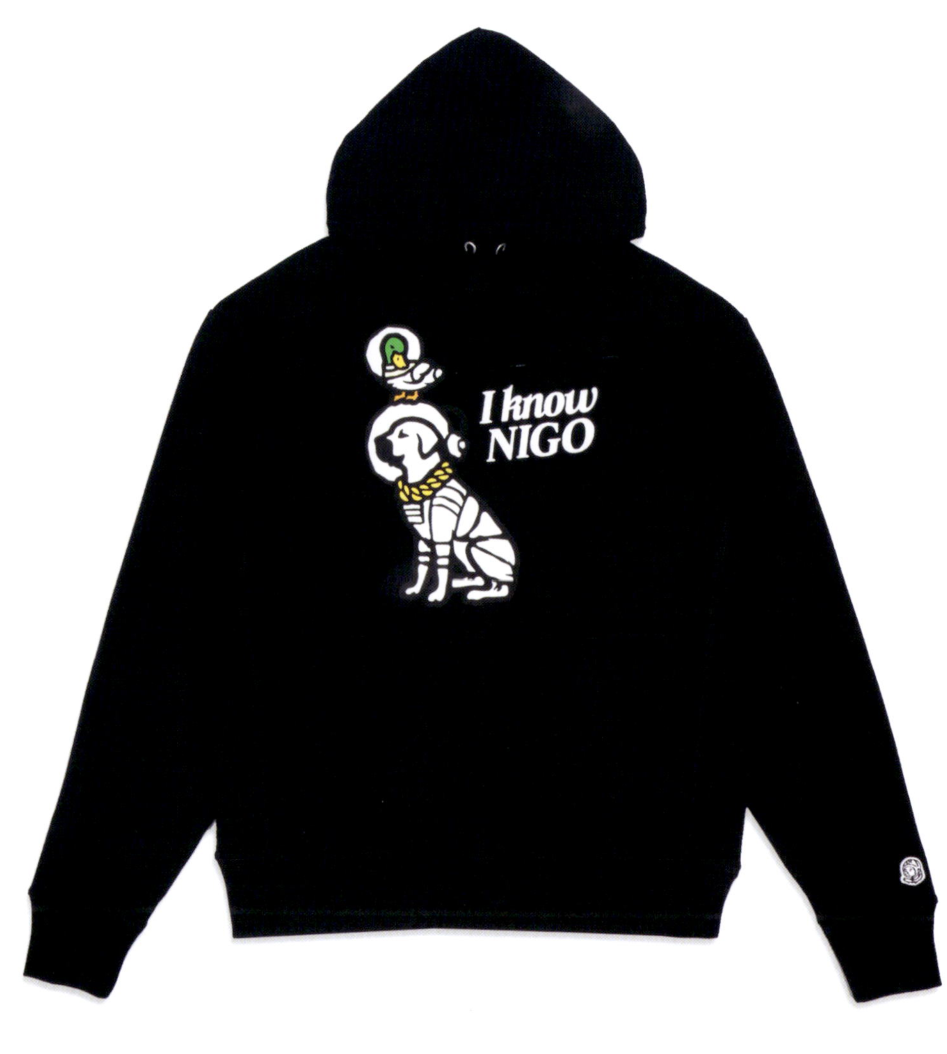
I know
NIGO

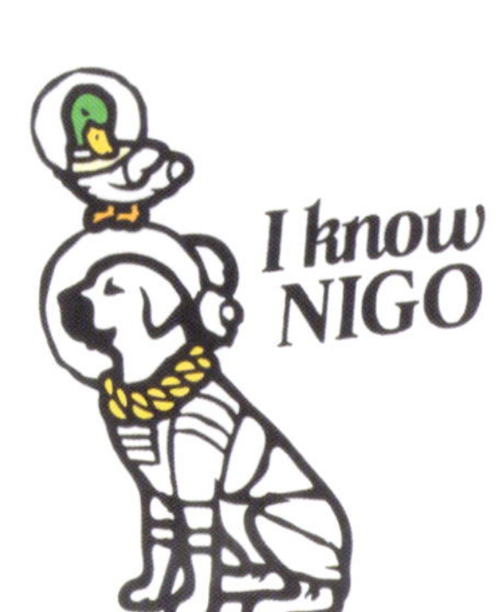
I know
NIGO

I Know NIGO® x Billionaire Boys Club hoodies & t-shirts

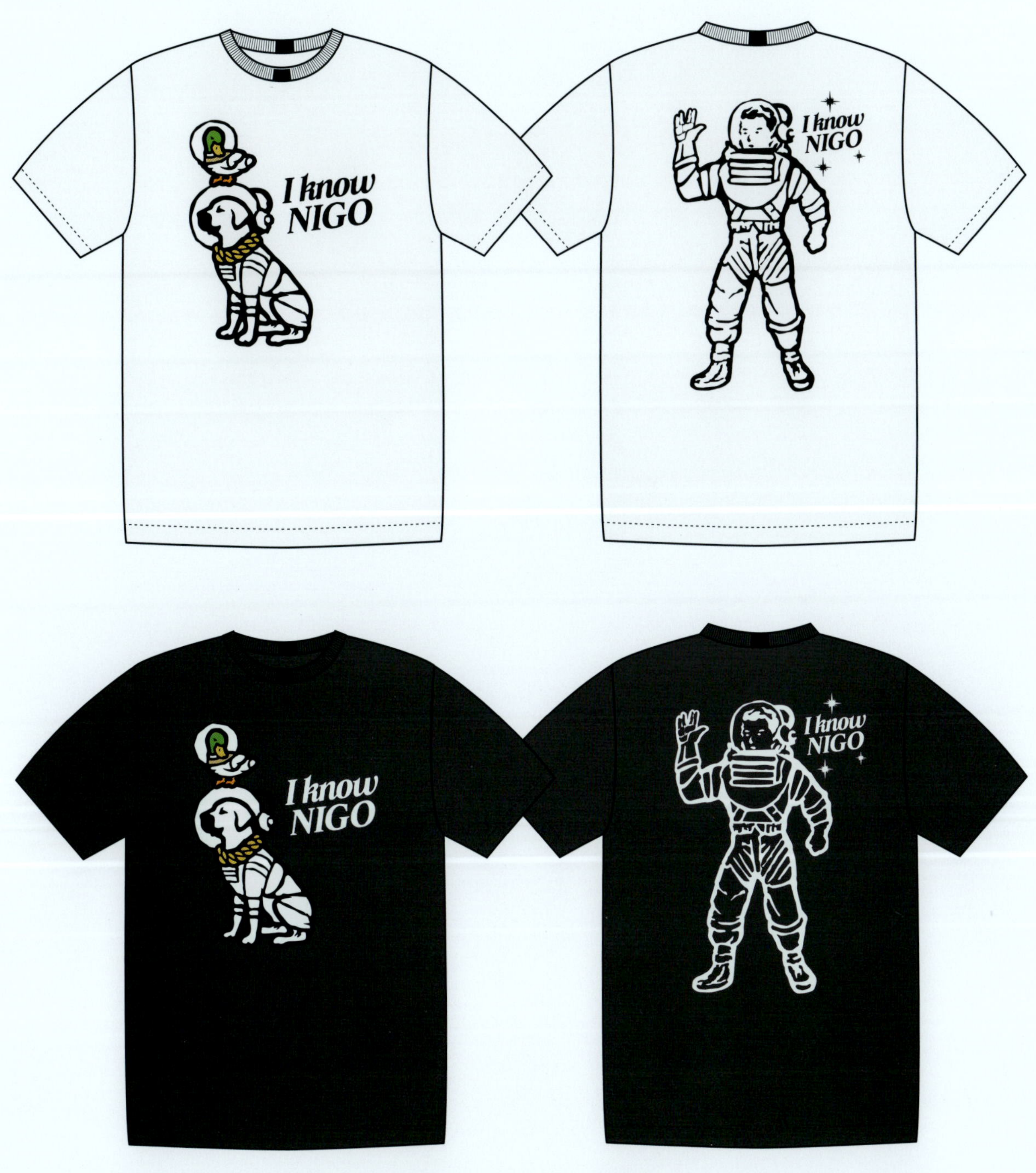

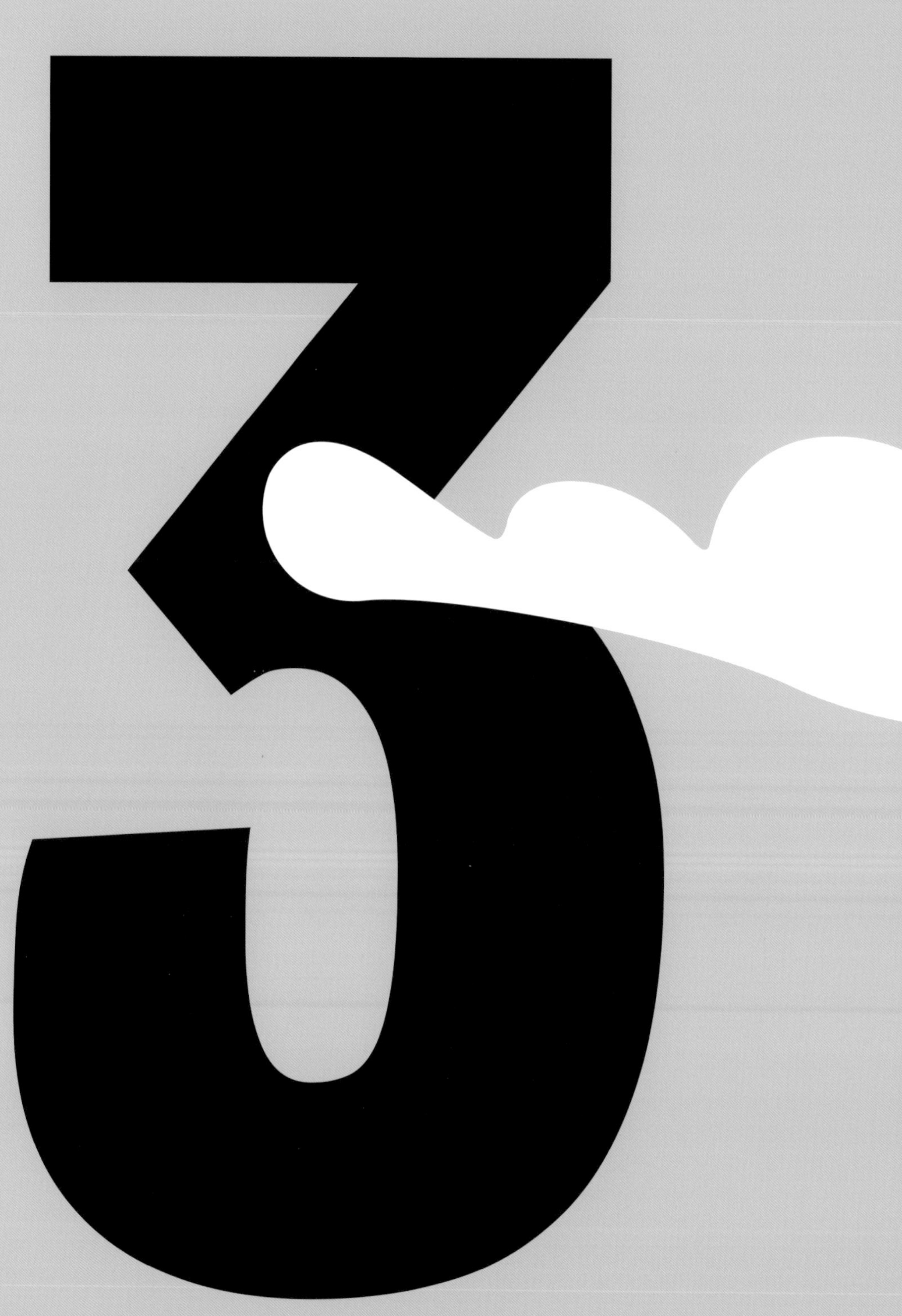

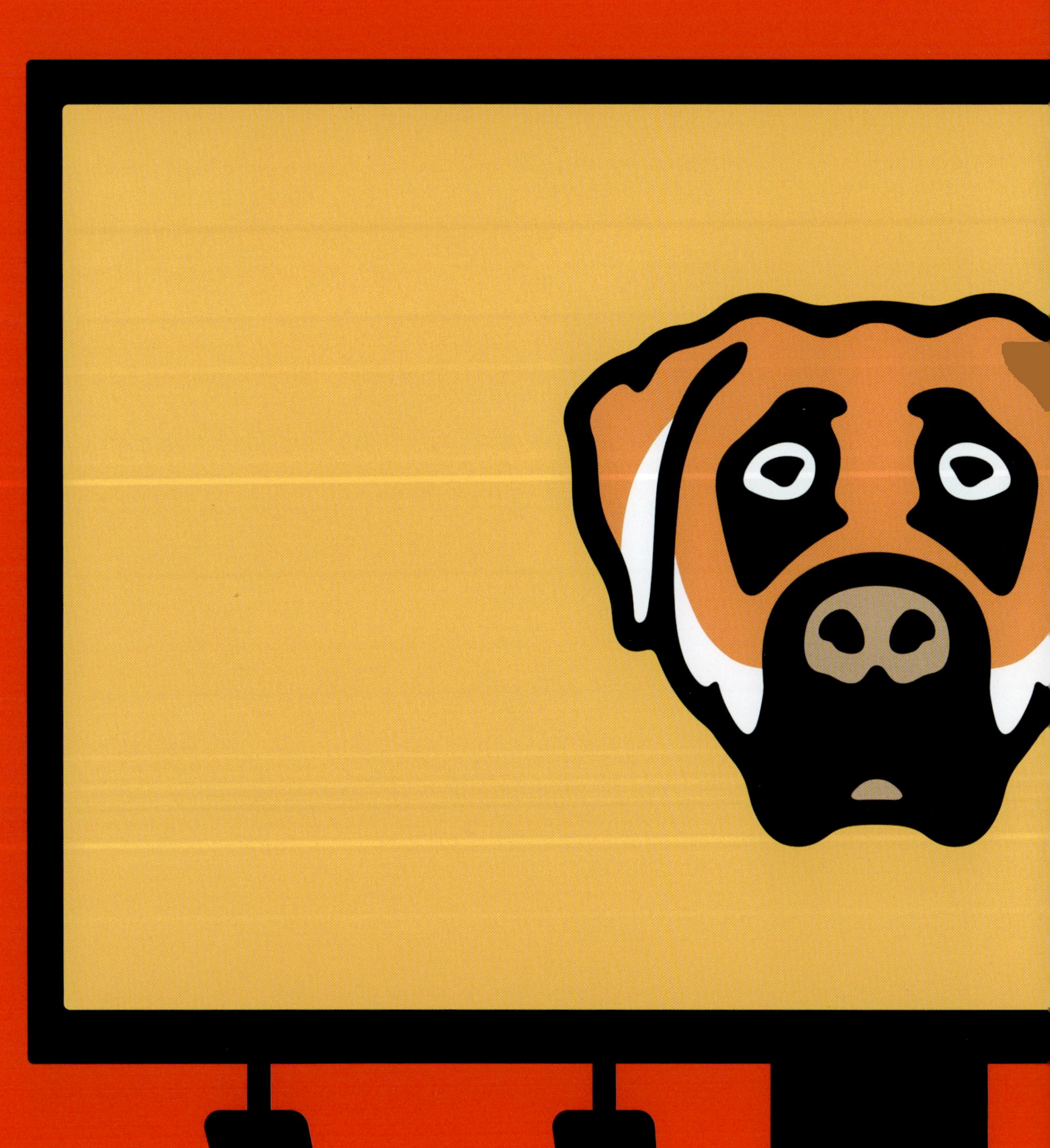

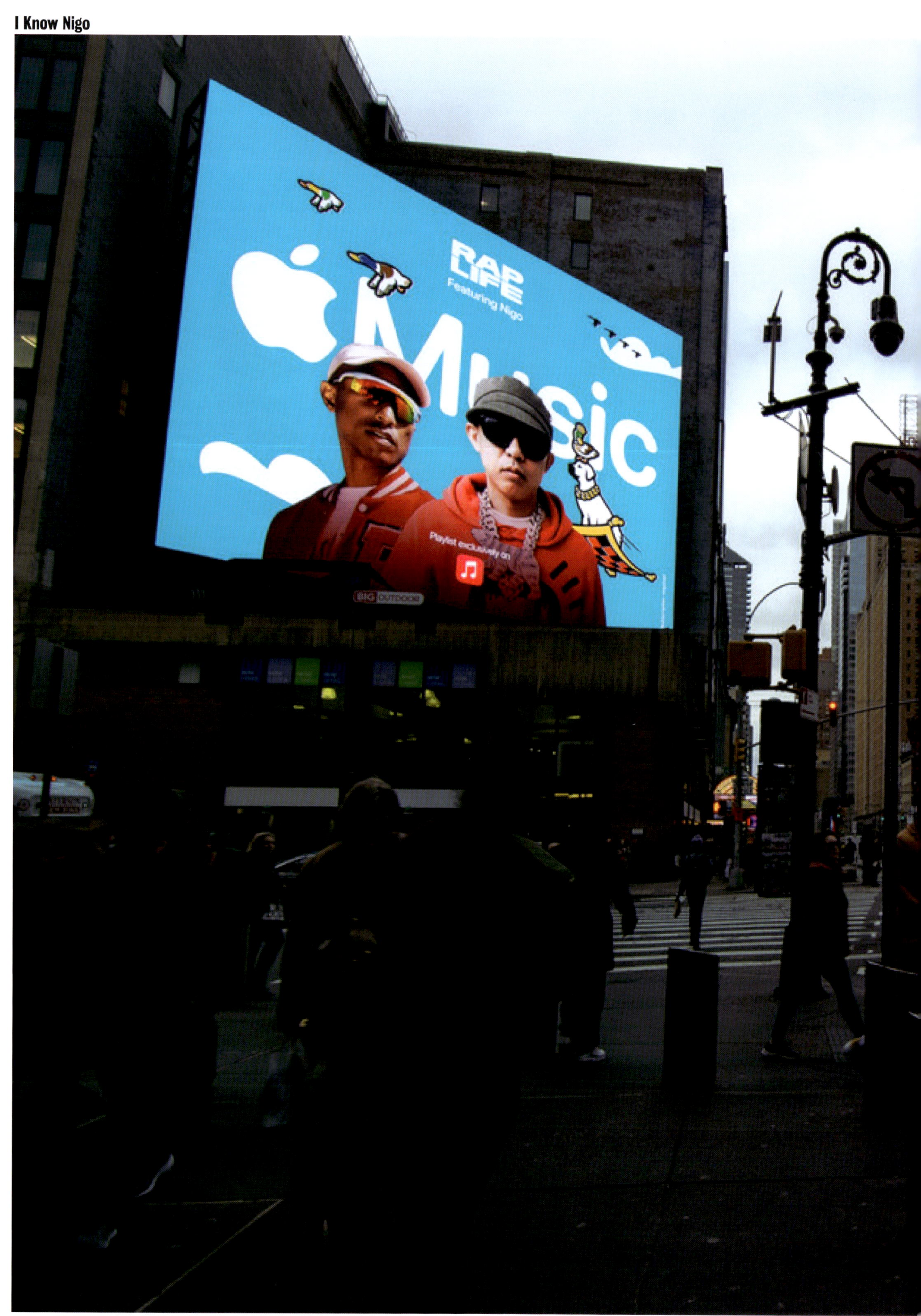

RAP LIFE
Featuring Nigo
Music
Playlist exclusively on
BIG OUTDOOR

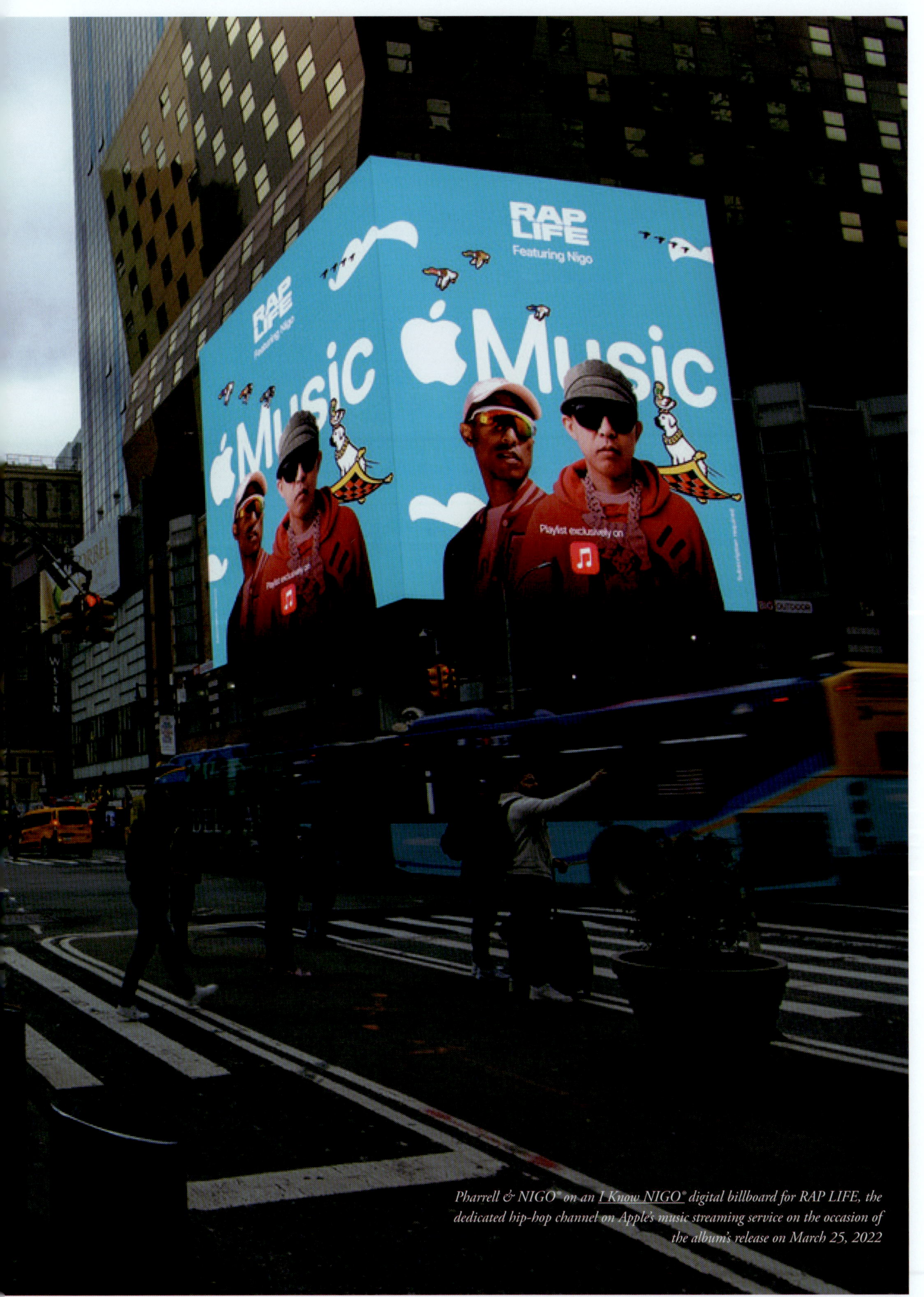

Pharrell & NIGO® on an <u>*I Know NIGO®*</u> *digital billboard for RAP LIFE, the dedicated hip-hop channel on Apple's music streaming service on the occasion of the album's release on March 25, 2022*

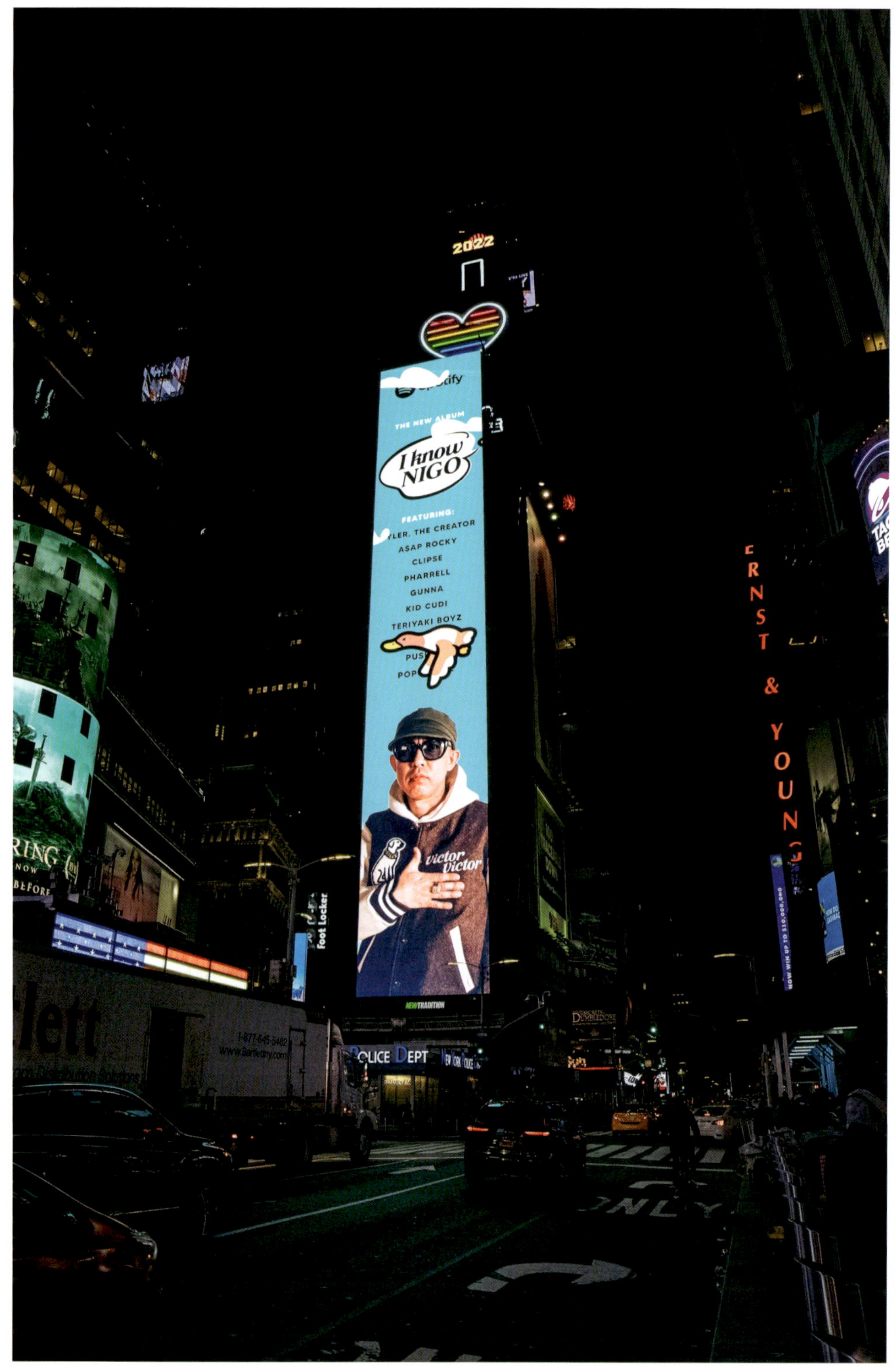

Spotify x I Know NIGO® digital billboard on the occasion of the album's release; March 25, 2022

NIGO® on a static billboard, Port Authority Bus Station, New York City

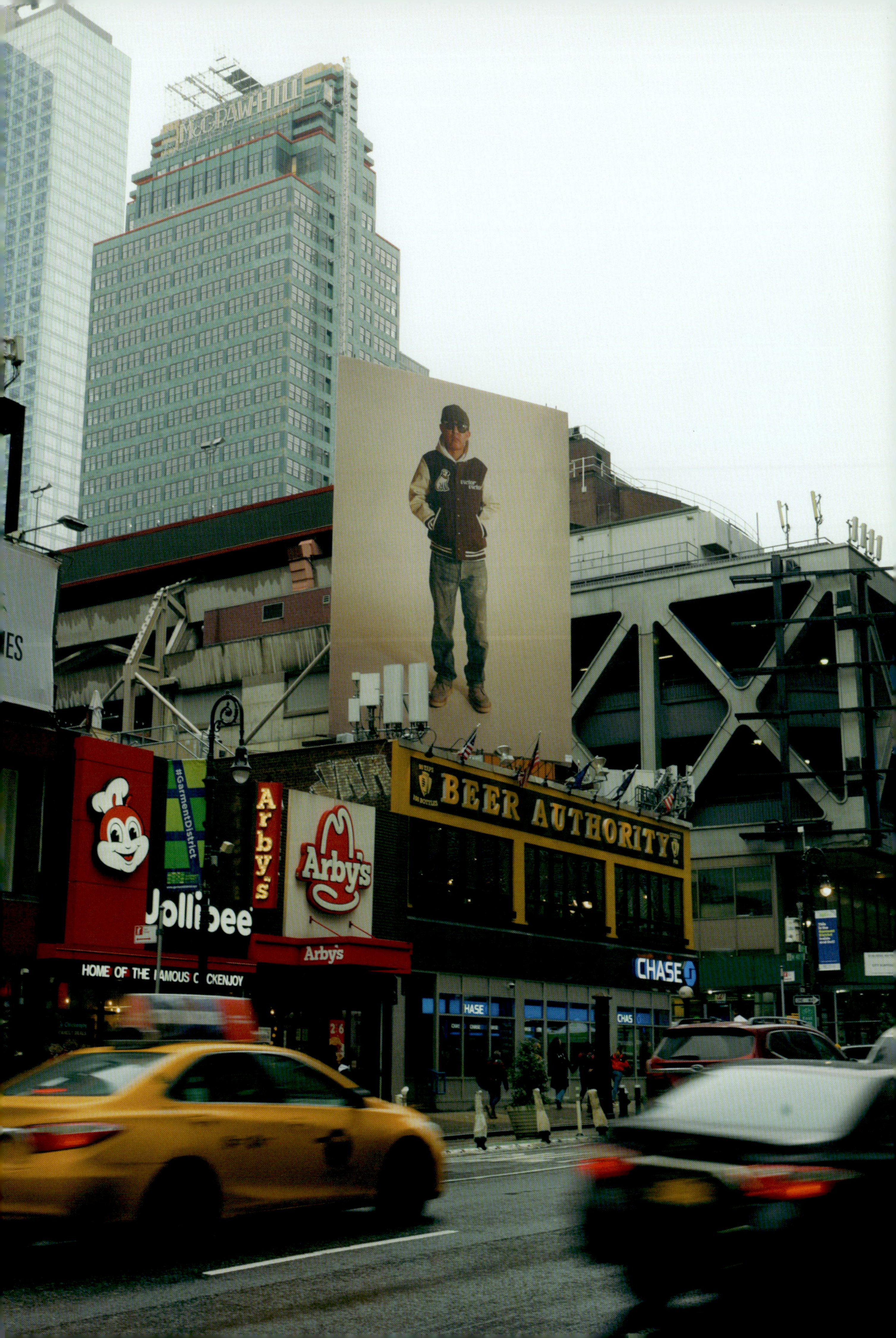
McGRAW-HILL
#GarmentDistrict
Jollibee
Arby's
Arby's
Arby's
BEER AUTHORITY
CHASE

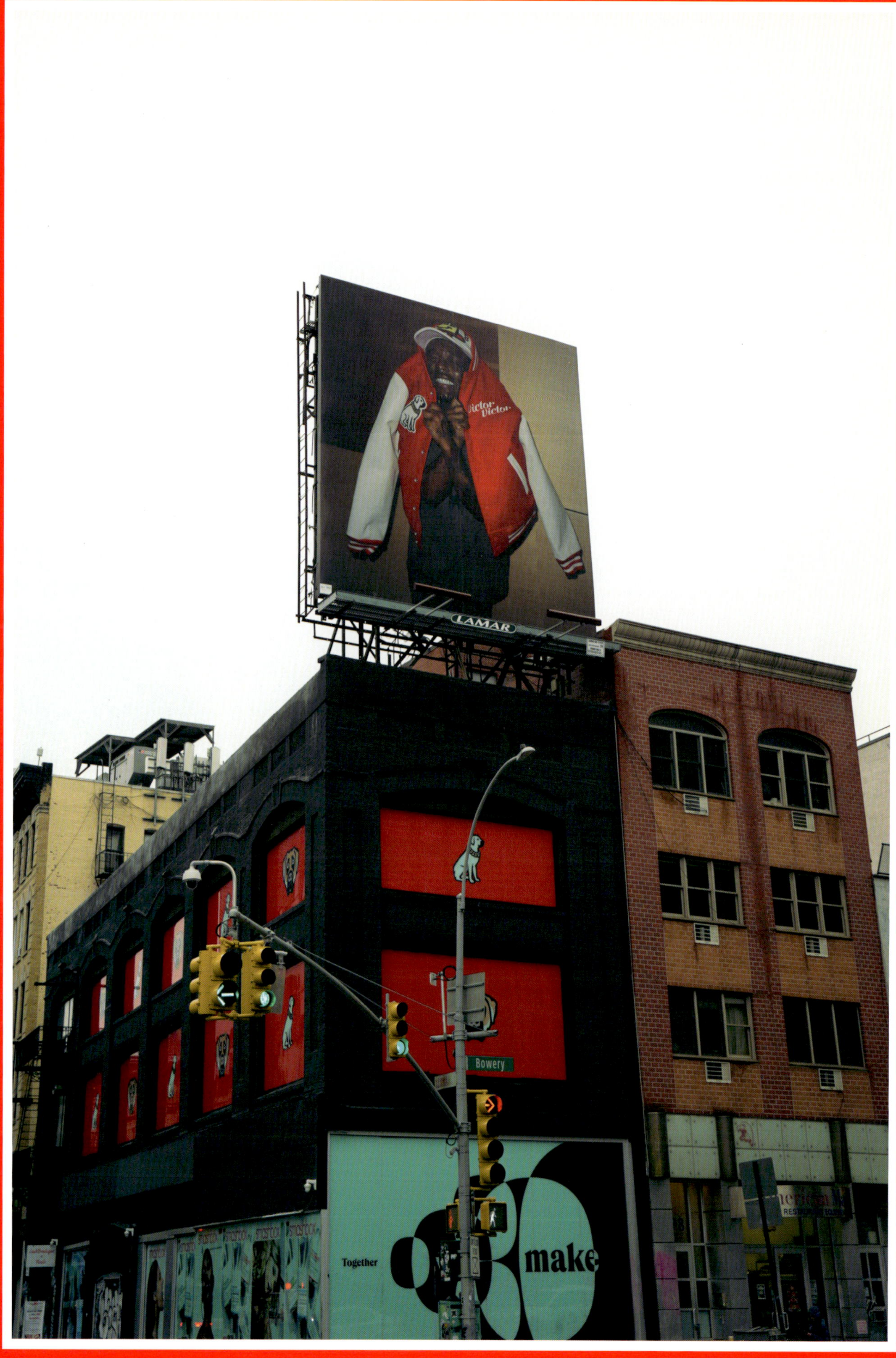
Victor Victor
LAMAR
Bowery
Together
make

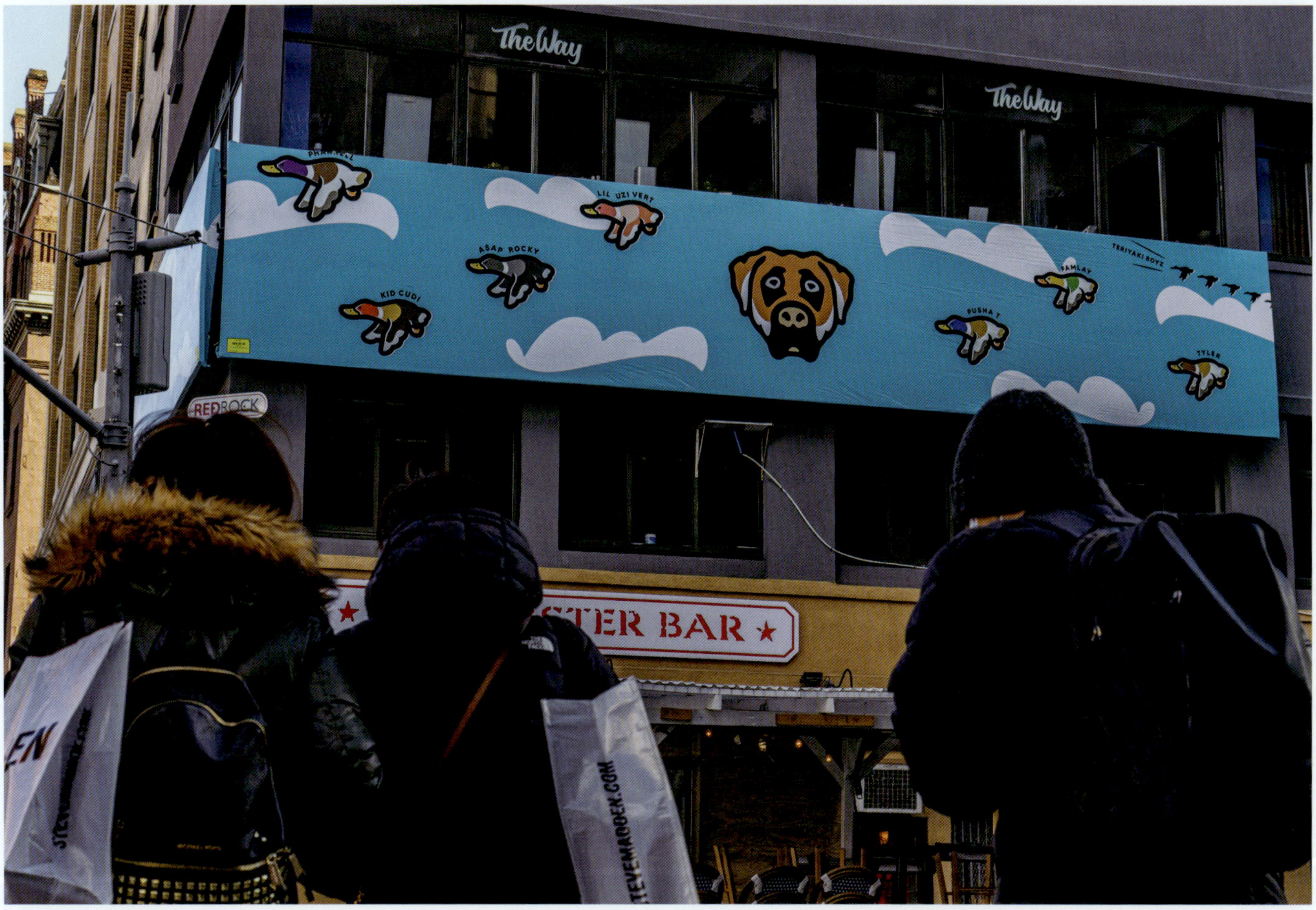

Page 164: Static billboard in Lower East Side, New York City, featuring Lil Uzi Vert, in advance of album release

Pages 165-167: I Know NIGO® static billboards in Chinatown, New York City, hinting at the upcoming album

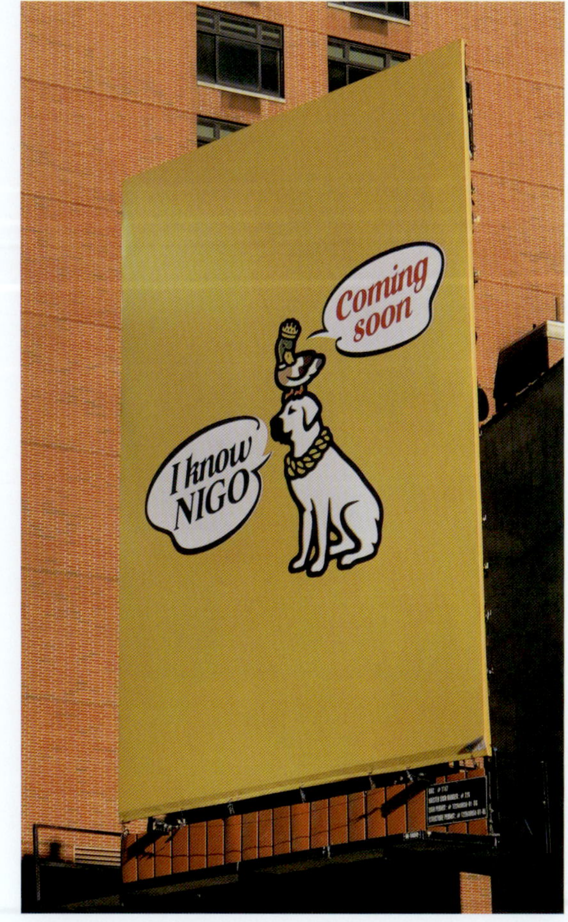

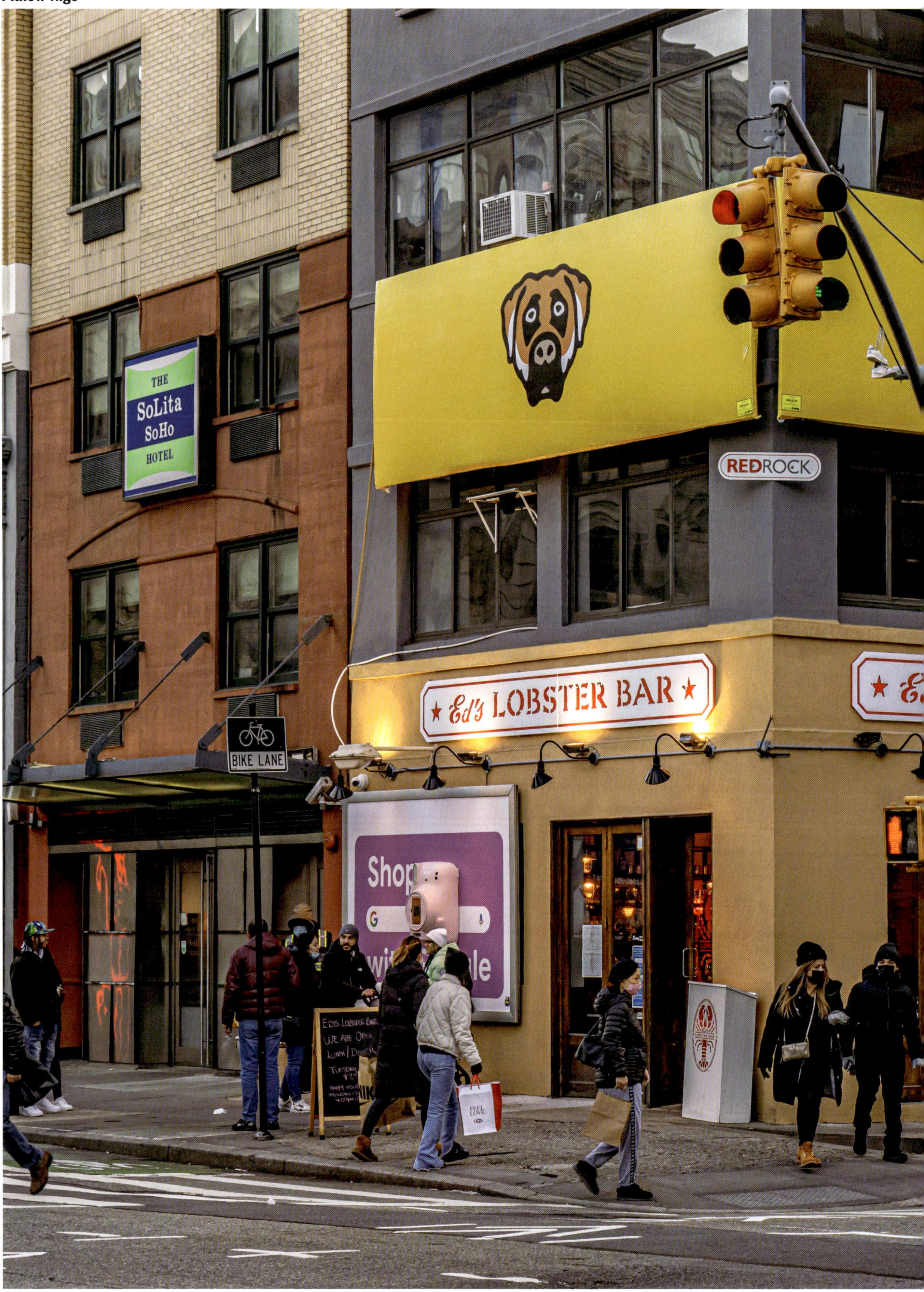
THE
SoLita
SoHo
HOTEL
REDROCK
Ed's LOBSTER BAR
BIKE LANE
Shop

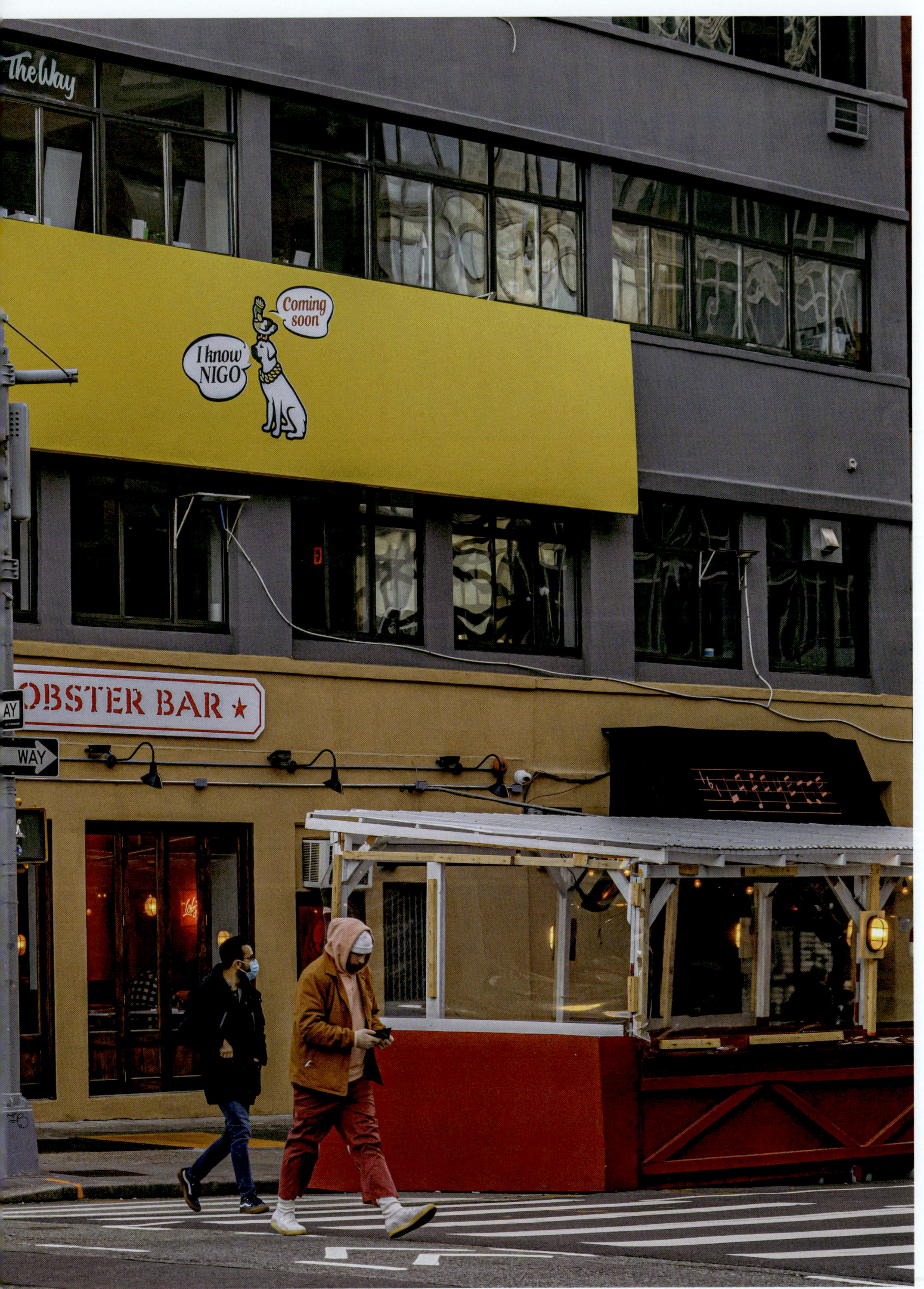

The Way
Coming soon
I know NIGO
OBSTER BAR
WAY

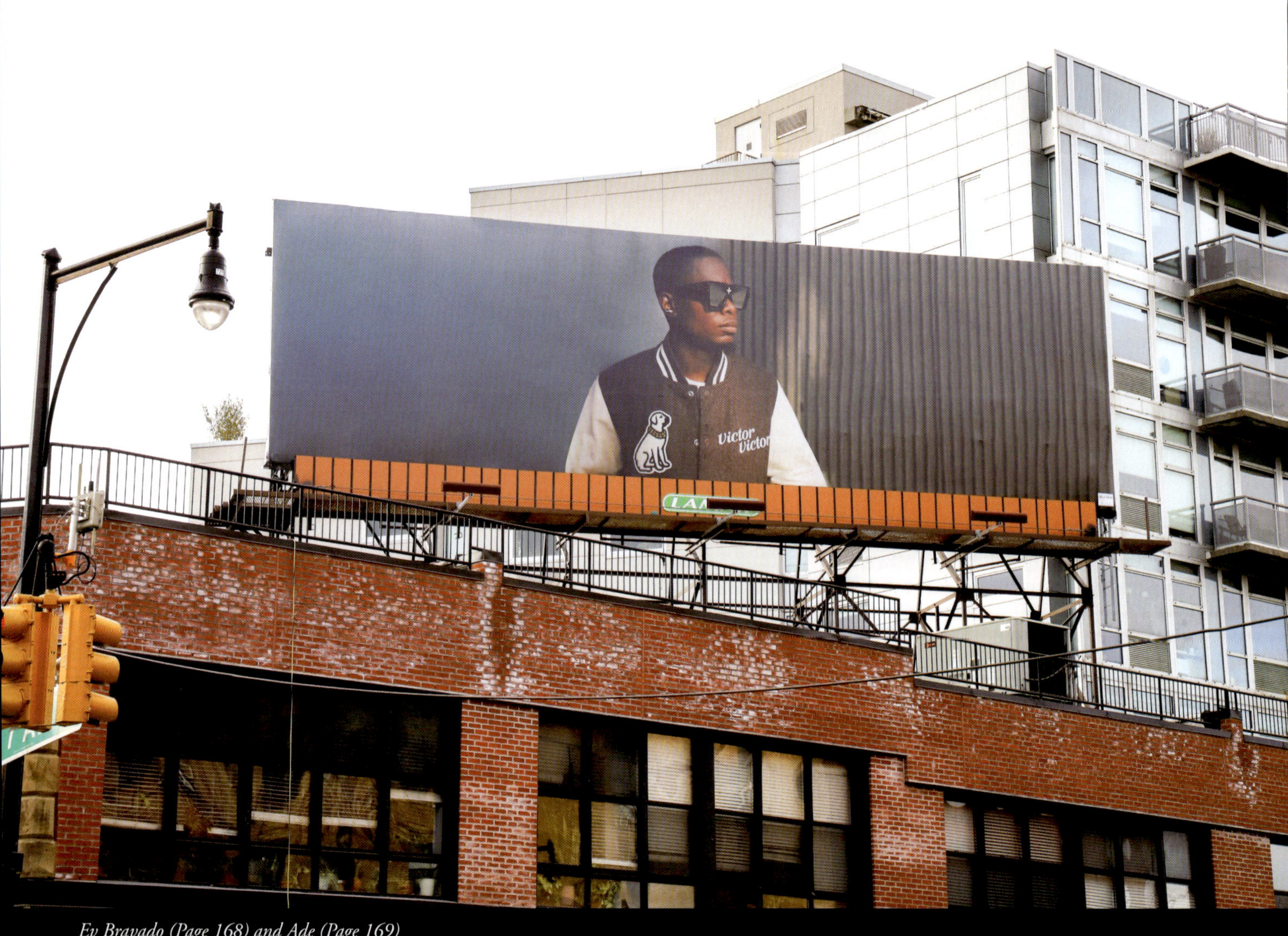

Ev Bravado (Page 168) and Ade (Page 169) in the VICTOR VICTOR varsity jacket produced by Human Made; static billboard at the Barclays Center, Brooklyn, New York

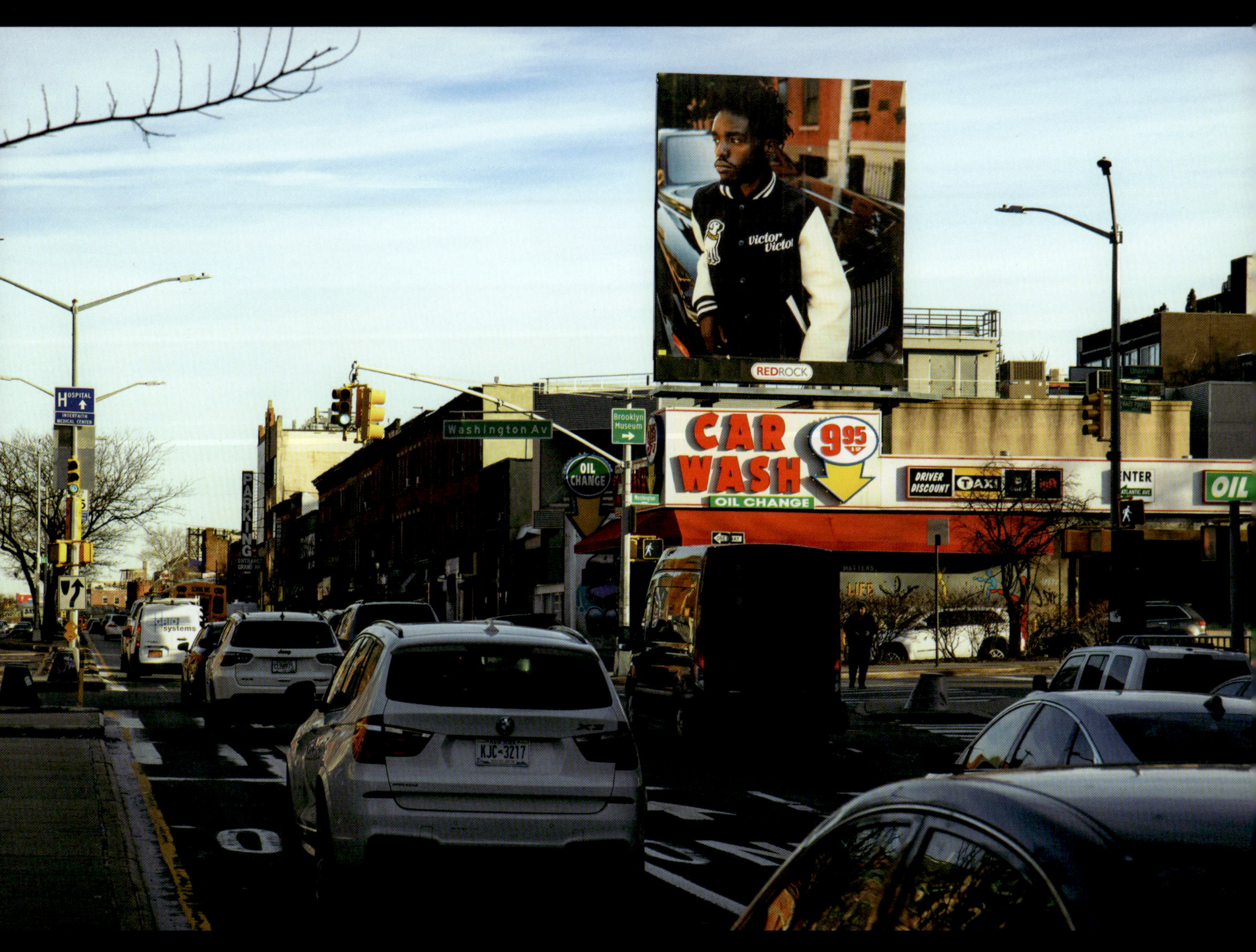
REDROCK
CAR WASH
OIL CHANGE
Washington Av
Brooklyn Museum
OIL CHANGE
PARKING
HOSPITAL
DRIVER DISCOUNT
TAXI
OIL

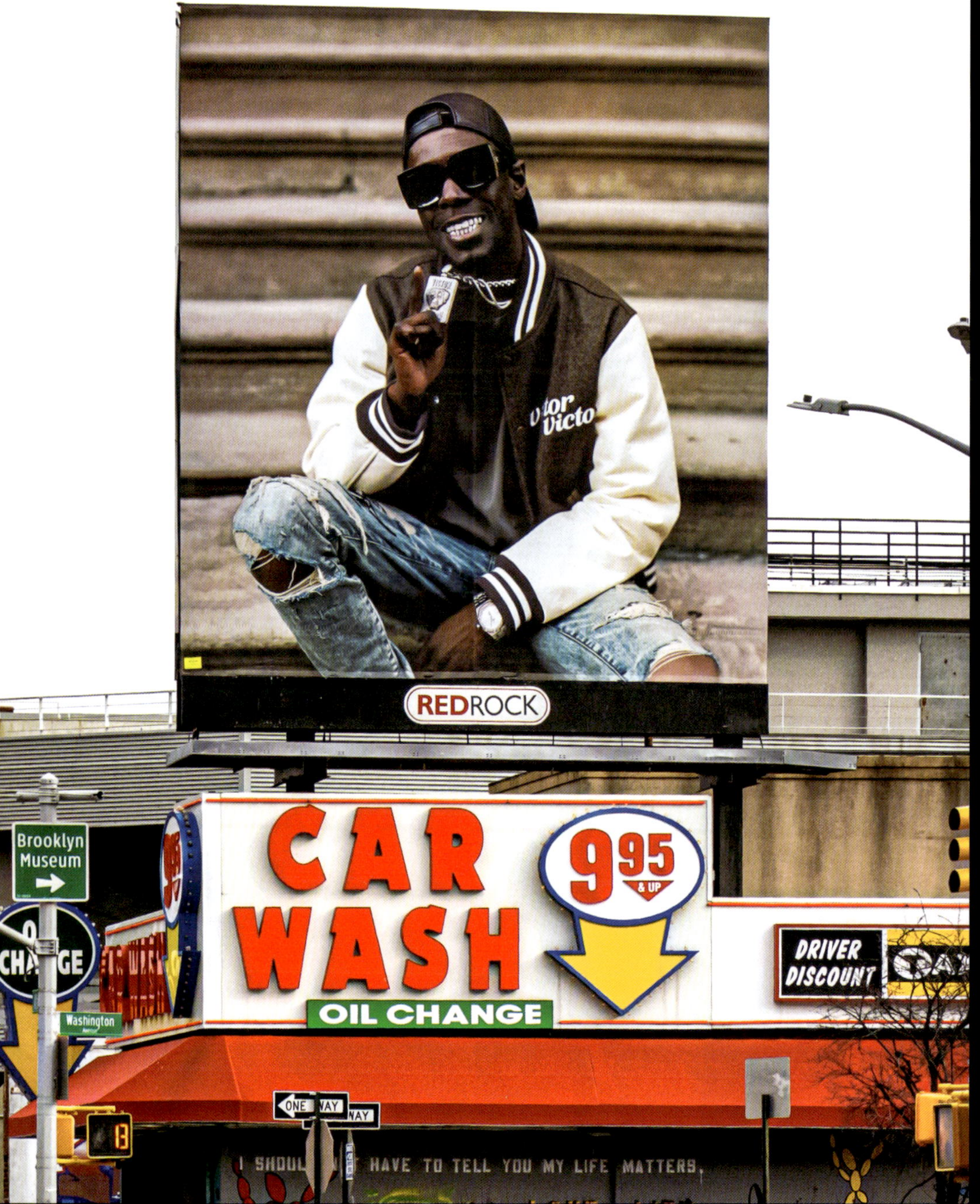

Rico Beats (Page 170) and Lil Jupiter (Page 171) in the VICTOR VICTOR varsity jacket produced by Human Made; static billboard at the Barclays Center, Brooklyn, New York

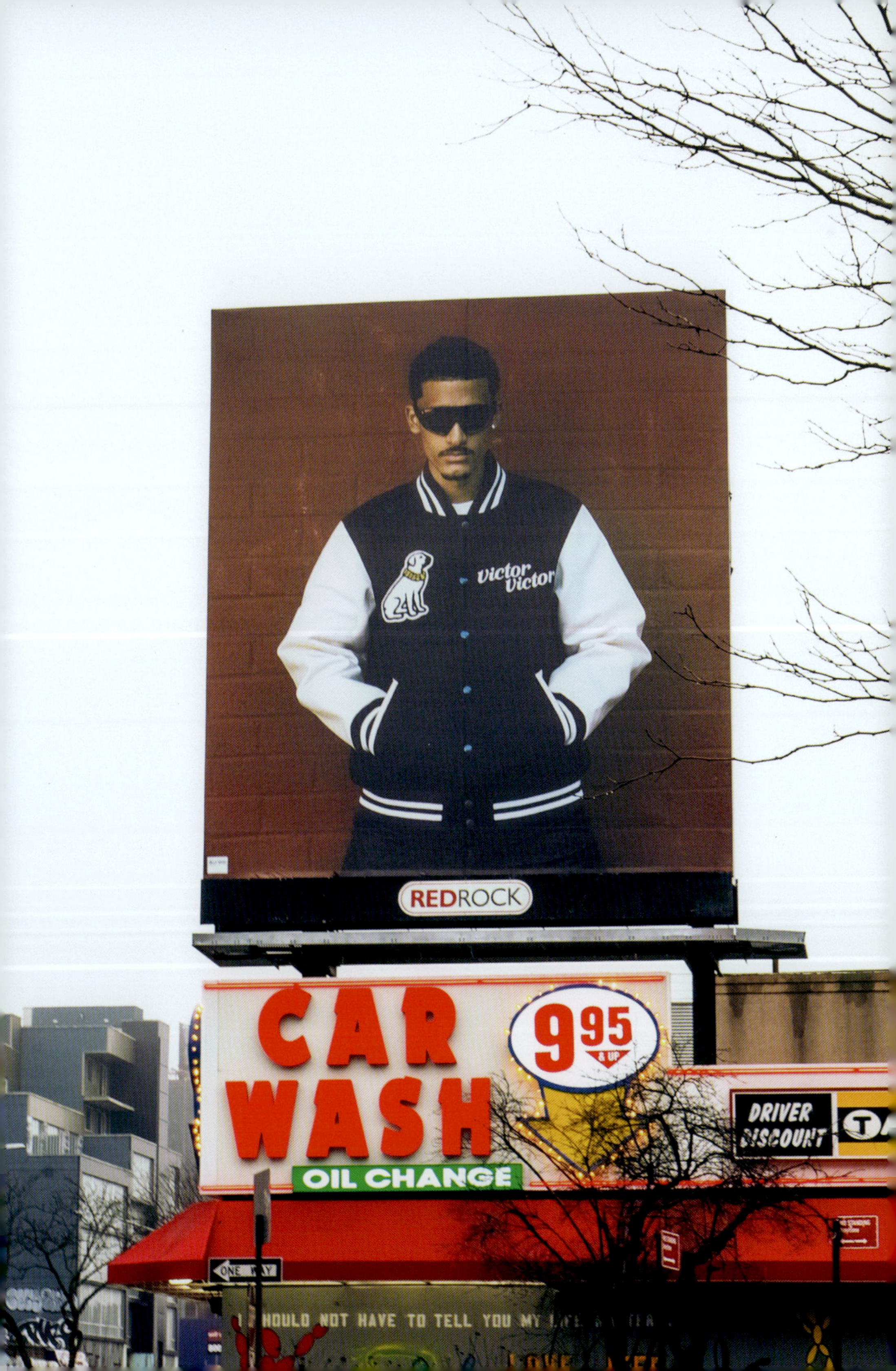

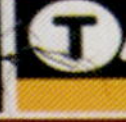
victor
Victor
REDROCK
CAR
WASH
9.95
& UP
OIL CHANGE
DRIVER
DISCOUNT
ONE WAY

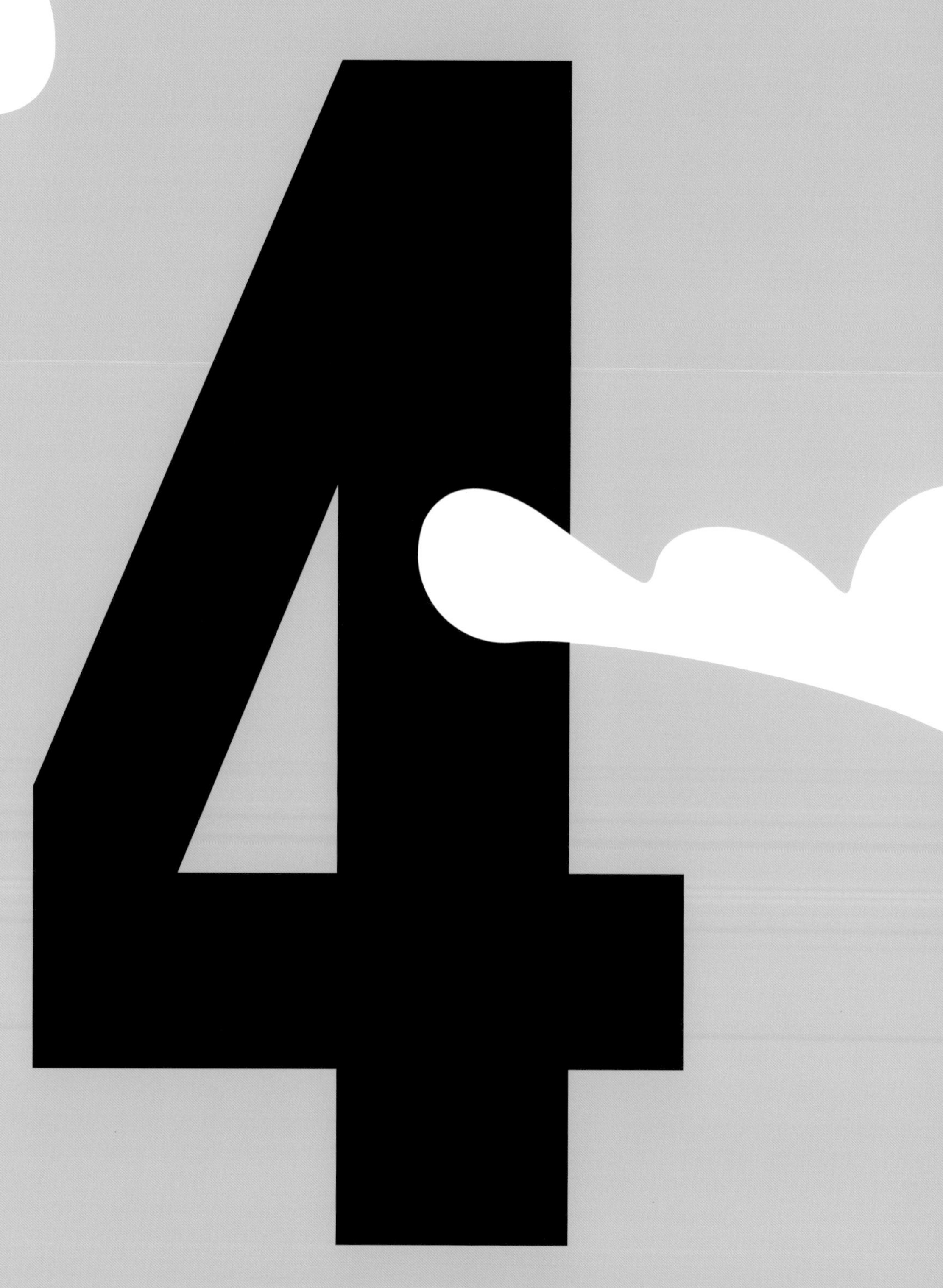

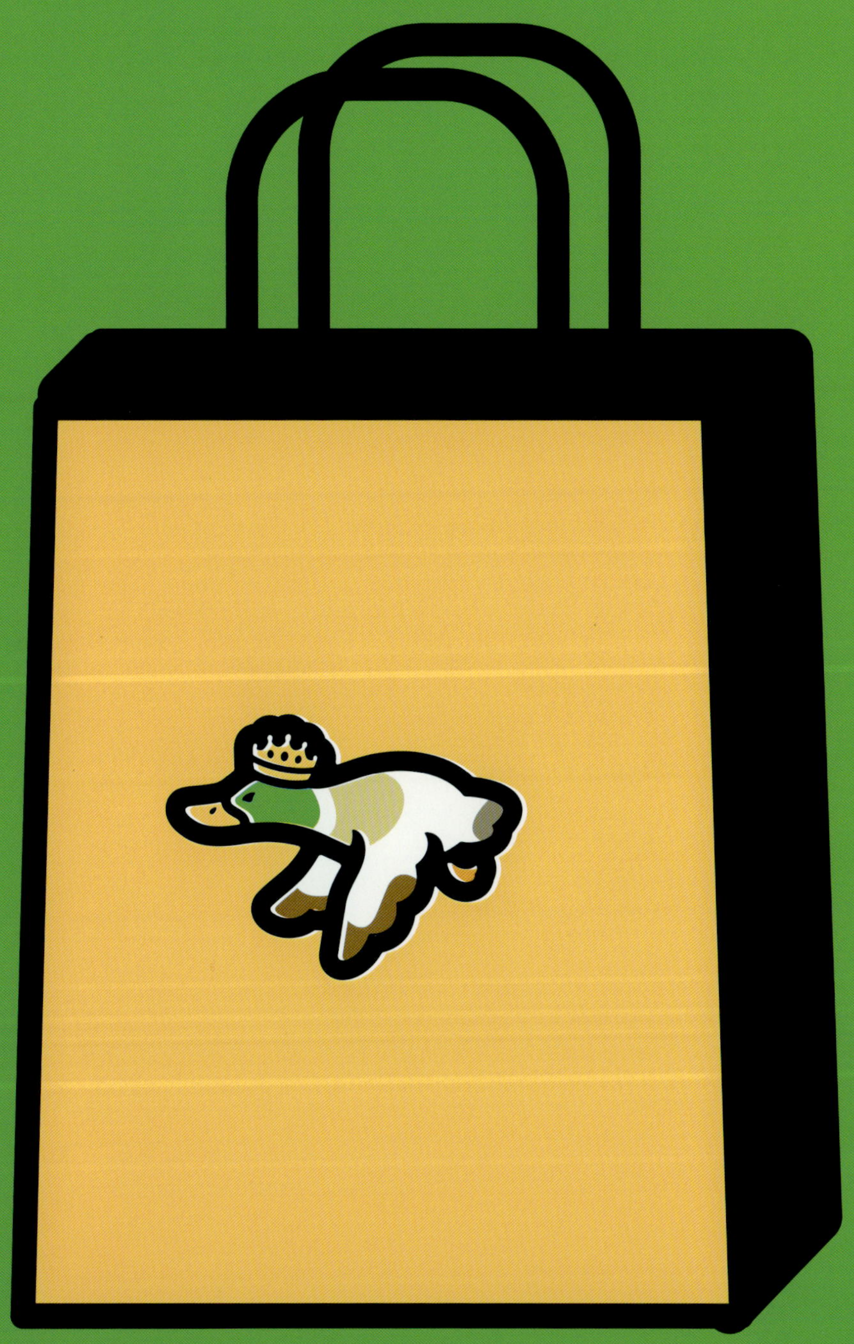

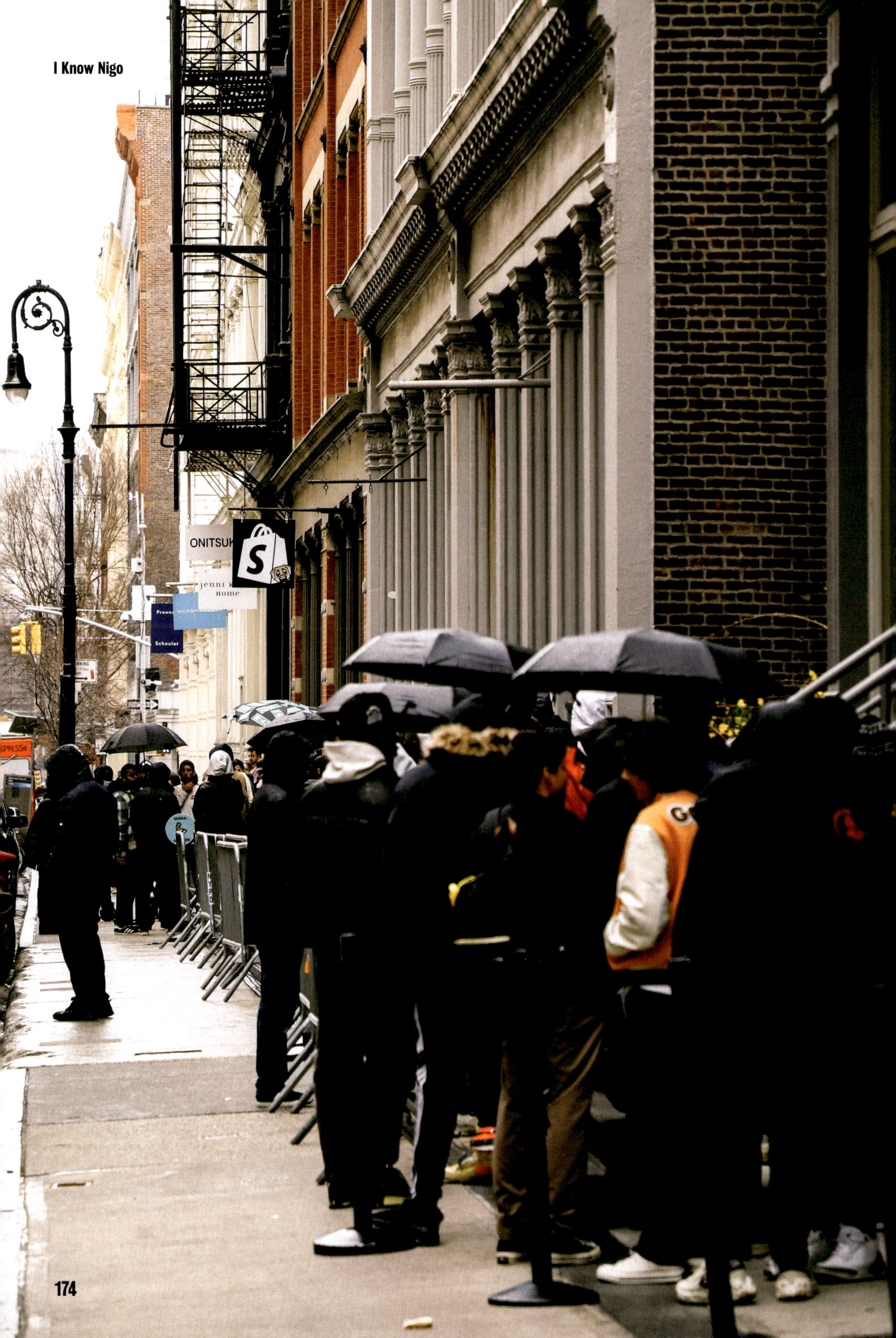

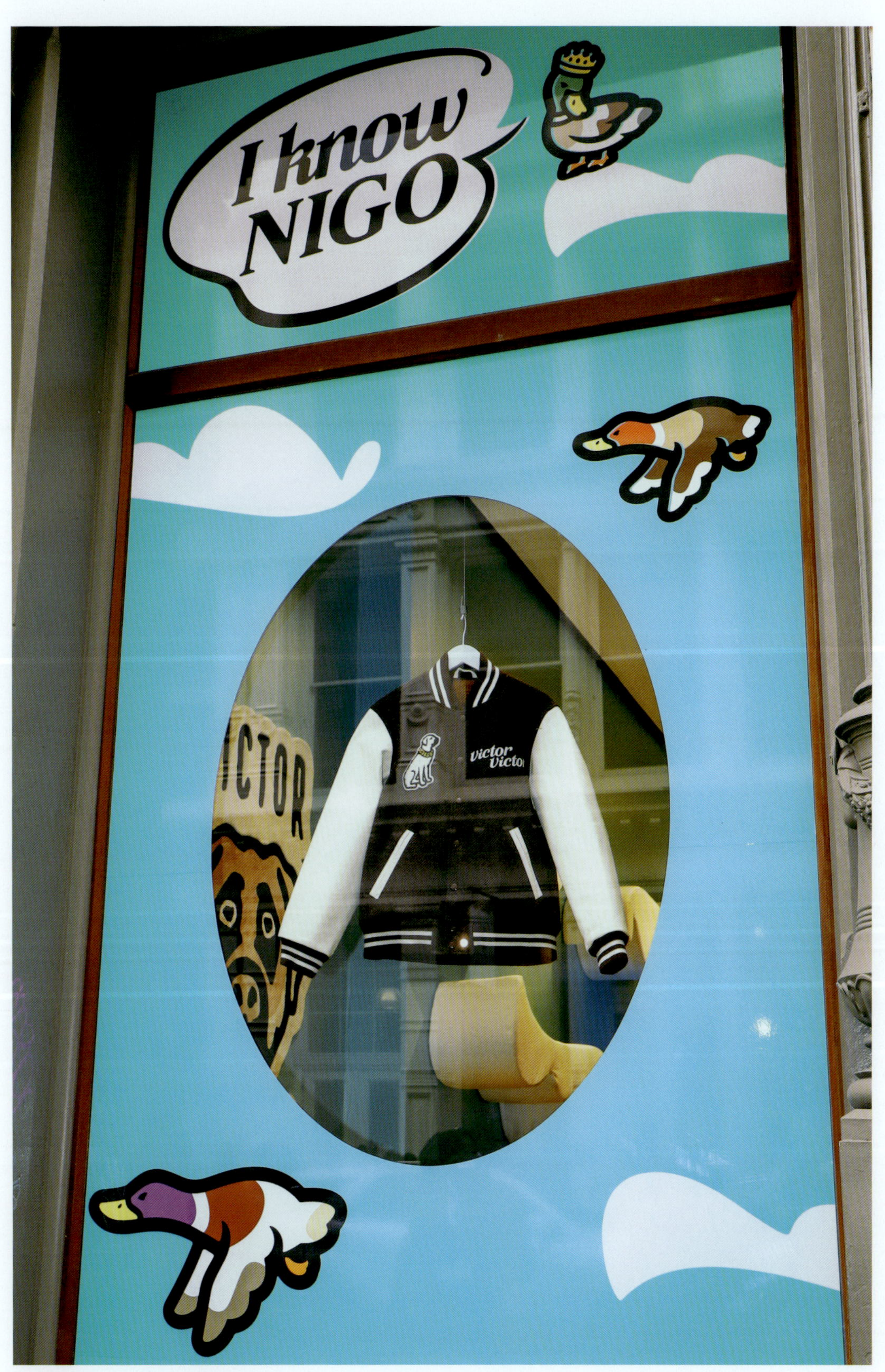

Images from the I Know NIGO® pop-up in partnership with Shopify, which opened in Soho, New York City on March 26, 2022

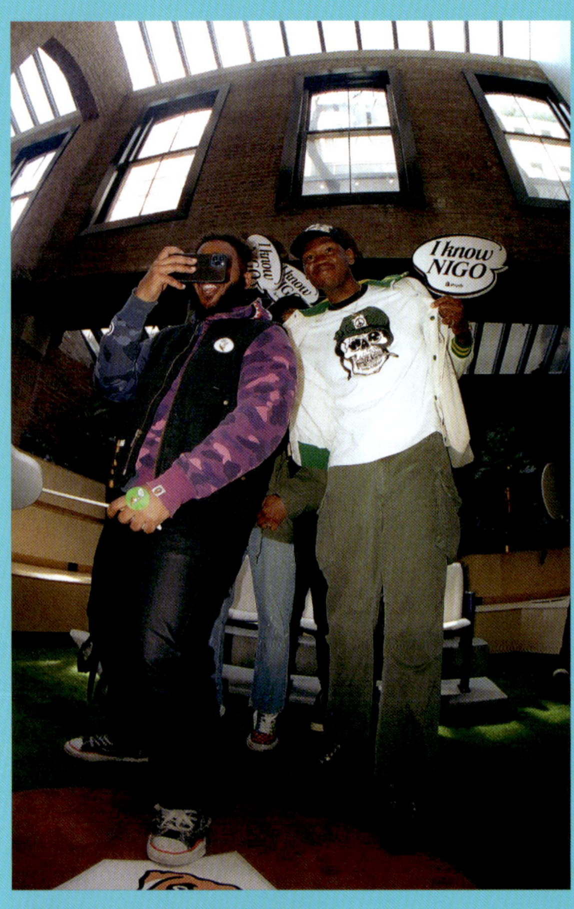
I know
NIGO

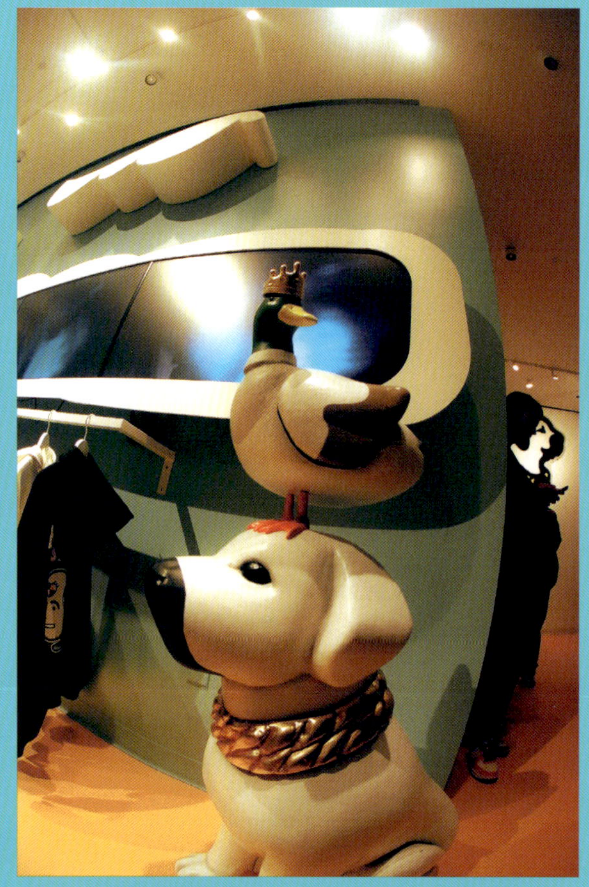

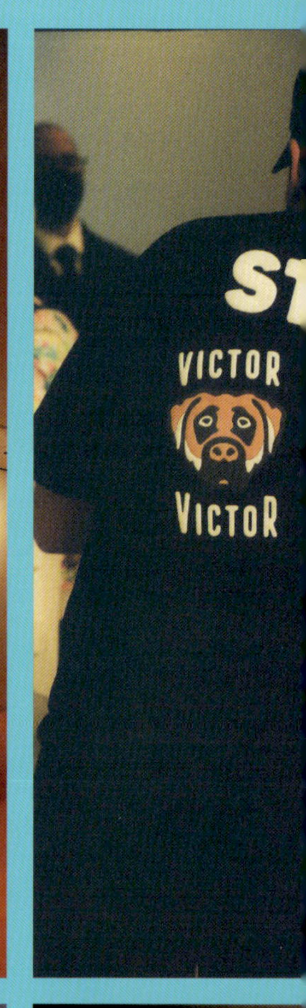
VICTOR
VICTOR

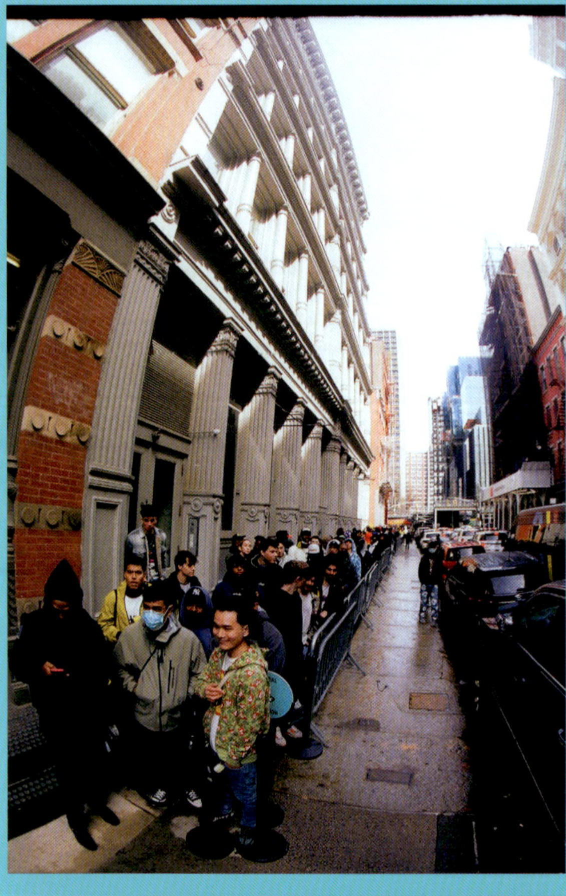

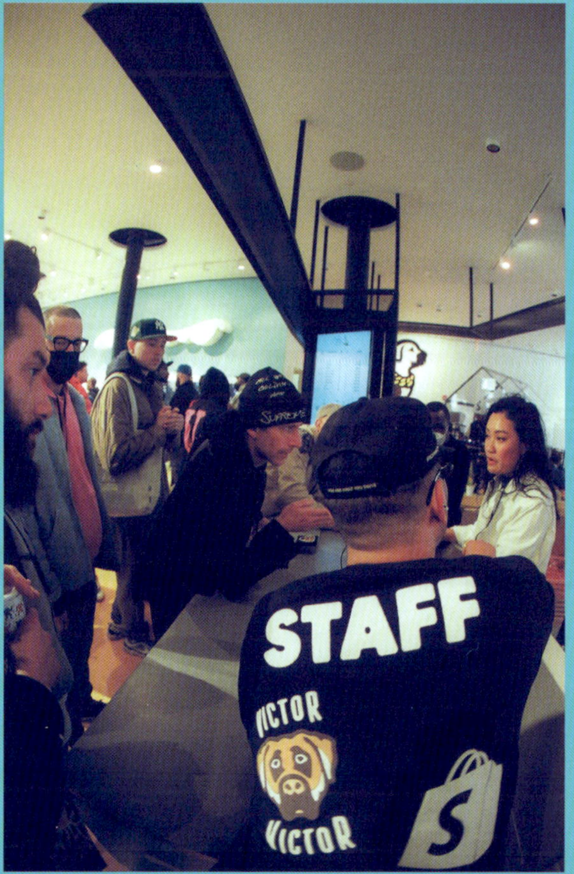
STAFF

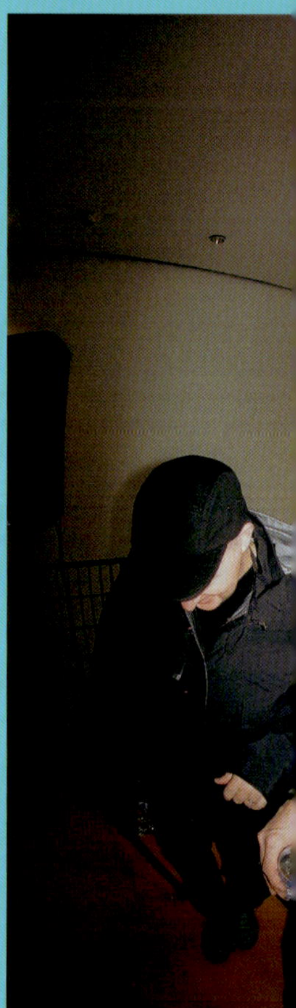

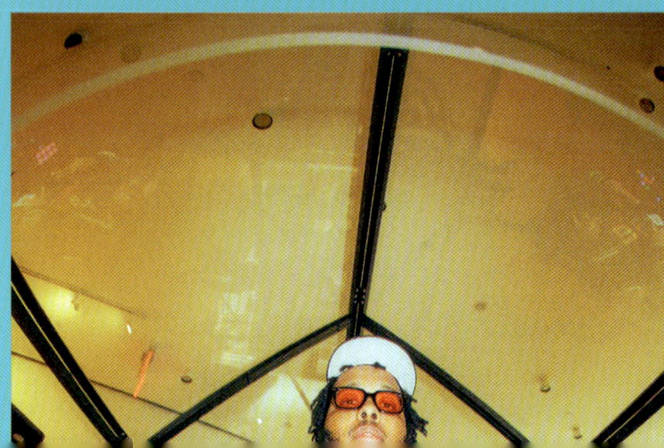

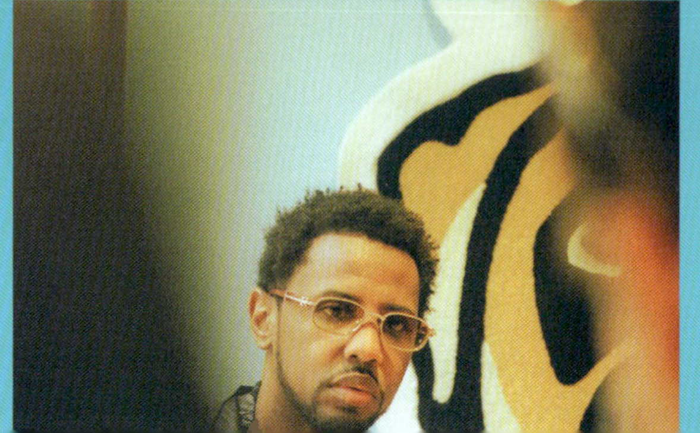

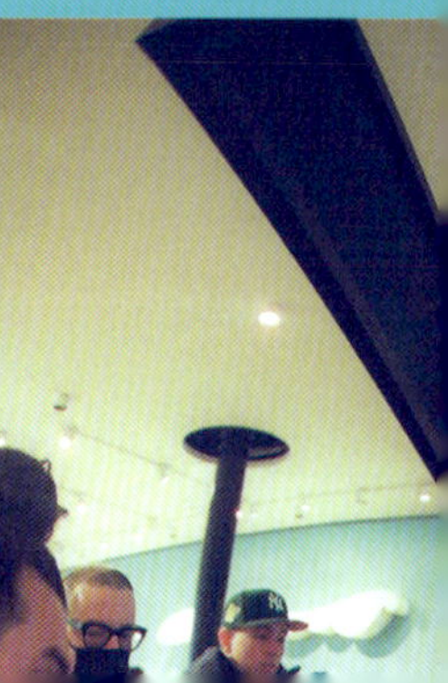

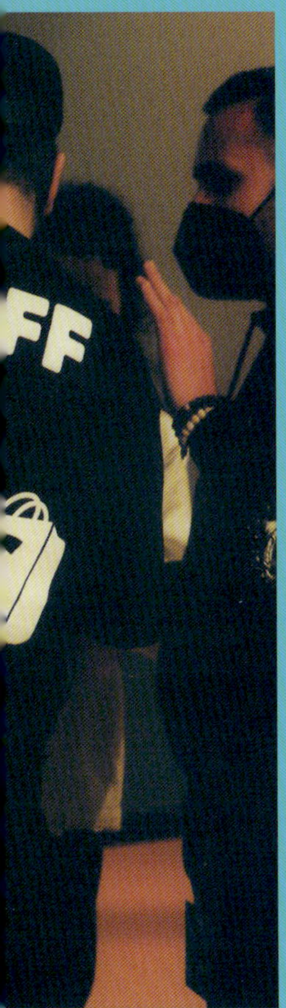

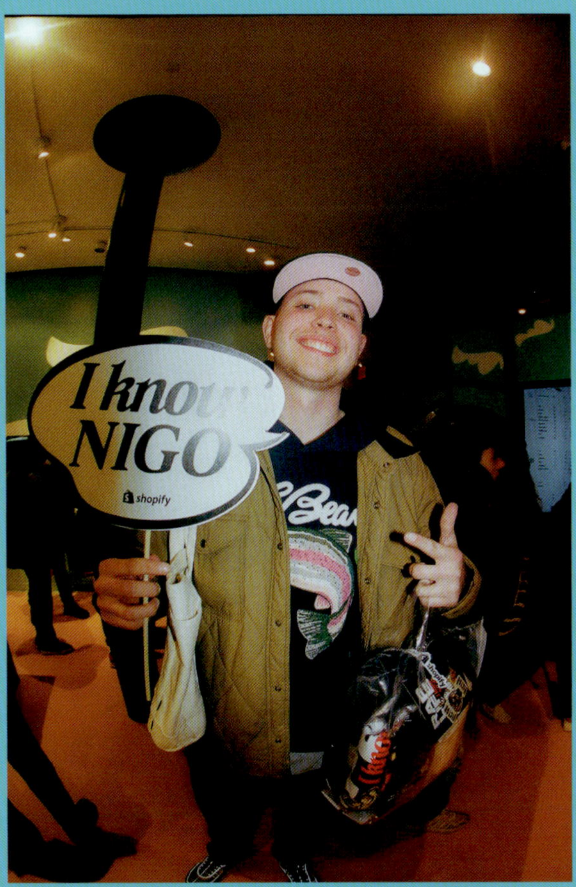
I know NIGO
shopify

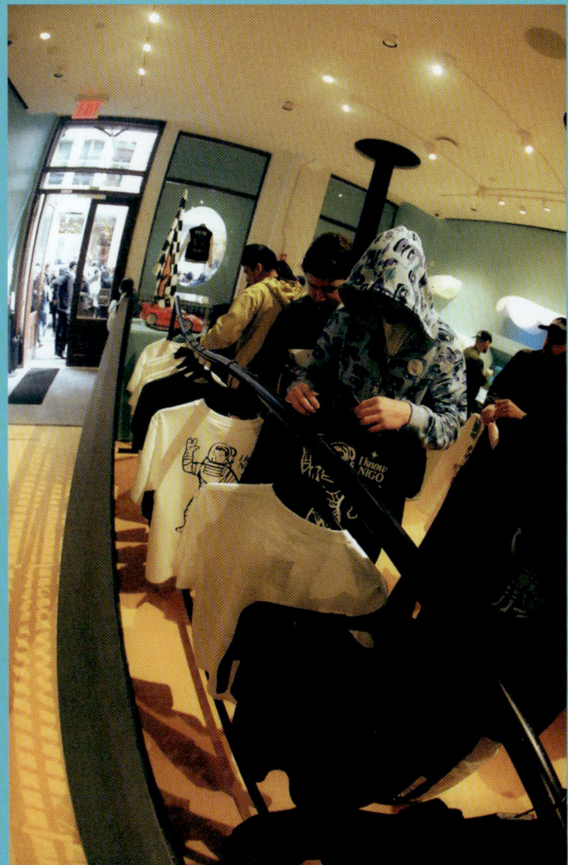

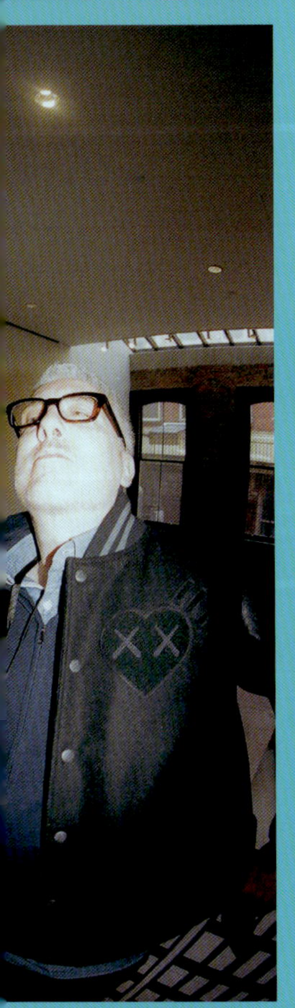

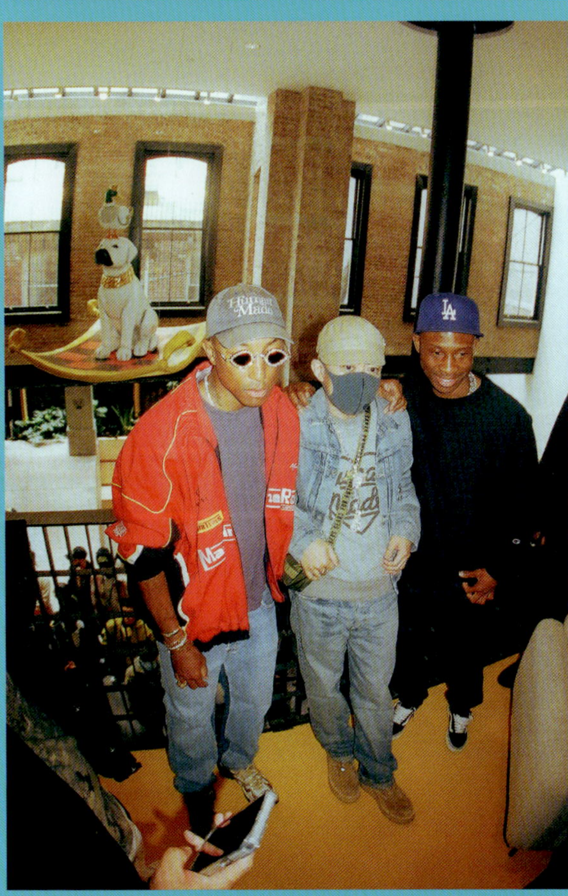

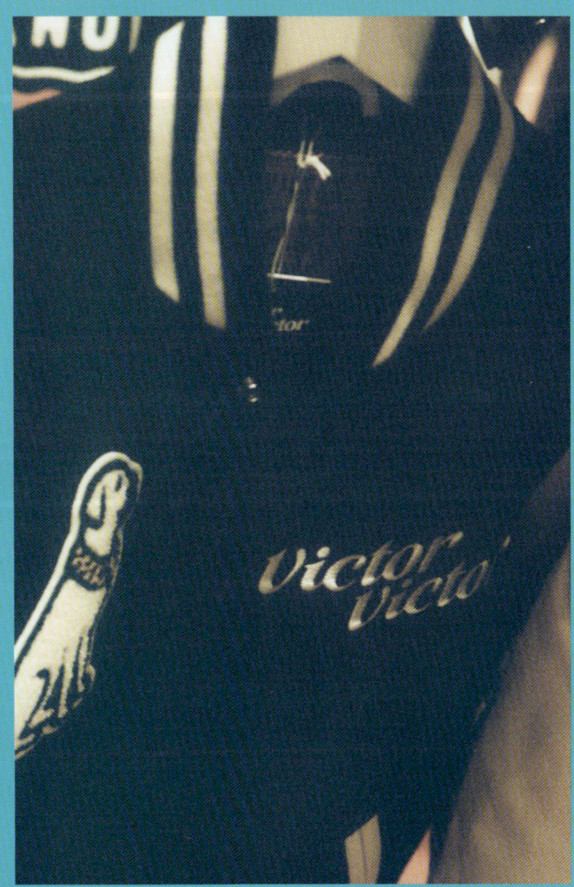
victor victo

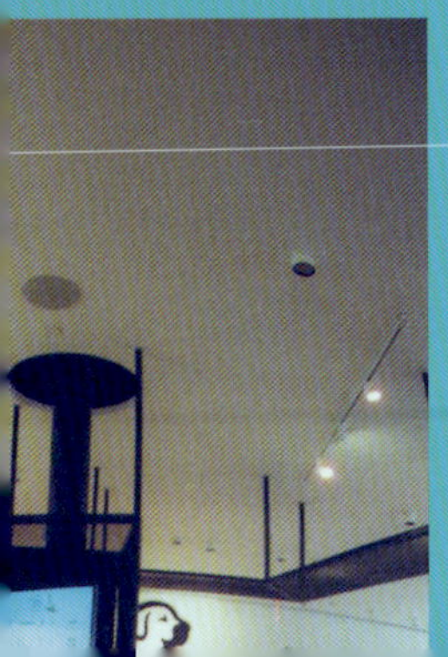

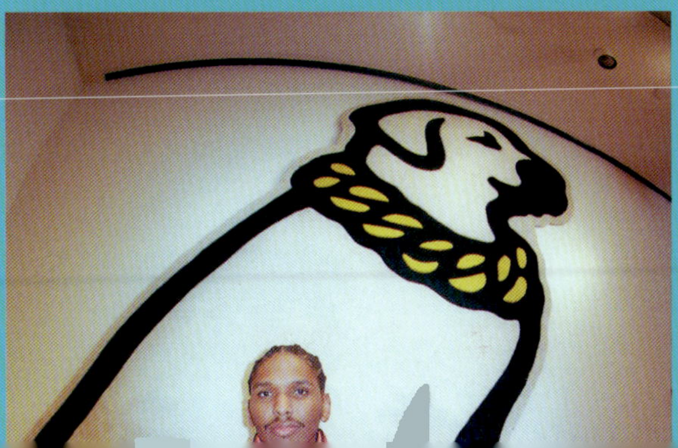

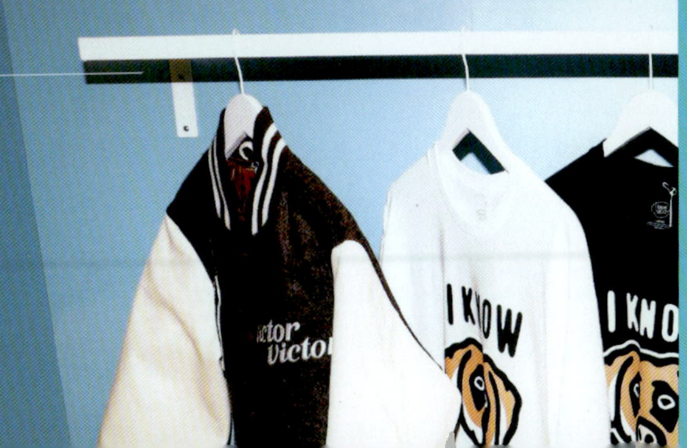
I KNOW

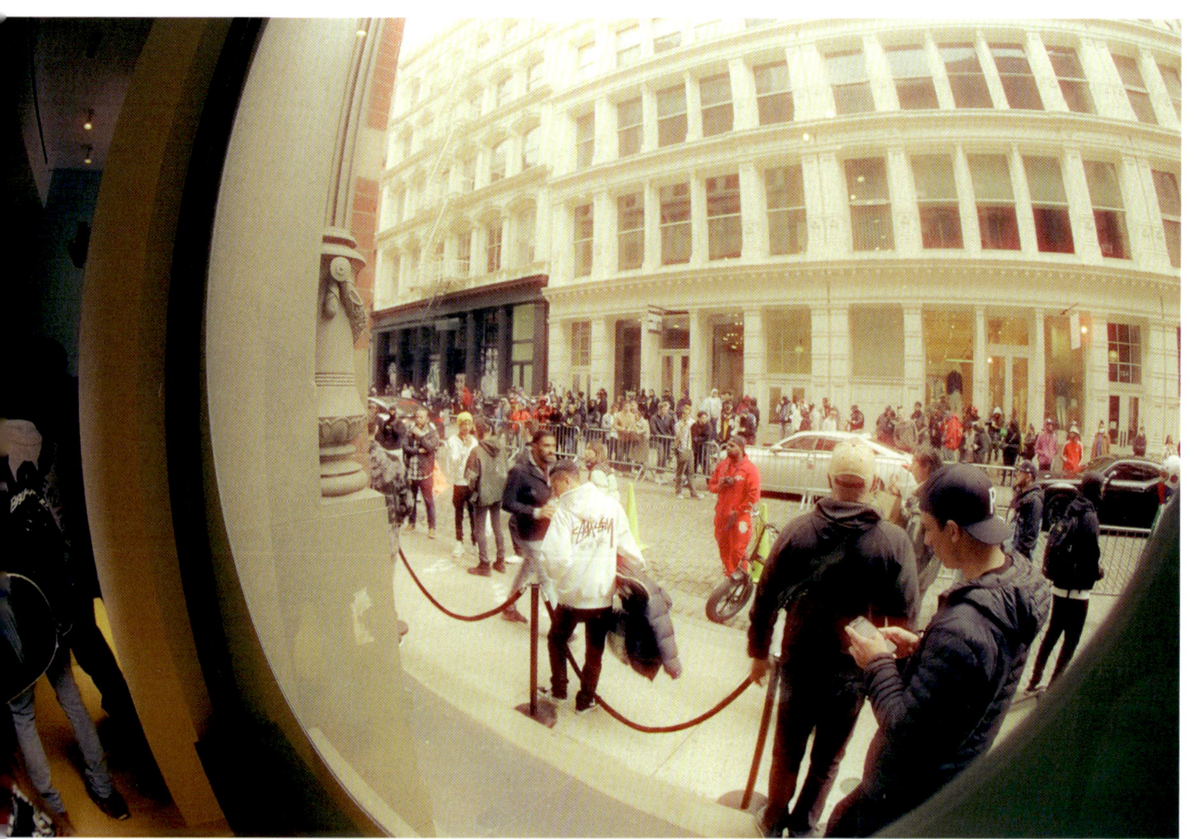

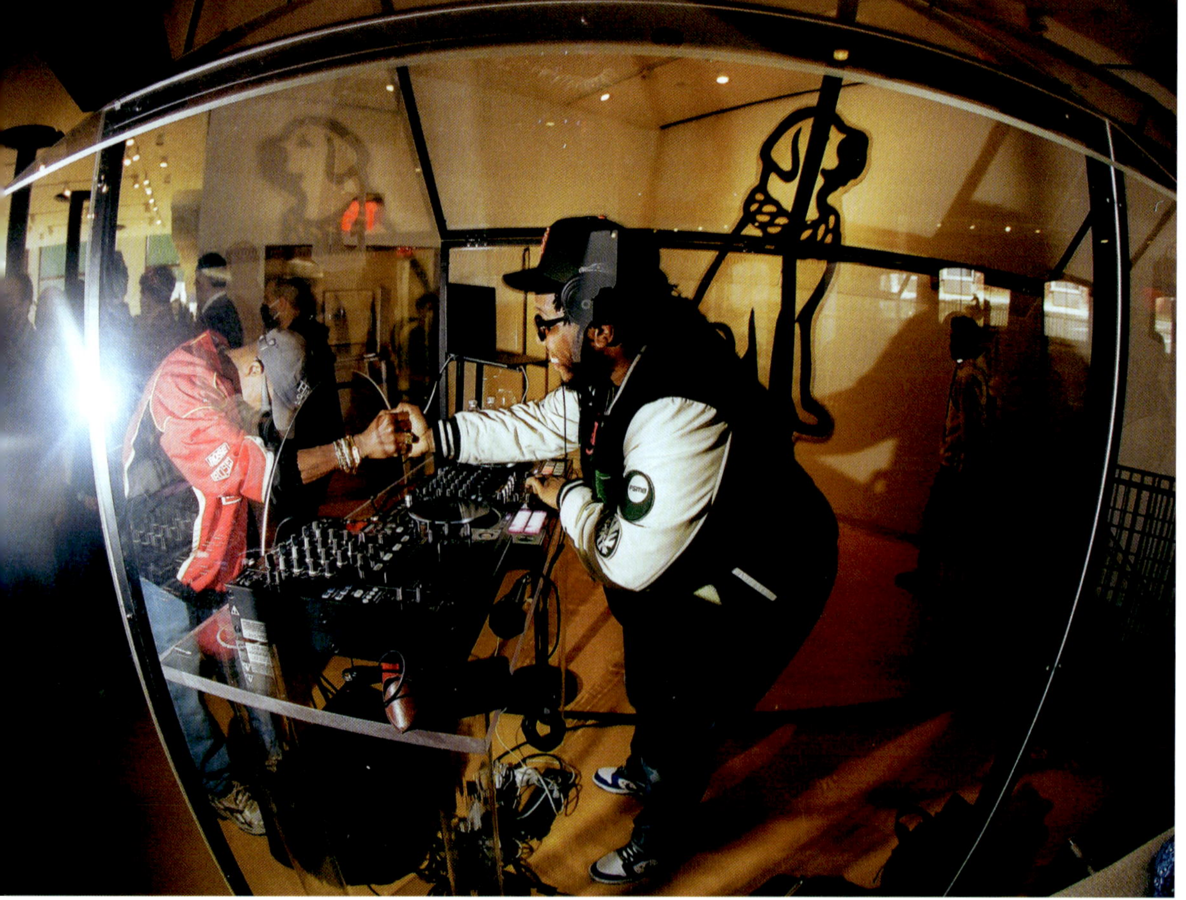

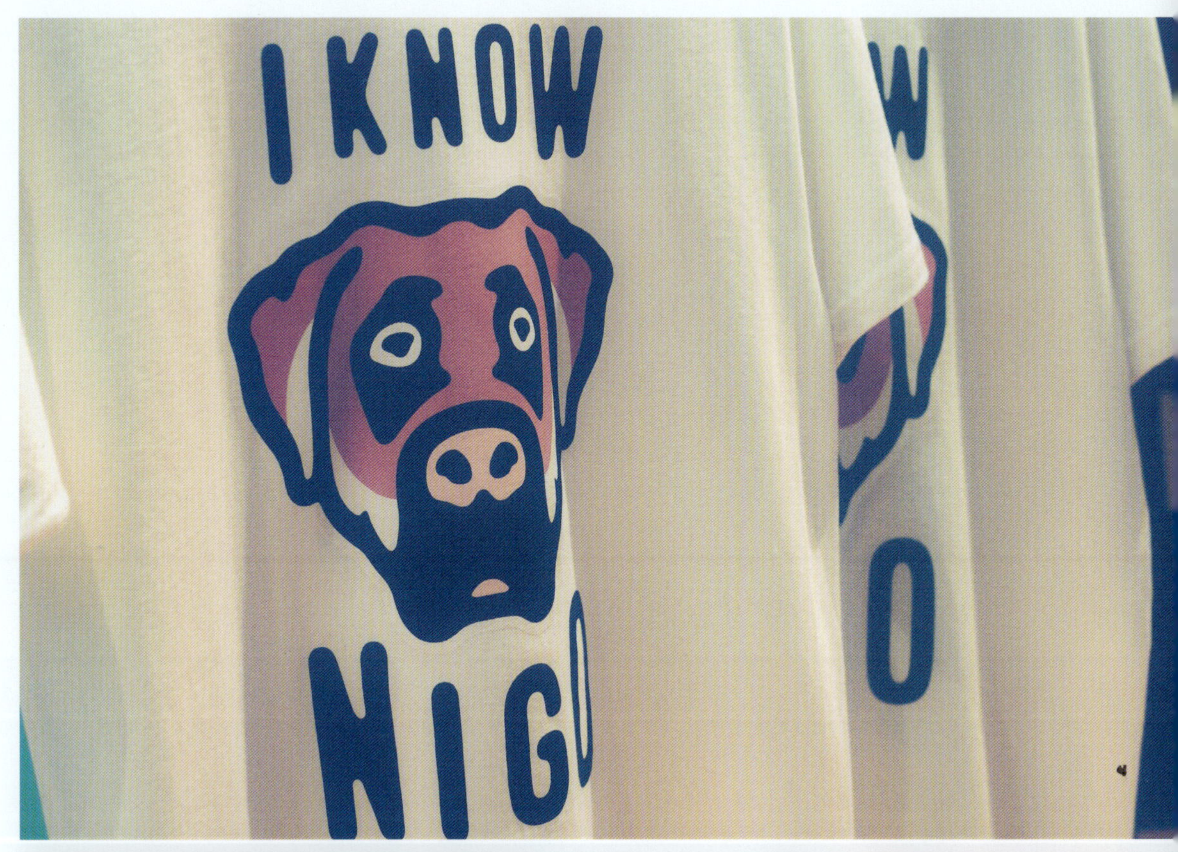
I KNOW
NIGO

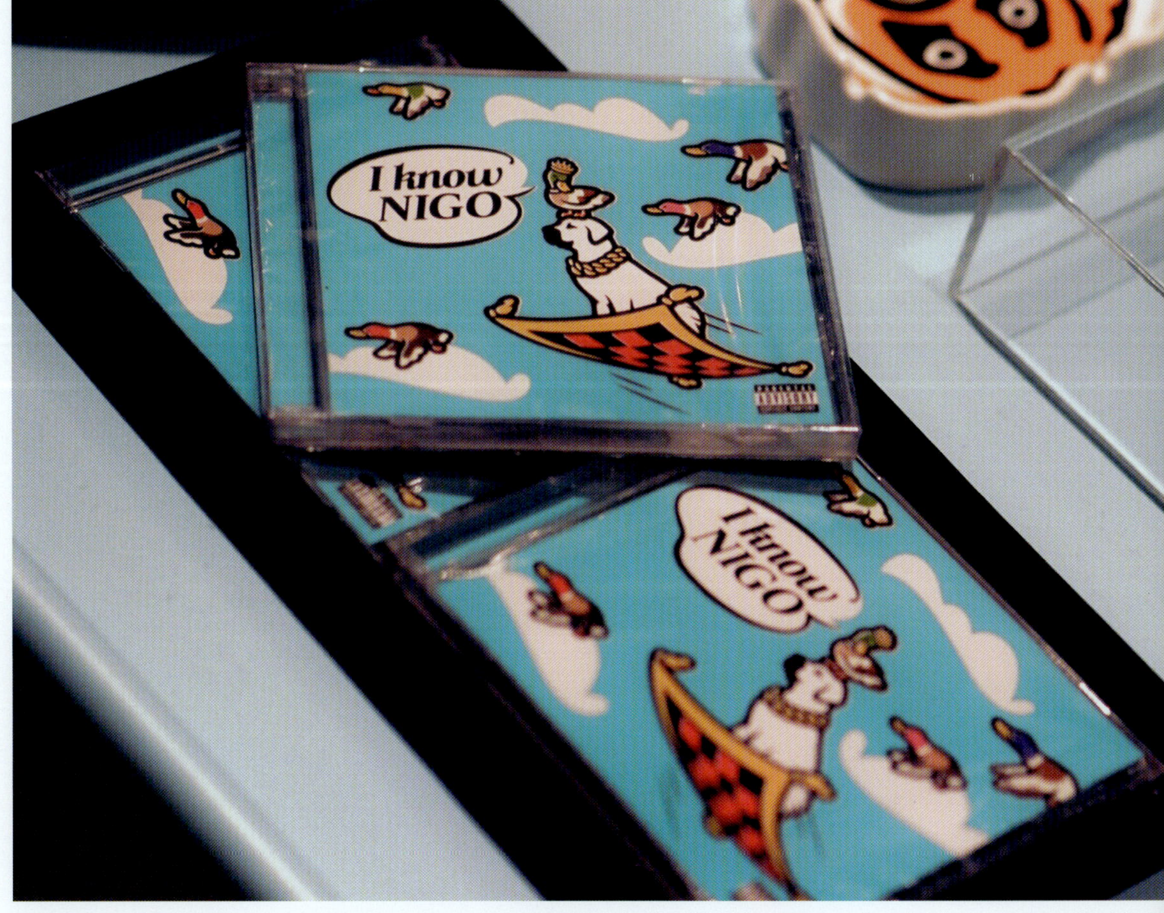
I know
NIGO

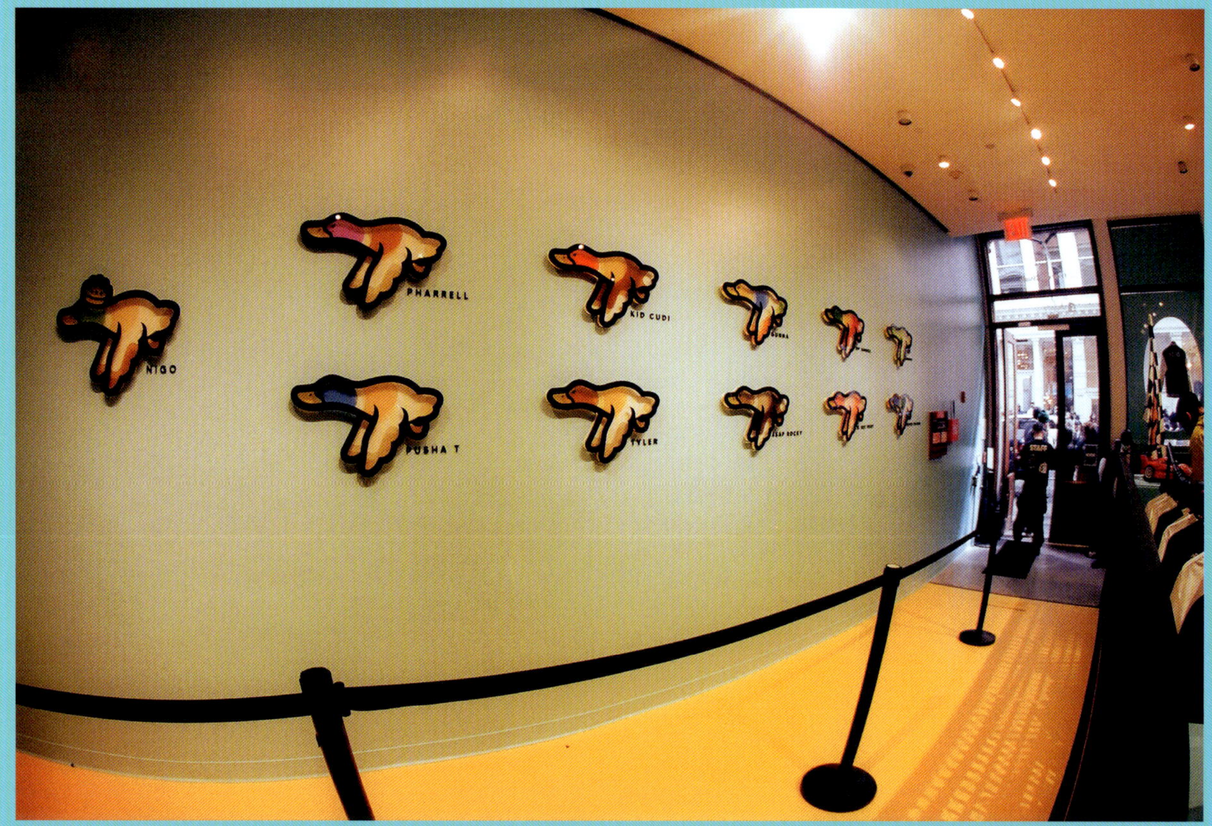
NIGO
PHARRELL
KID CUDI
PUSHA T
TYLER
ASAP ROCKY

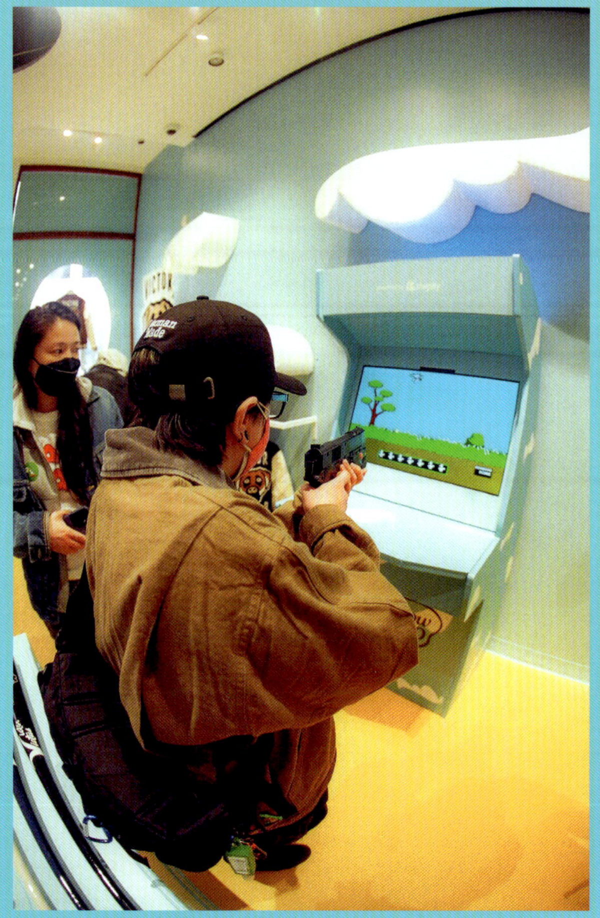

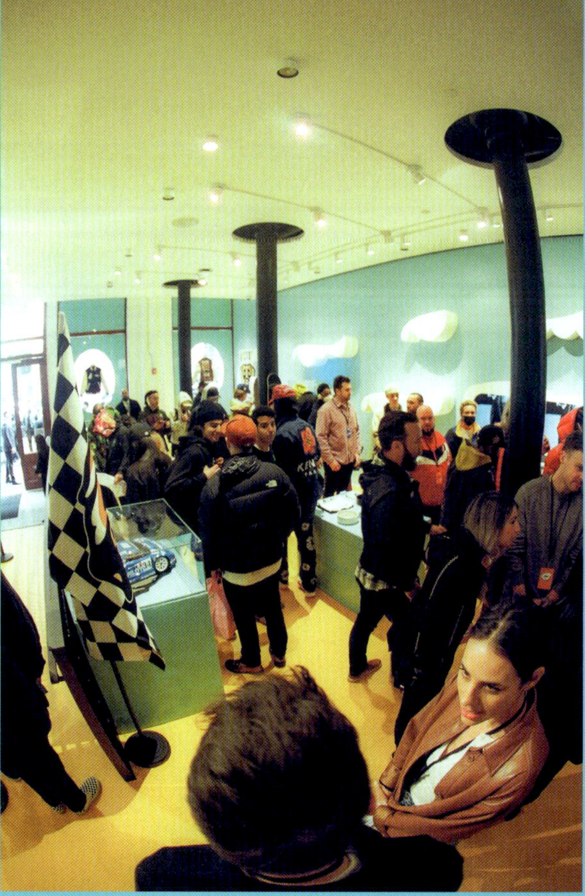

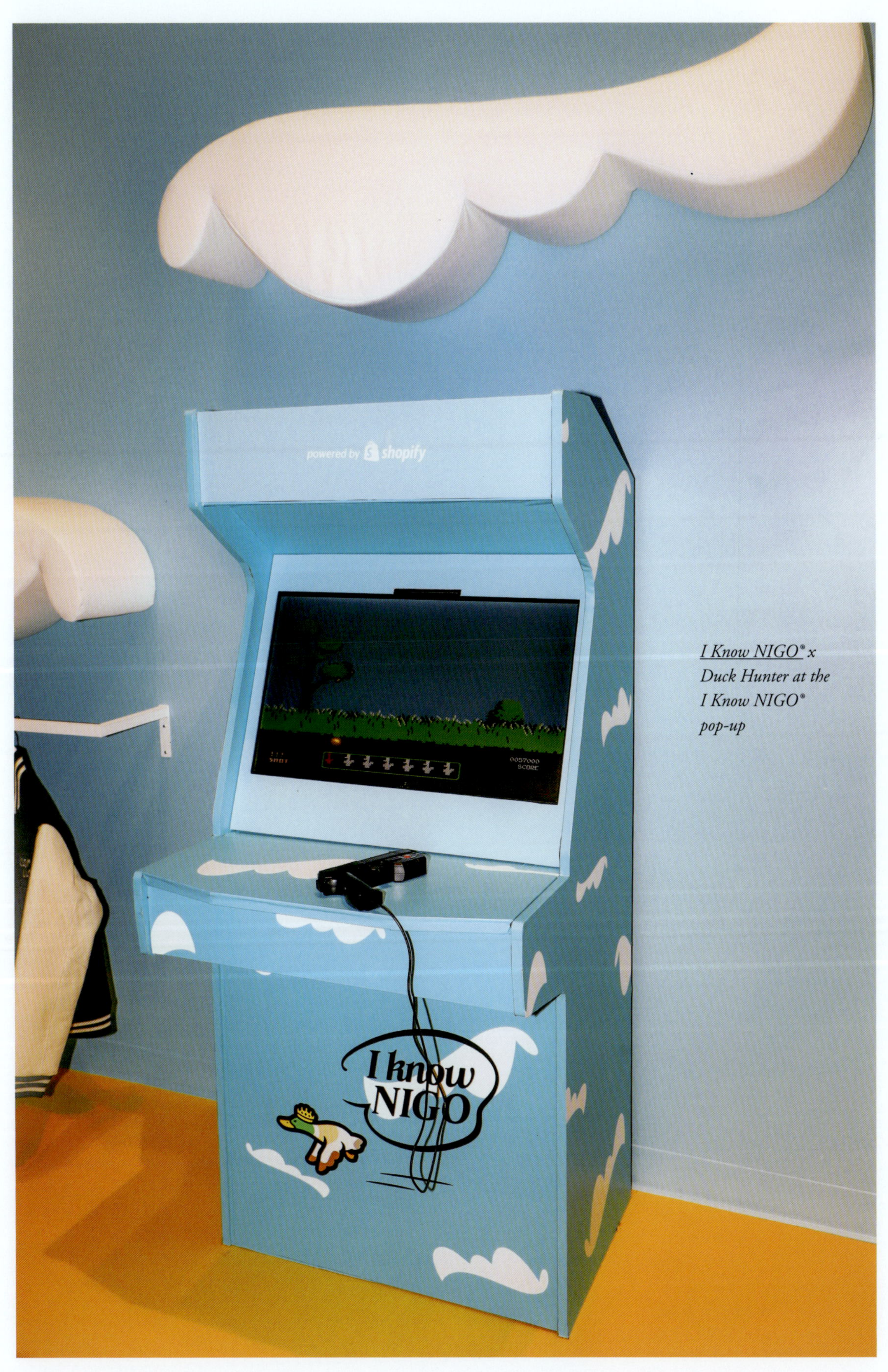

I Know NIGO® x Duck Hunter at the I Know NIGO® pop-up

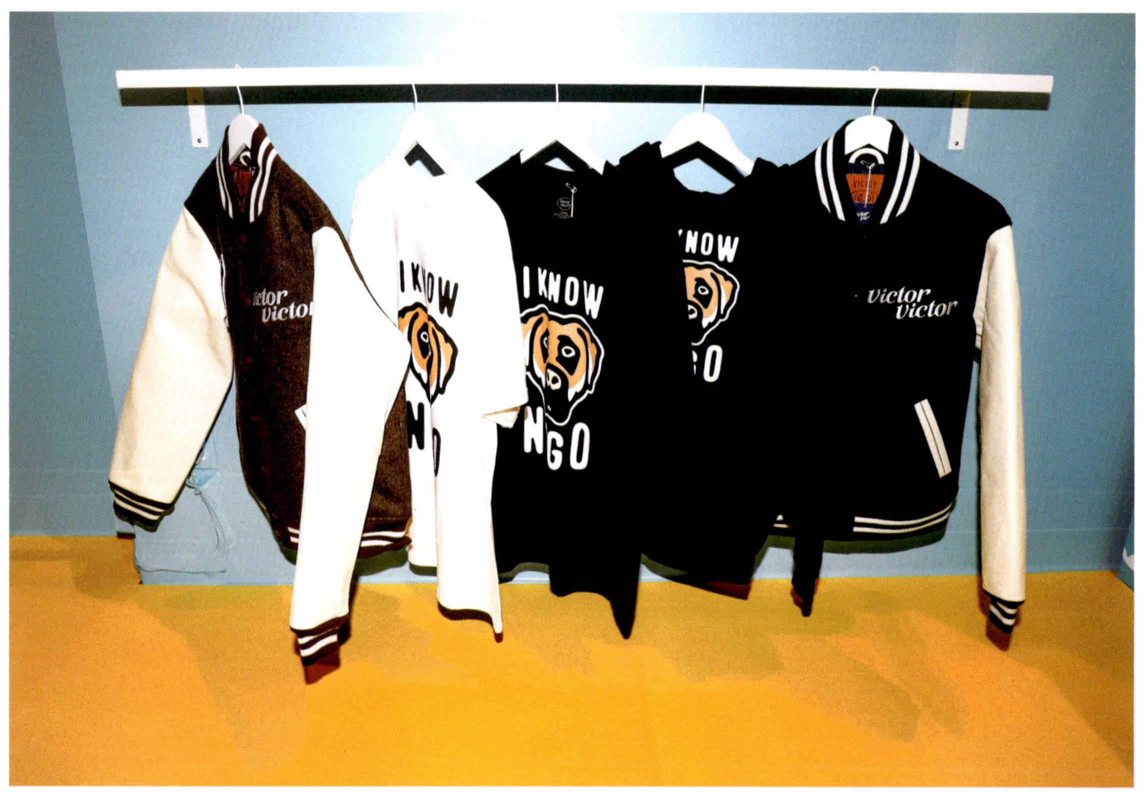
Victor
Victor
I KNOW
NGO
I KNOW
NIGO
KNOW
GO
Victor
Victor

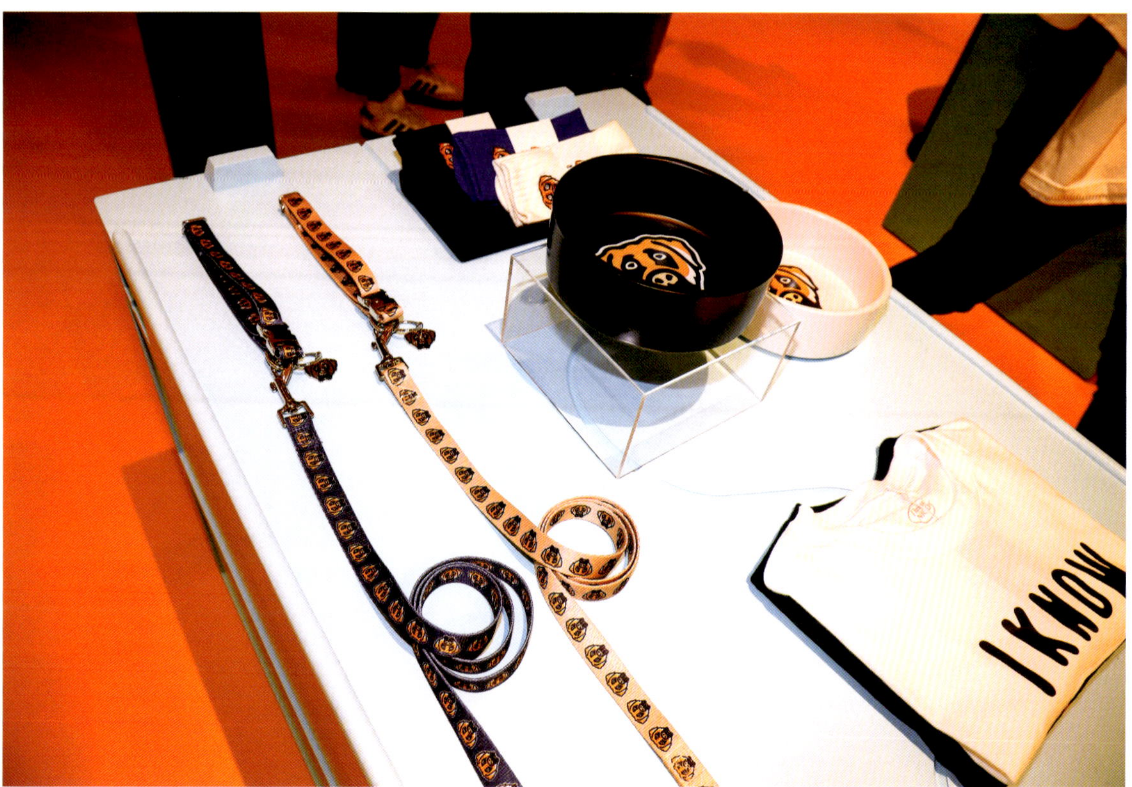
I KNOW

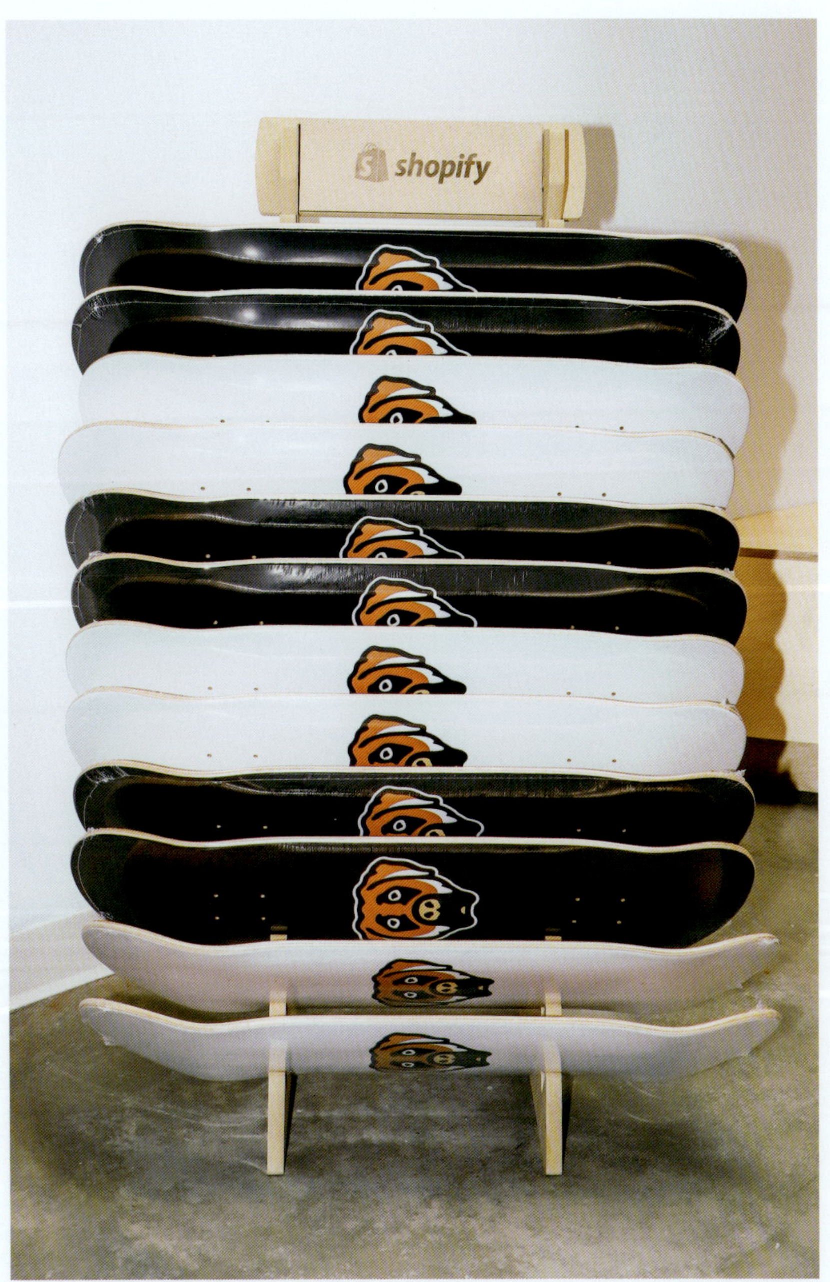

VICTOR VICTOR skate decks and other items such as the I Know NIGO® varsity jacket and other collaborative goods were made available for the first time

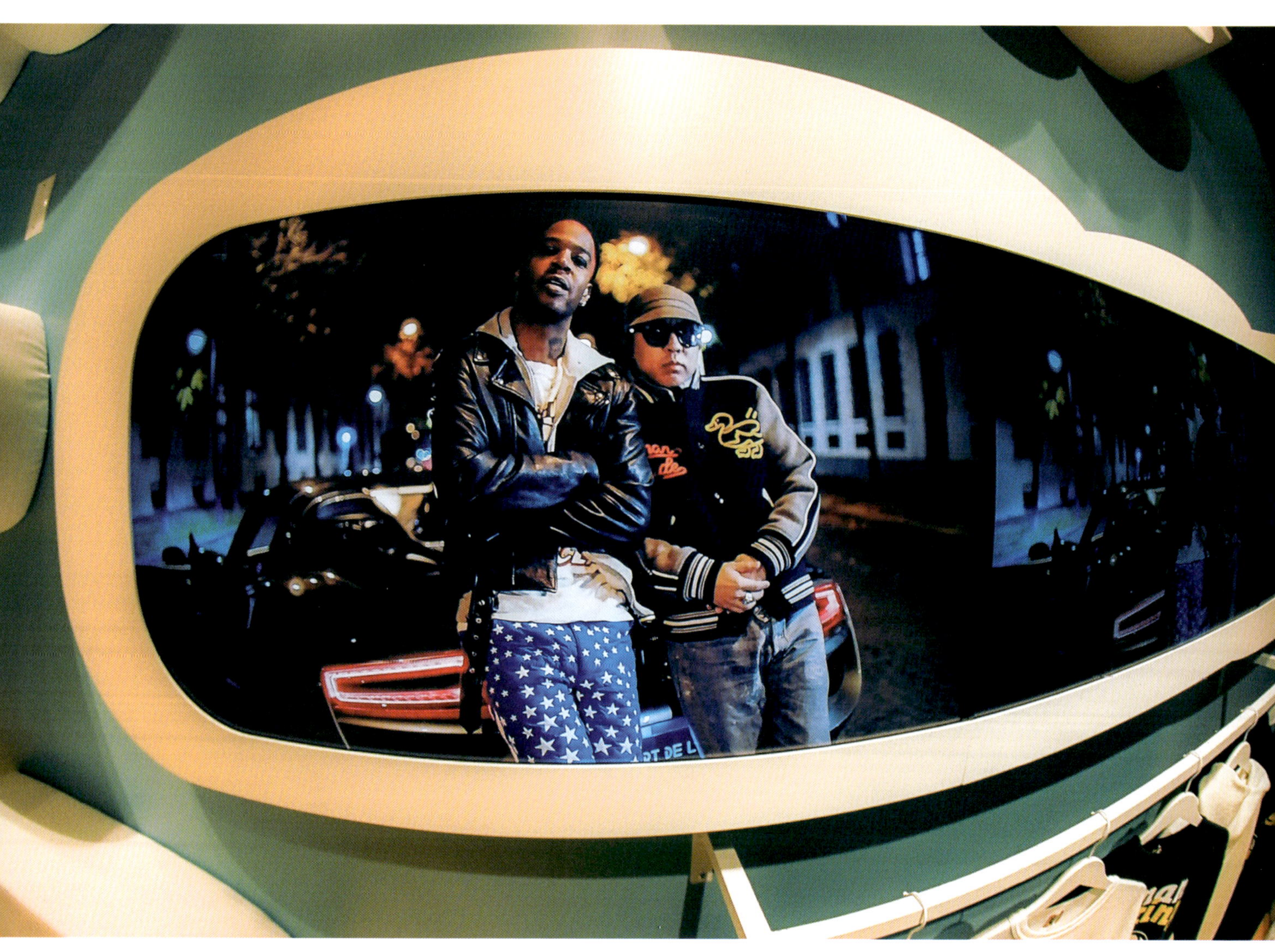

Kid Cudi and NIGO®, still from the "WANT IT BAD" video shoot, Paris, November 2021

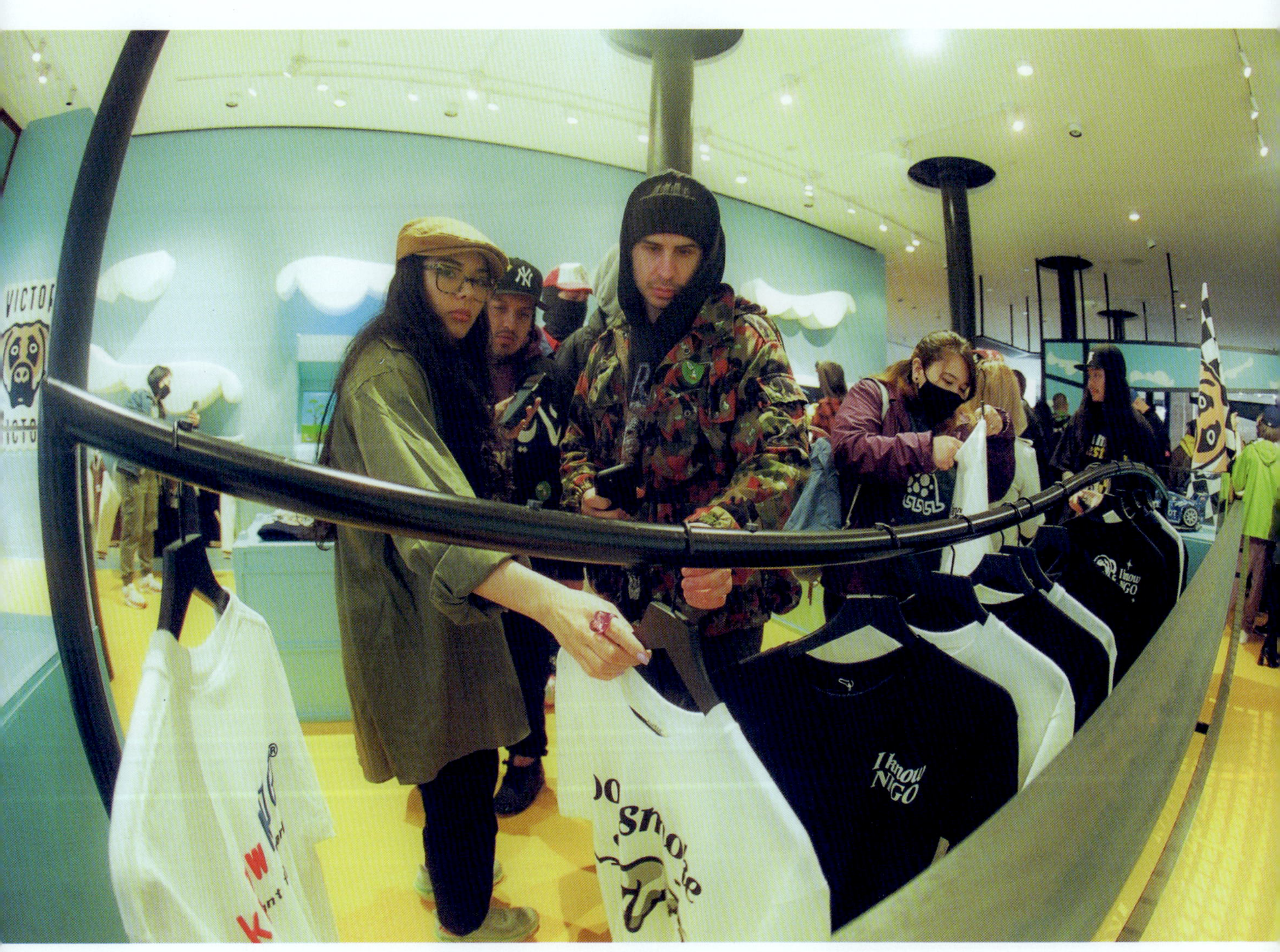
VICTOR
I know NIGO

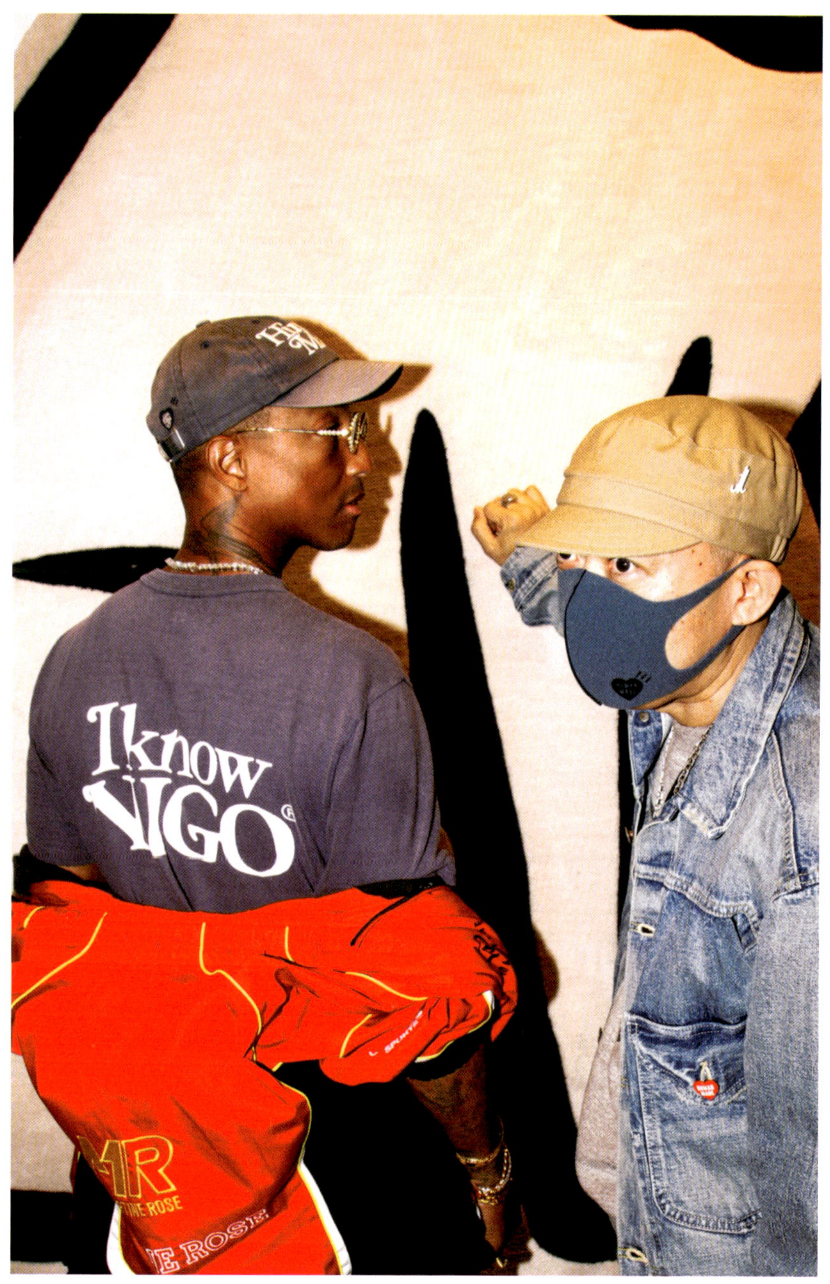

Pharrell & NIGO® at the
I Know NIGO® pop-up

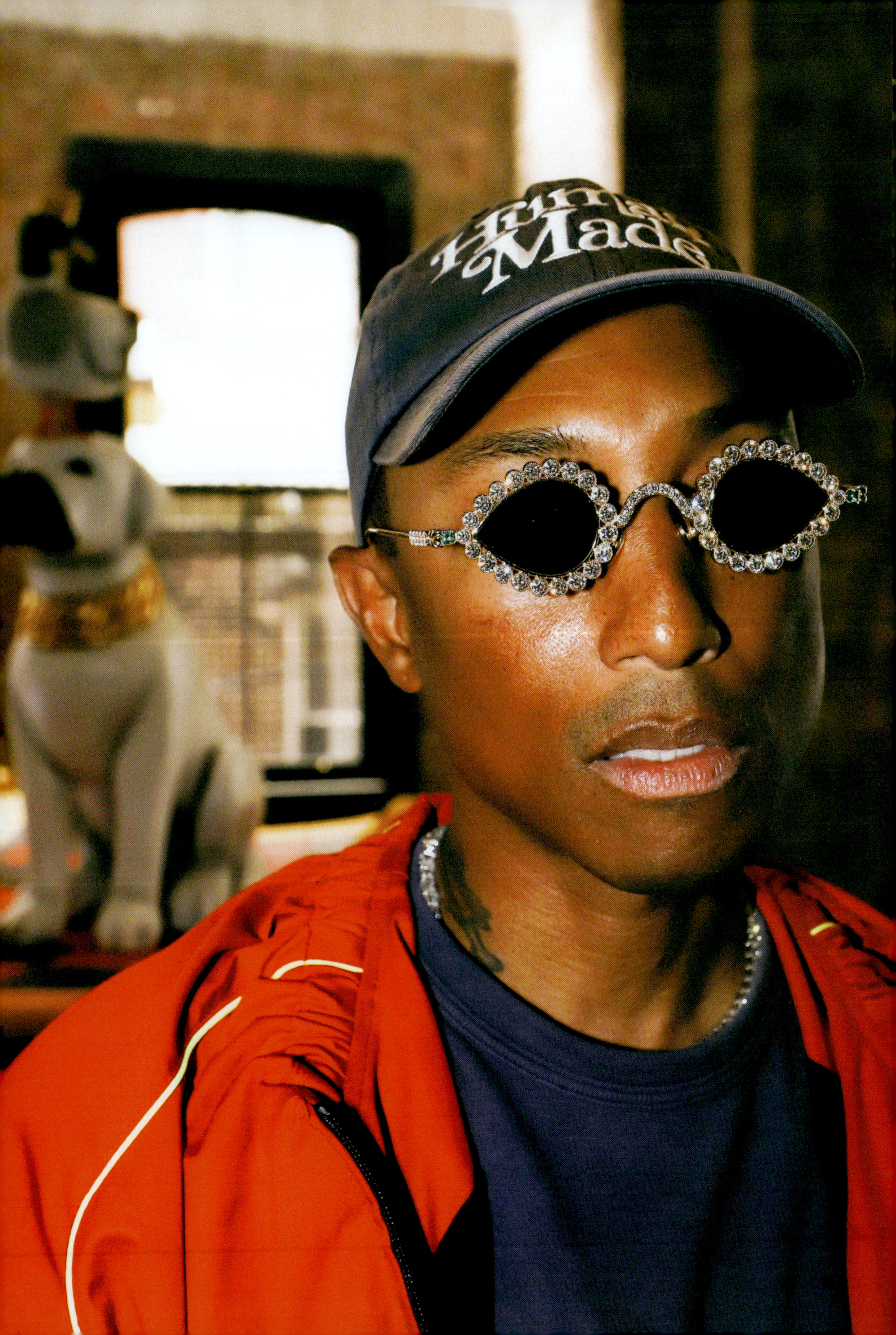
Made

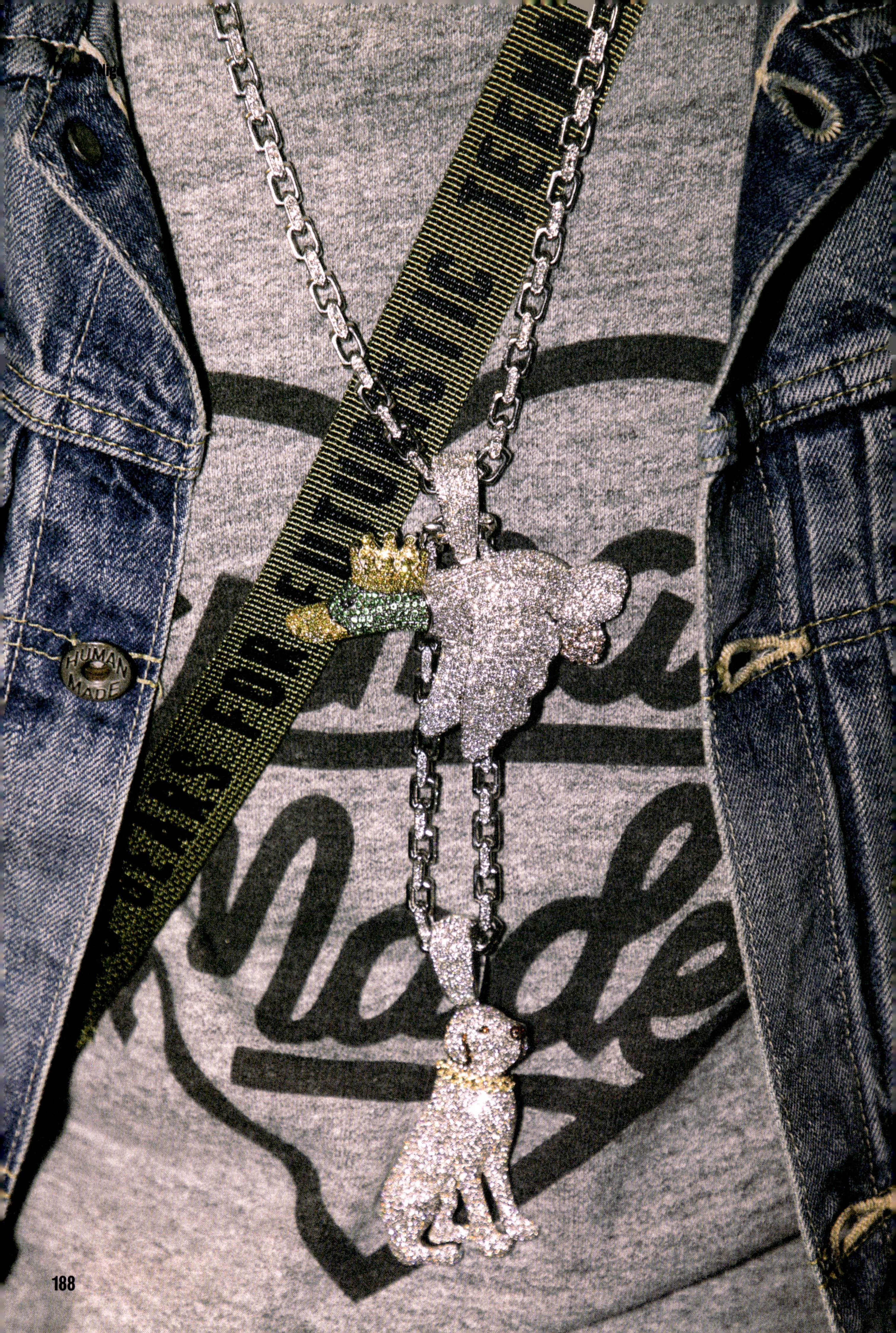
HUMAN
MADE

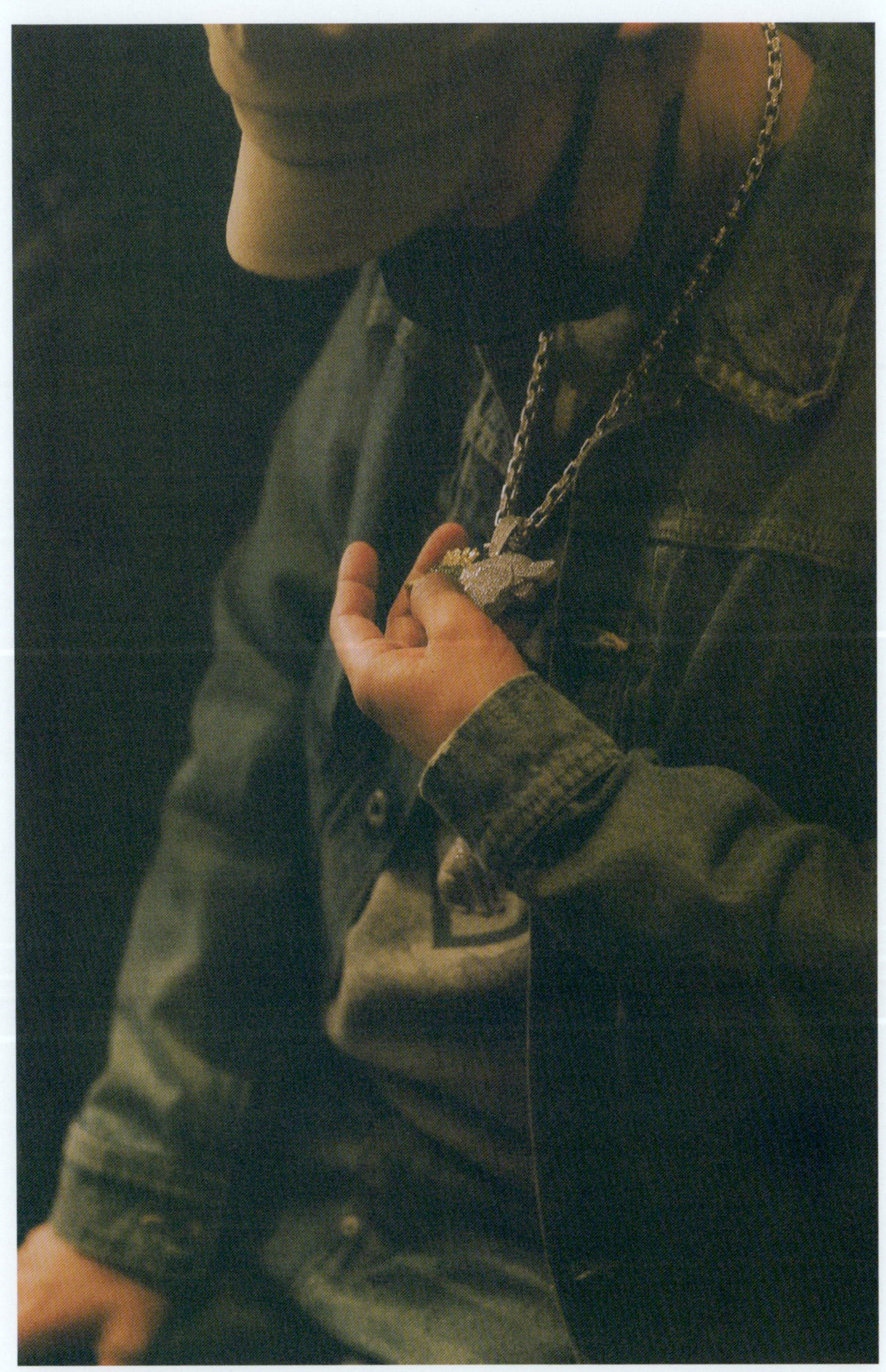

NIGO® x Jacob & Co custom
I Know NIGO® & VICTOR
VICTOR pendants

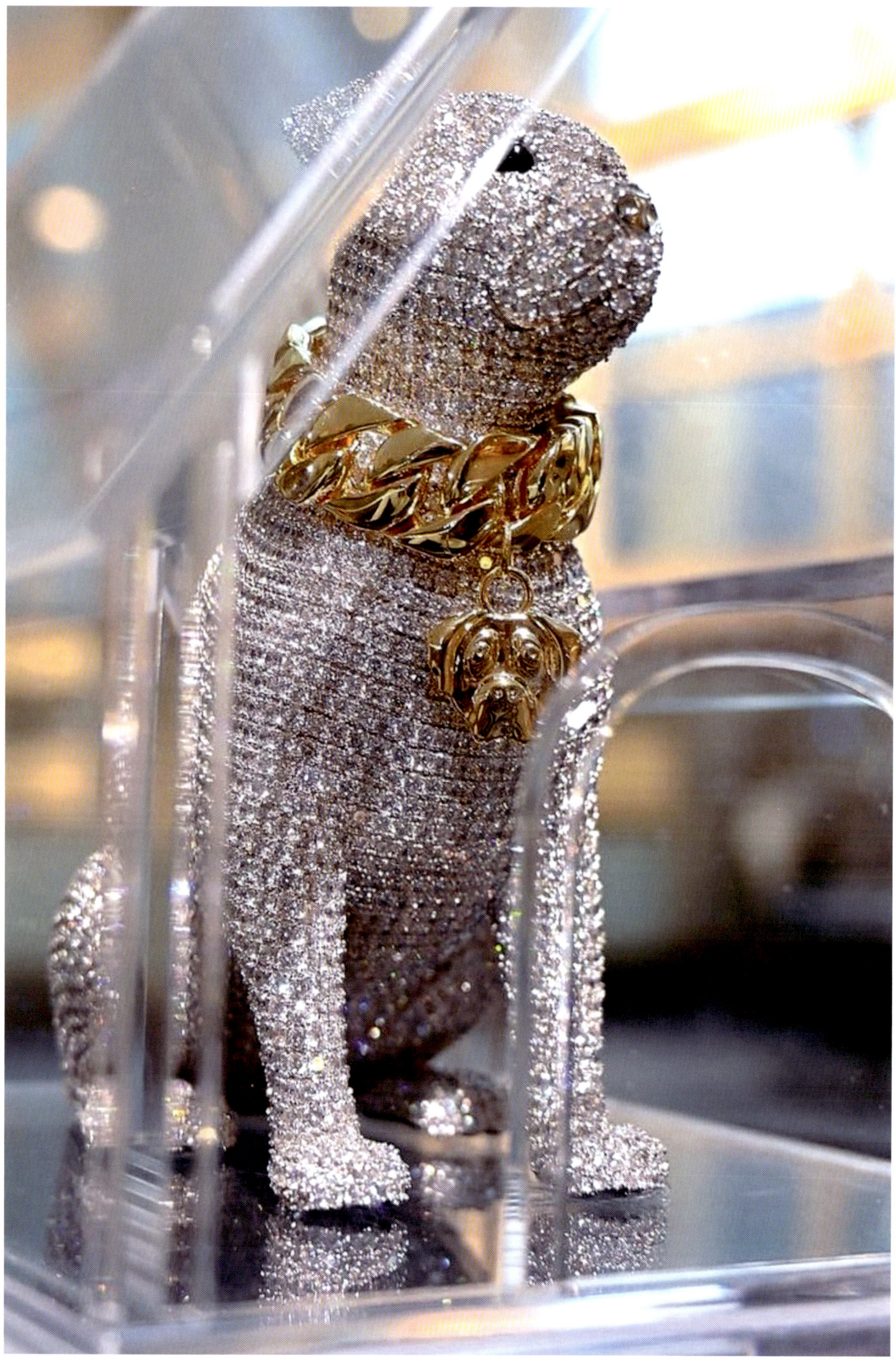

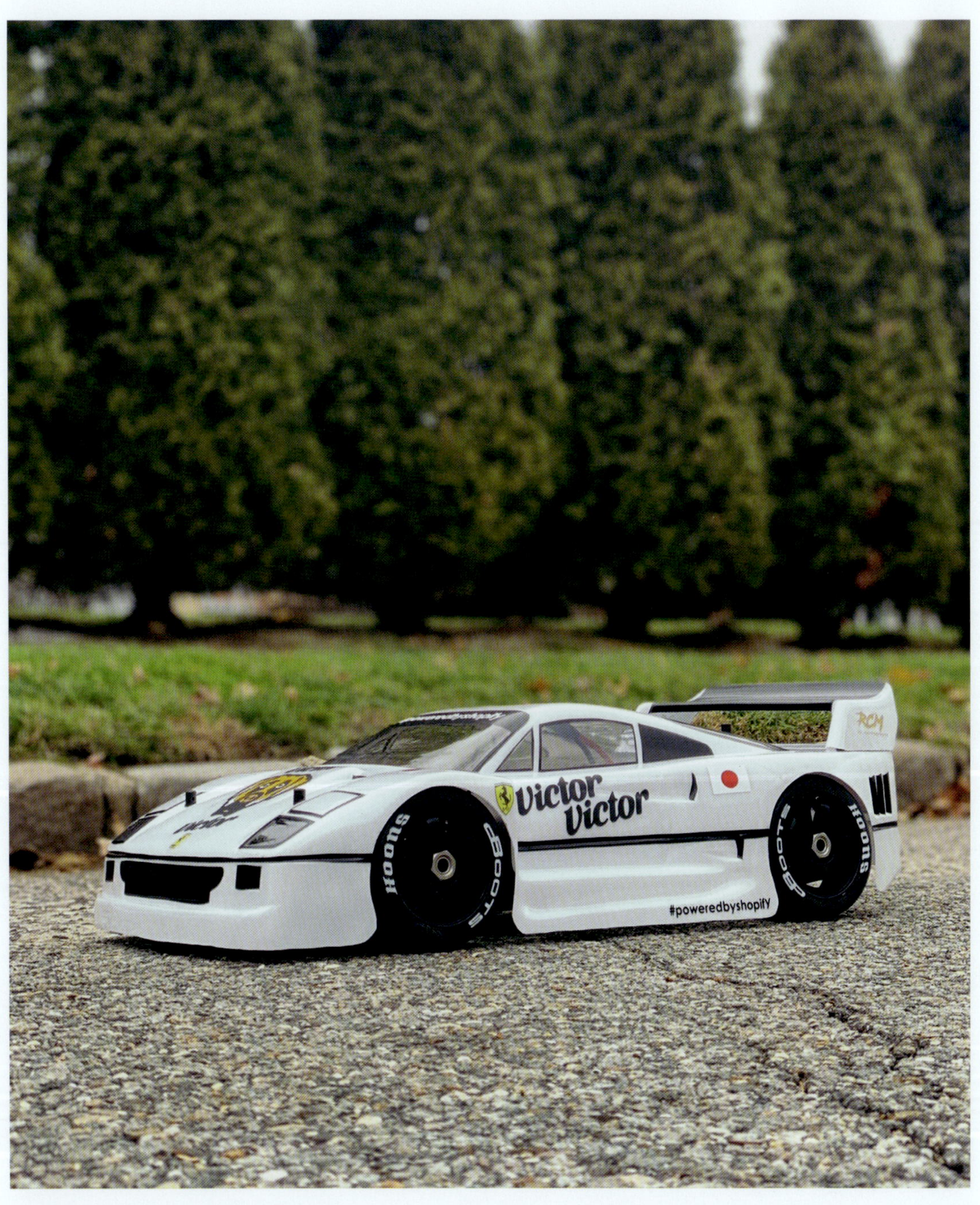

VICTOR VICTOR decorative dog mascot & doghouse at the I Know NIGO® pop-up; custom RC Car

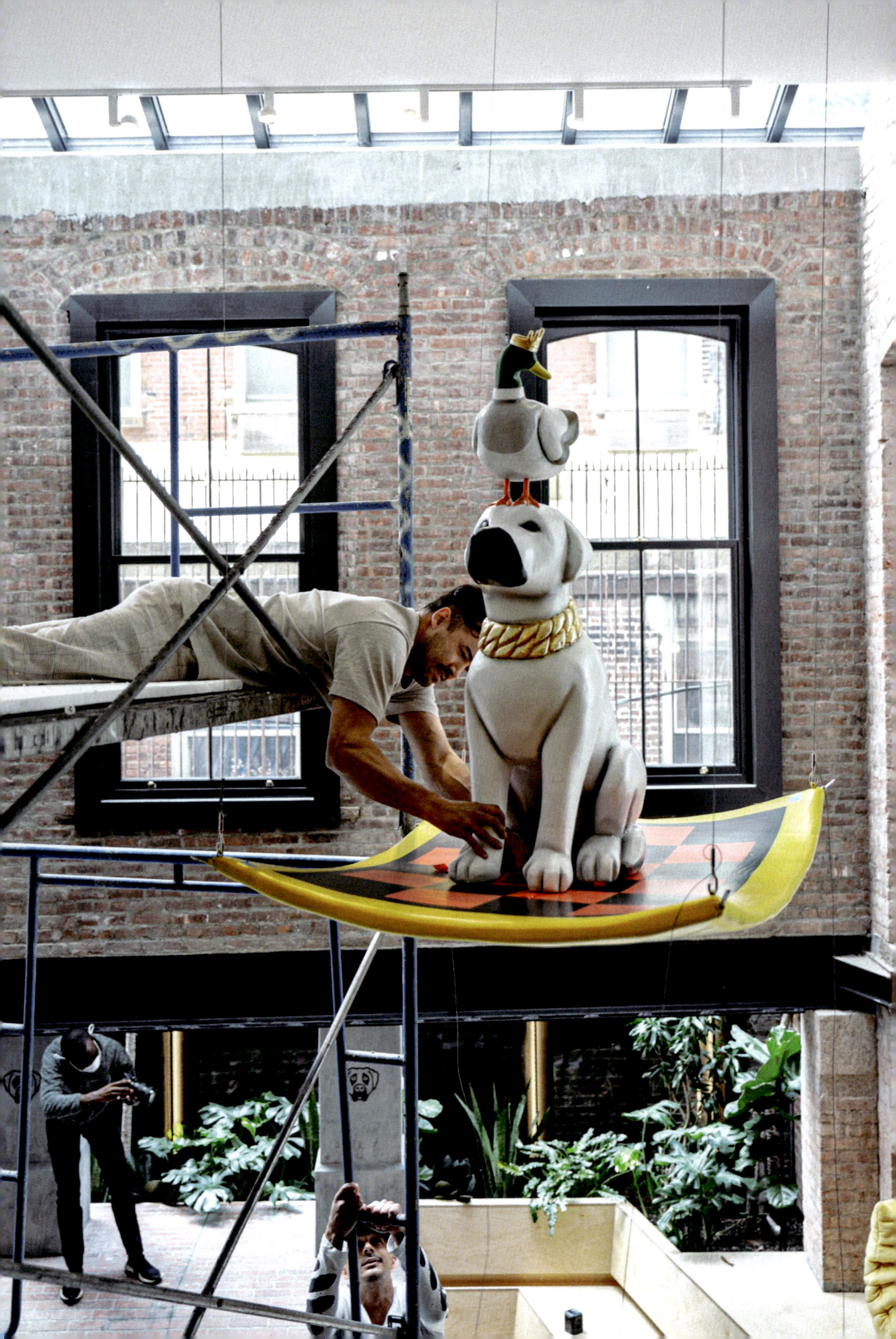

Behind the scenes of the construction of the I Know NIGO® pop-up, designed by AWGE, with the effigies built by Anthony Hart

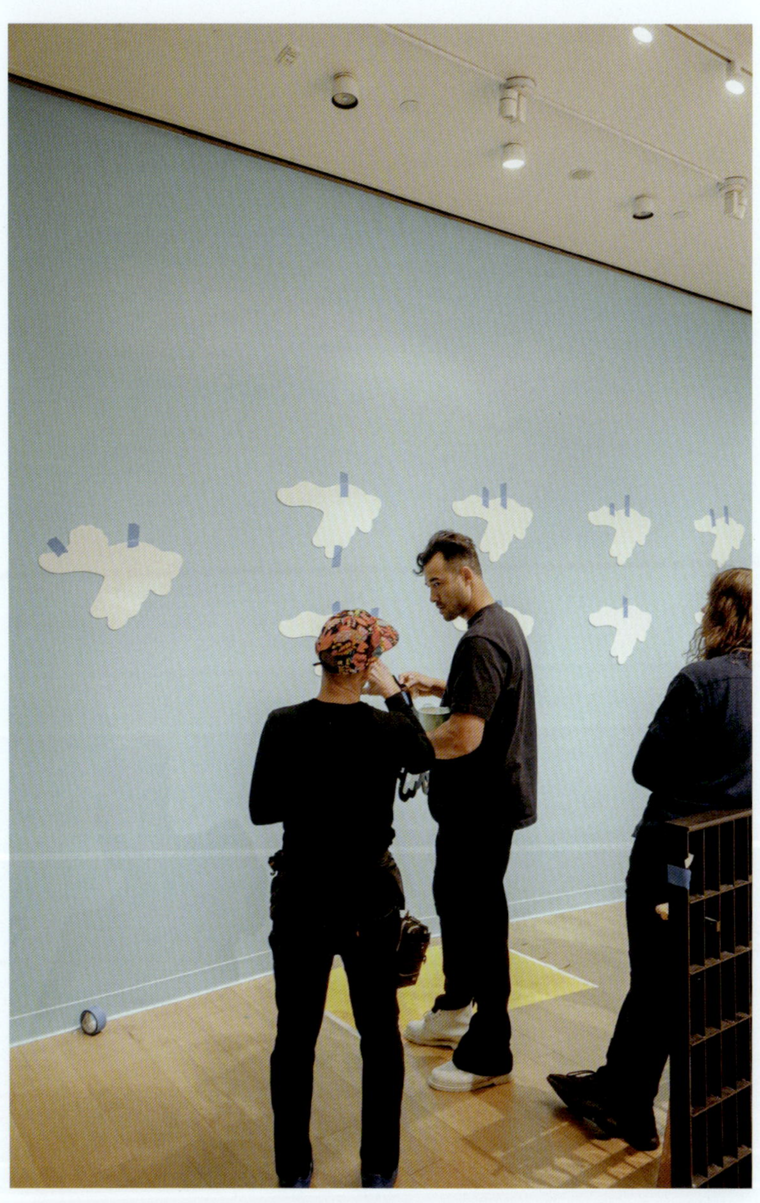

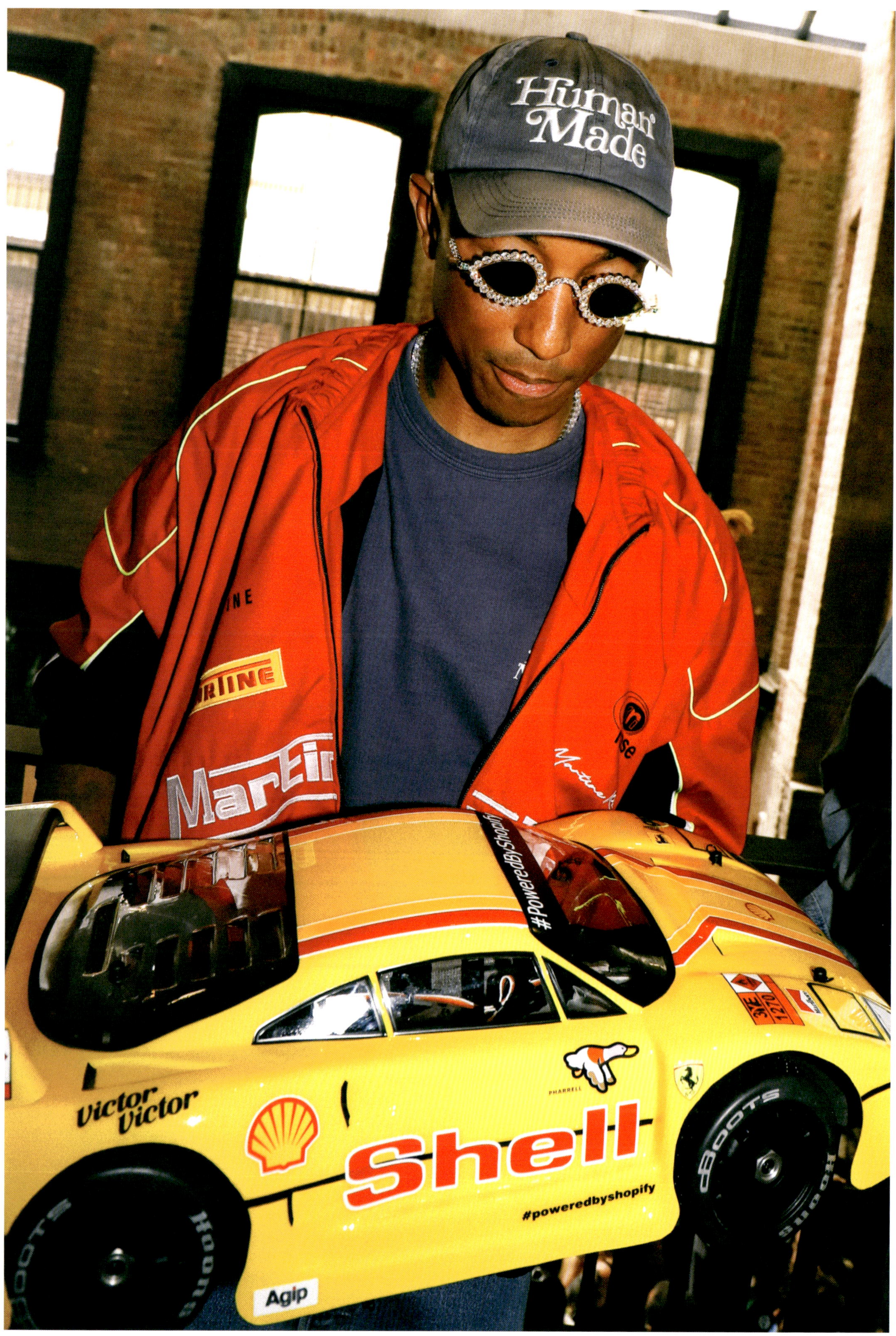
Human Made
Victor Victor
Shell
#poweredbyshopify
Agip

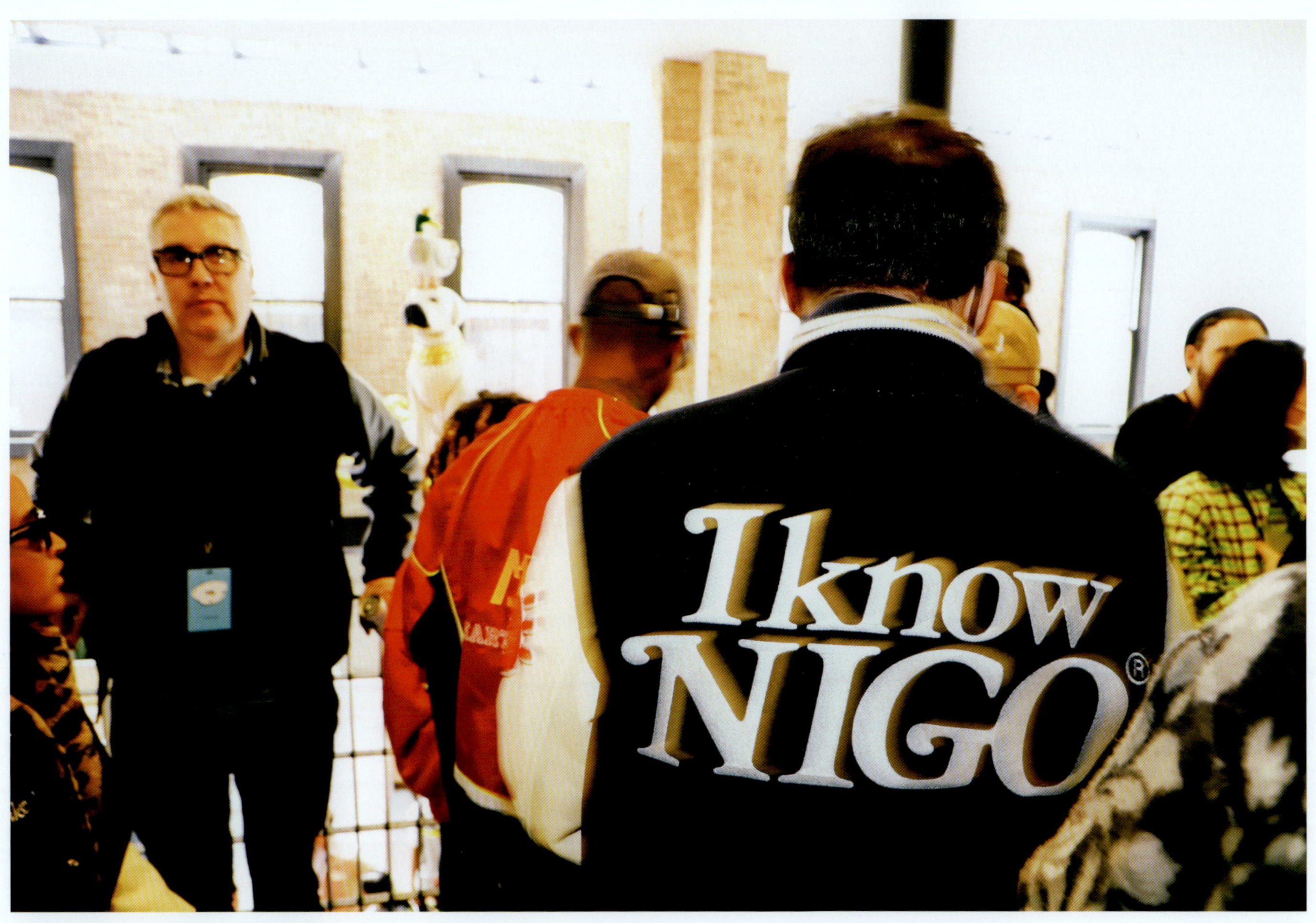

Pharrell with an alternate colorway of the custom RC Car; Friends & Family *I Know NIGO®* *x Human Made varsity jacket*

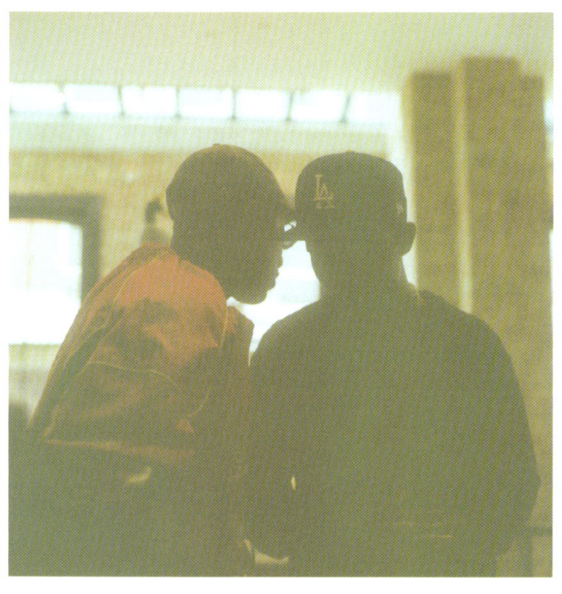

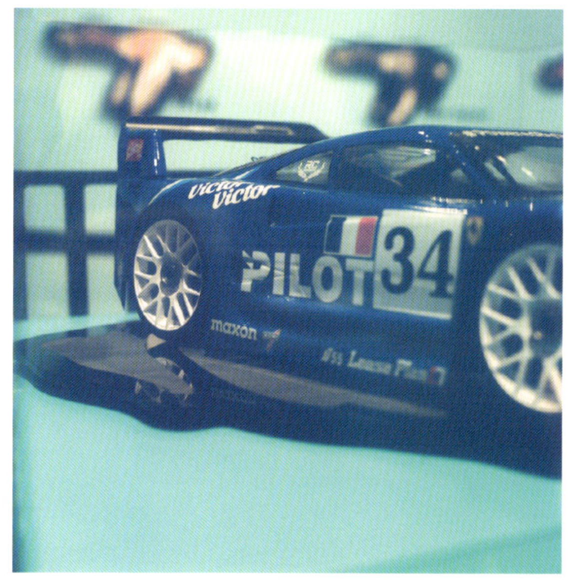

Victor
PILOT 34
maxon

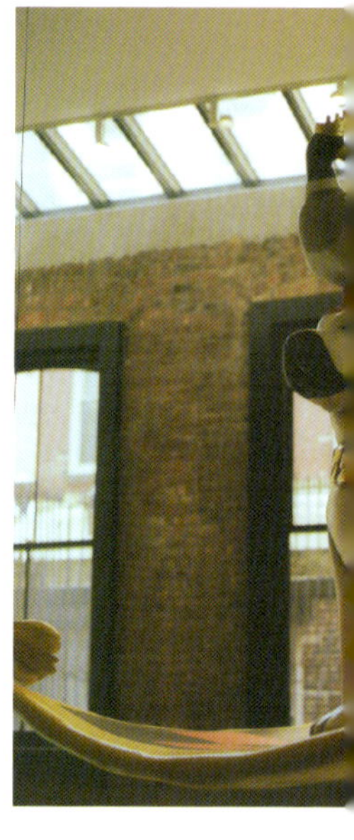

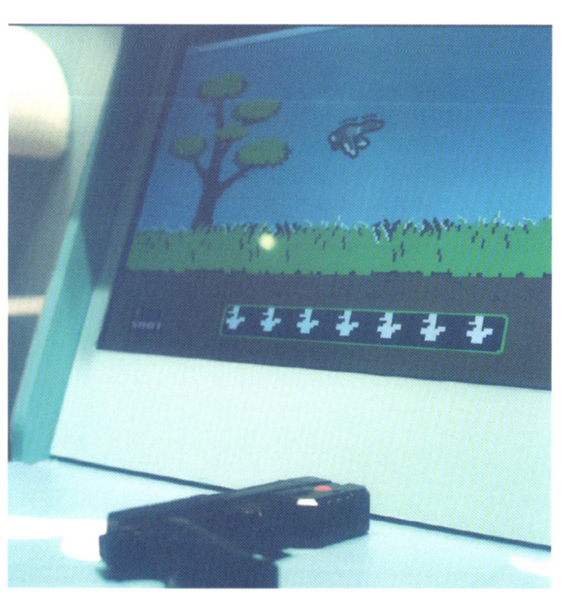

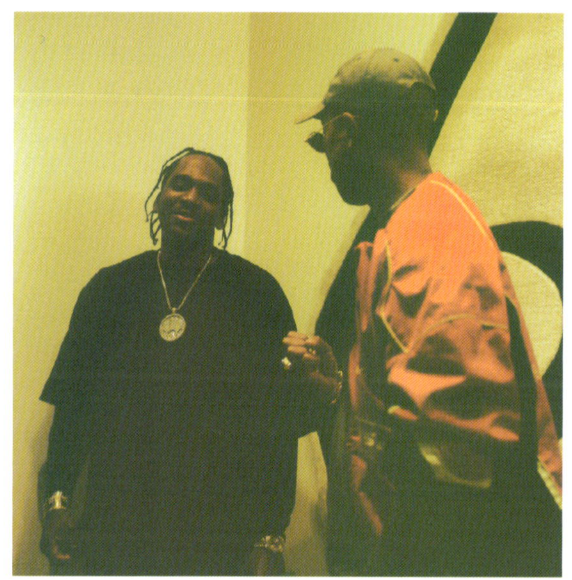

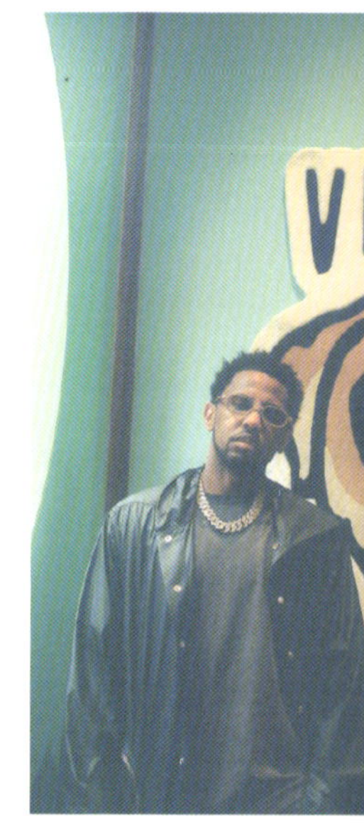

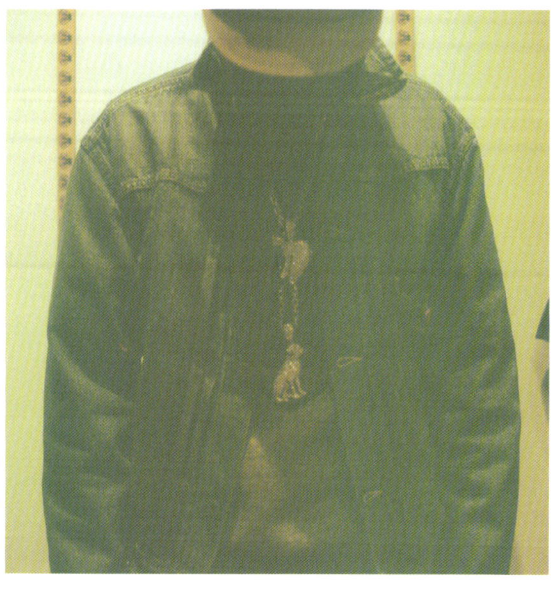

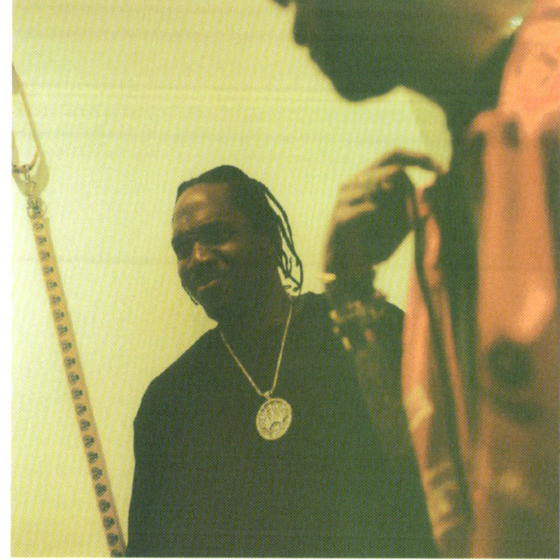

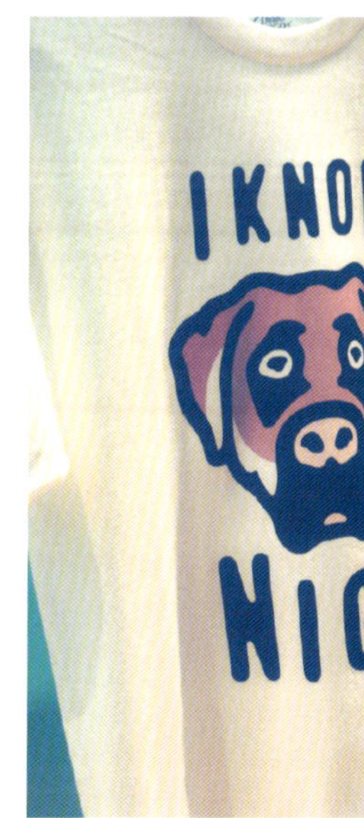

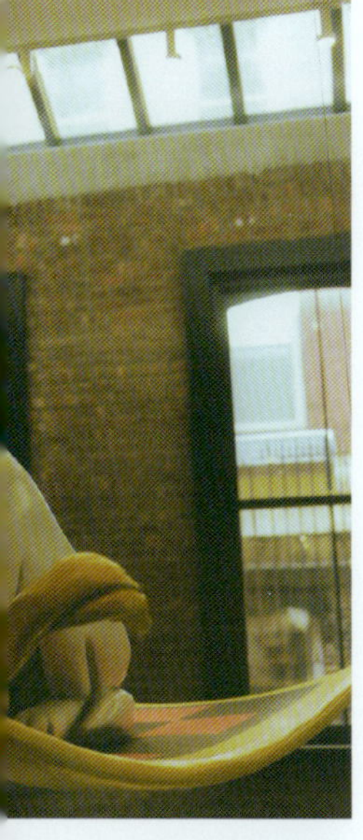
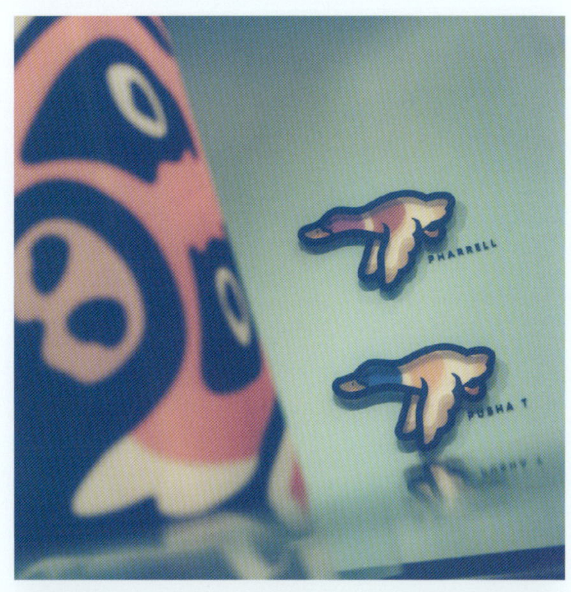
PHARRELL
PUSHA T
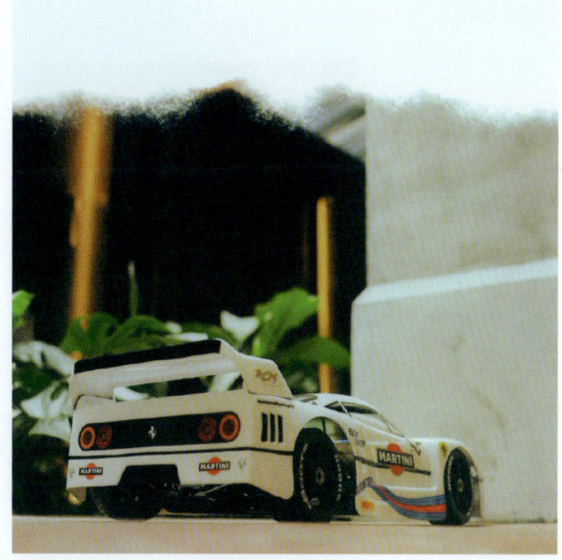
MARTINI
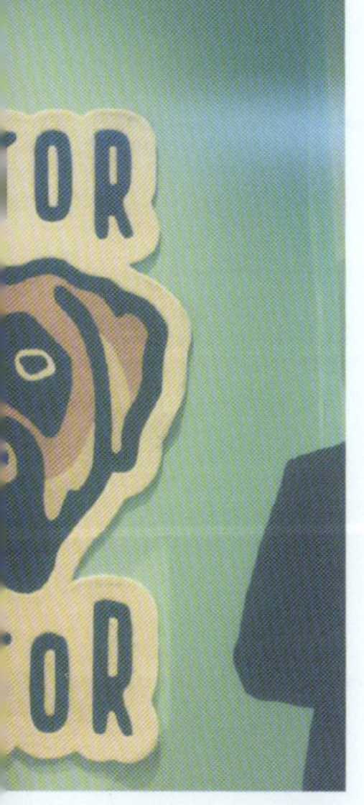
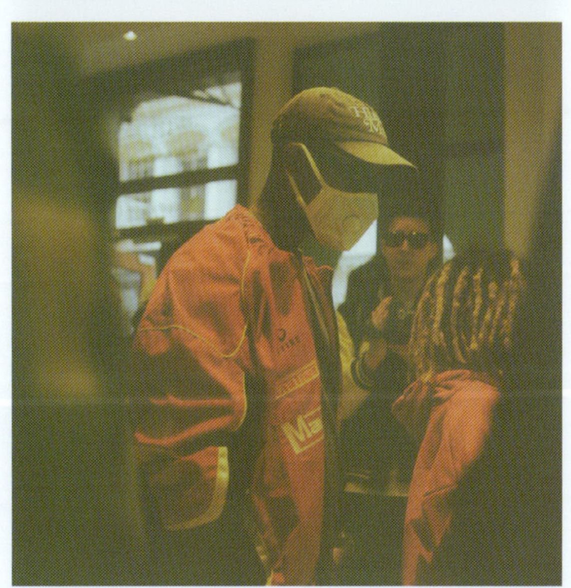
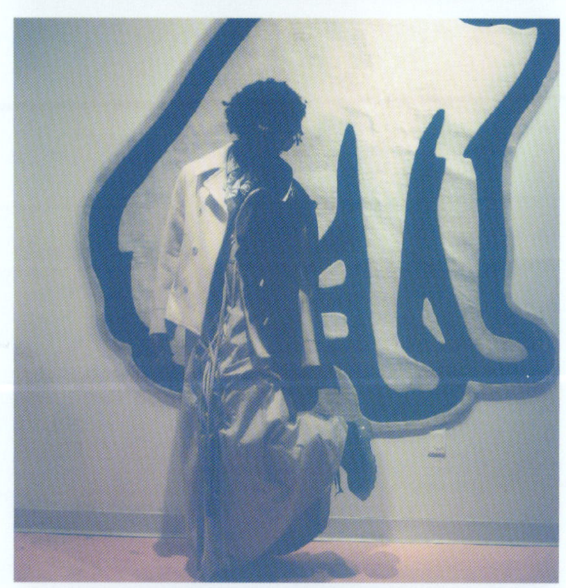
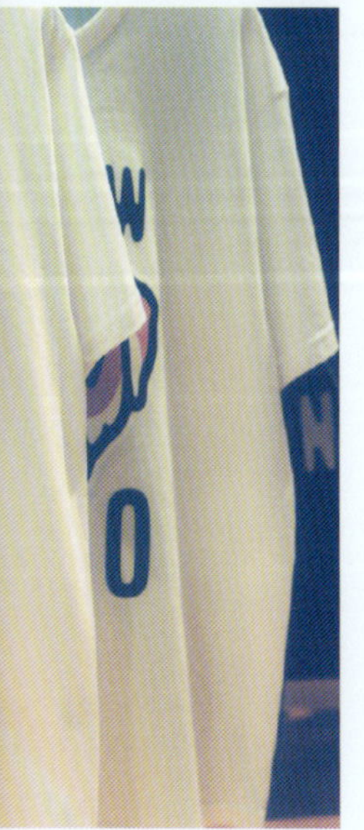
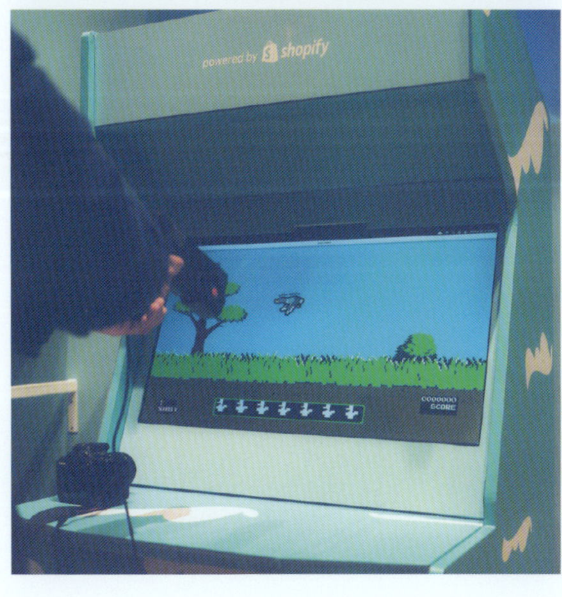
powered by shopify
SCORE
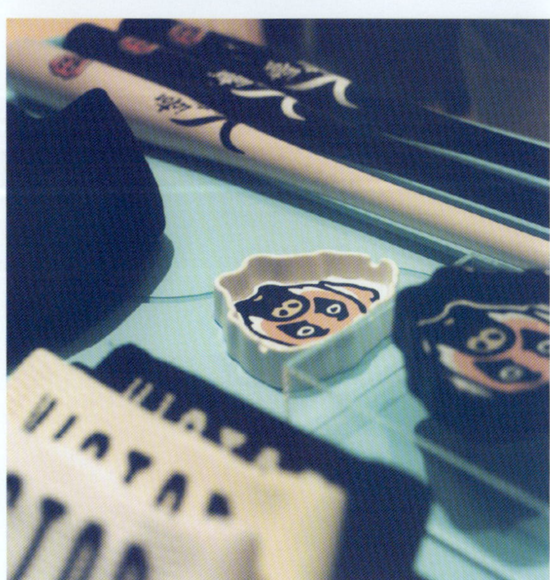

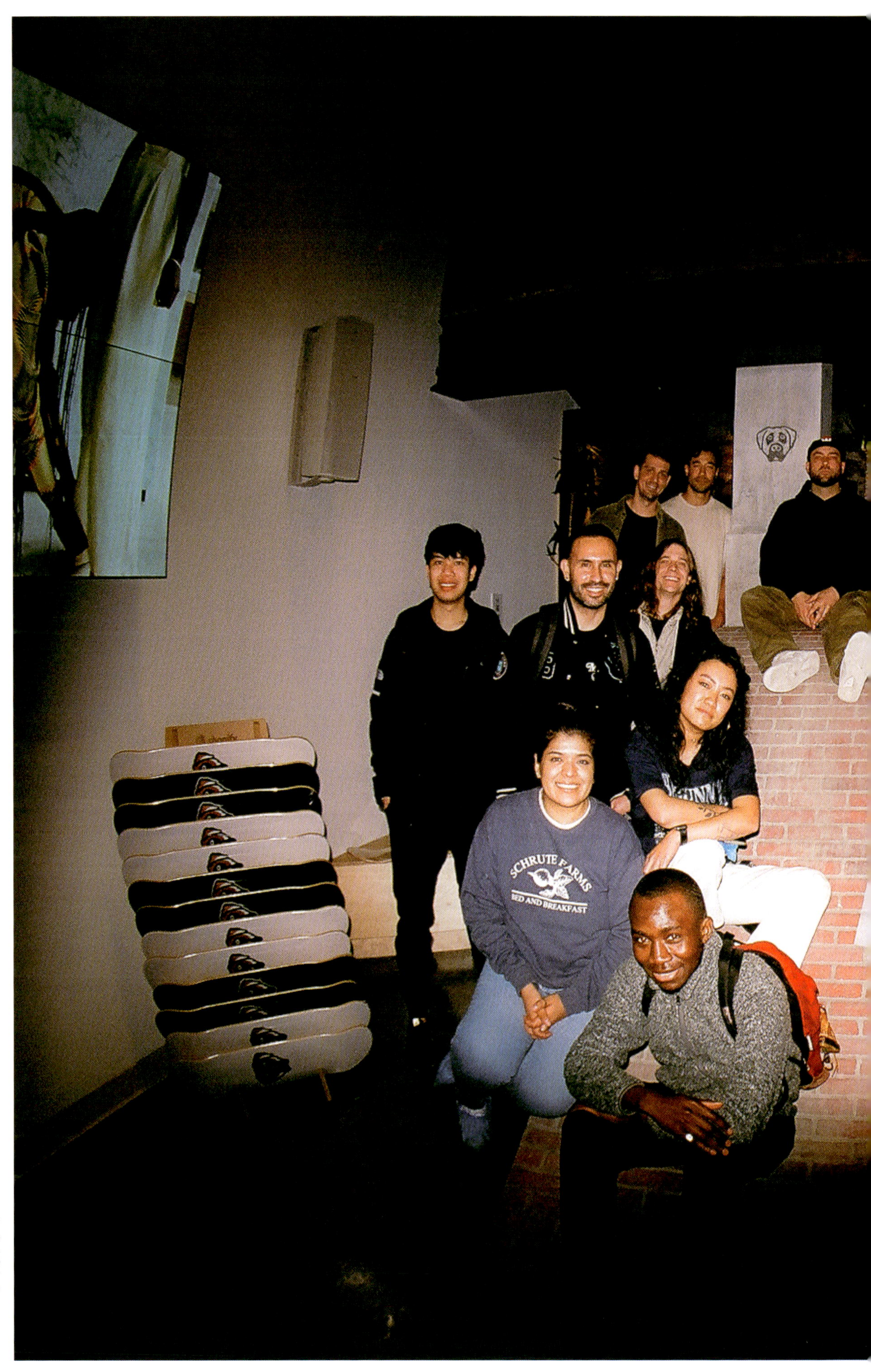

The team at Shopify at the I Know NIGO® pop-up

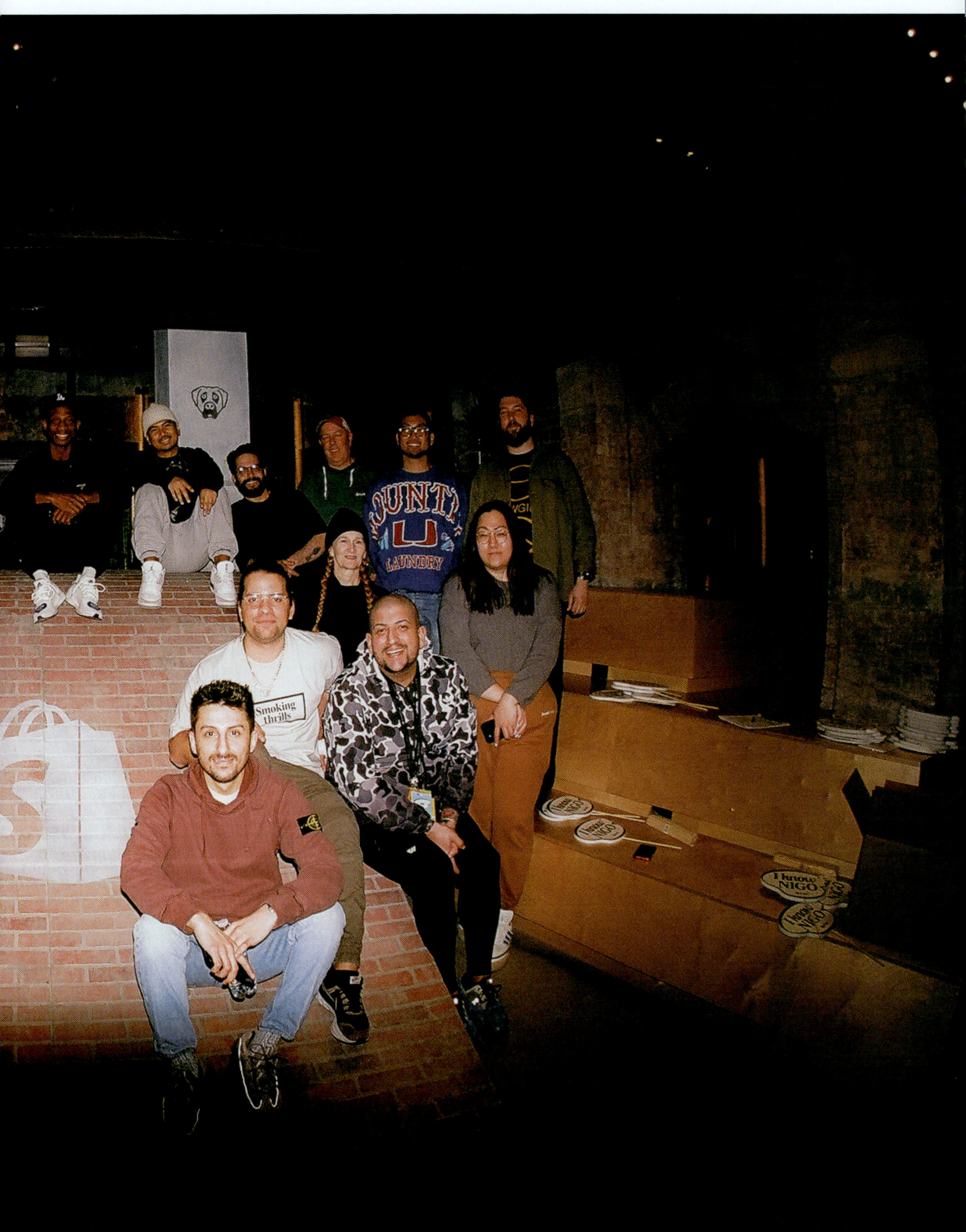
LAUNDRY
Smoking
thrills
I know
NIGO

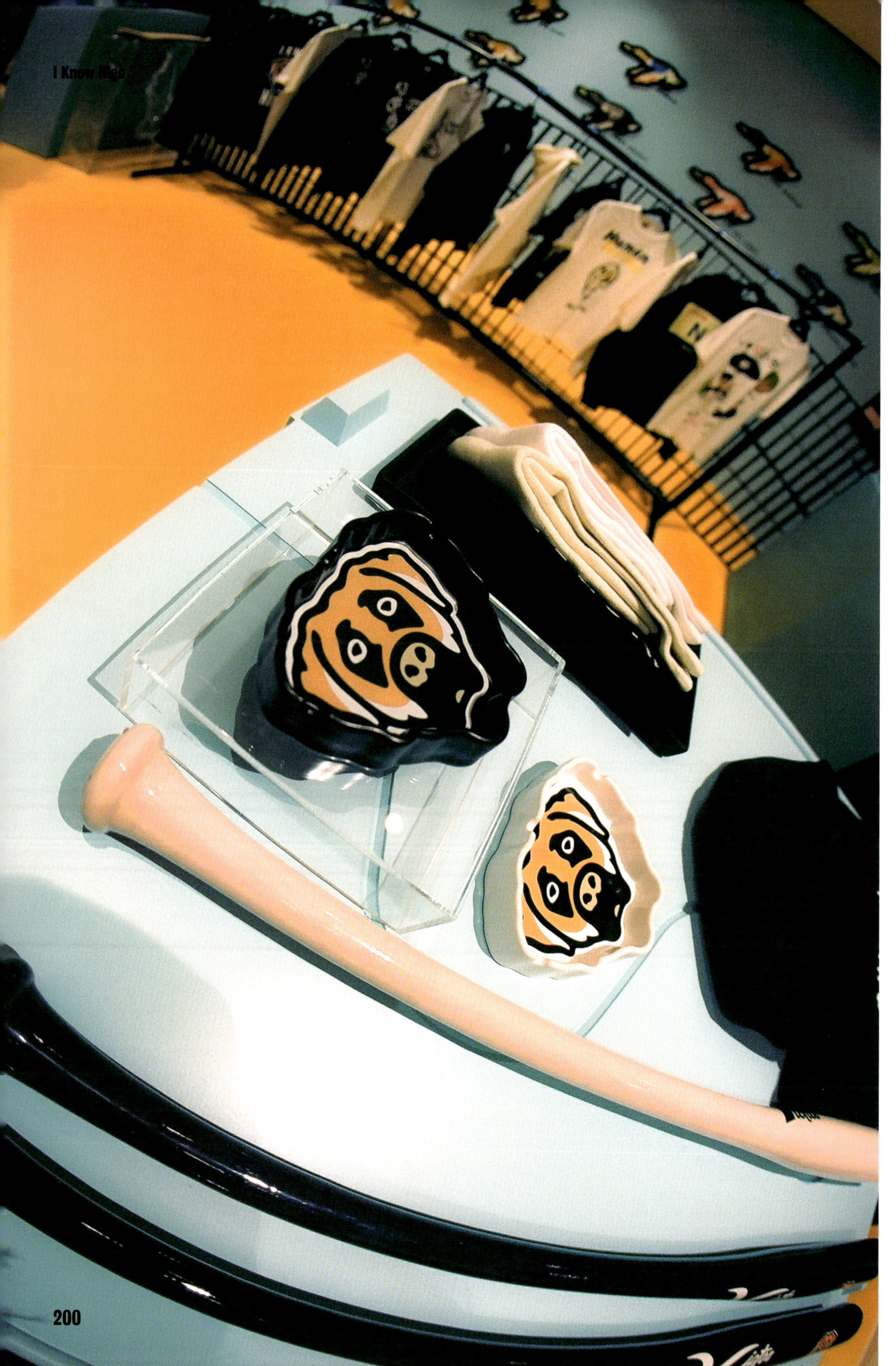

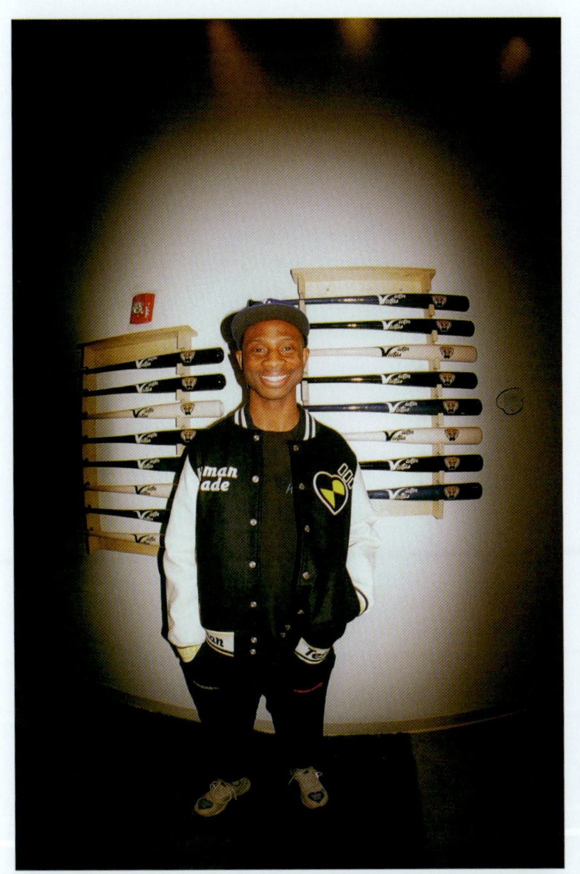

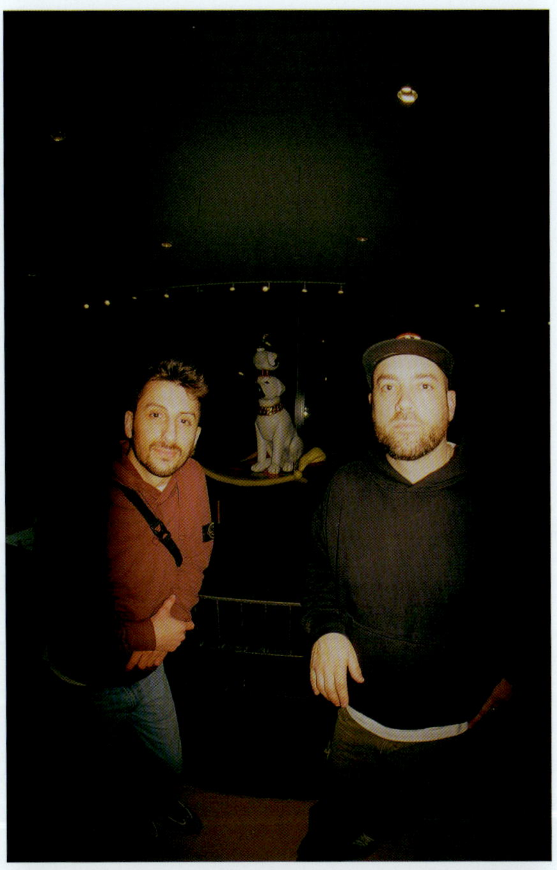

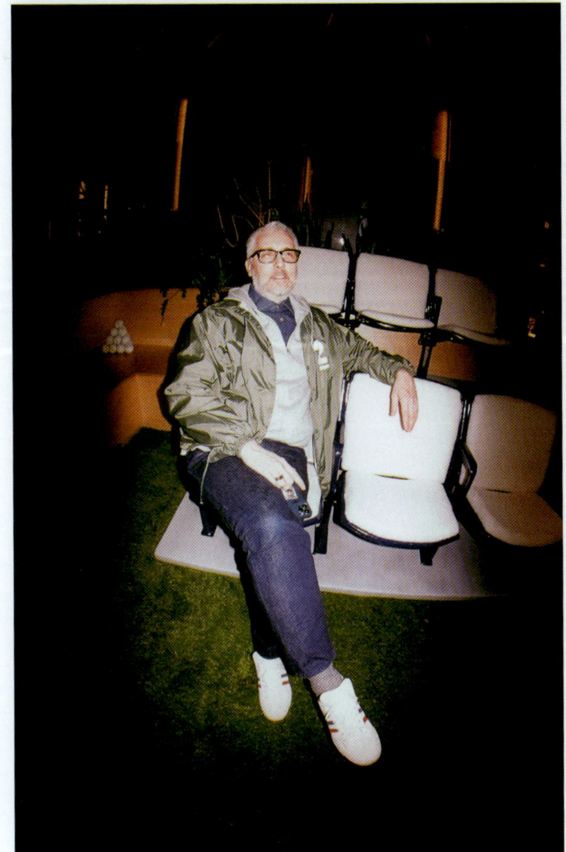

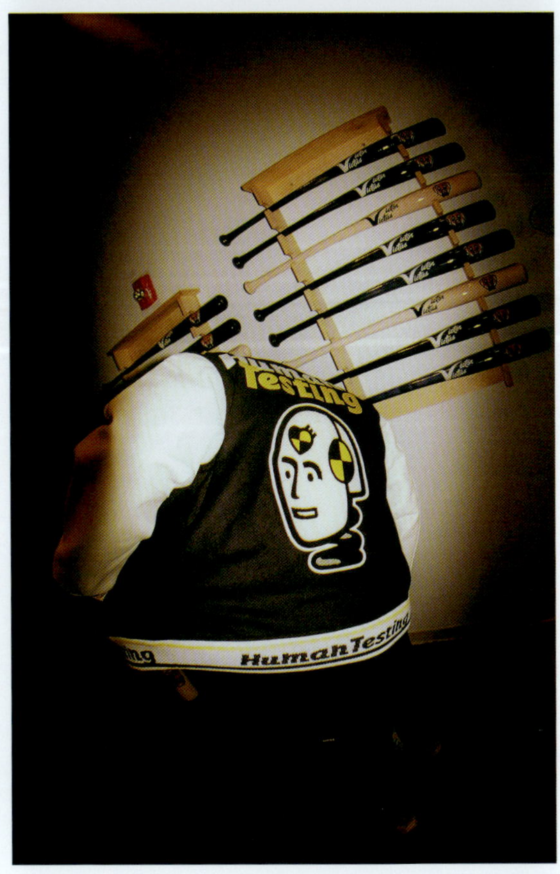

VICTOR VICTOR baseball bats in partnership with Victus

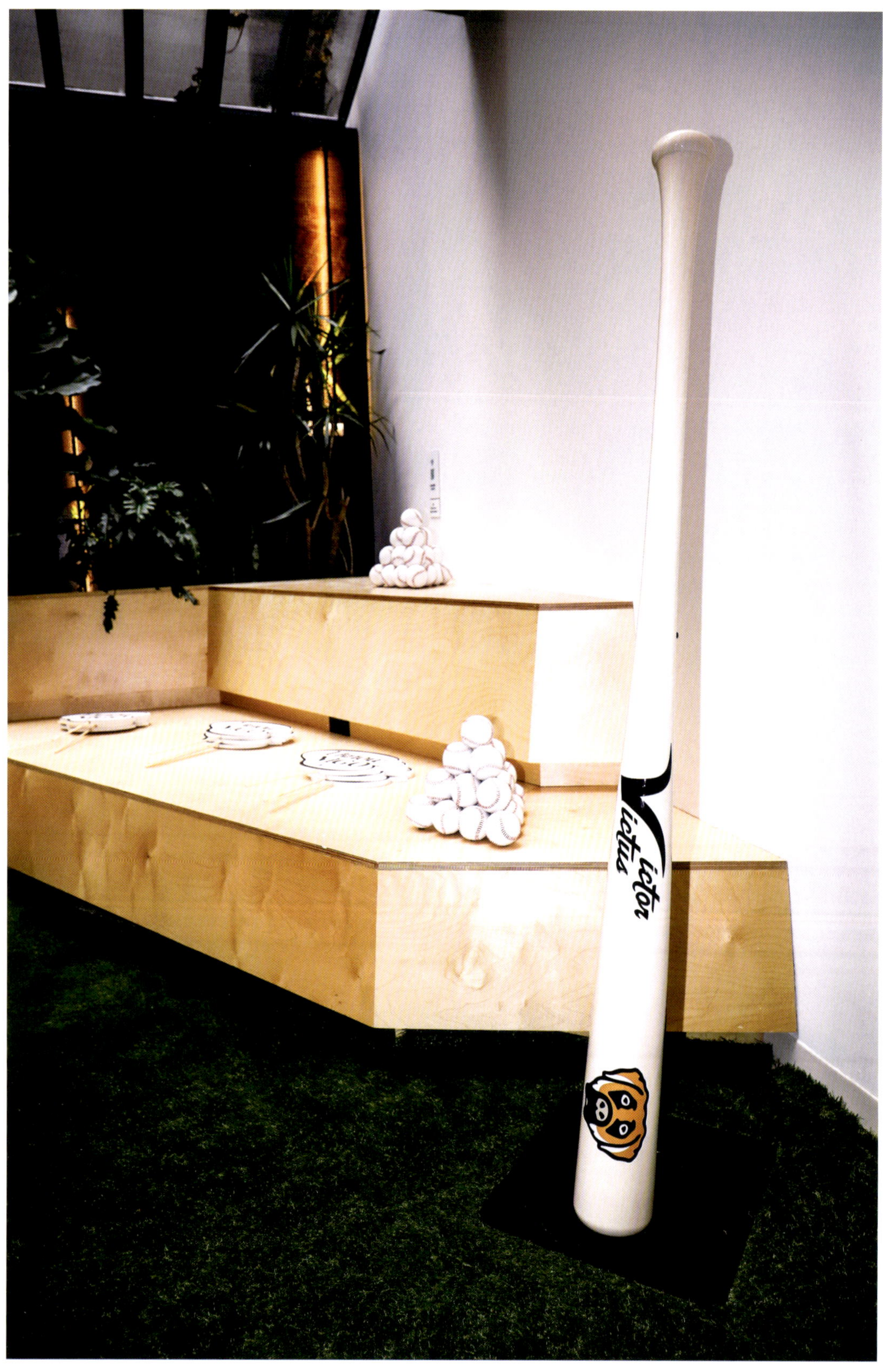
Victor
Victus

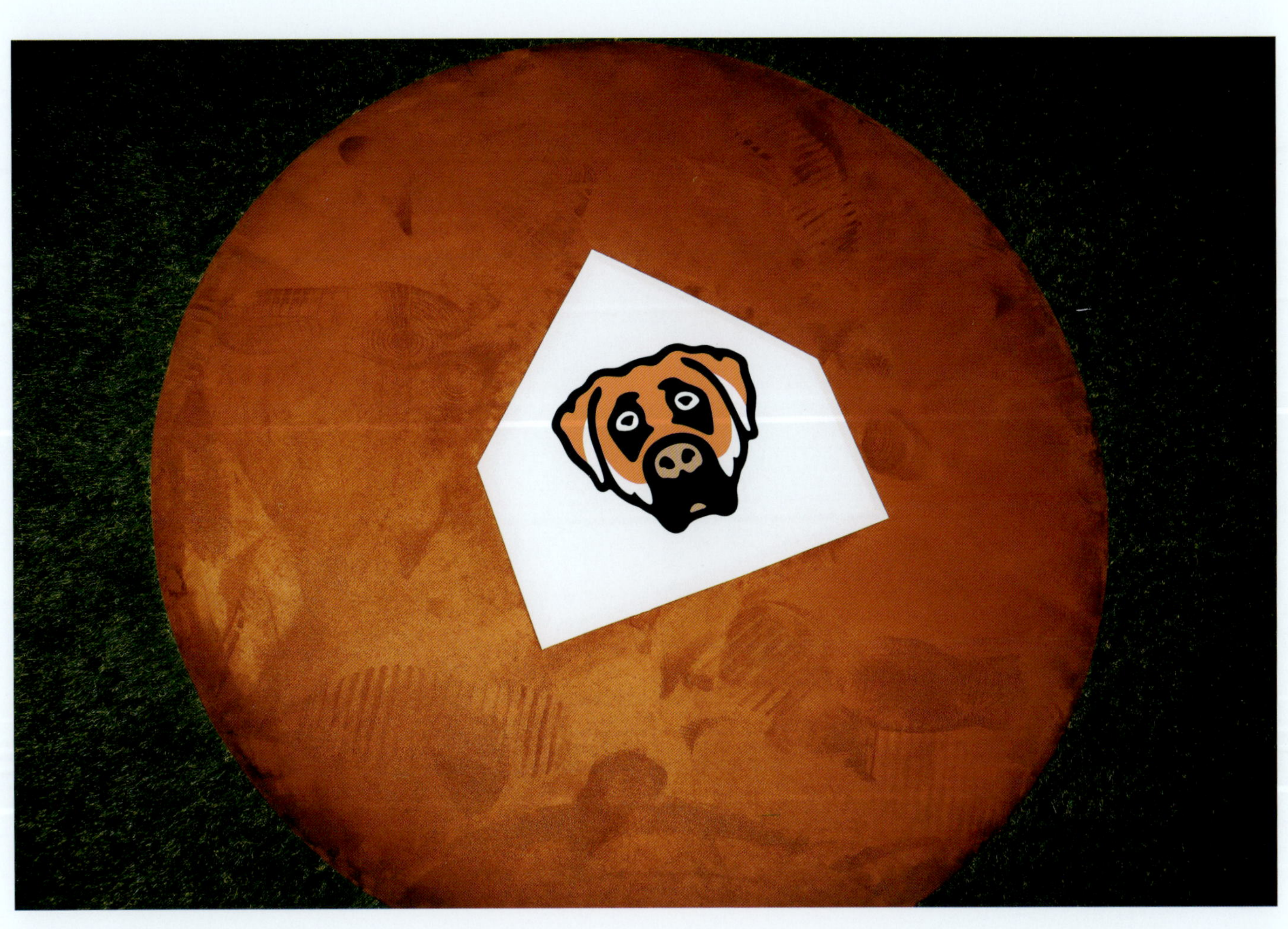

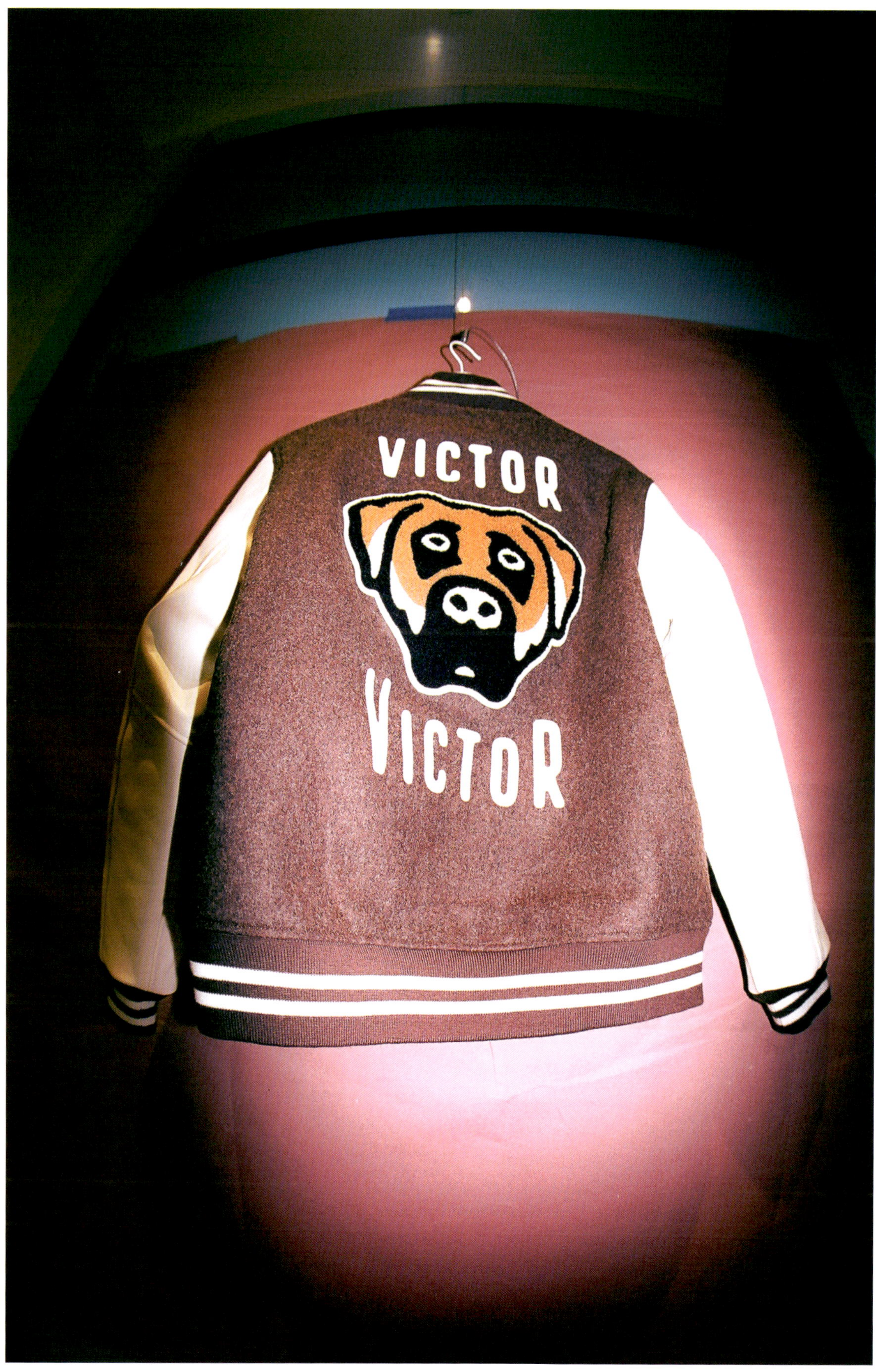
VICTOR
VICTOR

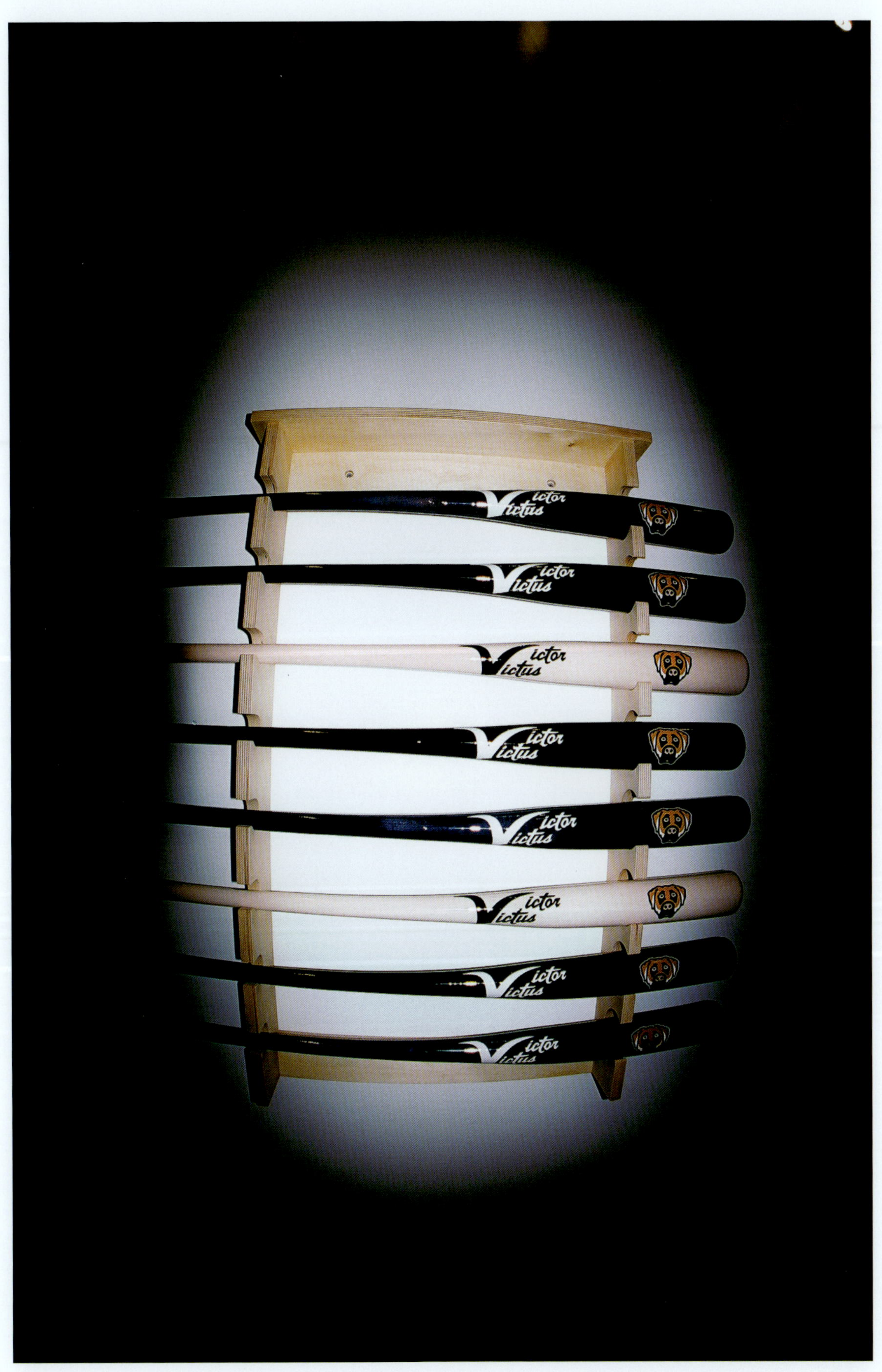
Victor Victus

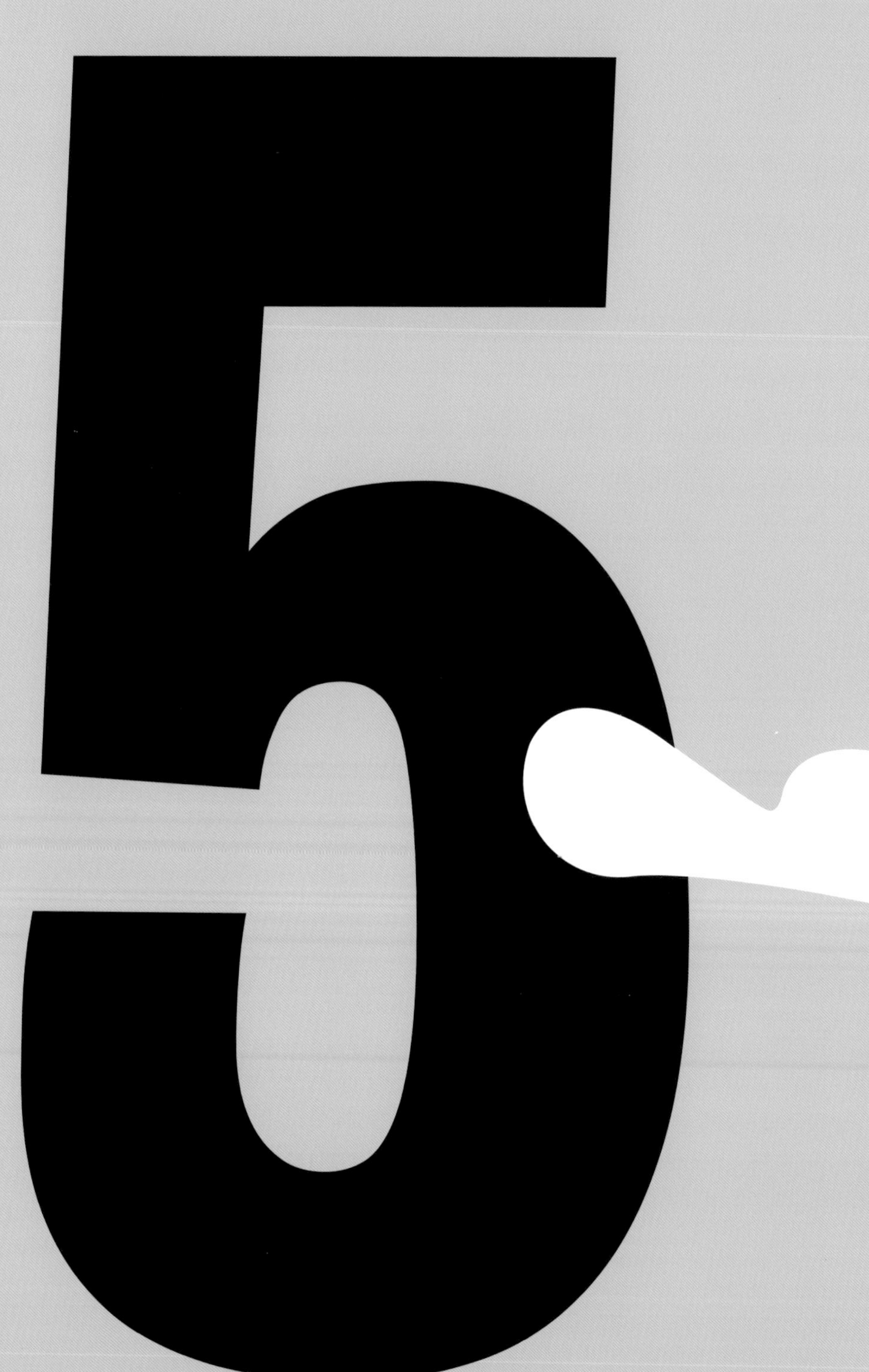

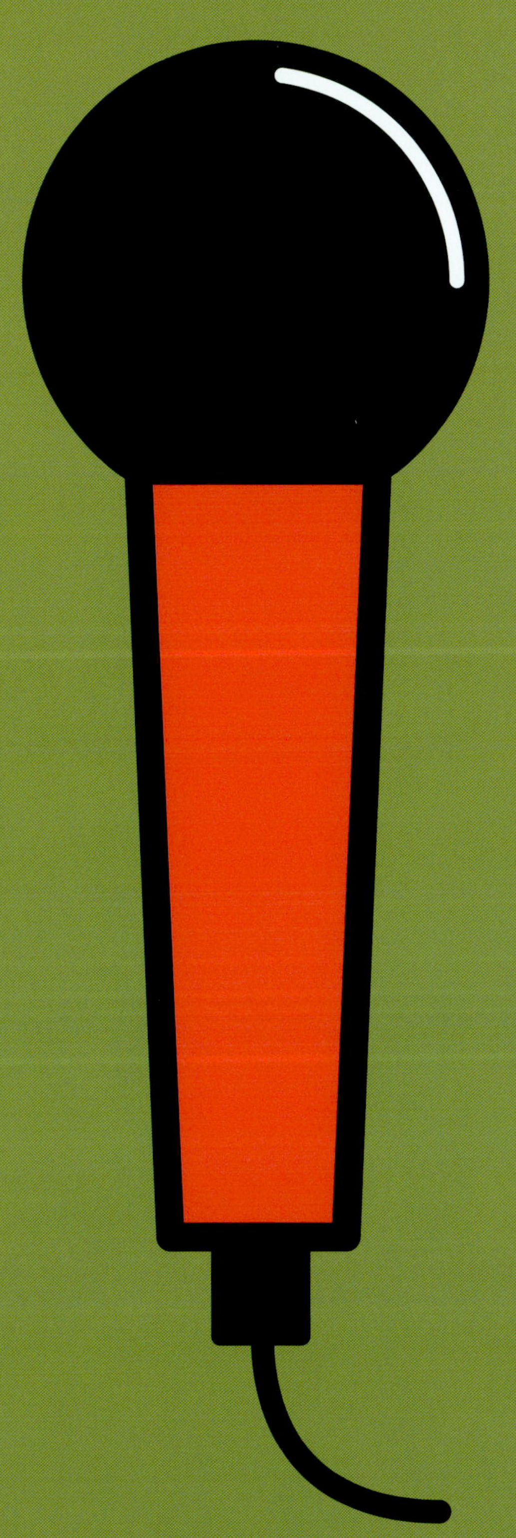

Steven Victor, NIGO® & Verdy at ComplexCon, November 20, 2022, Long Beach, California

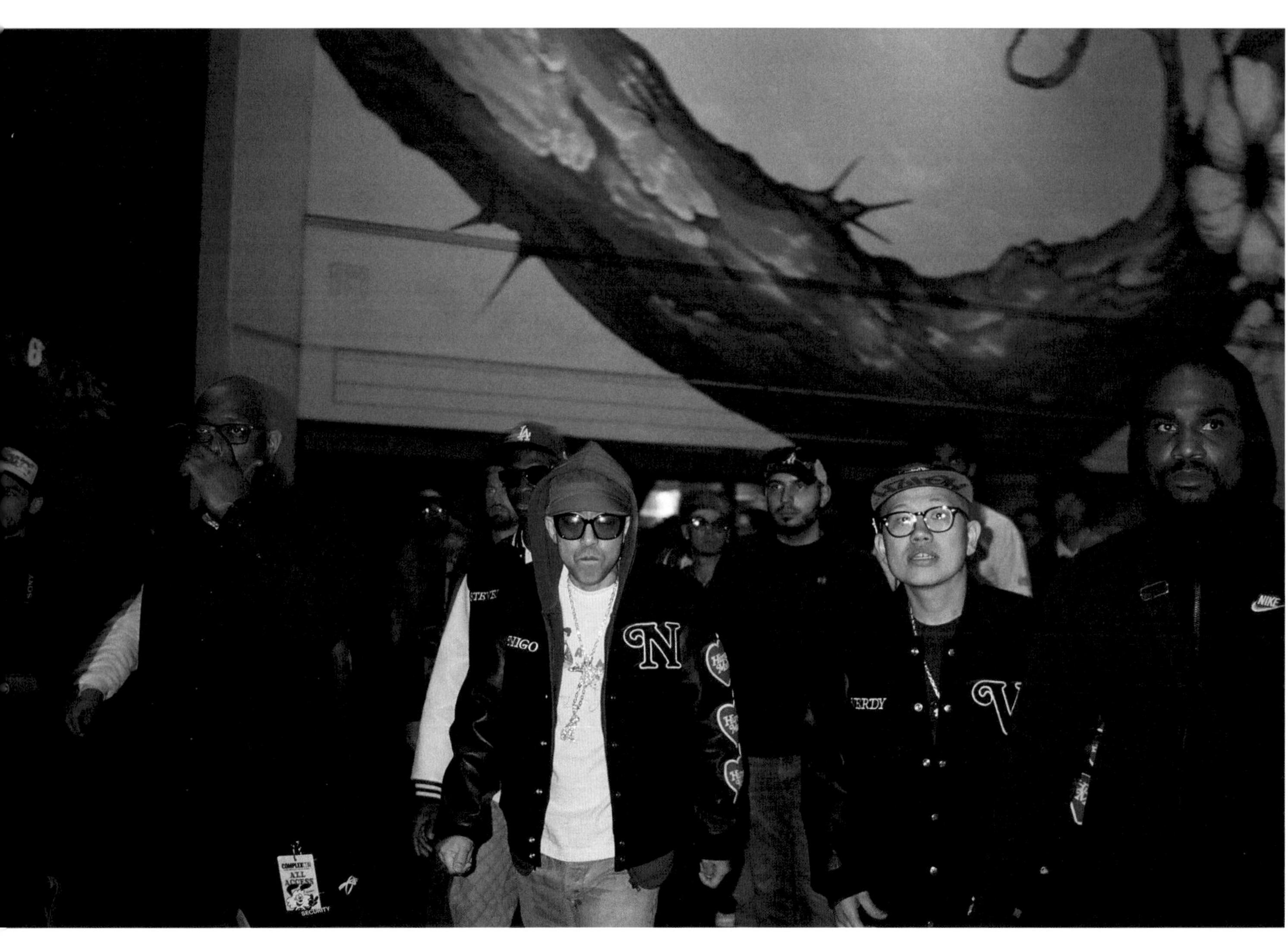

I Know NIGO® was the musical guest for ComplexCon 2022. NIGO® DJ'd a set featuring performances by Clipse, Pusha-T, Ski Mask the Slump God, Kodak Black, TERIYAKI BOYZ®, & Lil Uzi Vert

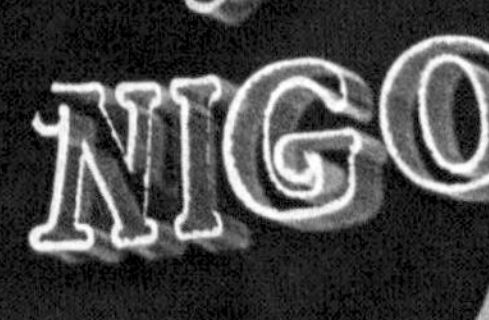
NIGO

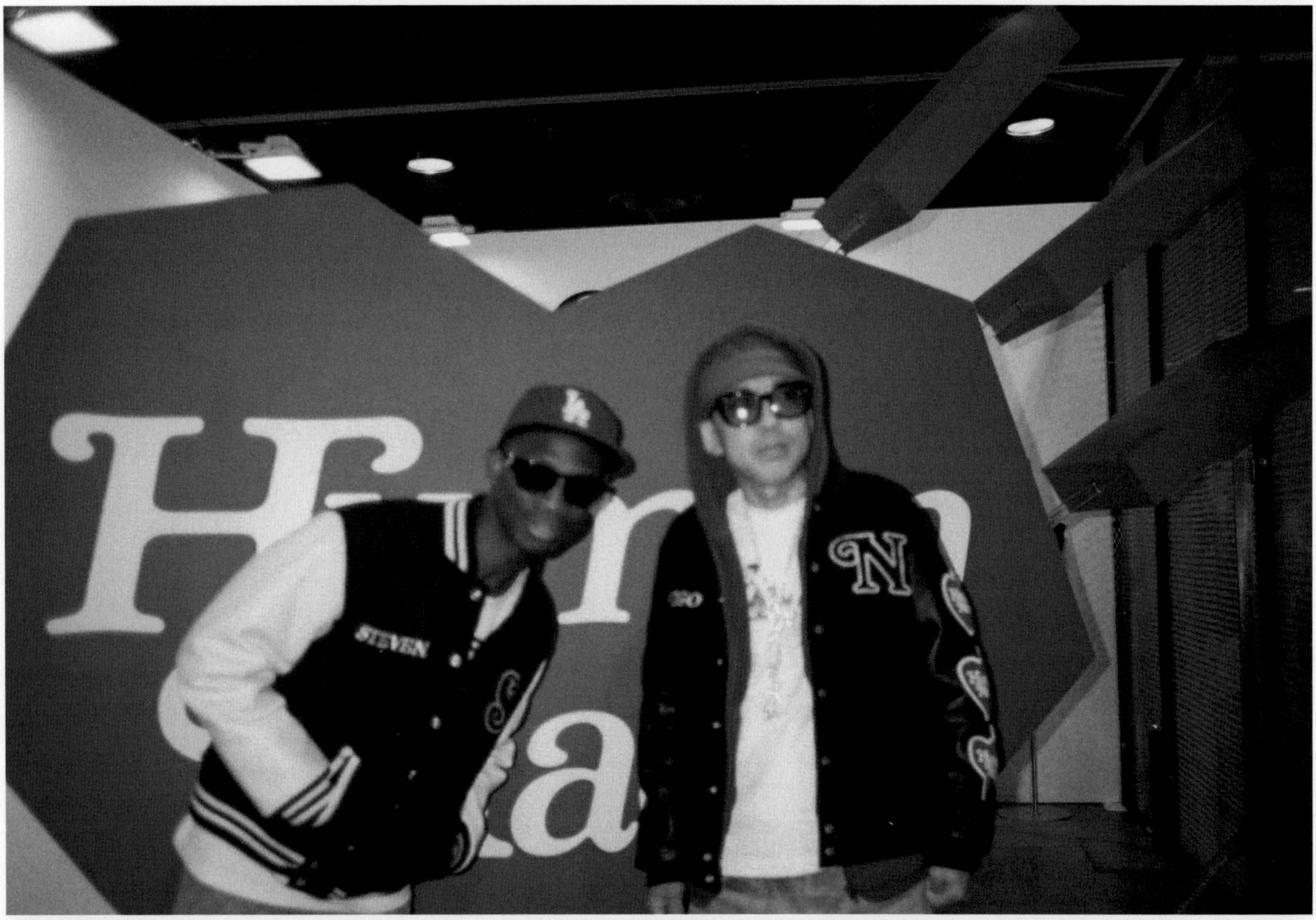

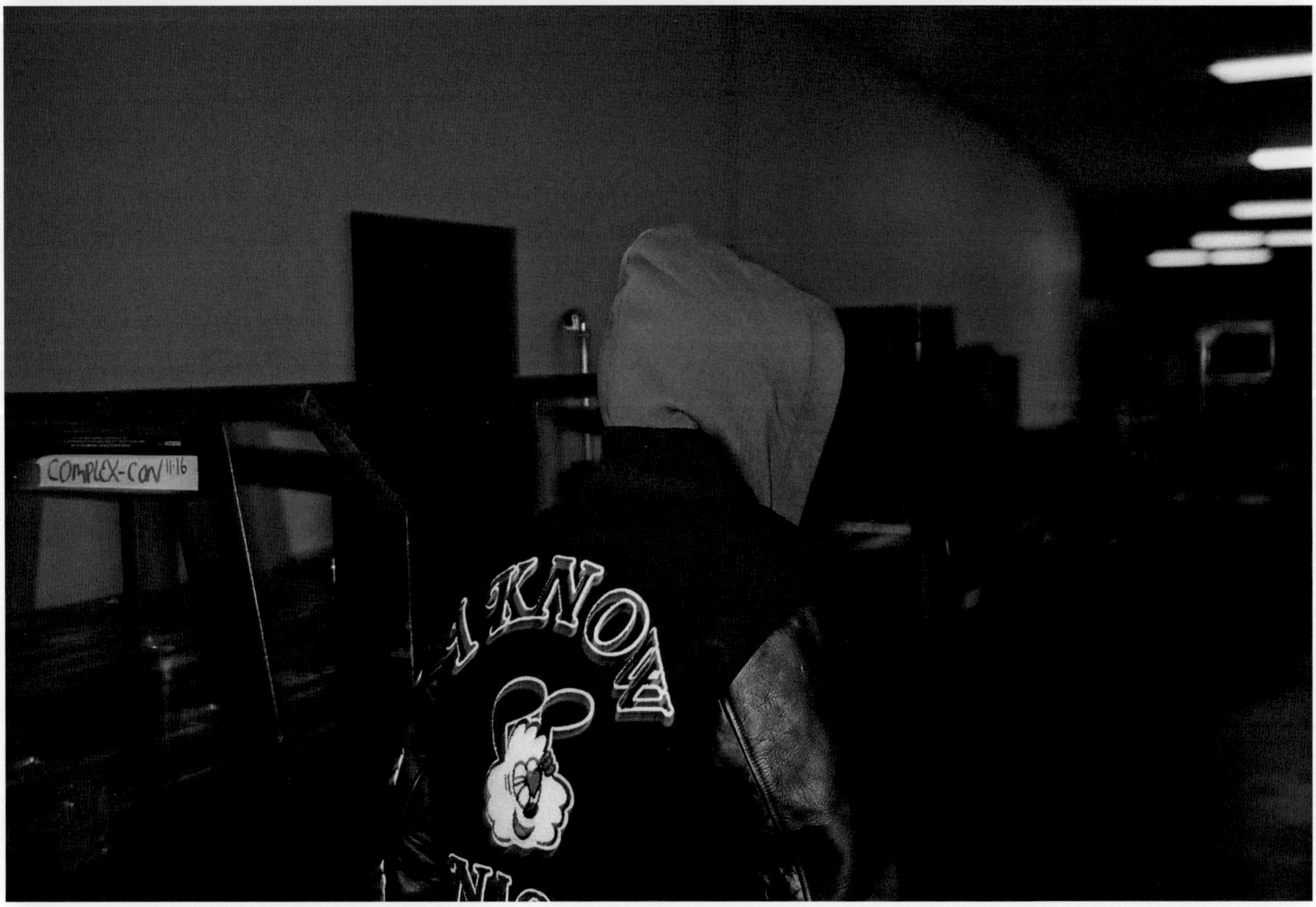

I Know NIGO® x Human Made x Verdy Friends & Family varsity jacket, designed for ComplexCon 2022. Worn by No Malice, Pusha-T, Steven Victor & NIGO®

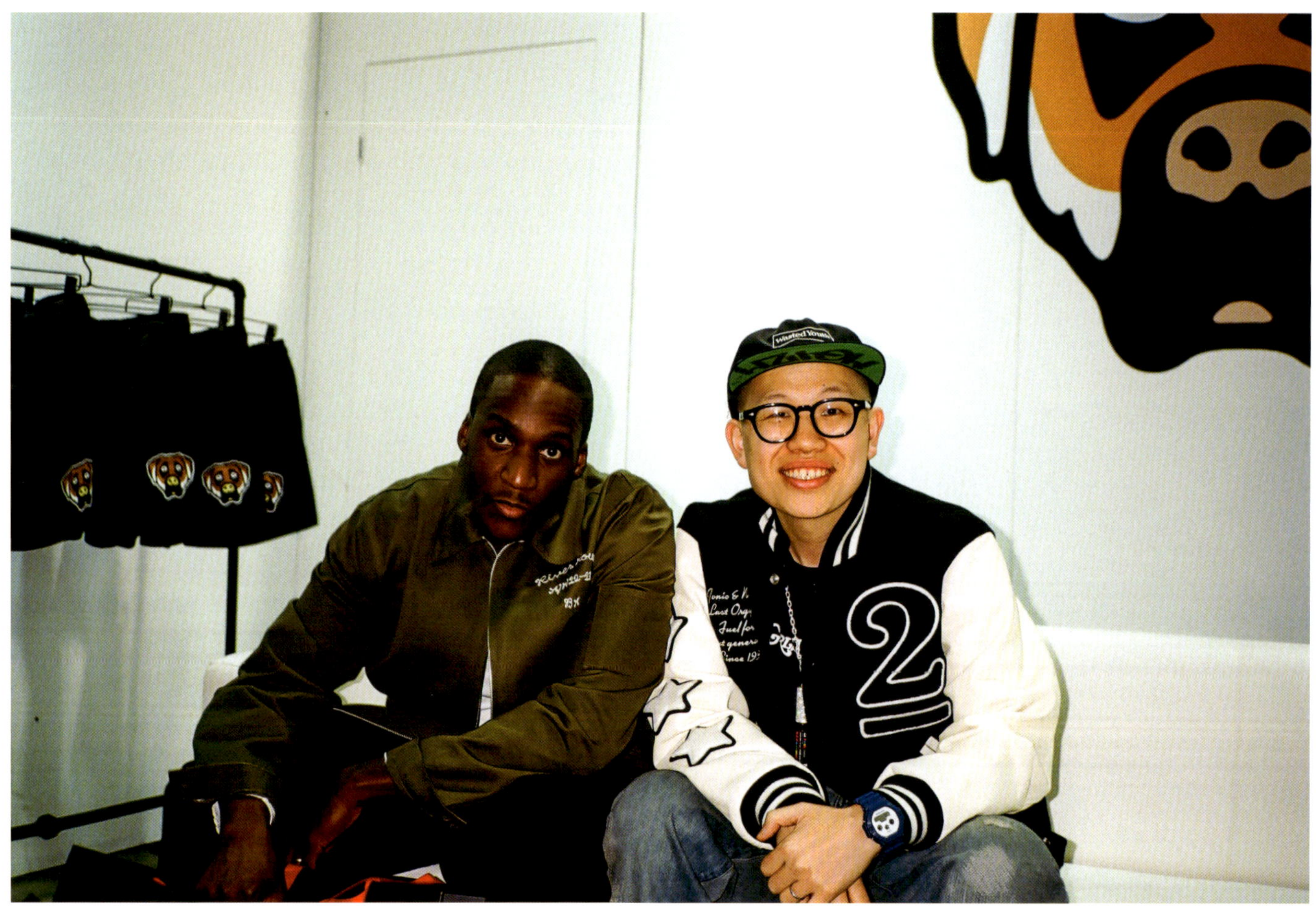

Verdy & Clipse stop by the VICTOR VICTOR Booth at ComplexCon 2022, with Steven Victor

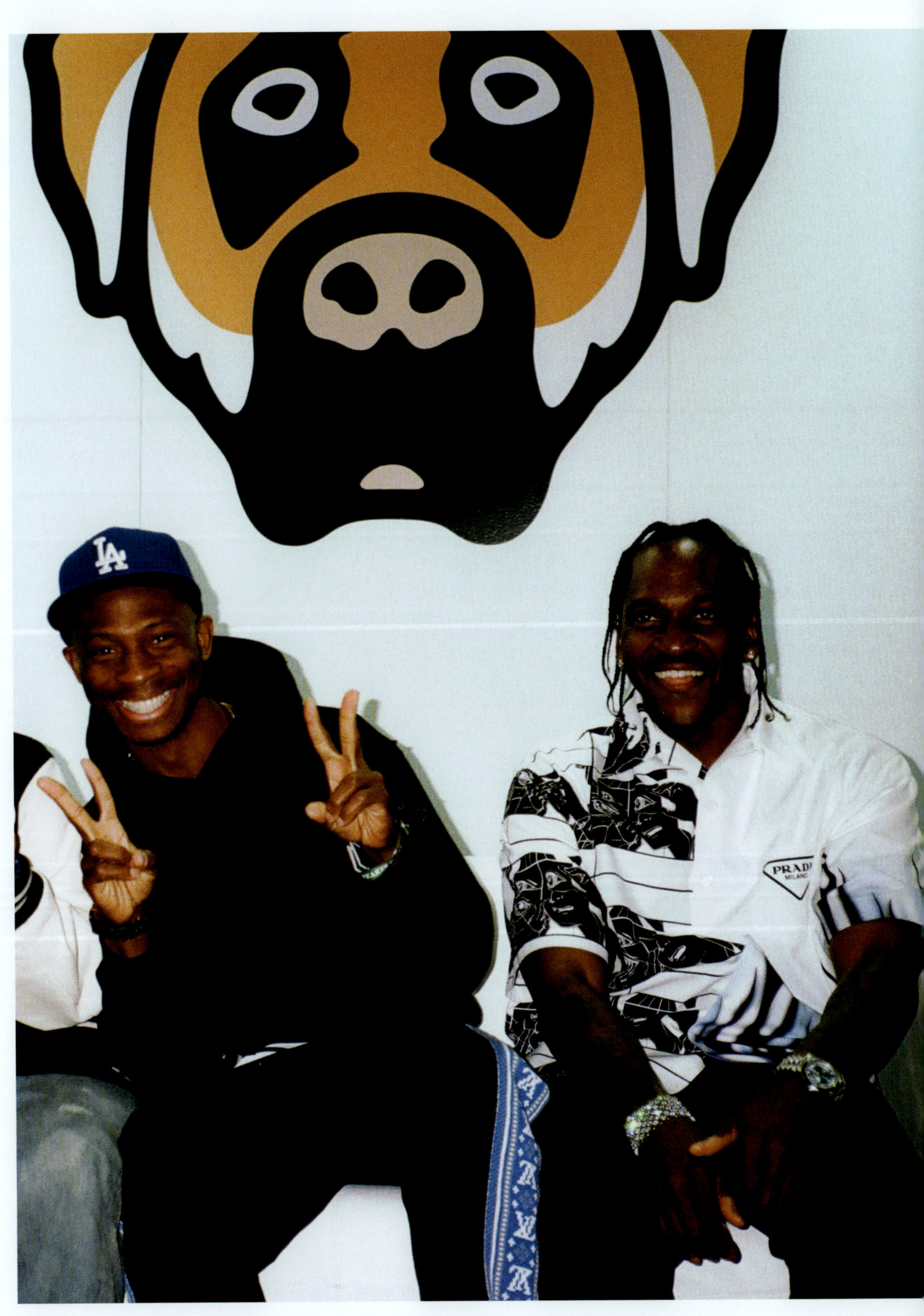
LA
MILANO

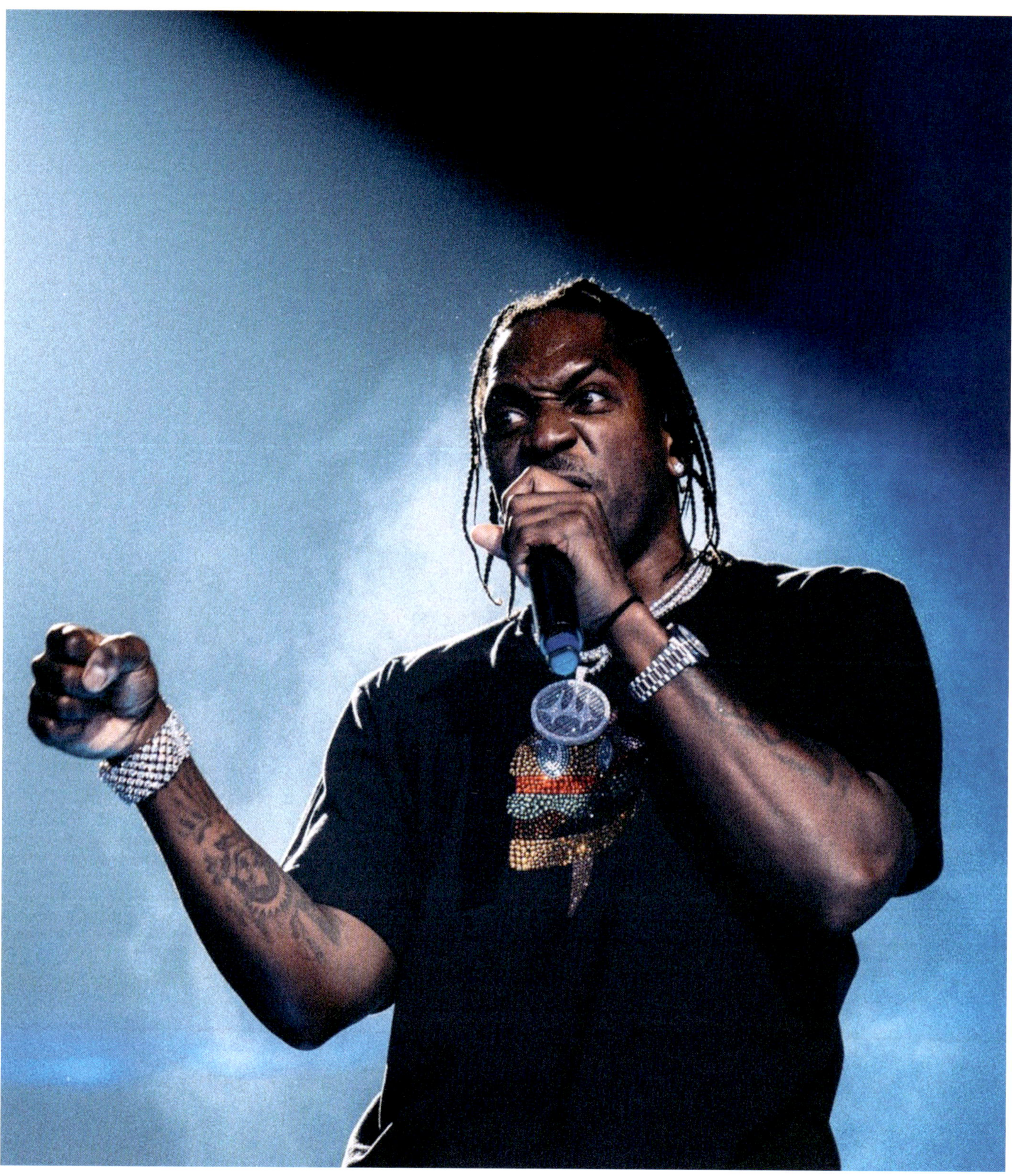

Pusha-T performing at ComplexCon
2022

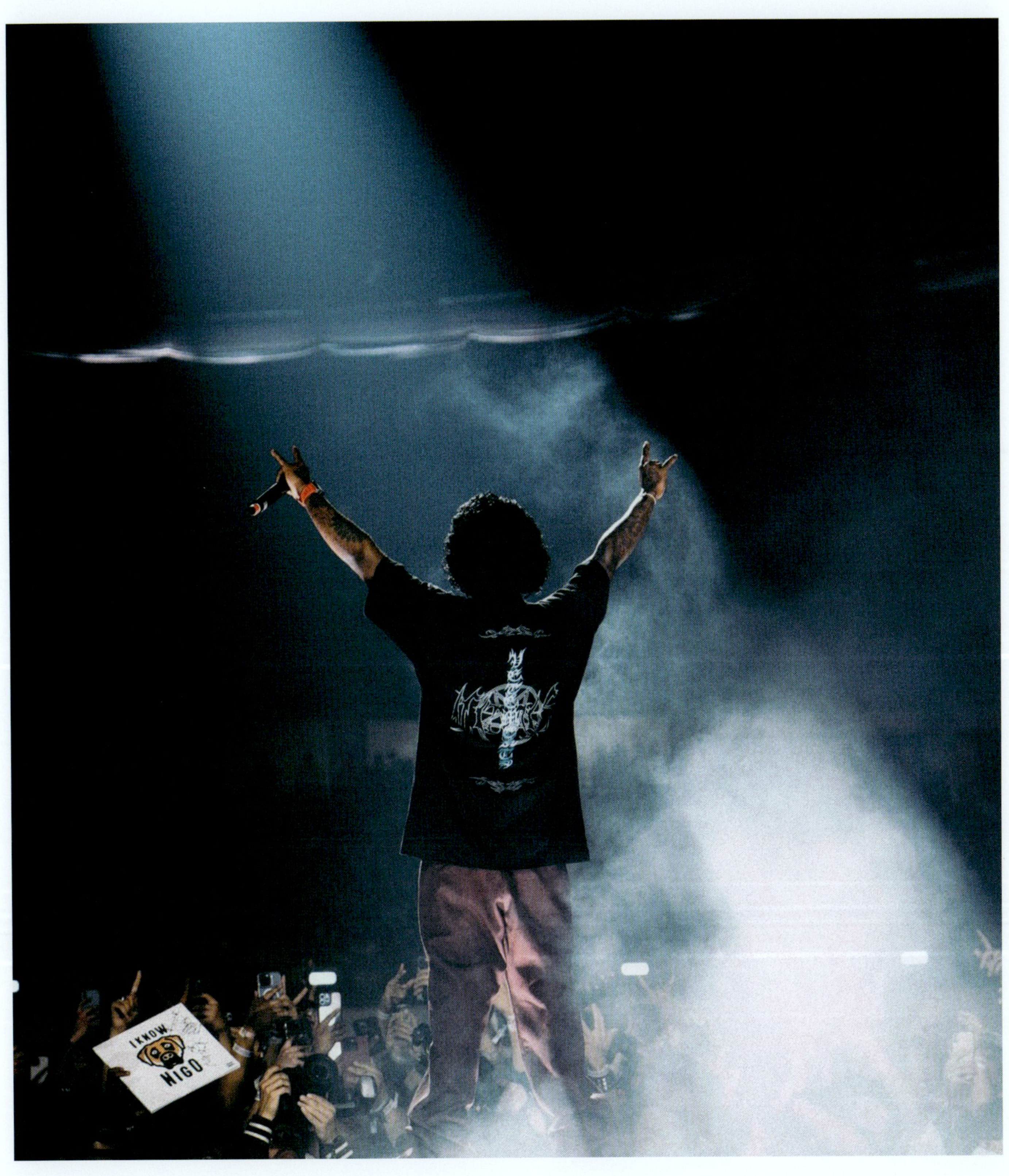
I KNOW
NIGO

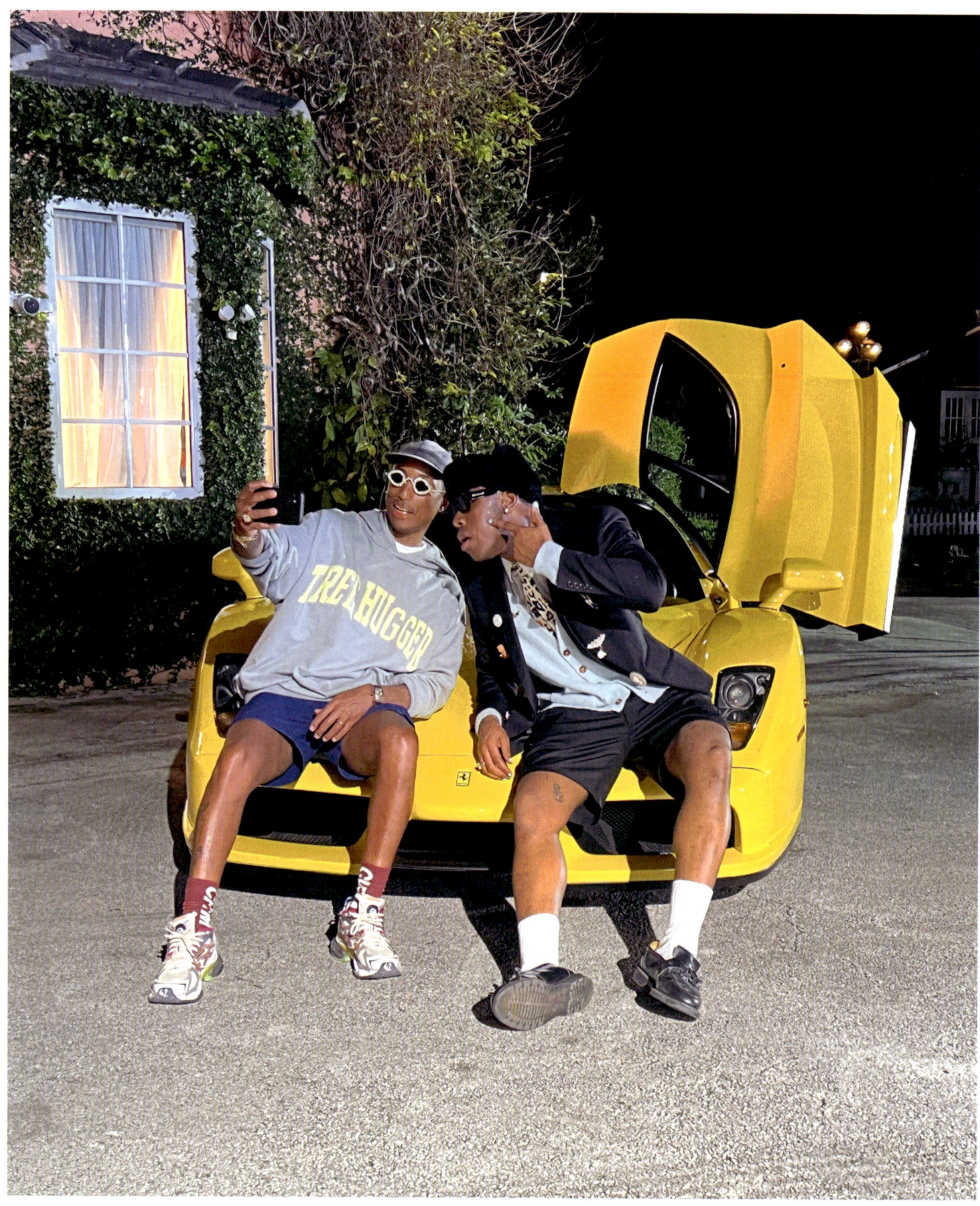

Behind-the-scenes image from the video shoot for "Come On, Let's Go" with Tyler, The Creator and Pharrell, 2022; Tyler, The Creator performing the song live in Miami, 2022

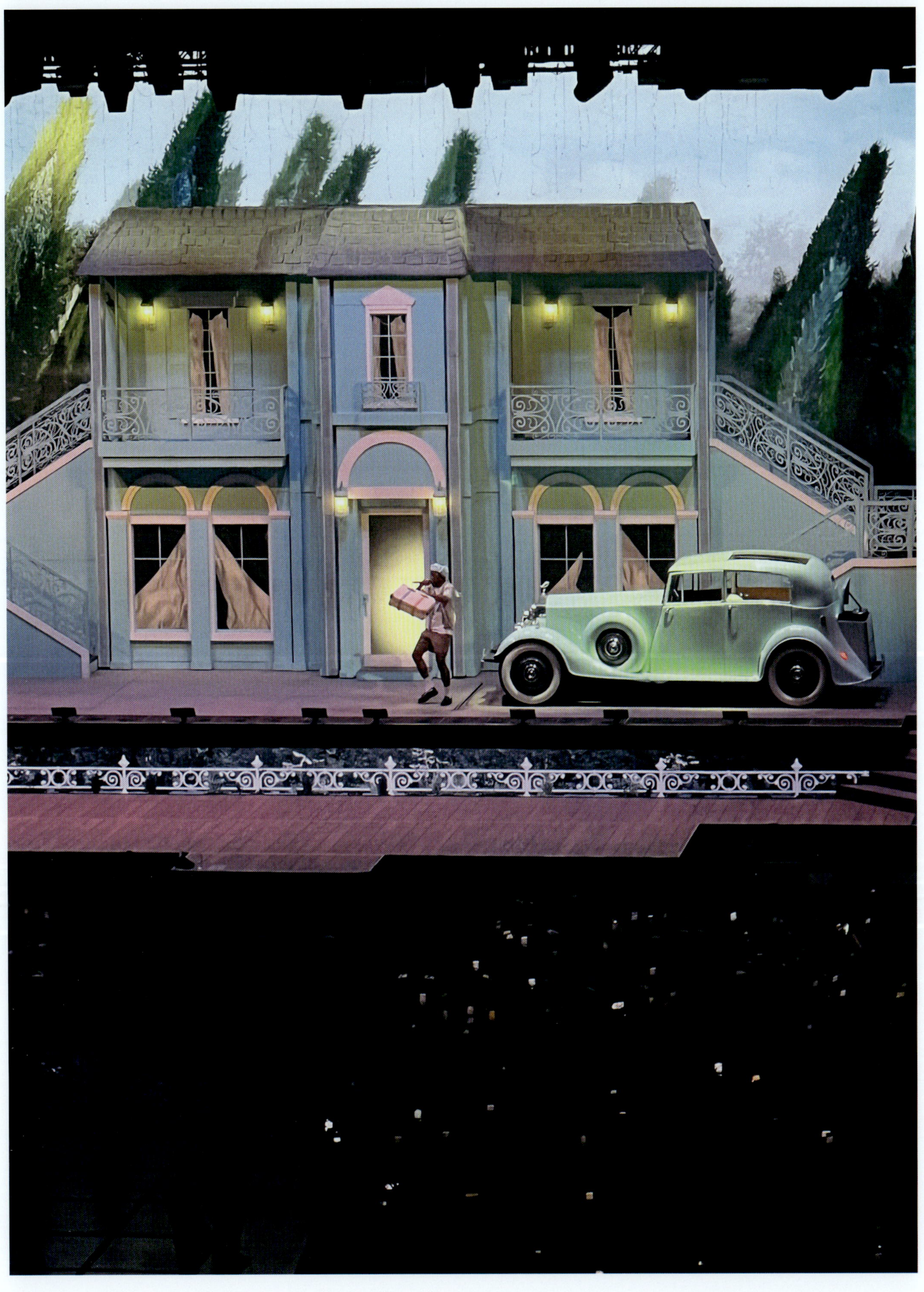

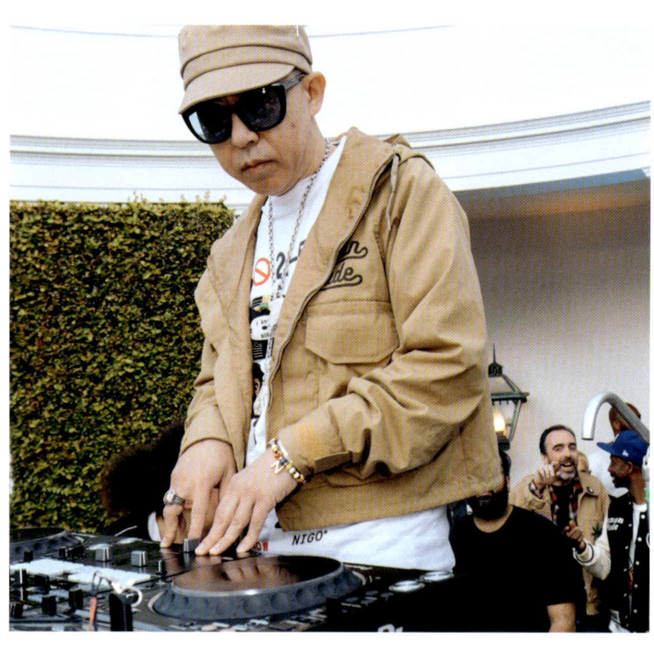

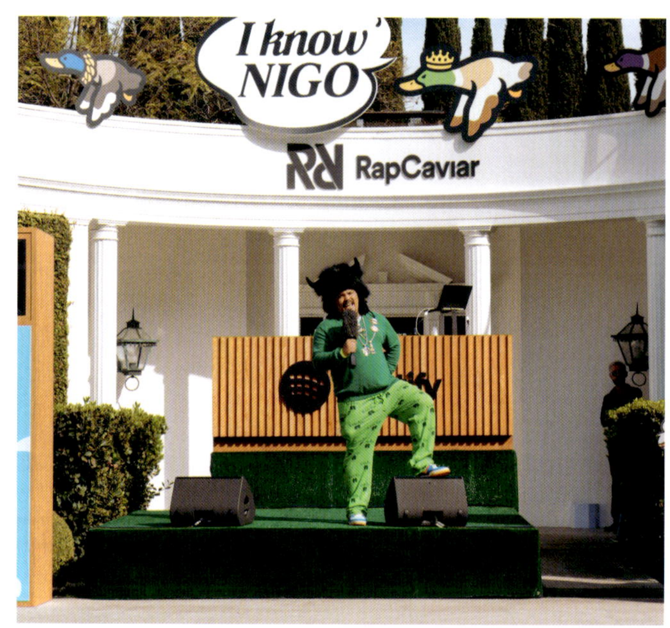

NIGO®, Pharrell & Kerwin Frost at the I Know NIGO® x Spotify / RapCaviar Pool Party at Kelly Wearstler's Los Angeles estate, March 31, 2022

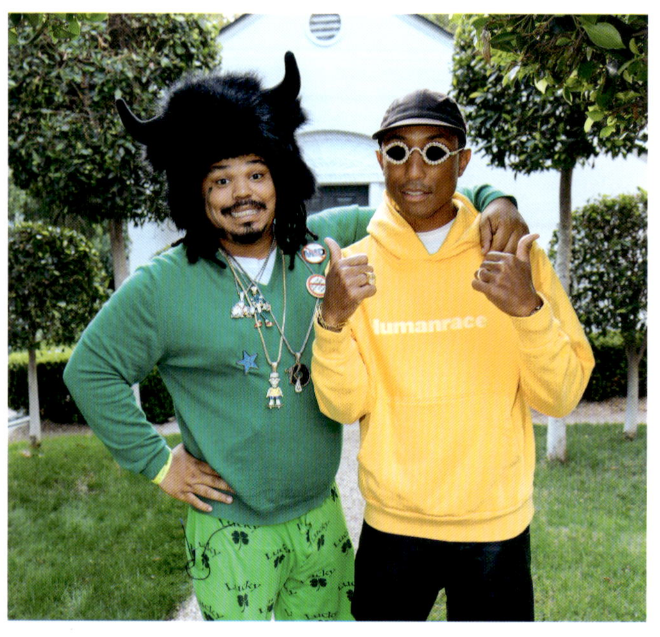

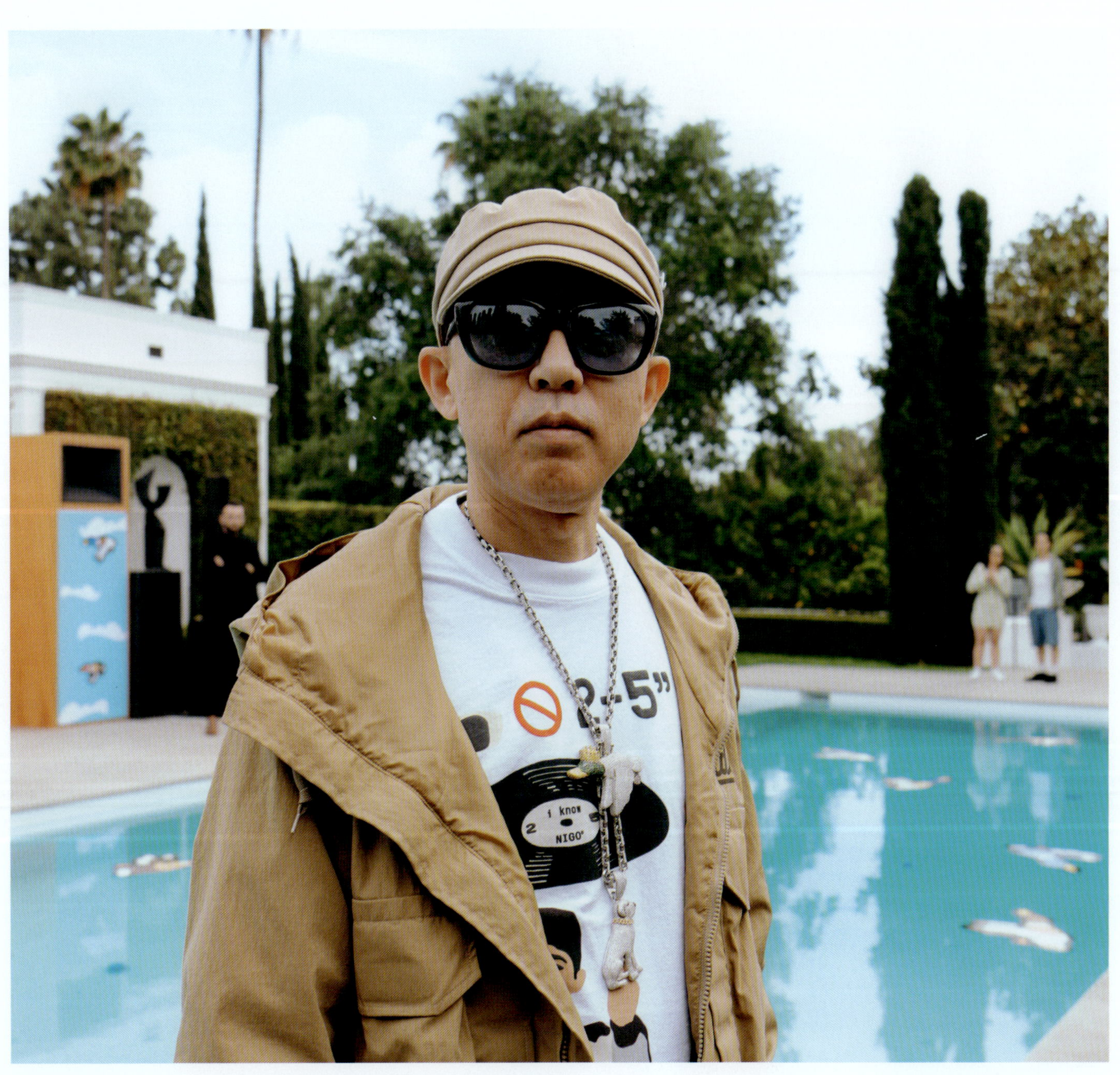
i know
NIGO

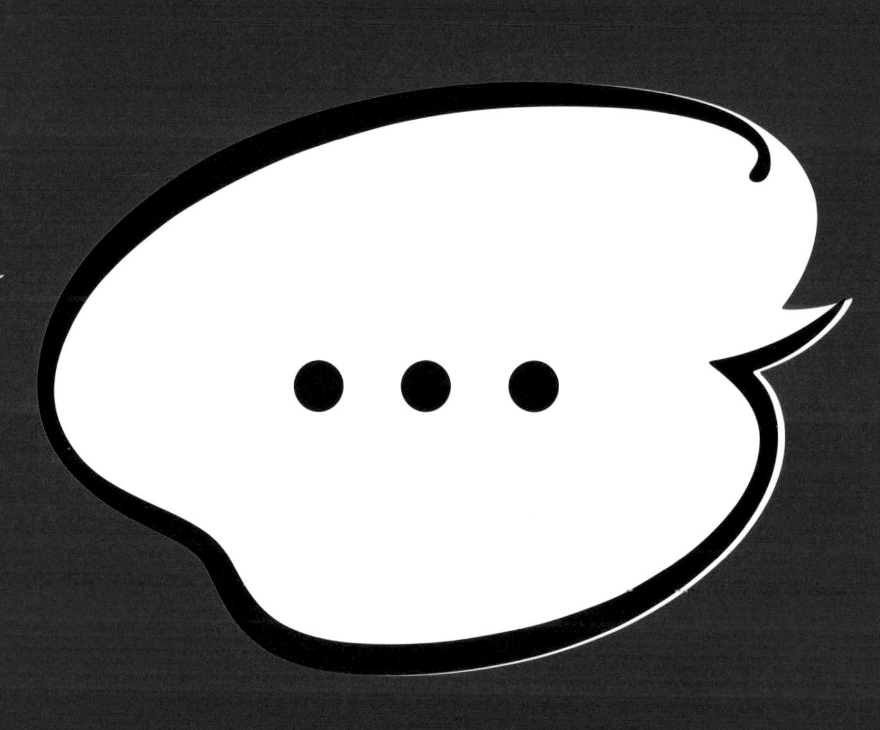

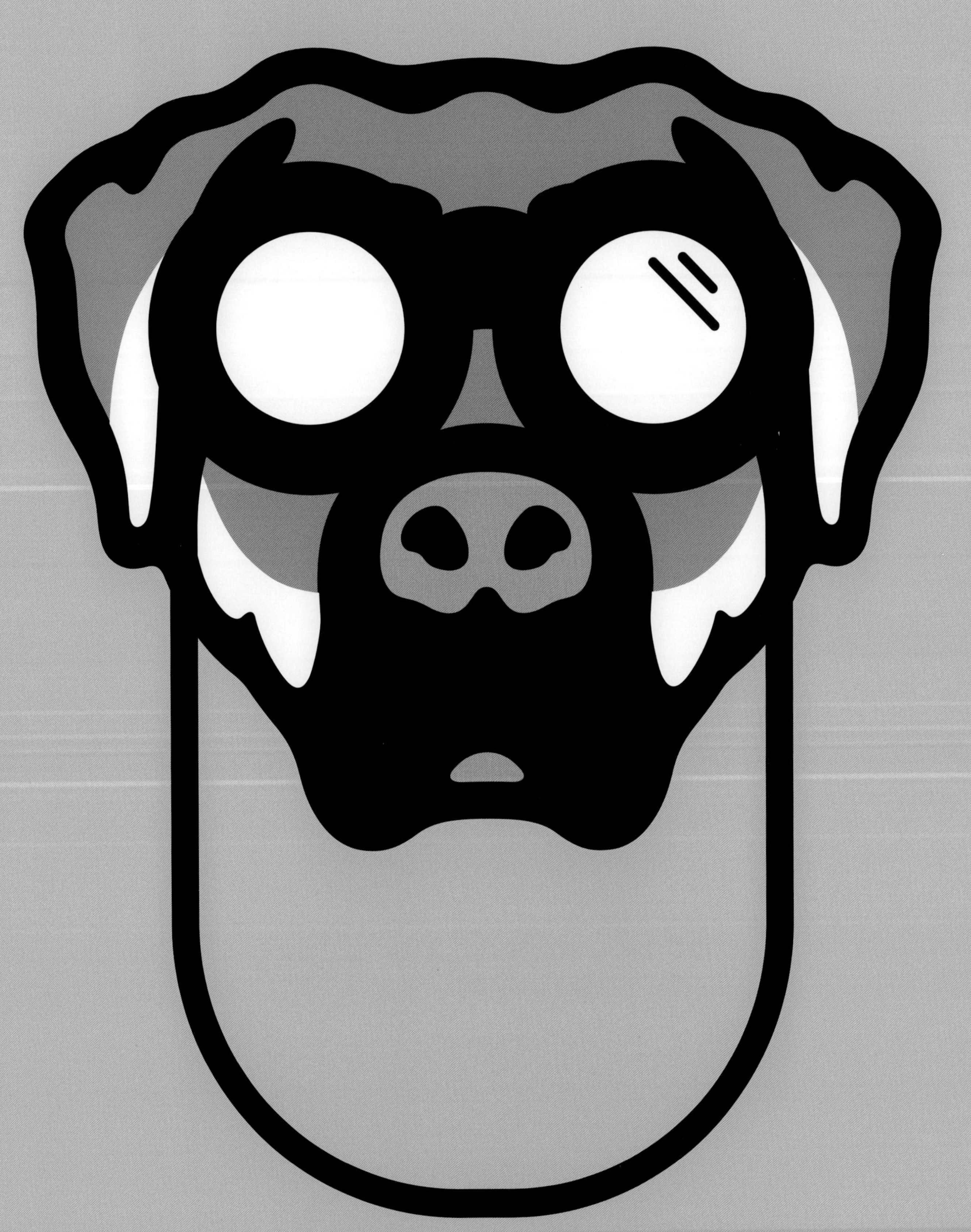

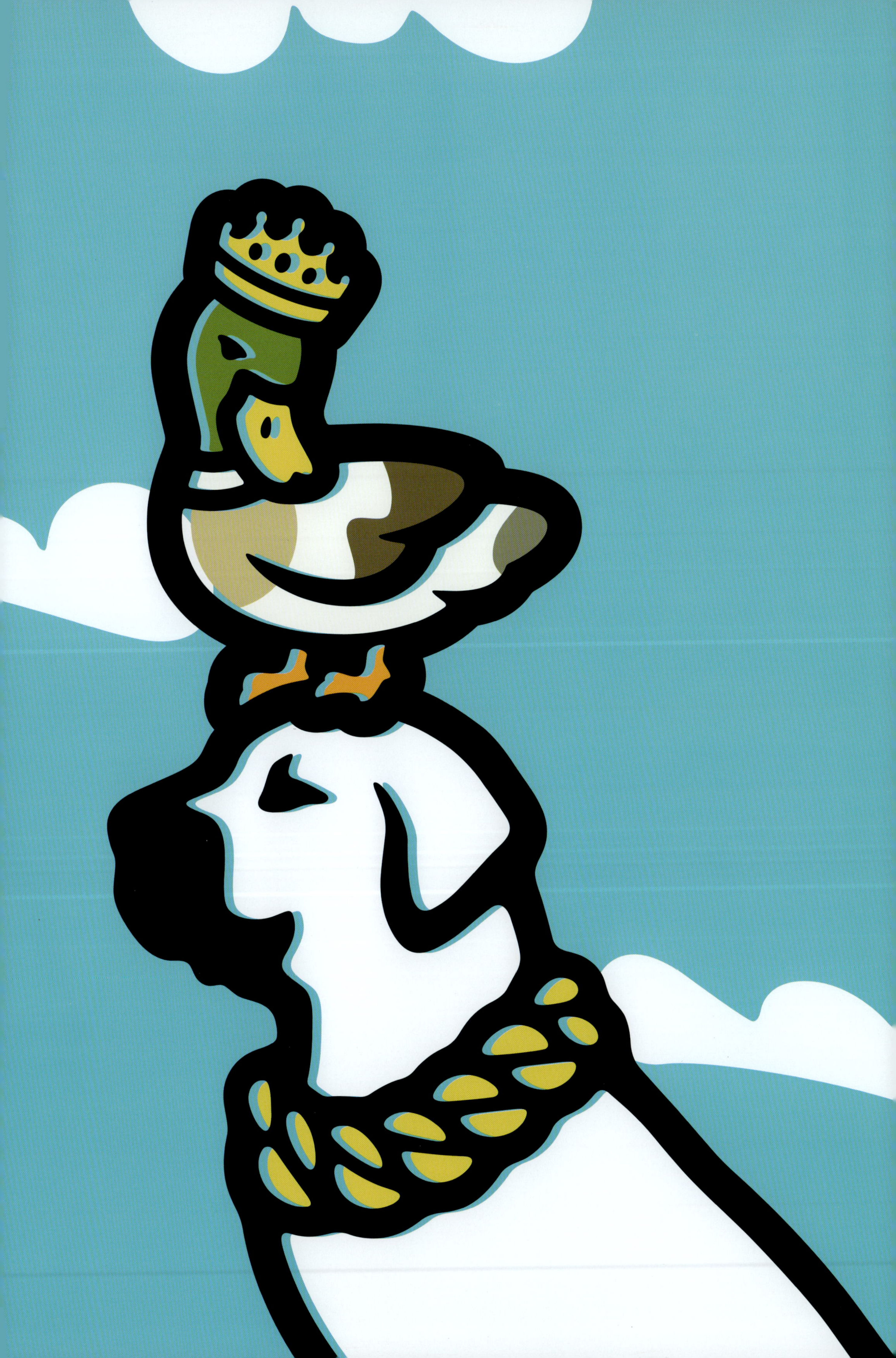

ALBUM CREDITS

I Know NIGO®
Executive Producers: Steven Victor & Pharrell
Art Direction & Design: NIGO®
Creative Direction: AWGE
Management: Daniel Doyle
A&R: Ben Lust
Legal: Christine Calip Victor
Marketing: Shiv Pandya, Kevin McMullan & Xiarra-Diamond Nimrod
A&R Coordination: Ben Lust & Bryan Montesano
Business Affairs: Daniel Getz, Antoinette Trotman, Ian Allen, Corey Williams, Rachel Meisner, Jenna McPhail, Stephanie Joseph & Scott Sherman
Sample Clearances: Deborah Mannis-Gardner for DMG Clearances, Inc.
Package Production: Jenny Beal, Michelle Ayabarreno & Eric Neuser

ILLUSTRATION CREDITS

Every effort has been made to gain permission from copyright holders and or photographers, where known, for the images reproduced in the book, and care has been taken to caption and credit those images correctly. Any omissions are unintentional and appropriate credit will be included in future editions if further information is brought in writing to the publisher's attention.

Original cover illustration and related artwork: NIGO® & Human Made
Additional illustrations by Oliver Munday and Paul Spella

10-11: Tomohiko Tagawa, Courtesy of Human Made
13: Daniel Doyle
14: Bladimir Corniel
19-20: Harrison Boyce
25: Courtesy of NIGO®/Human Made
26: Bladimir Corniel
27-29: SHOTBYCONES
30-38: Bladimir Corniel
40-41: Harrison Boyce
42-45: Bladimir Corniel
46-47: Harrison Boyce
48: Harrison Boyce
49: Bladimir Corniel
50-52: Bladimir Corniel
53-54: SHOTBYCONES
56-57 : Bladimir Corniel
58-60: SHOTBYCONES
62: Harrison Boyce
63-64: Bladimir Corniel
65-69 : Harrison Boyce
70: NIGO®
71-87: SHOTBYCONES
88: NIGO®
90-91: Courtesy of TERIYAKI BOYZ®
95: Courtesy of Victor Victor Worldwide, Universal Music Group
96-97: Courtesy of Human Made
100-101: Harrison Boyce
102-103: Courtesy of Human Made
104-105: Harrison Boyce
109-113: Courtesy of Human Made
114-117: Thomas Nguyen
118-123: Courtesy of Human Made
126: SHOTBYCONES
128-135: Courtesy of Human Made
136-137: Designed by NIGO® for Apple Music Rap Life
139: Oliver Cannon Boyce
140-141: Courtesy of Human Made
142 Harrison Boyce
143: Courtesy of Human Made
144-145: Courtesy of Shopify
147: Courtesy of Human Made
148-155: Courtesy of Shopify
156-157: Courtesy of Billionaire Boys Club
160-161: Courtesy of Apple Music
162-171: Oliver Cannon Boyce
174-175: Garrett Bruce
176-177: Bijan Sosnowski
178-188: Garrett Bruce
189: Bijan Sosnowski
190-191: Provided courtesy of Shopify
192-193: Courtesy of Shopify
194-195 Garrett Bruce
196-197: Bijan Sosnowski
198-199: Provided courtesy of Shopify
200-205: Bijan Sosnowski
208-213: Brendan O'Connor
214-215: Tony Huynh
216-217: Andrea Rojas
218-219: Courtesy of Spotify

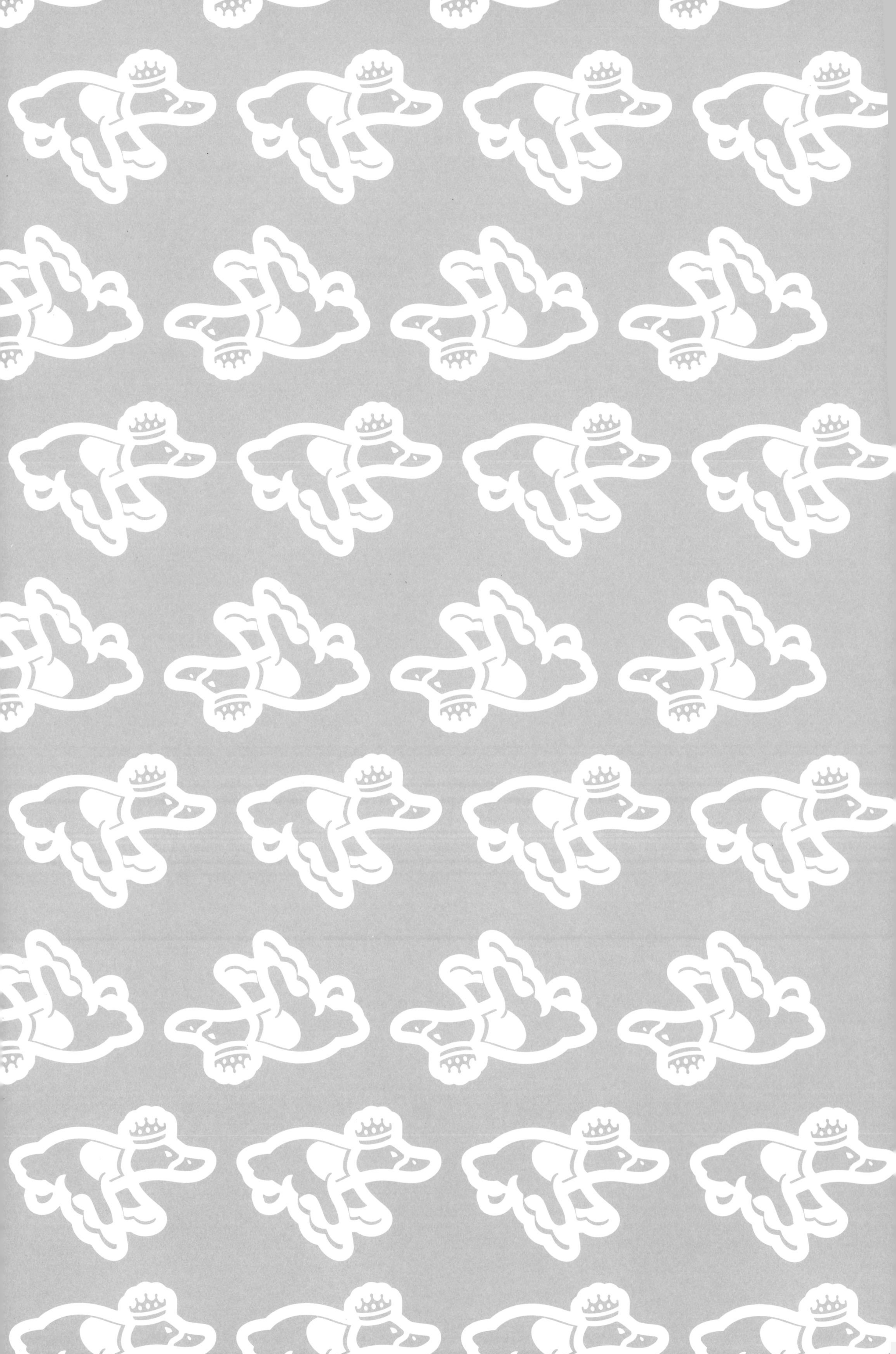